A TREATISE ON
STAIRBUILDING AND HANDRAILING

STAIRCASE, CREWE HALL, CHESHIRE.

Frontispiece.

A TREATISE ON
STAIRBUILDING AND HANDRAILING

CONTAINING NUMEROUS EXAMPLES ILLUSTRATING THE CONSTRUCTION OF THE VARIOUS
CLASSES OF WOOD STAIRS, BOTH FOR HOUSES AND PASSENGER SHIPS, AND OF
STONE STAIRS ; WITH A COMPLETE COURSE OF HANDRAILING, SHOWING
EASY, ACCURATE, AND ECONOMICAL METHODS OF GETTING OUT
AND PREPARING WREATHED HANDRAILS ; ALSO AN
APPENDIX CONSISTING OF A SHORT COURSE OF
PLANE AND DESCRIPTIVE GEOMETRY
BEARING ON THE SUBJECT

INTENDED FOR THE USE OF HOUSE AND SHIP JOINERS, MASONS, BUILDERS, ARCHITECTS
AND FOR STUDENTS IN TECHNICAL SCHOOLS PREPARING FOR THE EXAMINATIONS
OF THE CITY AND GUILDS OF LONDON INSTITUTE AND OF THE
SCIENCE AND ART DEPARTMENT IN CARPENTRY AND
JOINERY AND BUILDING CONSTRUCTION

BY

WILLIAM MOWAT, M.A.

*Science Master, School of Science and Art, Barrow-in-Furness. Late Examiner in Ship Joinery to
the City and Guilds of London Institute*

AND

ALEXANDER MOWAT, M.A.

Science Master, School of Science and Art, Barrow-in-Furness

13 14 15 16 17 18 19

A TREATISE ON STAIRBUILDING AND HANDRAILING
With new additions.

ISBN 0-941936-02-3

LC 85-6916

Linden Publishing Co. Inc.
3845 N. Blackstone
Fresno CA 93726

In memory of S. Linden
33 Craven St., Strand
London

LINDEN PUBLISHING

The Woodworker's
Library

INTRODUCTION

STAIRBUILDING has been called the "head of the joiners trade" The art dates back to 6000 B.C., and in the beginning, was developed as an exterior addition to a building. It quickly became evident there was an inherent military aspect to the art and stairs became important defensive positions in fortifications. By the 11th century England had developed the narrow, circular, interior keep stairway. Stone was the major choice of construction and the military aspect was still in full evidence. The division of dextral and sinistral, right curving and left curving stairs, may have developed by taking into account the ability of the righthanded swordsman to defend or attack while holding onto the railing with the left hand.

Years would pass between the use of the narrow, defensible stairway and the common use of the grand central stairway of later times. As the need for military defense declined, stairs were constructed with more social comfort in mind. By the 14th century, spiral stairs in wood became common, and by the 17th century excellent examples of stairway construction could be found. Some authorities have described double spiral staircases, so constructed that two people might pass one another without meeting or seeing the other.

With the continuing decline in the need for defensive consideration, the grand central staircase came to the fore. Individual wealth increased and the arts and crafts became available to those who could afford to construct the large country manors so prevalent in England. Stairway development moved quickly from heavy timber construction to flat sawn boards and extensive decorative work with dramatic changes in balustrades, both in construction and decorative enhancement.

The late nineteenth century is considered by many to be the golden period in the art of stair building. Peter Nicholson had developed his mathematical system and at last staircasing and handrailing could be reduced to an art available to the master and journeyman carpenter and joiner. Books became available which offered instruction as well as design, and the art prospered. Nicholson had raised the art of stair-building and handrailing to a science. Nicholson's system was based on sections of solids, and the development of these sections into the lines for handrailing. From this body of work there evolved numerous books on stairbuilding and handrailing, all based to some degree, either by elaboration or refinement, on Nicholson's original system.

Two famous authors to succeed Nicholson were James Monckton and Robert Riddell. Riddell reduced the new science to a method which enabled the common, though skilled, carpenter to construct a wide range of staircase designs. However, problems still plagued the late 19th century literature on the subject. Although Monckton, Riddell and many others, claimed to have systematized Nicholson's work and reduced it to a level easily understood by the skilled carpenter and joiner, the actual texts they produced were difficult to read, the plates were, in some instances, poorly reproduced, and the works in general required an evangelical dedication by the reader.

In 1900 the Mowats published their book, "A Treatise on Stairbuilding and Handrailing". It soon became the foremost text on the subject, and has remained one of the most lucid, best illustrated and authoritative works on the art and science of stairbuilding and handrailing.

Richard Sorsky
Fresno California
1985

PREFACE

In preparing this treatise we have aimed at placing in the hands of students and craftsmen a complete course of instruction in the principles and practice of stairbuilding and handrailing, embracing all the technical information required in general practice.

The subject has been arranged in three divisions:—Part I. treating of the construction of wood stairs; Part II. handrailing; and Part III. stone stairs.

We have endeavoured to present the more elementary parts of the subject in as simple a manner as possible, for the benefit of beginners, and at the same time have tried to treat each branch as fully and comprehensively as would make the book of some service to stairbuilders, and to architects, in the planning out and designing of stairs.

With these objects in view, great care has been taken to illustrate the subject by a series of well-detailed practical examples, which would present the various points of construction in progressive order of difficulty, and which would, in some measure, serve as guides in the preparation of new designs. In all cases the illustrations of staircases have been given in full detail, and to a sufficiently large scale to enable the nature of the design, and the arrangement of the various parts, to be readily and clearly comprehended; and these, in most cases, have been supplemented by enlarged drawings of the more important parts, showing the methods of forming the principal joints and connections.

A special feature of the book is the section devoted to the construction of stairs for passenger ships, a portion of stairbuilding practice which, as far as the writers are aware, has not been treated of in any previous publication.

In practical handrailing, with the view of making the descriptions anent the various examples as direct and concise as possible, the theoretical matter has been given in two preceding chapters. In these copious explanations are given of the principles involved in the various operations, which, together with the numerous illustrations, it is hoped

may tend to obviate the peculiar difficulties experienced by beginners,
and help forward more advanced students in acquiring a thorough
mastery of this admittedly difficult though highly interesting branch of
joinery.

The ordinary method of describing the ellipses of the " face mould,"
i.e. by means of a trammel guided on the principal axes, has been adopted
in most of the practical illustrations; but by regarding the ellipse as a
particular case of the hypotrochoid, we have shown that to each pair
of lines passing through the centre of the ellipse, as well as to the
principal axes, there belongs an appropriate trammel which may be used
for striking out the curve, and hence that the ellipses of the face mould
may be drawn by trammels guided on the springing lines.

These extensions of the trammel principle, which we presume may
be new to most craftsmen, are discussed and illustrated at the end of
Chapter XII, and more generally in the geometrical appendix.

As any general work on handrailing would now necessarily be
regarded as incomplete without some reference to the system by square
or normal sections, two chapters have been devoted to its elucidation.
This system, however, though it has numerous able advocates, and
presents many points both instructive and interesting to handrailers, is
nevertheless attended with practical objections which render it unlikely
that it will ever become so general in practice as the more simple
cylindric system, and consequently the latter has been treated of at
much greater length.

Although an intimate knowledge of handrailing may not be absolutely
essential to the stair designer, some acquaintance with its leading
principles must prove of the greatest use to him in attaining the best
results.   In fact, it is common experience that architects too often show
in the arrangement of their plans, even of the most ordinary class of
geometrical stairs, an entire absence of appreciation of the points that
conduce to a satisfactory handrail.   This is seen more particularly in
stone stairs in the often unduly crowding together of the steps round
the wells and in the placing of intermediate landings.   If the practice
was more generally followed by architects of drawing developments,
showing the " falling lines " that would result from their plans, as suggested in this work, the defects alluded to would be readily detected,
and the crippled forms of handrails so often met with, even in the better
class of buildings, avoided.

How far the objects aimed at have been realized in the following
pages is of course a matter entirely for others to judge, and the authors

can here only express a hope that the publication of the volume may serve the useful purpose of bringing more forcibly home to artisans who may be engaged in staircase work the great advantages, not only in point of accuracy but in economy of time and material, that follow from the application of geometrical principles as compared with the results obtained from the employment of those "rule-of-thumb" methods too often adopted in the workshop.

It only remains to acknowledge our indebtedness to Mr. John Murray, the publisher of Barry's "Lectures on Architecture," and to the owners of the copyright of that work, for their permission to reproduce the drawing of the "Crewe Hall staircase" which appears as the frontispiece.

All the other illustrations have been specially prepared for this work.

For much kindly encouragement, and for valuable help in arranging the book, we have to thank the publishers, Messrs. George Bell and Sons, who have been at great pains to present the subject matter in the most suitable form.

A list of the principal works consulted will be found following the contents.

WILLIAM MOWAT.
ALEXANDER MOWAT.

SCHOOL OF SCIENCE AND ART,
    Barrow-in-Furness,
        January, 1900.

SAFETY REGULATIONS APPLICABLE TO STAIRBUILDING AND HANDRAILING

All readers are advised to consult national and local regulations relating to the construction of handrails and staircases. This book has been reproduced from an original edition published in 1900 and is intended to illustrate how staircases and handrails were constructed at that time. The instructions, designs and other data contained in this book may not conform with present industry safety standards.

CONTENTS

PART I.—STAIRBUILDING

CHAPTER I

CHAPTER II

CHAPTER III

CHAPTER IV

CHAPTER V

HALF-TURN NEWELLED STAIRS

CHAPTER VI

HALF-TURN GEOMETRICAL STAIRS

CHAPTER VII

HALF-TURN GEOMETRICAL STAIRS—*continued*

CHAPTER VIII

STAIRS FOR PASSENGER SHIPS

CHAPTER IX

STAIRS FOR PASSENGER SHIPS—*continued*

SIDE-FLIGHT STAIRS

CHAPTER X

STAIRS FOR PASSENGER SHIPS—*continued*

CIRCULAR STAIRS

CHAPTER XI

MISCELLANEOUS ILLUSTRATIONS OF STAIR STARTINGS AND BALUSTRADES —CHARACTERISTIC EXAMPLES OF NEWEL STAIRCASES OF THE SIXTEENTH AND SEVENTEENTH CENTURIES

PART II.—HANDRAILING, THEORETICAL AND PRACTICAL

CHAPTER XII

HANDRAILING (THEORETICAL)

REMARKS AND DEFINITIONS—The problem of handrailing—A difficult branch of joinery—A knowledge of geometry necessary to efficiency—Practice as well as theory essential. *Technical terms*—Wreaths, ramp, level easing, swan-neck,

CHAPTER XIII

HANDRAILING (THEORETICAL)—*continued*

DETERMINATION OF FACE MOULDS AND BEVELS

CHAPTER XIV

HANDRAILING (PRACTICAL)

THE WAY TO MAKE A QUARTER-CIRCLE WREATH

CHAPTER XV

HANDRAILING (PRACTICAL)—*continued*

CHAPTER XVI

HANDRAILING (PRACTICAL)—*continued*

CHAPTER XVII

HANDRAILING (PRACTICAL)—*continued*

COMPLEX CASES OF WREATHS (EASINGS FORMED ON WREATH PIECE)

CHAPTER XVIII

SYSTEM OF HANDRAILING BY NORMAL SECTIONS

CHAPTER XIX

SYSTEM OF HANDRAILING BY NORMAL SECTIONS—*continued*

PART III.—STONE STAIRS

CHAPTER XX

GENERAL DETAILS OF CONSTRUCTION

CHAPTER XXI

CONSTRUCTION OF SPIRAL AND ELLIPTIC STAIRS

Remarks on winding or spiral staircases—*Spiral stair with solid newel formed by ends of steps*—Disposition of steps in plan. *Spiral stair (geometrical)*—Practical problems involved in the construction of winding stairs—Remarks—Application of the moulds in the preparation of steps. *Elliptic staircases*—Forming the soffit—An approximate method of determining the soffit lines.

CHAPTER XXII

TERRACE STAIR WITH STONE BALUSTRADE

General arrangement—Development of long balustrade—Nature of the heading joints in the plinth and capstone of the balustrade—Moulds for marking out the plinth blocks—Directions for working one of the plinth blocks—Moulds for marking out the wreathed capstone of balustrade—Directions for applying the moulds and working a length of the capstone of balustrade—Observations on the method—Preparing the capstone when the heading joints are plane surfaces.

APPENDIX

PLANE AND DESCRIPTIVE GEOMETRY

General observations.

PLANE GEOMETRY.

Measurement of Angles.

PLANES.

Traces of a Plane—Horizontal Trace—Vertical Trace.

SECTIONS AND DEVELOPMENTS.

LIST OF PRINCIPAL ILLUSTRATIONS

LIST OF
THE PRINCIPAL WORKS CONSULTED IN THE PREPARATION OF THIS TREATISE

Newlands' Carpenter and Joiner's Assistant.
Tarbuck's Encyclopædia of Carpentry and Joinery.
Nicholson's New Carpenter's Guide.
Rivington's Notes on Building Construction.
Riddell's Handrailer and Stairbuilder.
Creswell's Staircasing and Handrailing.
Colling's Practical Treatise on Handrailing.
Monckton's Stairbuilding and Handrailing.
Wood's Practical Stairbuilding and Handrailing.
Marwick's Staircases, Historic and Artistic.
Goldthorp's Handrailing by the Square Cut.
The American Stairbuilder and Instructor.
Stairbuilding, Encyclopædia Britannica.
Gwilt's Encyclopædia of Architecture.
Barry's Lectures on Architecture.
Wilson's Carpentry and Joinery.
Mitchell's Advanced Building Construction.
Nash's Old English Mansions.
Purchase's Stonecutting.
Mahan's Stonecutting.
Warren's Problems on Stonecutting.
Fletcher, B. and H., Carpentry and Joinery.
Robson's Domestic Building Construction.
The Professional Building Journals.

PART I.—STAIRBUILDING

STAIRBUILDING

CHAPTER I

GENERAL REMARKS AND PRELIMINARY DEFINITIONS

A STAIR (literally an ascent, from the Anglo-Saxon word *Staeger*, to ascend) is a series of steps arranged on an incline to enable ascent and descent to be conveniently made from one level to another.

The term *staircase* is generally used to denote the whole structure, including the supporting framework and balustrade.

Some writers on this subject, for example, Newlands, define staircase as " the apartment in which the stair is placed;" and, again, Gwilt, in his "Encyclopedia of Architecture," defines staircase as an "enclosure formed by walls or partitions, or both, for the reception of an ascent of stairs."

In some standard works on Architecture no distinction is observed between the words stair and staircase, both terms being used synonymously to signify the whole structure.

It would perhaps tend to greater clearness to use the term *stairway* to denote the space set apart for the reception of the stairs; *staircase* to mean the whole mechanical structure, and to restrict the term stair more particularly to the combination or set of steps.

Staircases are generally built either of stone, concrete, iron or wood. These materials differ so widely from one another in their physical properties, that when they are used for constructive purposes, as in stairbuilding, the forms of the component parts and the modes of combining them that prove suitable for one of these materials are not applicable to any of the others. The constructive details of stairs therefore necessarily vary with the material employed.

The special characteristics possessed by each of the materials mentioned recommend its use in preference to the others in certain situations. Thus, stairs built of stone are most suitable for public buildings where there is much traffic, for all exposed situations, and generally wherever strength and durability are required. While, again,

B

iron stairs may be used for situations where economy of space and of material, as well as some degree of fire resistance, are the essential requirements. Iron is also the most suitable material for the construction of spiral staircases that have to stand in open areas, free from supporting walls. In the United States iron is very extensively used in the framework of staircases in association with other materials, such as slate, tile, marble, etc., for the treads.

Wood stairs are used in almost all situations, but being more liable to decay are not so well adapted as either stone or iron for external construction. They are almost universally employed for the internal stairs of domestic buildings, being not only well adapted to the special purpose, but also in harmony with the other interior furnishings. Wood has a softness and elasticity which do not belong to the other materials. The steps do not become smooth through wear, and prove a source of danger, as is the case with stone or iron. On this account wood stairs can always be used with greater freedom and security. In large "tenements" the exits from the upper floors should not depend on wood stairs, these being quickly destroyed in the event of fire, unless the steps are formed of solid blocks of hardwood, built into the wall at both ends, or some form of fireproof construction with wood adopted. In ships, wood is almost exclusively used for both inside and outside stairs, although in cases where extra strength is required iron is sometimes used in combination with wood as supports.

Although the present treatise is primarily devoted to the technique of wood staircasing, or work that would generally be performed by joiners, many of the considerations and principles laid down in the following pages are applicable to all stairs of whatever material they may be constructed.

Before proceeding to classify the different forms of stairs, and to describe and illustrate their construction, it will be convenient to define all the important terms that have a meaning peculiar to the subject.

The **step** of a wood stair consists of two parts, the one termed the *tread*, and the other the *riser*.

The **tread** is the horizontal part of the step upon which the foot is placed.

The **riser** is the vertical part of the step, and connects the front of one tread with the back of the next below it.

Nosing is the outer edge of the tread which projects beyond the outer face of the riser. It is usually rounded, chamfered, or moulded, and when so treated is termed a *moulded nosing*.

The **going** of a step is the horizontal distance between the outer faces of two consecutive risers. This term is not often used, the distance referred to being generally spoken of as the "width of tread," or shortly, the "tread" (see Fig. 1).

Rise.—The vertical distance between the upper surfaces of two consecutive treads.

Fliers.—Steps of uniform or parallel width used in the straight portions of stairs.

Winders.—Steps that are narrower at one end than the other. They are employed in turning corners or going round curves.

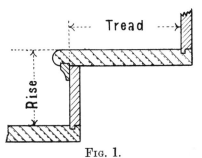

Fig. 1.

Flight.—A succession of steps uninterrupted by a landing.

Landing.—A horizontal platform introduced in the course of the ascent as a convenient resting-place, and affording a means of effecting a change of direction of the stair. It thus forms the termination of one flight as well as the start for the next.

If a complete half turn has to be made on the landing between the termination of one flight and the start of the next, it is then termed a *half-space landing* (see Figs. 16 and 19), and if only a quarter turn, it is called a *quarter-space landing* (see Figs. 9 and 11).

The term "landing" is also applied to the portion of the floor (or of the deck in ships) immediately adjoining the top or bottom of a stair.

The going of a flight.—The horizontal distance between the faces of the first and last riser of a flight. Sometimes also called the *run* of the flight. In circular stairs the measurement is made on a line 15 inches to 18 inches from the handrail, over the narrow ends of the steps.

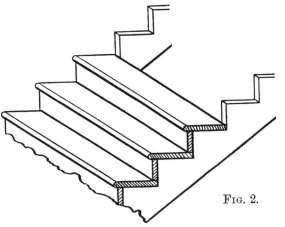

Fig. 2.

Strings or stringers.—The raking or inclined pieces which support the ends of the steps. Of these there are several sorts.

1. *Cut strings* are simply notched out on their upper edges to receive

the treads and risers, as shown by Fig. 2. They are only used for the roughest class of stairs.

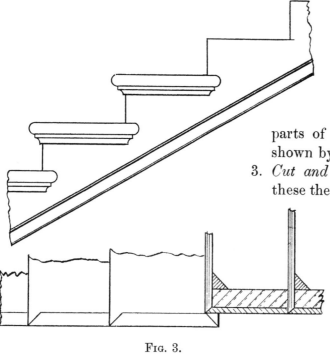

2. *Cut and mitred strings.*—These are notched out as in the preceding, but the ends of the risers are mitred against the vertical parts of the notches. This is shown by Fig. 3.

3. *Cut and bracketed strings.*—In these the ends of the risers mitre with "ornamental brackets" nailed to the face of the string. An example is given by Fig. 4.

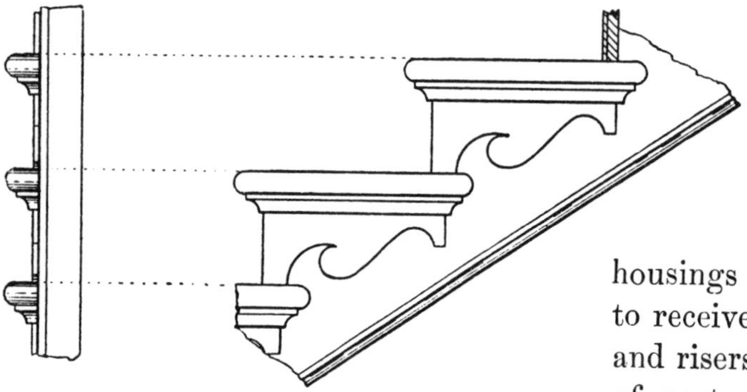

4. *Housed strings.*—The upper edges of these strings, instead of being notched out as in the previous examples, are made parallel to the lower edges, and housings cut in the inner sides to receive the ends of the treads and risers. An inside elevation of part of a housed string is given by Fig. 5.

FIG. 3.

FIG. 4.

5. *Open and close strings.*—The examples Figs. 3 and 4 are often designated "open strings," as opposed to that given by Fig. 5, which is frequently called a "close string."

6. *A wreathed string* is one that, while it follows the inclination of the stairs, winds round a vertical cylindric surface. For example, the strings of a spiral staircase, or again the curved string carried round the well-hole of a geometrical stair are wreathed.

7. *Rough strings.*—These are rough scantlings, fitted below the steps between the finished strings, to provide additional support and stiffening to the stair, rendered necessary when it exceeds three or four feet in width. *Carriages,* and sometimes *spring-trees,* are terms also applied to these timbers.

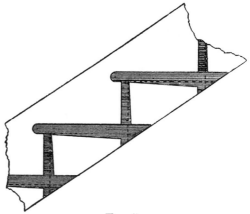

Fig. 5.

Strings are also distinguished by their relative positions, as "outer string," "front string," "well string," "wall string," in ships "bulkhead string;" the meanings of which being obvious no explanations are required.

Easings.—The curves formed on the edges of strings, where they meet at different inclinations, or, again, where a pitched string joins in with the level skirting, are called "easings," and may be parts of circles or any other agreeable curves.

Well, well-hole.—The clear, vertical, central space round which the stair turns.

Stair-handrails are rounded or moulded bars for holding on to by the person ascending or descending the stair. They are placed over the ends of the steps, at a height from them convenient for the hand to grasp, being made to conform throughout their length to the inclination of the stair.

Balusters are light pillars for supporting the handrail and for filling up the space between the latter and the stair steps, to prevent persons from falling through.

Balustrade.—The framework formed by the combination of rail and balusters.

Newels.—The posts or columns used in some kinds of stairs at the turnings to connect the handrails and strings of adjacent flights.

The term newel is also applied to the post or final baluster, at the bottom of a stair, which terminates a balustrade. In a spiral staircase built round a central post or pillar the post is referred to as the "newel."

Curtail or scroll step.—The bottom step of a stair is so named when one or both of its ends project beyond the strings so as to stand under the spiral scrolls of the handrail, with which they should be made to partly agree in plan (see Fig. 119).

Bullnose step.—The bottom step of a stair projecting as above, but having its ends semicircular (see Fig. 11). The step shown in Fig. 44 with quarter circle end is also sometimes called a "bullnose."

Commode step.—A combination of two round-ended steps, one above the other, standing under a newel at the start of a stair, as in Fig. 184.

CLASSIFICATION OF THE VARIOUS FORMS OF STAIRS.

All stairs may be referred to either of two classes:

1. STRAIGHT STAIRS or those which continue in the same direction throughout the entire ascent.

2. TURNING STAIRS, *i.e.*, stairs that change their direction in the course of the ascent.

Class 1.—Sketch plans of straight stairs are given by Figs. 6 and 7. They are generally continued in one flight from top to bottom as in

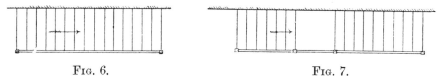

FIG. 6.   FIG. 7.

Fig. 6, unless in cases where the height to be attained is considerable, when it may be desirable to introduce a landing, as in Fig. 7.

Class 2.—Several subdivisions may be made of this class: first, having regard to the amount of turning; second, the construction or manner in which the turns are made. Thus we have (1) quarter-turn stairs; (2) half-turn; (3) three-quarter-turn; and (4) one-turn stairs, according as the whole change in direction between the first and last riser is one, two, three or four right angles. Again, they may be classed either as *newel stairs* or *geometrical stairs*, this being the more common classification. In the former, newels are the leading feature, being employed at the turnings to connect the strings and handrails of separate flights, as well as at the terminations of the stair balustrade. In the latter, in place of newels at the turnings, the strings of adjacent flights are continued into each other, being connected by a wreathed portion which stands over a definite curve in plan, usually a portion of a circle. This curve may extend the full length of the string, which is then wreathed throughout as in circular stairs (see Figs. 13 and 27), where the turning begins with the stair starting, and is continued uniformly to the top. The characteristic feature of geometrical stairs is therefore the continuity of strings and rails, the formation of which depends on geometrical principles, and hence the name.

The term geometrical as applied to stairs had originally a less general application than is implied in the definition we have just given. It was restricted to such stairs as were supported at one side by a wall and at the other by a continuous string.

We may now refer to the sketch plans Figs. 8 to 27, which are introduced at this stage for the purpose of illustrating the principles of classification explained above.

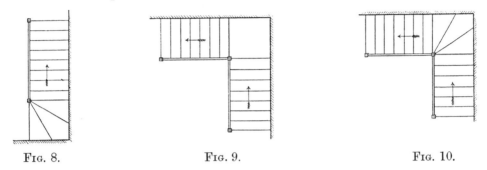

FIG. 8.　　　　FIG. 9.　　　　FIG. 10.

(1) **Quarter-turn stairs.**—The group shown by Figs. 8, 9 and 10 may be described as quarter-turn newel stairs, as they are shown with newels at the turnings into which the strings would be framed; while the next group, Figs. 11 to 13, would be properly distinguished as quarter-turn

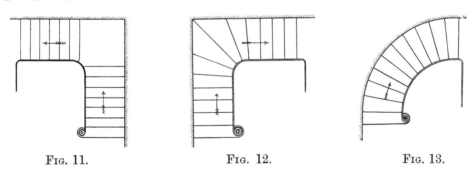

FIG. 11.　　　　FIG. 12.　　　　FIG. 13.

geometrical stairs, the strings and rails being continued without interruption from start to termination.

The separate stairs in each group show differences in their arrangement at the change of direction. Thus Figs. 9 and 11 have a quarter-space landing, and Figs. 10 and 12 are provided with winders in the quarter-space, one or other arrangement being adopted according as either convenience or economy of plan space is the principal consideration.

The characteristic of the stair in Fig. 13 is that the turning commences at the bottom and continues uniformly to the top, the entire stair being composed of winders (excepting the first step), and from this feature they are often referred to as "winding" stairs, or "circular" stairs.

Figs. 14 and 15 may be described as quarter-turn side-flight stairs, as they have two side flights branching off from the common landing,

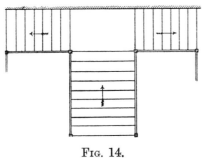

FIG. 14.

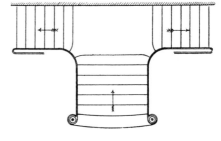

FIG. 15.

each being at right angles to the centre flight. They are distinguished from one another also in the one being a newel and the other a geometrical stair.

(2) **Half-turn stairs.**—These form a numerous class, and are usually of one or other of the types illustrated by the plan sketches, Figs. 16 to 25.

The first and second groups represent *newelled* stairs, and the others *geometrical*. Of the former, two kinds may be distinguished.

(a) *Dog-legged.*—These are shown by Figs. 16, 17 and 18, and are so named from a fancied resemblance that the side elevation presents to the bent form of a dog's hind leg. They have no well, the

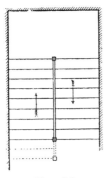

FIG. 16.

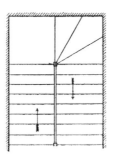

FIG. 17.

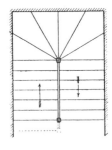

FIG. 18.

outer strings and rails of the forward and backward flights being directly over one another. Three varieties of the dog-legged stair occur, as represented by the sketches, Fig. 16 having a landing in the half space, and Fig. 18 winders, while Fig. 17 is shown with a landing in one of the quarter spaces, and three winders in the other.

(*b*) *Open Newelled.*—In these there is a clear vertical space or well left between the progressive and retrogressive flights ; so that two newels are required instead of one as in the case of the dog-legged,

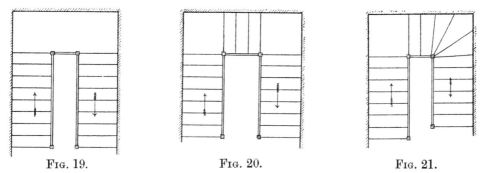

FIG. 19.   FIG. 20.   FIG. 21.

admitting of a cross-string and rail being framed into between them to continue the balustrade across the well.   The width of the well is often

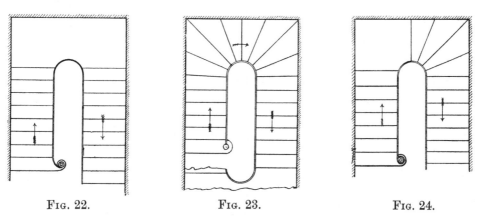

FIG. 22.   FIG. 23.   FIG. 24.

such as to allow a definite cross flight to be formed between the quarter spaces, as in Figs. 20 and 21.

Various arrangements may, according to the circumstances, be made between the two flights, but those illustrated by Figs. 19, 20, 21, are the most common.

Of course, the term "open newel" is not confined to stairs making a half turn, but one or more quarter turns may be added, the whole inclosing a square or rectangular well.

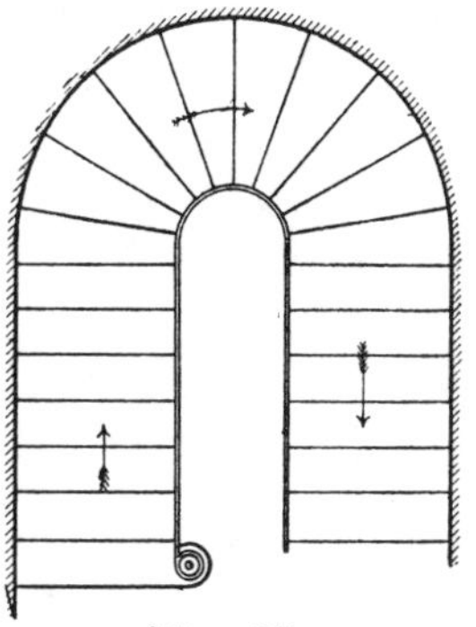

Half-turn Geometrical stairs.—Figs. 22 to 25 illustrate the usual variations in the arrangement

FIG. 25.

of these stairs.   The landings and winders have to be so placed in the well as to produce agreeable curves in the strings and handrails.

C

(3) **Three-quarter turn stairs.**—Only one example of this class is given by Fig. 26. As in the preceding groups, differences occur according as there are landings or winders at the turns. The illustration, it will be seen, is the plan of a geometrical stair with landings in the half and quarter spaces.

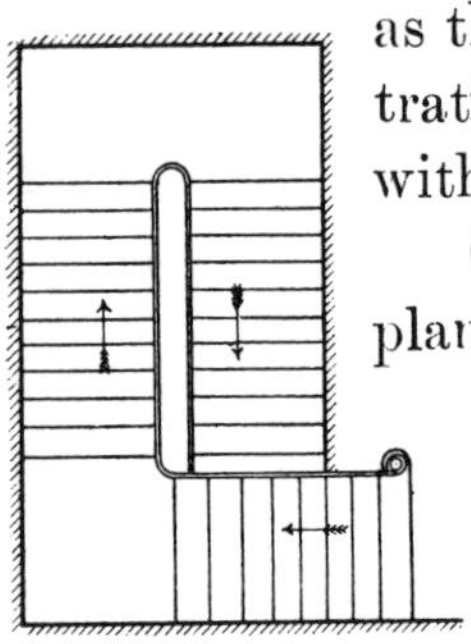

Circular staircases.—Stairs may be so named when the plans of the strings conform to circles or arcs of circles. They are, of course, included in the general classification that we have just made; thus the example, Fig. 27, would be described as a "whole-turn winding stair." Another example of the class making a quarter turn, Fig. 13, has already been noticed.

FIG. 26.

They also receive other names, as "Spiral stairs," "Helical stairs," "Wheeling stairs."

Several points of difference may be noted in stairs belonging to this class. For example, the inner or converging ends of the steps may be either supported and cased into a finished string encompassing a well of greater or less diameter, according to circumstances, or they may be housed into a solid central newel, round which the stair is built. Again, the outer or divergent ends of the steps may be supported by a wall and wall string, as in the illustration Fig. 27, or the stair may be completely detached from any wall, and self-supporting.

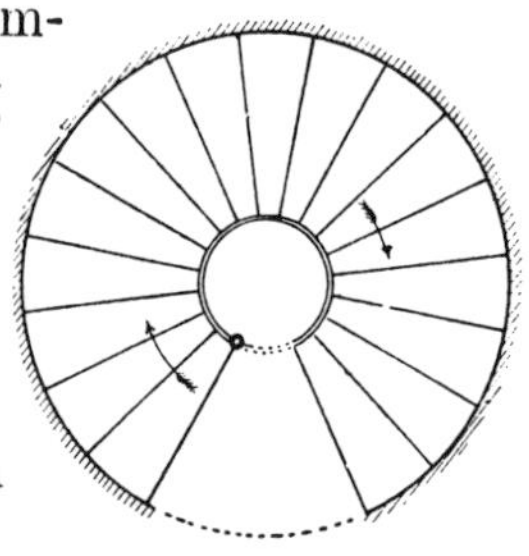

FIG. 27.

Elliptic staircases are those that have the plan lines of the strings parallel to or equidistant from an elliptic curve, the position of which on the plan should be so chosen as to give the best appearance to the whole. It is generally convenient in practice to make this guiding ellipse the plan of the centre line of handrail at the well. The other curves made equidistant from it—measured along the normals—are, of course, not ellipses, but only agree with the guiding ellipse in having the same centres of curvature, or, in other words, the evolute of the ellipse is also the evolute of all the other curves that are parallel to it. A plan of an elliptic stair making rather more than a half turn is given by Fig. 27a.

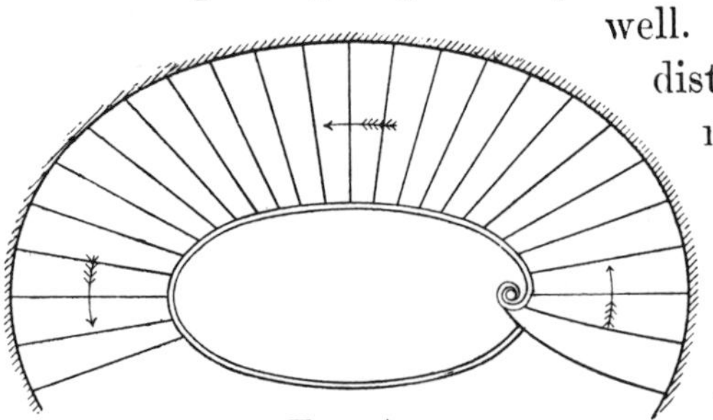

FIG. 27a.

Bracket stairs is a name applied to stairs with "open strings," which have ornamented brackets fitted below the ends of the treads.

Many other varieties of plan arrangements might be added to the illustrations, but to give more would not serve any useful purpose here, as sufficient examples have been given to show the principle of classification, and to enable the student to assign any stair of ordinary form to its proper class.

CHAPTER II

General remarks.—It is of the utmost importance in preparing the designs of a building, or in planning out the internal arrangements of passenger vessels, that sufficient space be allocated to the principal stairs, so that they may be made to meet in all respects the requirements of the place and circumstances.

Their positions also should be suitably chosen, so as to be easily accessible and convenient for the traffic.

In ships there is some palliation for the naval architect allocating to the staircases restricted plans, where the whole accommodation is necessarily limited, and where every portion of space is of so much value; and, besides, the conditions are such as to require every one on board to submit to some inconvenience, and to be prepared to exercise caution in getting from one deck to another. But in dwelling-houses there should be no such restricting conditions, especially as it will often be found that had only a slight re-arrangement of the plan been made it would have resulted in adding a couple of feet or so to the " going," which would have made the stair satisfactory, and would not have interfered much with other conveniences. Often a very little plan space will make all the difference between a good and a bad stair.

It is not uncommon to find in dwelling-houses, which are otherwise convenient, stairs that are narrow, steep, ill-constructed, badly planned, and even dangerous, and to which the name " chicken ladder " would be much more appropriate than staircase.

In important buildings the degree of appropriateness of the stair structure to the situation and surroundings affords a very good means of measuring the skill and ability of the architect. It is very commonly admitted that no other part of the interior of an edifice exercises to the same extent his ingenuity and skill, or makes so great demands upon his resources, or affords him so much scope for architectural display and effect.

An eminent architect[1] has said that "nothing marks more clearly than the design of the staircase the difference between an architectural composition and a builder's box," and strongly advises young architects to study the planning and designing of staircases.

Every new situation calls for distinct treatment and new designs. A staircase designed so as to be fitted in every way to the peculiarities of its position will not be, in all respects, suited to another, although the conditions may be somewhat similar. The capacious and elaborate staircases appropriate in a palatial public building would be out of place in a private mansion, and the grand staircases of ocean liners would only be occupying useful space in vessels designed for less important passenger traffic.

Any ornamentation or embellishment should be appropriate and in harmony with the surroundings, and should not be realized at the expense of utility and convenience.

In the ordinary run of work which really forms the greater part of what the stairbuilder is called upon to execute, the architect does little more than set apart the necessary stair space, and give a few details, leaving all the internal arrangement of steps, etc., to be worked out by the practical man.

We will now discuss some practical points and rules that have to be attended to in staircase design and construction.

1. **Width of flights.**—In determining the width of stairs general reference will, of course, be made to the size and quality of the building or the ship, as the case may be; but principally to the exigencies of the position and the traffic.

Main staircases should never have the steps less than 4 feet long, so that two persons meeting on the stair may easily pass each other without experiencing any inconvenience. On the other hand, they may extend to a length of 8, 10, or even 12 feet in *grand staircases*.

Again, the width of *ordinary stairs* should not be much less than 3 feet even for small cottage-houses.

Where two or more flights lead to and unite in a single flight, the capacity of the latter should be equal to that of the other two combined, since it has to accommodate their united traffic. Thus in a stair of the type shown by Figs. 14 and 15, if the width of each of the side flights is, say, 3 feet, the central one should be about 6 feet. In many cases of stairs of this class, when the centre flight exceeds 9 feet in width, it is divided in the middle by a light handrail.

[1] Professor Barry.

In theatres and similar buildings the lower flights of stairs should be proportionately widened to accommodate the fresh accessions of persons poured into them from the different levels. The regulations of the London County Council require a minimum width of 4 feet 6 inches for 400 persons, and this width to be increased by 6 inches for every accession of 100, up to a maximum width of 9 feet.[1] In such buildings wide stairs are to be deprecated, it being safer to multiply the number of separate stairs. For schools 4 feet should be about a maximum width.

2. **Pitch of stairs.**—This is an important point, as upon the pitch or angle of inclination will chiefly depend the ease and safety of the stair.

Down to a certain limit the less the inclination the easier is the stair to ascend. When, however, the angle of inclination is too small—say less than 27°, or one vertical to four horizontal—it would in some respects prove inconvenient, as the ascent, though easy, becomes too tedious, and any one with ordinary activity would experience a feeling of impatience at the slowness of his progress up or down, and would probably be tempted to take two steps at a time.

On the other hand, when the pitch exceeds 45° the stair can no longer be described as an easy one, even though the steps may be properly proportioned and arranged in the best possible manner on the stair slope. Farther, when the angle of inclination reaches 60° the stair is then both a difficult and a dangerous one, and should not be allowed for dwelling-houses, except in situations where it has only to be used on occasion and with due caution, and where an ordinary trap ladder might answer the purpose.

It may be of interest to observe that although a stair of moderate pitch is much easier to ascend than one that is decidedly steep, the total energy expended in the one case is just as much as in the other, being in each case the mechanical work performed in raising one's own weight through the vertical height between the floor levels. Thus, for example, a person weighing 10 stones, or 140 lb., in ascending a stair-case communicating between two levels 10 feet apart, has to perform $140 \times 10 = 1{,}400$ foot pounds of mechanical work, no matter what be the angle of slope.

3. **Length of flights and position of landings.**—For an easy stair it is necessary also to introduce landings at proper intervals in the height, as long flights prove tiresome. A flight of steps should not, if possible,

---

[1] See regulations made by the London County Council under the Metropolis Management and Building Acts Amendment Act, 1878.

contain more than ten or twelve steps, and not less than two. An isolated or single step at any point should not be introduced.

Staircases consisting of several flights will prove all the pleasanter to ascend, and also look all the better, if the same number of steps is placed in each flight. This consideration is especially worth attending to in half-turn stairs of two straight flights. In ascending, the experience of the lower flight forms a rough gauge in one's mind of what the length of the upper should be, and if the latter should contain a few more steps than the former the top will always be anticipated before it is reached, and *vice versâ*.

But however desirable a symmetrical arrangement may be, it cannot always be attained, because the lengths of the flights will, in general, have to accommodate themselves to the position and heights of doors, staircase windows, and other conveniences that may intervene in the stairway.

Landings introduced into spiral staircases between floors should, if possible, be avoided, as they interrupt the continuity of the helical curves, detracting from the graceful appearance which these stairs present, and which is one of their chief recommendations. This is one of the exceptional cases in which it may be justifiable to sacrifice some ease and convenience for the sake of appearance.

4. **Position of winders.**—In the stairs of public buildings, such as town halls, assembly rooms, churches, schools, theatres, etc., which at times may have large crowds to accommodate, winders should never be employed. In these suitable landings should be placed at all the changes of direction.

Winders joined to a straight flight should, if at all possible, be arranged at the *bottom* of the flight, not at the top.

5. **Arrangement of steps.**—The width of the treads should be equal, and in stairs which have both winders and fliers in their length they should be of a uniform width along a line of ascent, about 15 to 18 inches from the handrail. It is customary in good stairs to make the bottom step wider than the rest, one or two succeeding steps being graduated till the general width is reached. The rise of the step should never vary in the length of a flight, but be made strictly uniform, none higher or lower than the rest. Any difference in the rise always produces a disagreeable feeling to any one using the stair, and may even be attended with danger.

In stairs with winders the ends of the steps round the well should be properly arranged and graduated in width, increasing towards the fliers, so as to avoid sudden alterations in the pitch, and thereby produce easy and graceful curves in the strings and handrails.

It has been recommended by some eminent authorities on architecture to give a slight slope or tilt (about $\frac{3}{16}$ inch to a width of 12 inches) to the upper surface of the steps—being made lower at the nosings—instead of what is the more general practice, to place them horizontal. This however introduces considerable irregularity into the construction, and the advantage to be gained by its adoption is not by any means apparent.

6. **Relation of width of tread to rise.**—There are several rules used in the practice of stairbuilding for determining the ratio of width of tread, or what is sometimes termed the *going* to the rise, these rules giving results which agree more or less closely with one another. They all conform to the general maxim that the greater the width of tread the less should be the height of the rise, it being common experience that stairs having steps which are both wide and high require a great exertion to climb.

Rule I.—It is found by experience that $5\frac{1}{2}$ inches is a convenient rise for a step 12 inches wide; consequently a step of these dimensions may be taken as a standard for regulating those of other steps. Assuming that for other sizes of steps the tread and rise vary from that of the standard in inverse proportion, we get:

$$\text{Tread} : 12 :: 5\tfrac{1}{2} : \text{Rise}$$
$$\text{or Tread} \times \text{Rise} = 12 \times 5\tfrac{1}{2} = 66.$$

It therefore follows that

$$\text{Rise} = \frac{66}{\text{Tread}}$$

$$\text{and Tread} = \frac{66}{\text{Rise}}.$$

Hence the rule may be stated thus:—*Divide the constant number 66 by the width of the assumed tread, and the quotient will be the rise;* or, again, if the rise is assumed, *divide the constant 66 by it, and the quotient will be the required width of tread.*

Example.—With a tread of 8 inches the rise would thus be $\frac{66}{8} = 8\frac{1}{4}$ inches; and, again, with a rise of 7 inches, the tread would be $\frac{66}{7} = 9\frac{1}{2}$ inches nearly.

We give several geometrical constructions for finding the same result graphically.

1st Method.—Draw any two lines at right angles to each other, as D A and C B, intersecting at O, Fig. 28. From O mark off O A = $5\frac{1}{2}$ inches and O B = 12 inches, the rise and tread respectively of the approved standard step.   Set off O D equal to the assumed tread, join B D, and through A draw A C parallel to B D; then O C is the required rise.

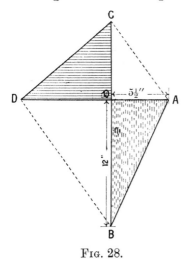

If the rise is assumed and the tread required, the given rise would be marked off as O C, and C A joined, when a parallel to it through B gives OD the width of tread sought.

2nd Method.— Draw a rectangle O A B C, Fig. 29, the sides being equal to the standard tread and rise respectively as shown.

Then (a), *given the tread to find the*

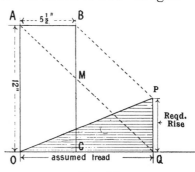

FIG. 28.

FIG. 29.

rise. From O lay off along O C produced a distance O Q, equal to the given tread, and at Q set up a perpendicular.   Draw B P parallel to A Q, intersecting the perpendicular in P.   P Q is the required rise, and P O Q the pitch of stair. (*b*) *Given the rise to find the tread*.   From B set off the distance B M, equal to the given rise.   Join A M, and produce it to cut O C produced in Q; then O Q is the tread required.

3rd Method.—The rule requires that whatever the sizes of the tread and rise may be, when they are multiplied together, their product must equal 66.   A well-known property of the circle, namely, that *the rectangles on the segments of any two intersecting chords are equal,* may be used to find a series of treads and risers related in this way, and its application, as will be seen, is simple.

Draw a straight line A C B, Fig. 30, making A C 12 inches and C B 5½ inches, the dimensions of the standard step.   From C draw,

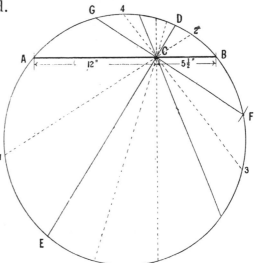

FIG. 30.   DIAGRAM SHOWING TREADS AND RISES FOR VARIOUS SIZES OF STEPS.

at any angle with A B, a line C D, making it equal to either the tread or the rise (say the rise).   Describe a circle passing through the three points,

A, D, and B (see Problem 6, Appendix); then D C, produced to meet the circle in E, gives C E the required tread corresponding to the given rise C D.

By using the same diagram the sizes of any other suitable step may be found. Thus, let the tread be 9 inches: set the compasses to 9 inches, and with C as centre cut the circle at F as shown; then by joining F C and producing it to meet the circle in G gives C G, the rise required.

The student will observe that all chords drawn through C, as 1 2, 3 4, etc., are divided at that point into two parts, which will give treads and rises properly proportioned to one another for any size of step included in the limits of the circle, since the product of any two segments is equal to $A C \times C B$, or $12 \times 5\frac{1}{2} = 66$.

Rule II.—Another simple rule, which gives somewhat different results from the preceding, especially in the case of *narrow* steps, is as follows:—*The tread added to twice the rise equals* 23. Thus, according to this rule

A tread 11 inches wide requires a rise of 6 inches

,,	$10\frac{1}{2}$	,,	,,	,,	,,	$6\frac{1}{4}$	,,
,,	10	,,	,,	,,	,,	$6\frac{1}{2}$	,,
,,	$9\frac{1}{2}$	,,	,,	,,	,,	$6\frac{3}{4}$	,,
,,	9	,,	,,	,,	,,	7	,,
,,	$8\frac{1}{2}$	,,	,,	,,	,,	$7\frac{1}{4}$	,,
,,	8	,,	,,	,,	,,	$7\frac{1}{2}$	,,
,,	$7\frac{1}{2}$	,,	,,	,,	,,	$7\frac{3}{4}$	,,
,,	7	,,	,,	,,	,,	8	,,

The above rule is identical in principle with that given by Blondel in his "Cours d'Architecture," his formula in general terms being:

$$2h + w = p$$

Where h = the height of a step in inches

w = the width   ,,   ,,

and p = the average pace in inches of a man walking on level ground.

Rule III.—A third rule which is generally considered to give good proportions is the following:

Take, as in Rule I., a step 12 inches $\times 5\frac{1}{2}$ inches as a standard, *and for each 1 inch added to or deducted from the tread, deduct from or add to the rise $\frac{1}{2}$ inch respectively.* Thus a tread of 11 inches wide would have a rise 6 inches, and one of 10 inches a rise of $6\frac{1}{2}$ inches, and so on for other widths.

It is hardly necessary to point out that when the going of a stair, as well as its height, is fixed, the above rules for finding out the relation of tread and rise cannot always be strictly carried out; but of course the stairbuilder should approximate to them as nearly as the circumstances of the particular case will allow.

7. **Lighting.**—It is essential for safety that a staircase be adequately lighted at all parts, but particularly at the approach to the top, as well as at the turnings, since it is at these parts that accidents are most likely to occur. The light is furnished either by a skylight at the top or by windows in the sides of the stairway, and sometimes both these means are employed in the same staircase. The most equally diffused and satisfactory light is that obtained by skylights, a construction which readily lends itself to architectural display and effective ornamentation, and also adds loftiness and airiness to the stairway. It is difficult to get a properly diffused light by means of windows in the sides of the stairway; but these are in some respects preferable to skylights, as they are cheerful, and if favourably situated may afford a pleasant look-out from the stairs.

8. **Headway.**—Another point requiring attention in the planning out of stairs is that there be sufficient headway provided when one flight passes under another, or below a trimmer or a landing, so that the tallest person may be able to move up and down with perfect freedom. This will be amply secured if there be a clear space of from 6 feet 6 inches to 7 feet between the obstacle and the nosing line of the steps, measured at right angles to the pitch line of the stairs (see Fig. 74).

The headway thus obtained gives more clearance, measured vertically, in steep stairs than in those of ordinary pitch; and in the former case a smaller distance than 6 feet 6 inches would suffice. In no case, however, should the headway be less than 7 feet, measured vertically at the front edges of the steps.

9. **Strength.**—Only good sound timber, thoroughly seasoned, should be used in the construction of staircases. The several parts should be securely joined together, so that the whole structure may be rigid, and no creaking result from the movement of persons upon it. It is of some importance also that the strength of a stair should be *apparent* as well as real, in order that those ascending it may do so with a feeling of security. This points to the desirability of having, as far as possible, the structural arrangements and supports for the stair conspicuously shown.

KINDS OF WOOD USED IN STAIRS.—In staircase construction the kinds of timber chiefly used are oak, teak, mahogany, and walnut, pitch pine, red and yellow pine.

The first four, the hard woods, are used for the best class of stair-cases, while the soft woods, being cheaper and more easily worked, are used for all parts of inferior stairs, and also for the rough, covered scantlings of the framework of stairs of all sorts.

Oak.—Of the hard woods oak is the most generally used, and when of the best quality probably no other timber answers the purpose so well. It is strong and durable, and when the " silver grain " is well marked has a rich mottled appearance.

When newly wrought it has a clean, bright colour, but grows darker with age. The historical and picturesque newel staircases of the Elizabethan period were generally made of home oak, and present day architects seem to favour traditionally this timber. Oak is easily bent into any curved form by steaming, hence it is well suited for the bent facings of strings round the wells of geometrical stairs.

Teak.—The properties of teak make it admirably suited in many respects for staircase work; like oak, it is strong, durable, and elastic, and it resists well the tear and wear to which stair steps, under the usual conditions of traffic are subjected. It shrinks little, and is not nearly so liable to warp and twist as oak, and, besides, is more easily worked. The lighter varieties of teak have a fine colour, and admit of a high degree of polish. The surface also is not easily disfigured. The best qualities however are more expensive than oak or mahogany, and this places some restriction on its use.

Some of the characteristic properties of teak render it better adapted for the construction of ships' stairs than any other timber.

Mahogany.—This timber is not very extensively employed in the construction of house stairs, though its use is frequent for those of all kinds of passenger vessels. It is, however, much used by the house-builder for the handrails of staircases that are otherwise constructed of pine wood, and is a very fit material for this purpose, being of a nature that makes it easily moulded and worked up to a smooth surface.

The best qualities of mahogany have a fine bright red-brown colour, and the wood is susceptible of taking on and retaining a brilliant polish, which makes it highly ornamental; and, besides, it is fairly strong and durable.

Walnut.—Italian walnut is sometimes used for the balustrades of stairs of the highest class.

This wood when smoothed and polished shows good figure and a rich dark colour. It is, however, rather dark for staircase work, and, besides, is a very expensive wood.

American walnut is frequently used for the same purpose in passenger ships. It is much cheaper than Italian, but not so highly ornamental.

Pitch pine is often used for house stairs as it is a very cheap timber, and its appearance when polished or varnished is another recommendation. It is, however, unreliable in some other respects, as it shrinks and warps, causing the joints to open, even when it has been fairly well seasoned. A pitch pine stair has never to the expert that appearance of strength and solidity that is presented by those that are made of hard wood. This wood is hardly ever adopted for staircases on board ships, except for the rough carriages and framework.

CHAPTER III

CONSTRUCTION OF STRAIGHT STAIRS

Remarks.—A straight staircase being the simplest and most elementary form of stair structure that can be employed, it will be convenient to commence this, the technical part of our subject, with an example of one of this class, and proceed by easy stages to those of greater complexity.

Stairs of this kind are easily constructed, since all the parts that enter into their formation are, in general, straight, their essential component parts being a series of parallel steps supported by a pair of straight string-boards, and no curvilinear, wreathed, or twisted work involved. The operations, therefore, of setting out and making them are of a comparatively easy and straightforward character, and consequently can be produced cheaply as compared with other forms. They are very common in the ordinary class of cottage-houses.

They in many respects prove very convenient, but obviously require a greater length of plan space than those which change their direction in the course of the ascent.

Refer now to the illustrations. Fig. 32 represents the plan of a straight stair built against a wall, an approximate sketch of which, to a small scale, would be given on the general plan of the building.

Fig. 33 is a plan of the joists of the upper floor, showing how they would be trimmed round the opening.

A sectional elevation on the line A A is given by Fig. 31, from which it will be observed that the outer string that receives the ends of the steps in housings is framed in between two newels, the upper newel being fastened directly to the face of the trimmer joist, and the bottom one to the floor. The other string is attached to the wall, and the soffit or under side of the stair is finished with plaster.

We will now describe briefly the taking account of, setting out, and performing the principal operations in connection with the making of a stair such as that represented by the simple example before us.

Principal measurements required.—These are (1) the *height* from

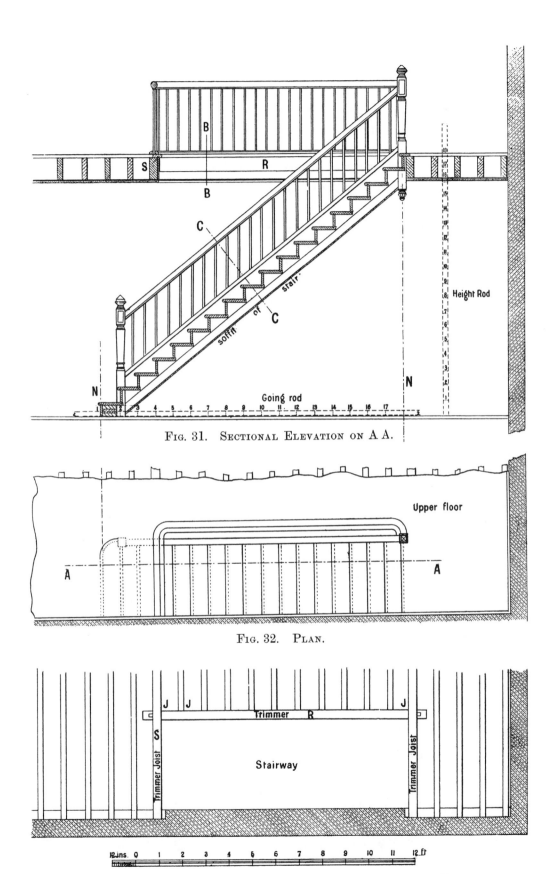

B

S   R

B

C

soffit   of   stair

C

N   Height Rod   N

Going rod
1 2 3 4 5 6 7 8 9 10 11 12 13 14 15 16 17

FIG. 31. SECTIONAL ELEVATION ON A A.

Upper floor

A   A

FIG. 32. PLAN.

J J   Trimmer   R   J

S

Trimmer Joist   Stairway   Trimmer Joist

12 ins. 0   1   2   3   4   5   6   7   8   9   10   11   12 ft

FIG. 33. PLAN SHOWING THE ARRANGEMENT OF TRIMMERS, ETC.

the top of one floor to that of the next; (2) the *going* of the flight; and (3) the *width* of the stairs.

1. The exact height of the storey should be taken at the building (if already erected) by means of a batten, called a "height rod," or "storey rod," as shown on the right of Fig. 31. Otherwise the height will be marked on the rod as measured from the plans of the building.

2. The going of the flight is next marked on another rod. Since this dimension, as we have already explained, is the horizontal distance between the faces of the first and last risers, their positions have of course to be first determined; but it may be observed here that the going—unlike the height, which is fixed—may often be varied, within certain limits, from that given in the original plan, if it is found that by so doing a better ratio of tread to rise would be obtained.

In the illustration (Fig. 31) the going is the distance between the two vertical lines N, N through the riser faces, and the rod on which it is marked is shown lying on the floor.

3. It is usual also to prepare a third rod, showing the distance between the strings, length of steps, depth of housings, thickness of strings, position of newels (if any), and any other particulars which may be required for the stair, such as the position of carriages, etc.

Division of rods for tread and rise.—Being now furnished with the height and going of the stair, the next operation is the division of these dimensions into such a number of steps as will give a tread and rise properly related to each other.

Begin by assuming what might be regarded as a width of tread suitable for the circumstances, and space it off along the going rod (Fig. 31) from N to N with a pair of compasses. Of course, the assumed width will have to be increased or diminished till it divide N N exactly.

The height marked on the storey rod is then divided into the same number of equal parts, *plus one*, which gives the rise corresponding to the assumed tread.

The *rise* and *tread* thus found should now be tested by any of the rules given in the preceding chapter. Thus, by Rule I., if the number found by multiplying them together is about 66, the arrangement may be taken as satisfactory. Otherwise a re-division of the rods will have to be made by taking out a step, or adding one more as required, till a tread and rise properly related to each other have been determined.

The same object may be attained by dividing the height rod first into such a number of equal parts as will give what may be considered a suitable rise, and then dividing the going into the same number of equal parts, *minus one*, to obtain the corresponding tread, and applying the rule as before.

If the stair starting is not confined strictly to a definite position, but may be varied a few inches in one direction or in the other, it would in that case be more convenient to adopt the latter course, namely, to assume a suitable rise and divide the height rod first. Then divide 66 by the rise—given by one of the equal divisions of the rod—and the quotient will be the width of the corresponding tread, which, when spaced off on a rod to the correct number (one less than the number of risers), will show if a suitable starting point for the stair results.

If the starting so found is outside the prescribed limits, the operation will have to be gone over again with a greater or less number of steps as required to bring the first riser to a suitable position.

Some may prefer to find the most suitable rise and tread wholly by arithmetic from the measurements of the height and going without employing rods. Thus, in the example before us, the height is 10 feet 5 inches = 125 inches; and the going is 13 feet 1 inch = 157 inches. Assuming now a trial rise of 7 inches, then the number of rises in the height $= \frac{125}{7} = 17\frac{6}{7}$. We may choose, therefore, between 18 rises at a height of $\frac{125}{18} = 7$ inches (nearly), and 17 rises at a height of $\frac{125}{17} = 7\frac{3}{8}$ inches (nearly).

Taking 18 rises, the number of treads is of course 17, and therefore the width of tread $= \frac{\text{going}}{\text{No. of treads}} = \frac{157}{17} = 9\frac{1}{4}$ inches nearly. Since $9\frac{1}{4}$ inches $\times$ 7 inches $= 64\frac{3}{4}$, these dimensions may be regarded as satisfactory. On the other hand, if 17 rises and 16 treads were taken, the width of tread would be $9\frac{13}{16}$ inches exactly, which multiplied by the corresponding rise, namely, $7\frac{3}{8}$ inches, gives 72·4.

The first supposition, therefore, namely, 18 rises and 17 treads, gives the better proportion, and is the arrangement adopted in the drawing.

Although arithmetical operations may be employed and the rods dispensed with, for practical purposes it is always better, even in the most simple cases, and avoids mistakes occurring, to draw in the two rods as already explained, the one with divisions corresponding to the number and height of the rises, the other showing the number and width of the treads. These rods will prove serviceable also for setting out other dimensions, as for example, the positions of the trimmers.

Drawings required.—The size and number of the steps being now

E

determined, it would be an easy matter to draw out a complete plan
and elevation as shown in Figs. 31 and 32, though for a staircase of this
kind it would only be a waste of time to do so. All the drawings
necessary are full-sized details of some of the more important parts, such
as a step or two at the top and bottom of the stair, showing the position
and arrangement of the newels, trimmers, etc. On these drawings will
be shown also the width and sections of strings, thickness of steps and
risers, and their connecting joints.

Setting out straight strings.—Stair strings, particularly straight ones,
are generally set out with what is called a "pitchboard," an article much
used in stairbuilding and handrailing. It is simply a set-square, or right-
angled triangle (Fig. 34), having the tread and rise of step for its base
and perpendicular respectively, the hypotenuse representing the pitch

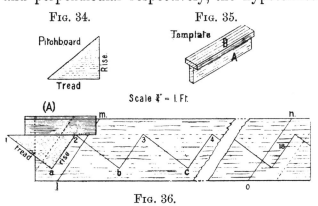

FIG. 34.   FIG. 35.

line of the stair. It
is usually made of a
piece of dry hard-
wood, and about $\frac{1}{4}$ to
$\frac{3}{8}$ of an inch thick.

We will take the
outer string of the
stair (Fig. 31) as an
illustrative example,
and as the method
therein shown will be

FIG. 36.

equally applicable to all straight strings, it will be unnecessary to again
describe the process with similar examples that follow.

First plane the upper edge of the string straight, and then nail two
pieces together to form a gauge or template, as shown in Fig. 35, the
width of the piece A being made equal to the distance of the intersections
of the faces of the treads and risers from the upper edge of the string, as
measured from the detail drawing, the piece B being simply nailed to its
edge to act as a fence.

Let now Fig. 36 be a portion of the lower end of the string; lay the
gauge on to its upper edge, $m\,n$, and place the pitchboard with its hypotenuse held close against the edge of the former, as shown at (A) Fig. 36,
the riser edge being of course kept toward the upper end of string.
Noting from the sectional elevation (Fig. 31) that the face of the second
riser is placed at the middle of the newel, the shoulder line ($m\,l$, Fig. 36)
of the tenon will be parallel to this line, and in advance of it half the
thickness of the newel, in this case 2 inches. The initial position of the

pitchboard must therefore be chosen to leave just sufficient length beyond the shoulder line to form the tenon.

Mark next the riser line, 2 *a* (Fig. 36), and then move the gauge and pitchboard together up the edge of the string till the lower angle 1 of the pitchboard coincides with the point 2. With a cutting-knife mark neatly and firmly the lines 2 *b* and 3 *b*. The gauge and pitchboard is again moved along to draw the lines 3 *c* and 4 *c*, and the operation repeated till the last riser, No. 18, is reached. The face of the last riser being in the middle of the top newel, the shoulder line, *n o*, of the upper tenon will be parallel to it and 2 inches in front of it.

The lines thus drawn on the string (Fig. 36) represent the upper sides of the treads and the outer faces of the risers, and the width of the housings are now marked off from them by means of two templates, T and R (Fig. 37), made to the forms of the ends of the treads and risers respectively, plus the requisite space for the wedges which are used as a means of fixing the ends of steps in the housings.

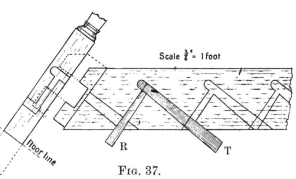

FIG. 37.

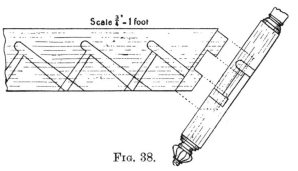

FIG. 38.

The wedges under the treads are made from $\frac{3}{8}$ inch to $\frac{1}{2}$ inch wide at the head, tapering to $\frac{1}{8}$ inch at the point, while those at the back of the risers are from a $\frac{1}{4}$ inch to $\frac{3}{8}$ inch at the head, and nearly $\frac{1}{8}$ inch at the point. They should be made out of dry, straight-grained wood.

The Figs. 37 and 38 represent the ends of the string at this stage, viz., with the housings drawn ready for trenching out and the tenons formed. The necessary housings, as well as the mortises, are also shown marked out on the newels.

For short string boards, instead of making a gauge, as explained above (Fig. 35), a straight-edge may be temporarily sprigged to the string as a guide to the pitchboard.

In any case care has to be exercised in placing the pitchboard accurately in its successive positions, as an accumulation of small errors made in the same direction may result in a very appreciable displacement of the lines of the last few steps.

A *steel square* is very often employed in place of a pitchboard for setting out stair strings of all kinds, and proves very handy for this purpose when the steps are of varying widths. Fig. 39 shows how it may be used to mark out a straight string, such as that in the present example. Insert the square (Fig. 39) into two saw cuts taken out of

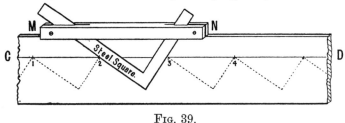

FIG. 39.

the ends of a piece of wood, as M N, and having adjusted the square to the angle of pitch, close the saw cuts firmly upon it by means of two screws, as shown. The distances 1 2, 2 3, 3 4, etc. (Fig. 39), each equal to the hypotenuse of the pitchboard, are spaced off with a pair of compasses along the line CD, gauged from the upper edge, and the tread and riser lines are then drawn through these points by means of the square as shown, the latter being kept to the proper angle by the fence MN sliding on the edge of the string.

Cutting out the housings.—The housings are usually cut out *by hand*, although sometimes in plain, straightforward work, and where a number

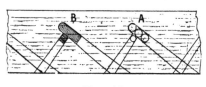

FIG. 40.

of stairs of the same kind are being made, a *machine* may be used with advantage. When cut by hand a few holes are bored out with a brace and centre-bit at the nosings and tops of risers, as at A, Fig. 40. These portions being then roughly pared out to the marks with a chisel, as at B in the same figure, enables a tenon-saw to be used for cutting the remaining parts of the sides of the trenches. The stuff is then roughly cleared away with a chisel, and a "router" used to take them to the exact depth, which is usually from $\frac{3}{8}$ inch to $\frac{1}{2}$ inch.

Preparation of steps.—For straight stairs, the steps being all of one size, the treads and risers can be almost entirely prepared with the machines to the specified sections, and made ready to clean off and put together: even in shops where there is no machinery, this part of the work, being of the very simplest character, can be performed by anyone without any special experience.

Whenever possible each tread and its riser should be jointed together, glued, nailed, and blocked at the bench separately, and the glue allowed to set before the stairs are put together.

Fig. 41 shows one of the steps put together, glued and blocked. It may be noted here that a special appliance, termed a "cradle," is often used as a means of cramping up the joint in the better class of stairs (see Fig. 42). In the present case it will answer well enough, after glueing the joint and knocking the tongue into the groove, to drive in two or three nails from the upper side of the tread to bring up the joint. A short lath, *ll*, should then be temporarily sprigged to the edges of the tread and riser, across the angle, as shown in Fig. 41, to keep them at right angles to each

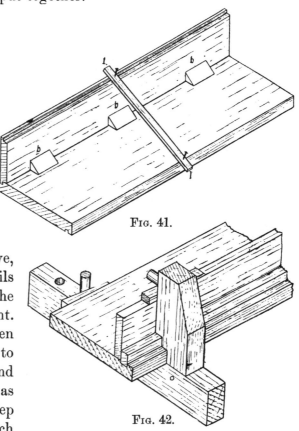

FIG. 41.

FIG. 42.

other until the blocks, *b b b*, are glued into the internal angle, and the whole joint properly set.

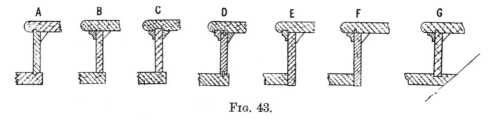

FIG. 43.

Joints between treads and risers.—The joint used in this stair is that shown at A (Fig. 43), the riser being tongued at both edges into the treads. Various other forms of joints are shown in Fig. 43, the most common being those given by C and E, where there is a cavetto below the nosing.

Bull-nose step.—Figs. 44, 45 and 46 illustrate three common methods of forming the riser at the round end of the bottom step. That shown in Fig. 44, namely, by bending the riser round the curve after being reduced at that part to the thickness of a veneer, makes the best job, and the description of the process is given in connection with the construction of scroll steps (Figs. 120, 121 and 122).

Fixing steps and strings together.—When the strings and steps have been prepared in the manner described above, the ends of the latter should be tried into their housings, and any necessary adjustments made to insure that they will fit properly when wedged up, care being taken to mark each step to its place before proceeding to the next.

Straight stairs may always be put together and nearly finished at the shop before they are taken to the building. Of course it will require to be seen to beforehand that they can be got into their place in the finished condition, otherwise they will have to be put together and wedged up *in situ*. In any case, however, it is better to leave the newels off till the stairs are being erected.

To proceed with the work of putting them together: first lay one of the strings on to a straight plank on the floor, and insert the ends of the steps into their proper housings in that string. Next lay the other string on to the top, and having all the steps thus entered into their housings in both strings,

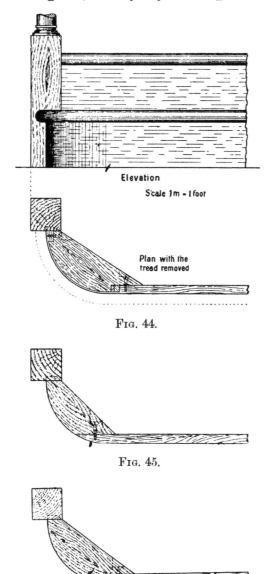

Elevation

Scale 1m - 1 foot

Plan with the tread removed

FIG. 44.

FIG. 45.

FIG. 46.

bring the whole hard up by means of struts from the ceiling, or from any other abutment advantageously situated. Where this cannot be done conveniently, place the plank and string upon low stools, instead of the floor, thus giving room for using cramps. If now the steps are perfectly square to the strings—which may be tested by applying a rod diagonal-wise across the steps— and the strings straight as well as their edges out of winding with each other, the wedges may be inserted and driven hard up. The backs of the treads being then screwed to the lower edges of the risers the struts may be removed, and the stair is ready for being fixed in its place.

Cross sections of stair and balustrade.—In this stair (Figs. 31-33) the handrail and balusters, as well as the capping on the outer string, are of the very plainest character. Enlarged sections of these parts, together with that of the wall string, are shown by ·Fig. 47, the latter being beaded on its upper edge to correspond

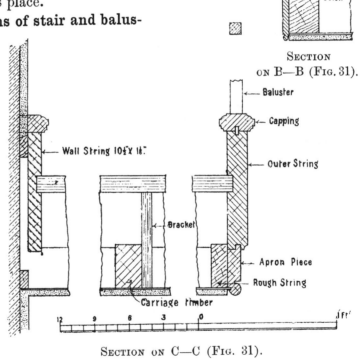

Section
on B—B (Fig. 31).

Section on C—C (Fig. 31).

Fig. 47.

with the skirting to which it joins on the landings.

Trimming joists.—An ·isometric sketch of the joints, J J (Fig. 33), employed in the trimming joists round the stairway is given by Fig. 48, this connection being referred to as a " tusk tenon."

The trimmer, S (Fig. 33), is kept at a distance from the wall beyond the width of the stair to allow the handrail to clear the finished nosing, about $1\frac{1}{2}$ inch. A section of the trimmer is shown at A (Fig. 47), in its relative position with respect to the handrail. Again the length of the opening has to be such as will give ample head room on the stair below the trimmer joist, S (Fig. 33).

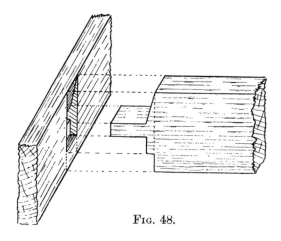

Fig. 48.

The construction of **straight stairs** for **passenger ships** is fully treated of in Chapter VIII., and may be profitably read by the student of stairbuilding at this stage, before taking up the more complex examples of staircases discussed in the next few chapters.

CHAPTER IV

CONSTRUCTION OF QUARTER-TURN NEWELLED STAIR, WINDERS AT THE STARTING

THE next example, which we illustrate to a small scale by a plan and two elevations (Figs. 49, 50 and 51), will form an easy introduction from straight to turning stairs.

Conditions as to space, etc., of stairway.—The outline of the plan (Fig. 50), it will be noticed, is oblong, and might suggest a straight staircase, but we suppose that the conditions of the situation render this form inadmissible. The doorway, M, at the top of the stair fixes the position of the top riser, and there would be too little space between it and the opposite wall for a straight stair of moderate pitch with the necessary room at the bottom to form a convenient approach. We require, therefore, to utilize the whole rectangular space for the ascent, and this is done by making the bottom steps winders, thus turning the direction of the stair outwards to face a passage which is supposed to run alongside the staircase. We have assumed also that the narrowness of this passage makes it undesirable to project the bottom winder beyond the width of the staircase.

The positions of the first and last risers being thus fixed, the problem now is to arrange the steps on the plan, so as to make the stair as safe and easy a one as possible under the prescribed conditions.

Laying-off the plan.—For a stair with winders it is necessary, in order to get their exact size and shape, and also for the preparation and setting-out of the strings and other details, that an accurate and full-sized plan be drawn out of at least the portion including the winders, and preferably of the whole, if not too large.

Having drawn the two lines A B and B C at right angles to each other (Fig. 50), to represent the walls, commence by marking out the square section, at E, of the bottom newel, placing it at the same distance from each wall, in this case leaving 3 feet clear, a dimension which will have been previously arranged and set out on the width rod along with other particulars. Next draw in the lines representing the faces of the top and bottom risers, 1 and 13 respectively, placing the latter about 1½ inch from the outer face of the newel post, so that the nosing of the tread will house into and not project beyond it. The upper newel, at **F** (Fig. 50), may now be drawn in at the same distance from the wall, **AB**, as the lower one, and projecting beyond the face of the top riser just far enough to receive the housing of the floor nosing. Draw also the lines representing the wall and outer strings, the former 1½ inch thick, and the latter 2 inches, and placed in the centre of the newels, as seen in Fig. 56. From the centre of the plan of the newel post, at the winders, with a radius of 16 inches, strike out the circular line of travel, and continue it in a straight line to the top of the stair parallel to the wall line. The stretch out of this line between the first and last riser faces of course represents the going of the stair, and all the steps, both fliers and winders, should be of uniform width measured along it. The length of this line may now be measured with a flexible batten, which should then be divided, along with the storey rod, precisely in the manner we have already explained for a straight stair (Chapter III.) in order to find the number and exact dimensions of the steps. These, in the present instance, divide out to twelve steps with 9-inch treads and 7¼-inch rises, the whole height being made purposely low to get the drawings within the limits of the page.

The " going batten," thus divided, is again laid upon the line of travel (Fig. 50), and the divisions on it transferred to the latter. The lines representing the faces of the risers are then drawn through these points, which must be taken as fixed and unalterable. The riser lines of the fliers are of course drawn at right angles to the going line. The direction of the riser lines of the winders, however, will require some consideration.

Balanced steps.—If these were drawn so as to radiate from the centre—in this case also the centre of the. newel—it would generally result in making the treads of the winders inconveniently narrow at that end: to as far as possible obviate this crowding at the newel, the riser lines should be swung round about the fixed points, as at A, B, C, D (Fig. 54), on the line of travel, out of the radial positions, so as to gain some additional width for these narrow ends of the winders, obtained, of course, at the expense of one or two of the adjoining fliers, which will be correspondingly narrowed at that end. The steps whose risers are thus placed obliquely to the line of travel of the stairs, so as to decrease the inequality of width between the ends of the winders and fliers, have been termed " dancing " or " balanced " steps.

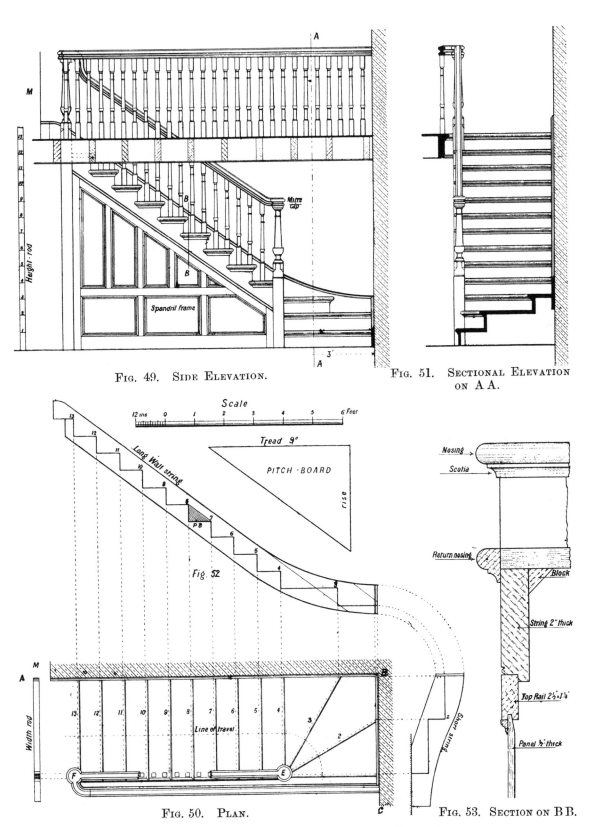

FIG. 49. SIDE ELEVATION.

FIG. 51. SECTIONAL ELEVATION ON A A.

Scale

12 ins 0 1 2 3 4 5 6 Feet

Tread 9"

PITCH · BOARD

rise

Long Wall string

P B

Fig. 52

Height · rod

Spandril frame

Mitre cap

Nosing

Scotia

Return nosing

Block

String 2" thick

Top Rail 2½" × 1¼"

Panel ½" thick

Width rod

Line of travel

Short string

FIG. 50. PLAN.

FIG. 53. SECTION ON B B.

FIGS. 49-53. DRAWINGS FOR A QUARTER-TURN NEWEL STAIR.

For the arrangement of the winders about the newel in the present example the student is referred to the enlarged detail (Fig. 56), in which it will be observed that the face of the fourth riser comes into the string just behind the newel post, and that a reasonable width is obtained for the narrow ends of the winders without encroaching on the adjacent flier. A reference to the elevation (Fig. 49) will make it apparent that, since the outer string is an open one, to have curtailed the end of the first flier in order to increase the width of the narrow ends of the winders would have detached the riser from the post, thereby leaving an unsightly opening, and cutting away a great part of the substantial connection

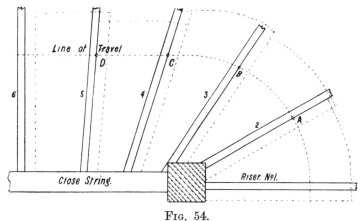

FIG. 54.

obtained between the string and newel.

Of course if a *close string* had been adopted it would have allowed greater latitude in the placing of the risers, and an arrangement

similar to that shown by Fig. 54 would then be preferable.

Elevation.—As we have already observed, it is seldom necessary for practical purposes to draw out a complete elevation, even for stairs of the most complex construction; but when a full-sized plan has been drawn it will not occupy much time to draw the principal lines of the elevation, projected from the plan, leaving out all minute details. For example, in Fig. 49 it would be an easy matter to draw in the main lines of the outside string, newels, and handrail, and also the outline of the spandrel frame, so that it could be made along with the stair. But, as a rule, a full-sized elevation would only be required to the extent of a small portion of the stair (a step or two) and balustrade at bottom and top, where the more important details occur.

Drawing in the newels.—An isometric view of the base of the lower newel, showing the requisite housings on its two inner faces, is given by Fig. 55. In order to mark out these housings, first draw on to the post the floor line with a square. Next, by means of the storey rod, applied as in the figure, mark the lines a, b, c, d, squaring them over to the adjacent face as required.

These give the lines of the upper surfaces of the four treads, which, as may be seen from the plan (Fig. 56), are each either wholly or partly housed into the newel.

Proceed now to set a gauge to the distance that the face of the first riser stands back from the front of the newel, that is O 1 in Fig. 56, and with it gauge off from the corresponding face of the newel (Fig. 55) the vertical line representing the front of the first riser. The other riser lines, 2, 3, are marked with the gauge in the same way, the distances being obtained from the plan as before. Otherwise the end of the post may be placed upon its plan, and the points 1, 2, 3 marked on the newel, and the lines of the riser faces projected up from these points.

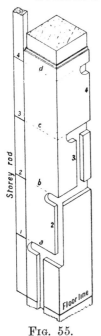

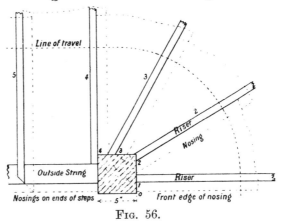

FIG. 55.

FIG. 56.

From these lines now drawn on the newel the width of the housings can be set off in the manner most convenient, while the nosings may be drawn out by applying the cut ends of the treads.

The positions of the mortises for the string, and the lines indicating the limits of the turning on both the newels, will be marked out from the full-sized partial elevation on which these particulars will have been arranged and shown, this part of the " setting-out " being only a matter, therefore, of copying or transferring the working lines from that drawing on to the stuff, requires no notice.

Setting-out the open string.—This is shown by Fig. 57, the operation being similar to that already explained for a close or housed string (see Fig. 36). Only it is more convenient in this case to work the gauge off the lower edge of the string, as the upper edge, having to be finally notched out, may be left in the rough condition.

It should be carefully noted, that since the ends of the treads project over the face of the string, and the ends of the risers are mitred to it, the lines drawn on the face of the string with the pitchboard represent the under sides of the treads and the faces of the risers, so that the width of the gauge (Fig. 57) has to be made equal to the distance of the intersection of these lines from the lower edge of the string-board.

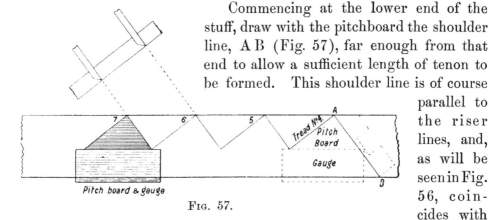

Commencing at the lower end of the stuff, draw with the pitchboard the shoulder line, A B (Fig. 57), far enough from that end to allow a sufficient length of tenon to be formed. This shoulder line is of course parallel to the riser lines, and, as will be seen in Fig. 56, coincides with the face of the fourth riser. Without moving the pitchboard (Fig. 57) draw the line for the tread No. 4. The gauge and pitchboard are then moved along to draw out the successive notches till the last riser, No. 13, is reached. The shoulder of the joint for the top newel is now drawn, being measured backwards 2 inches from the face of riser No. 13, and this completes the setting-out of the outer string.

Fig. 57.

Preparation of open string.—The tenons having been formed in the usual way, the notches are then accurately sawn out to the lines. This finishes the horizontal parts of the notches for the treads to rest on, but the vertical portions have to be recessed back the thickness of the risers, and the mitres formed as shown in Fig. 58.

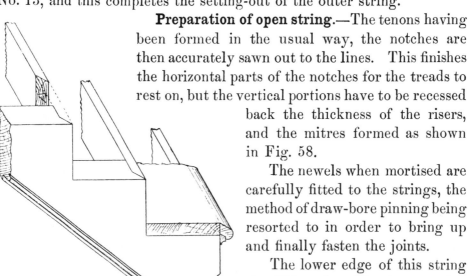

The newels when mortised are carefully fitted to the strings, the method of draw-bore pinning being resorted to in order to bring up and finally fasten the joints.

The lower edge of this string should be rebated for the reception of the spandrel framing, and the joint broken with a bead, as shown by the enlarged detail (Fig. 53).

Fig. 58.

When open strings are either painted on the outside, or partly covered with ornamental brackets, they may be cut out of narrower stuff by utilizing the triangular pieces cut from the notches, glueing these on in the manner shown by Fig. 59 to make the strings out to the requisite width.

Setting-out the wall strings. — The straight portion of the string where the widths of the steps are

FIG. 59.

uniform will present no difficulty to the student who has followed out the description of the operations involved in marking out a housed string for a straight stair, but it will be obvious that where winders occur, on account of their varying widths at the ends, the gauge and pitchboard cannot be applied in the same way.

It will greatly assist the beginner to obtain a clear knowledge of this part of the subject if he will project up from the plan the elevations of both the long and short wall strings, as seen in Fig. 52, using the respective wall lines, A B and B C, as ground lines, the widths of the treads in elevation being of course found by raising perpendiculars from the points where the several riser lines meet the inner faces of the strings. These perpendiculars give also the elevations of the riser faces, being coincident with them. Level lines drawn in between these perpendiculars, at their respective heights, give the several upper sides of the treads. The student should now cut the paper around the sides and top of these elevations so that each can be folded about its ground line into the vertical position. The paper thus folded up vertically fitly represents the walls, and also shows the strings in their correct relative positions with regard to one another and to the plan. In fact, a complete model of the stair in cardboard can be easily and quickly made in this way, standing over its plan, and such an exercise will prove very interesting as well as instructive.

Let us now turn our attention to Fig. 60, which is a plan of the lower part of the stair repeated here to a larger scale for easier reference. Before getting out the stuff for the strings, run out with chalk on the floor from this portion of the plan a rough elevation of the strings, as at (A) and (B) Fig. 60, in order to ascertain their approximate size and form, and what pieces will be required to make out their widths. The most economical arrangement for the present case would be that shown in the sketch, in which two pieces, C and D, are employed to make out the contour at the lower end of the long string, and to make the shorter string in one piece. Wall strings pieced up in this manner should have the component parts connected with tongue and groove joints well glued.

In marking out the long string for the housings it will be most convenient in this and similar examples to commence at the top and draw successively the several fliers, applying the pitchboard with gauge from

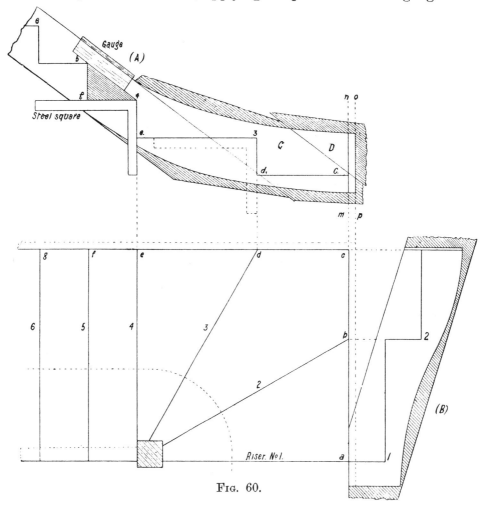

FIG. 60.

the upper edge in the usual manner. In Fig. 60 the pitchboard is shown at (A) in the position in which it would be employed in drawing out the lowest flier, No. 4, and riser No. 5. The gauge at this point is laid aside, and a steel square applied, as shown in the figure, to the edge of the pitchboard, or to line f 4, and the riser line 4 e drawn, making it equal to the rise. Next from e, Fig. 60 (A), square out the line e 3, making it equal to $e\,d$ in the plan, giving the line of the tread of the winder No. 3. Apply the steel square again, as shown by the dotted lines, to draw the riser 3 d, and finally set out $d c$ at right angles to it, the latter $d c$ representing that portion of tread No. 2 which is housed into this string. Draw the two lines $m n$ and $o p$ parallel to the risers, the former passing through c, and the latter at a distance from it equal to the thickness of the string, these lines representing respectively the outer and inner faces of the other string (B). The setting out of the lower string (B) will now present no difficulty, the operations being precisely similar to those just described. In fact, the one string may be regarded simply as a continuation of the other.

Lining off edges of String.—The nosings and widths of housings being marked out with templates, as in Fig. 37, it only remains to show how to draw the curves for the edges of the strings. For the upper edge bend a batten in a fair curve so as to pass as nearly as possible through points marked out at the same distance from each nosing as the edge of the straight part of the string is from those of the fliers, thus giving about the same margin above the nosings throughout the entire length of the string.

Care will have to be taken that the curved edges of both strings at their junction have the same height above the step No. 2, and ease properly into each other. They have also to be nicely eased into the skirting at top and bottom of the stair, and are ornamented with the same moulding (see Fig. 66), either planted on or stuck on the solid string. The lower edges may be cropped off so as to make the depth of the string about uniform, the waste stuff to be cleared away all round being shown in hatched lines in Fig. 60.

Different ways of forming Easings.—The length of the easing is of course arbitrary, and may be fixed according to taste; but it may be well to observe that generally a short easing will prove more pleasing to the eye than when the curve is made to extend far along the string.

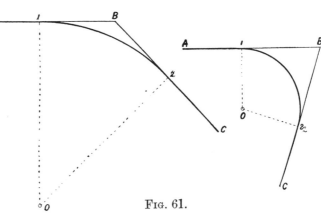

FIG. 61.

1. *By circular arcs.*—In Fig. 61 let A B C be the angle on which an easing is to be formed. From B set off equal distances, B 1 and B 2, and at these points

erect perpendiculars intersecting at O, which point will be the centre of the tangential arc.

2. *By parabolic curves.*—Let the points A and C (Figs. 62 and 63), be the terminations of the easing. Divide B A and B C into the same number of equal parts, and mark the points of division as in the figure. The lines joining the points with the corresponding numbers are tangents to a parabolic curve (see Appendix, Problem 22), and when the divisions are made small enough, these tangents will of themselves form the easing.

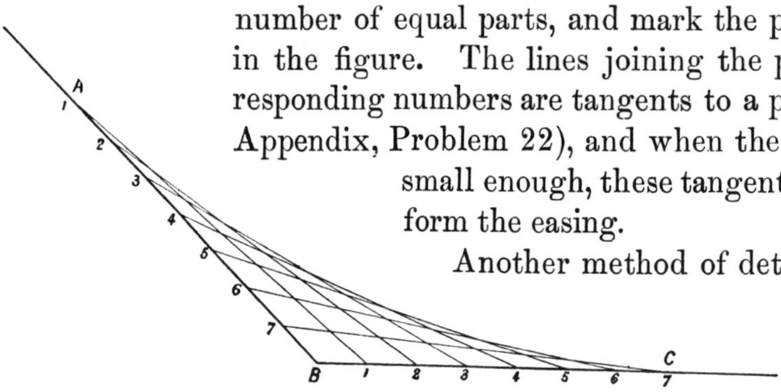

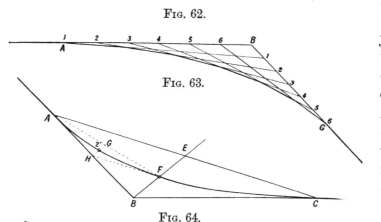

FIG. 62.

FIG. 63.

FIG. 64.

FIG. 65.

Another method of determining points on the parabola is shown by Fig. 64. Bisect the chord A C at E, and join E B; then F, the middle point of E B, is a point on the parabola. Again draw the chord A F, and through G, its middle point, draw GH parallel to B E. Bisect G H at the point 2; then 2 is another point on the curve. By drawing the chords A 2 and 2 F other two points may be obtained, and so on till as many points are determined as desired. Points on the curve F C on the right can be of course found similarly. Generally three intermediate points between A and C will be sufficient to enable the curve to be drawn by means of a batten.

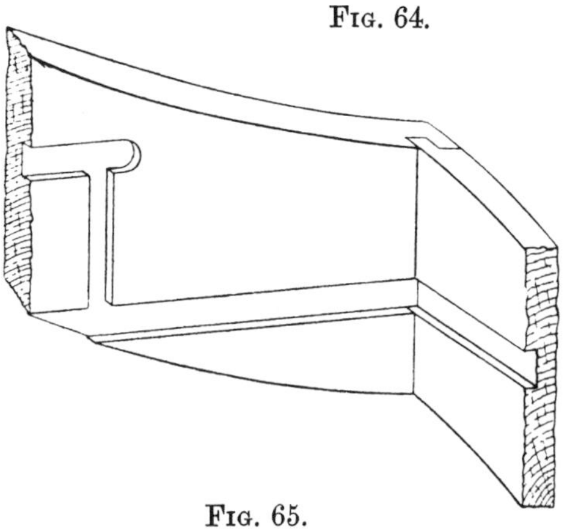

3. *By flexible batten.*—Very commonly easings are formed by bending a batten round into a curve to please the eye, or sometimes simply by drawing them in freehand.

Angle joint.—When two wall strings meet at an angle they are usually jointed together, as in Fig. 65, by forming a tongue on the end of one to fit into a corresponding groove cut out of the face of the other.

Preparing the winders.—It is a usual and convenient plan to take the winders out of the same width of stuff as works in suitably for the fliers, as it would not in general prove economical to cut them out of boards of the whole width, even though these were easily available. Consequently, two or more pieces, as required, are jointed together to make up the width, keeping the grain of the wood parallel to the nosing edge of the tread.

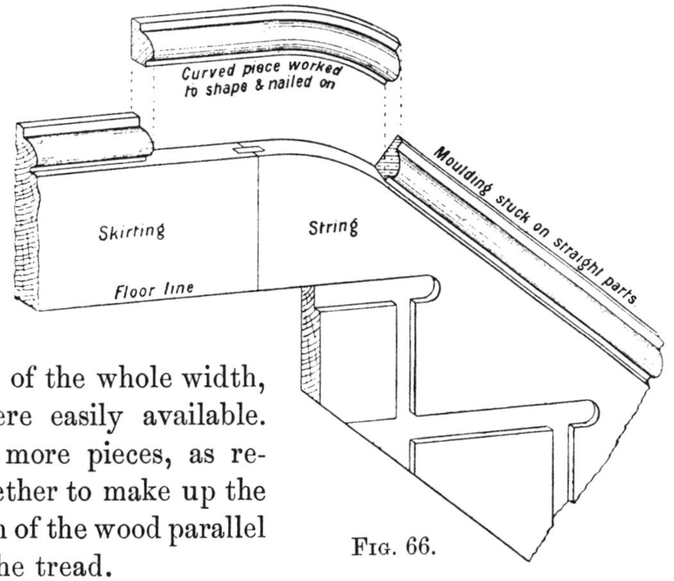

Fig. 66.

In getting out the winders approximate measurements are taken from the full-sized plan, so as to enable them to be roughly cut out to the shape from the boards. After being jointed and glued together, they are laid on to their plans (Fig. 60), and accurately marked out all round to the requisite size.

As the lines shown on the plan giving the form of the tread are generally only those of the fronts of the risers and inside faces of strings

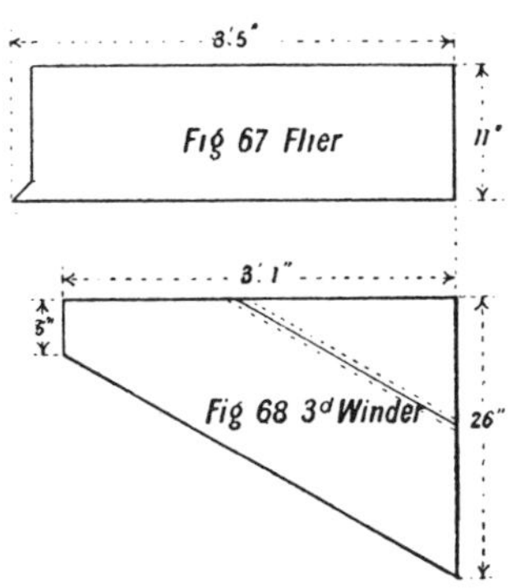

Figs. 67, 68. 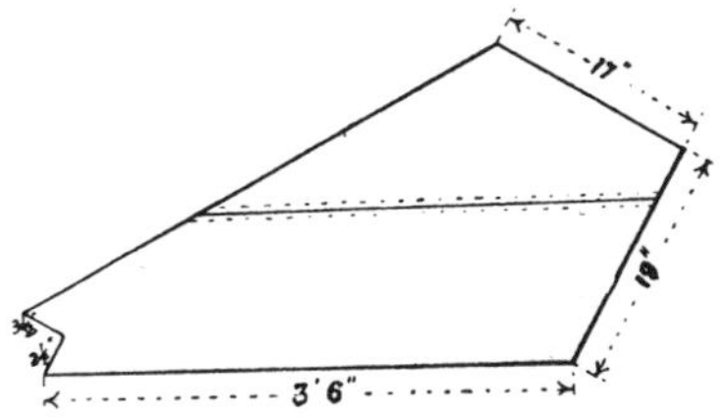   Fig. 69. 2nd Winder. 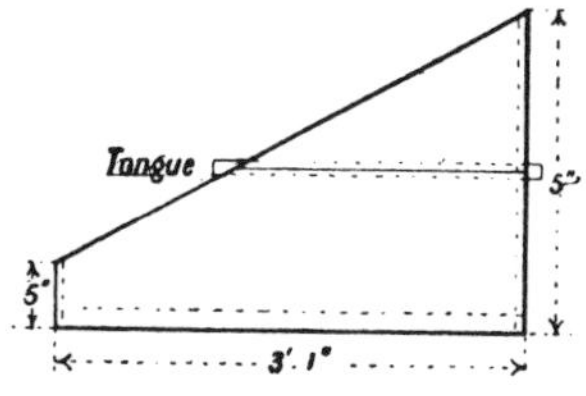   Fig. 70. 1st Winder.

and newels, the projection of the nosing over the riser, and in this case also the thickness of the riser at the back, as well as the depth of the housing, have to be added to give the extreme outlines for cutting.

Figs. 68, 69 and 70 give the three winders for the present example, showing them jointed up and cut to their exact size.

It will often be an advantage to nail a few strips of wood together to form templates or moulds for the exact extreme outlines of the winders, and these can be used both for cutting them out of the rough boards, and finally marking and trimming them to the exact size.

Fliers and return nosings.—Fig. 71 shows how these are prepared. It should be noted that the moulded nosing which projects beyond the front string is not formed on the end wood, but on a separate piece, and that for this purpose the end of the tread is cut off flush with the face of the string, as seen in Fig. 53, leaving only the nosing of the step projecting to form a mitre with the "return nosing," as at A in Fig. 71.

This not only avoids exposing the end wood, but also affords a ready way of concealing the means of fixing the balusters. The return nosing and scotia below it are usually made of one piece, the whole

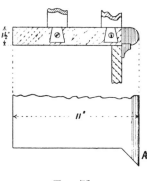

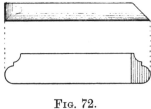

Scale 1½"–1 Foot

FIG. 71.   FIG. 72.   FIG. 73.
END OF TREAD.   RETURN NOSING.   NOSING IN POSITION.

moulding being returned on itself at the back of the step, as clearly shown in Figs. 72 and 73. The nosings would be, in this case, nailed on after the balusters had been fastened, the latter being dovetailed and screwed to the tread, as in Fig. 71.

Putting together and fixing stair.—No definite course of procedure which it would be desirable to follow in all cases can be laid down under this head, as much will depend upon the particular circumstances of the situation. But since work generally can be done better and more expeditiously at the shop, where presumably there is every appliance and convenience, than at the building, where the facilities are necessarily fewer, it may be laid down as a rule that stairs should be completed as far as possible before being taken to their places.

In the case before us it would prove an advantage if the whole stair could be put together at the shop, only requiring to be set into its place at the building.

Otherwise probably the portion embracing the two strings and the fliers could be so put together beforehand, leaving off the newels, winders, and short wall string.

The *separate operations* may be carried out as follows:

1. The treads and risers glued together and blocked, excepting those of winders, which should be left apart.

2. The steps fitted into their housings in the wall strings.

3. The outer ends of the steps next fitted to their places in the front string, and the riser mitres properly adjusted.

4. The long wall string, face uppermost, is now placed on a straight plank laid on the floor, and the ends of the steps inserted again into their proper housings.

5. The front string is then lifted into its place, and the steps brought hard up to it by means of handscrews or small cramps, applied so as to grasp the lower edge of the string, and a stiff scantling or batten laid upon the nosings.

6. Slanting screws are next driven through this string from the inside to fasten it to the treads and risers, or in the case of pine which is to be painted, "drive nails" inserted from the outside may be used instead.

7. The handscrews being removed, the steps are brought close up to their housings in the wall string by struts from the ceiling, or any other means found convenient, at the same time taking care to test if the stair is strictly square and out of winding.

8. Finally the wedges are driven up in the wall string, and the treads and risers blocked to the front string in the internal angles, as seen in Fig. 53; also the loose joints at the lower edges of the risers and backs of treads are secured with screws.

We may now assume that the stair is taken to the building in this condition, when the other parts would be added somewhat as follows:

In the first place fasten the top newel to the string, and let the whole down into its place. After this part of the stair has been levelled and set to the proper height, winder No. 3 can be slipped into its housings and the bottom newel driven on and secured. Winder No. 2 and riser No. 3 being next got into their housings, the short wall string is pushed up into its place; after which the first winder and the remaining risers can be inserted from the back.

CHAPTER V

I. Construction of Dog-legged Stairs

General observations.—A dog-legged stair may be described as a combination of two straight flights running in parallel but opposite directions without a well between them, or, in other words, the two flights occupy the full width of the stairway, the resulting construction being that the two outer strings and handrails are framed into the same newel at the turn, and stand directly over one another.

As compared with other types of half-turn stairs, the dog-legged is the most simple and economical, as it is easily constructed, and other things being the same, occupies less plan space. On the other hand, this simplicity of construction and space-saving is attended with some rather objectionable features; for example, the abrupt termination of the lower balustrade by the upper flight, against which it abuts, is not a good or pleasing arrangement, and leaves part of the stair without a handrail.

Further, stairs of this kind are not so light and airy as those where the flights encompass a well, and, though common in fairly good houses, would never be adopted for the best situations.

It will be instructive at this point if the student will turn back and compare the three varieties of the dog-legged stair given by Figs. 16, 17 and 18. Where sufficient space is available the arrangement of Fig. 16, in which the two straight flights are combined with a half-space landing, should be adopted, as it represents this class of stair in its best and most convenient form.

With the same width of tread as is used in Fig. 16, the height can be reached in a somewhat less plan by introducing winders in one of the quarter spaces, as shown in Fig. 17, and a still further reduction can of course be effected by adopting the arrangement given by Fig. 18, in which the whole half space is filled with winders.

To illustrate generally the constructive details of dog-legged stairs we have taken the first of the above varieties, the plan (Fig. 75) being the same example as is given by the sketch Fig. 16, but of course in greater detail and to a larger scale. Fig. 74 is a sectional elevation on the line AA, and Fig. 76 a front elevation.

The width of the stairway between the inclosing walls is 7 feet 6 inches, and the height to be attained is taken at 10 feet 10 inches.

General construction.—The stair starts with a flight of ten steps supported at both ends by housed strings, receiving further support at the middle from a rough carriage timber and brackets. The upper floor is reached from the intermediate landing by a shorter flight, consisting of eight steps of the same dimensions as the lower, and similarly supported.

In the plan (Fig. 75) the dotted lines, as in preceding examples, represent the fronts of the risers. A few of the treads in the lower flight and part of the boarding in the adjacent landing are omitted in the drawing, so as to expose the risers and constructive framework below. A portion of the upper floor is also shown, broken away to reveal the top trimmer and the stair starting. The landing or platform is 3 feet 6 inches wide, and constructed similarly to an ordinary floor. Common flooring boards are laid on light joists pinned into the wall at one end, and framed into a trimmer joist at the other, the latter spanning the stairway and let into the inclosing walls at each end. This is clearly shown in the plan (Fig. 75). The elevations (Figs. 74 and 76) further indicate the construction of the stair and arrangement of the component parts. It will be noted that the trimmers are placed so that the respective newels can be directly attached to them, as has already been illustrated (see Fig. 31).

Working drawings.—As heretofore, it is better to make out a full-sized plan showing the principal lines, as well as a partial elevation. To do this in the present case proceed as follows:

Marking rods.—Mark the height on a storey rod, as shown on the left of Fig. 74. Next cut a width rod to fit in approximately between the walls, as in Fig. 75, and from each end mark off the thickness of the wall strings. Having found the centre of this rod, set off on each side of it half the thickness of the newels, likewise that of the front string. Draw also lines on the rod to represent the depth of housings, thus giving the extreme length of the steps.

Take also on a going rod the distance XY, (Fig. 74) between the edge of the door at the stair starting and the back wall.

1. *Drawing the plan.*—With these dimensions commence the plan (Fig. 75) by drawing the outline of the surrounding walls. Next draw the section of the newel, B, placing it equidistant from the three wall

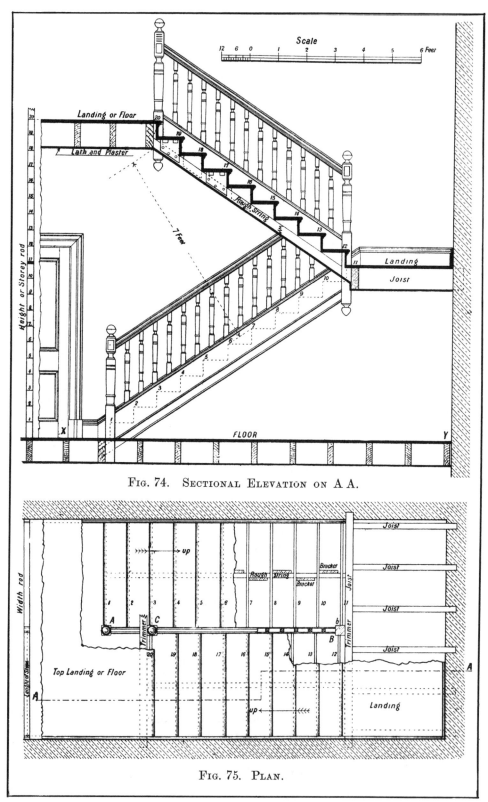

Fig. 74. Sectional Elevation on A A.

Fig. 75. Plan.

Elevation and Plan of Dog-legged Stairs.

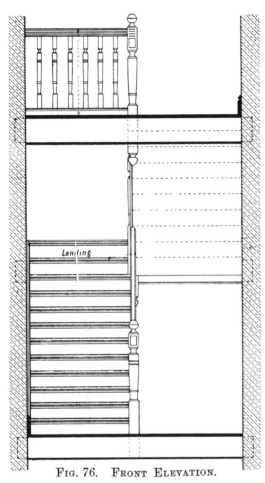

FIG. 76. FRONT ELEVATION.

lines, and close at the back of it, as shown in the figure, the trimmer of the half-space landing. A line drawn through the centre of the newel, parallel to the trimmer, represents the face of both the last riser of the lower flight and the first of the upper.

Suppose now after rough preliminary trials it is found that twenty rises at $6\frac{1}{2}$ inches, with a width of tread of 10 inches, will about suit the circumstances. Commencing at the riser, b, just drawn, space off with a pair of compasses ten treads of the assumed width, which number it will be found brings the stair starting to a position which just conveniently clears the door. This leaves eight treads to be disposed of in the upper flight. If now it is found that this number provides a suitable landing at the top of the stair, and also that it leaves sufficient head room below the top trimmer, the arrangement may be taken as satisfactory, and the riser lines finally drawn in at these divisions.

It need hardly be remarked that the plans of the riser faces in the upper and lower flights are in line with one another.

The plans of the bottom newel (A) and the top one (C) may now be drawn, placing them (as shown in Fig. 75) with their centres in line with the faces of the first and last risers respectively. This fixes also the position in plan of the top trimmer. Number the steps 1, 2, 3 . . . 20, as shown, and put the corresponding numbers on the storey rod.

2. *Elevation* (Fig. 74).—Draw the floor line XY, and place the storey rod as shown on the left of the figure. From the divisions on it, 1, 2, 3, 4 . . . 20, draw the horizontal lines intersecting perpendiculars projected from the corresponding riser faces, 1, 2, 3 . . . 20, in plan. This gives the lines of the treads and risers as shown in the

H

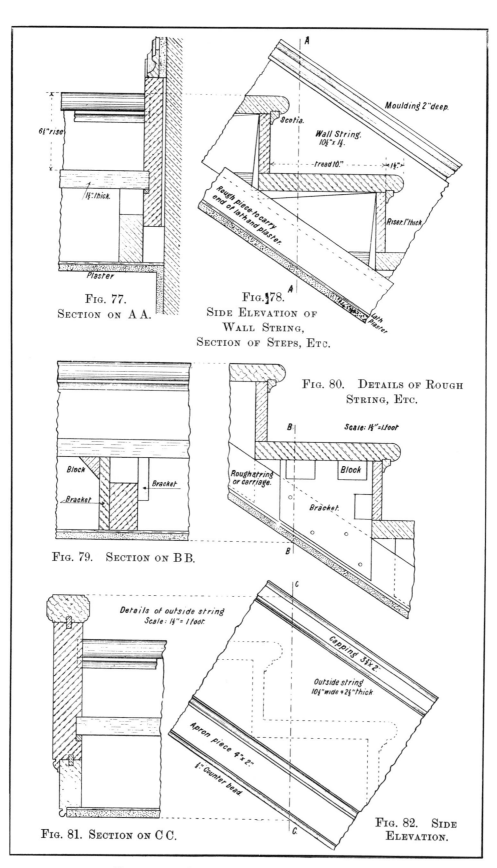

FIG. 77.
SECTION ON A A.

FIG. 78.
SIDE ELEVATION OF
WALL STRING,
SECTION OF STEPS, ETC.

6¼" rise

1¼" thick.

Plaster

Scotia.

Moulding 2" deep.

*Wall String.
10½" x 1¼.*

tread 10."

1¼"

*Rough piece to carry
end of lath and plaster.*

Riser 1" thick

*lath
plaster*

FIG. 80. DETAILS OF ROUGH
STRING, ETC.

Scale: 1½" = 1 foot

Block

Bracket

Bracket

FIG. 79. SECTION ON B B.

*Roughstring
or carriage.*

Block

Bracket.

*Details of outside string
Scale: 1½" = 1 foot.*

Capping 3½ x 2.

*Outside string
10½" wide x 2½" thick.*

Apron piece 4" x 2."

¾" Counter bead

FIG. 81. SECTION ON C C.

FIG. 82. SIDE
ELEVATION.

DETAILS OF DOG-LEGGED STAIR (FIGS. 74-76).

figure, the eleventh step being the landing. Next draw the lines representing the squared newels, projecting them up from the plan, and draw also the sections of the trimmers to which they are fixed.

The lines representing the strings and capping, as well as those of the handrails, should now be drawn, making them parallel to the nosing line; that is, the line in elevation passing through the points of intersection of the fronts of risers and tops of treads. The top of the handrail may be made about 2 feet 7 inches above the steps, measured on a vertical line standing over the face of the riser.

Of course the depth of the outside strings below the steps will depend in this case upon the depth of the rough carriages, which should be shown also in the elevation.

The lines now drawn in plan and elevation will enable the necessary material to be cut out, and also furnish particulars for setting it out; but as the scale of the drawings (Figs. 74-76) is so small that the details of the various scantlings and their principal joints and connections cannot be clearly delineated, enlarged drawings of these have been added, which will form the matter of the subsequent paragraphs.

CONSTRUCTIVE DETAILS.—1. **Wall string.**—Figs. 77 and 78 give full particulars of the wall string, and also show a section of the steps. The vertical section (Fig. 77) shows also the method adopted in this case of carrying the plaster below the wall strings, namely, by fixing a rough piece, from 1 to 2 inches thick and of the same depth as the rough strings, into the angle as shown, another method being to fix a strap to the wall with plugs (see Fig. 47). It will be seen also, from Fig. 77, that the stairs would be fixed previous to the walls being plastered, and the moulding on the upper edge of string afterwards planted on.

2. **Carriages.**—Figs. 79 and 80 give the details of the rough strings which are placed along the middle of each flight.

In stairs of not more than 3 feet 6 inches in width, and having treads of the ordinary thickness, the two strings furnish sufficient support to the steps. For wider stairs additional support is required, which is usually provided in the manner shown in the figure, by placing one or more—according to the width of the stair—rough scantlings below the steps, so that the lower angles of the latter may have a bearing upon them.

To further support the treads and connect them to the rough strings, brackets about 1 inch thick, made with the grain of the wood vertical, are either screwed or spiked to their sides, and well blocked to both treads and risers. These brackets may all be fixed on one side of the rough string, or alternately on opposite sides; that is, adjacent steps have the

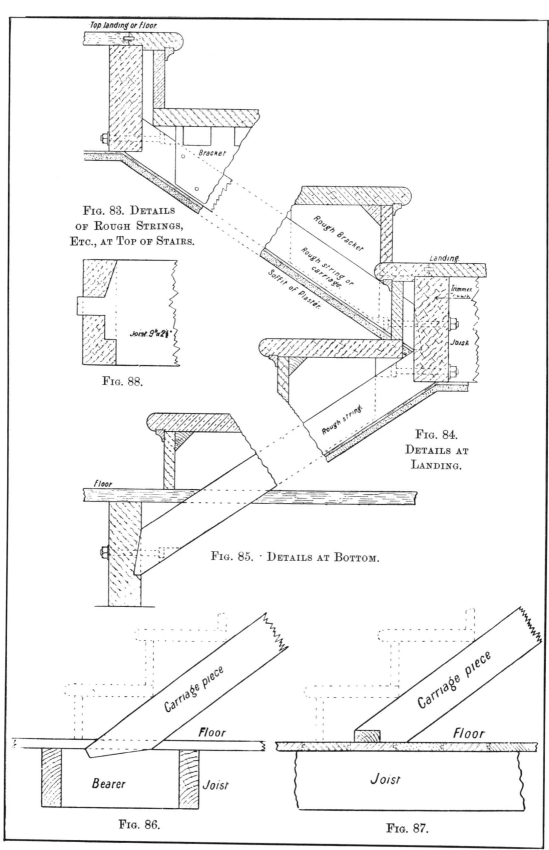

Top landing or floor.

Bracket.

FIG. 83. DETAILS
OF ROUGH STRINGS,
ETC., AT TOP OF STAIRS.

Rough Bracket

Rough string or carriage.

Soffit of Plaster.

Landing.

Trimmer.

Joisk.

Joist. 9" x 2½"

FIG. 88.

Rough string.

FIG. 84.
DETAILS AT
LANDING.

Floor

FIG. 85. · DETAILS AT BOTTOM.

Carriage piece

Floor

Bearer   Joist

FIG. 86.

Carriage piece

Floor

Joist

FIG. 87.

DETAILS OF DOG-LEGGED STAIR (FIGS. 74-76).

brackets on opposite sides, the latter arrangement being that adopted for this stair (see Fig. 75 at steps Nos. 8, 9, and 10).

These rough strings should be fitted in after the stairs have been erected. The manner of fixing them to the trimmers is shown by Figs. 83, 84, and 85, a "birdsmouth joint" being used at their upper ends and a bevel sinking at the other. Both joints are further secured with bolts, but these are frequently dispensed with for the light scantlings that may be used in short flights.

The adjoining sketches, Figs. 86 and 87, illustrate other two common, though less satisfactory, methods than the preceding of fixing these strings at the bottom.

Other methods of strengthening and stiffening wide stairs are discussed and illustrated in connection with subsequent examples, particularly in the section dealing with carriages of ships' stairs (see Figs. 142-5).

3. **Details of outer strings.**—Fig. 82 is a side elevation showing the thickness of the capping position of housings, etc. The vertical section (Fig. 81) on the line C C shows how the several parts are connected. In some respects it will prove convenient to have this string, as shown, made in two portions, since narrower stuff can be worked into it, which avoids the unnecessary labour of cutting housings much beyond the steps, where they are not required. The *apron piece* as it is termed—which makes out the depth of the string to the under side of the carriages, so as to receive the plastered soffit—has a *counter bead* run on the outer corner, and is connected to the housed portion with a rebated and "tongued and grooved" joint (see Fig. 81). It is driven on and tenoned along with the other portion of the string.

Drawing in the strings and newels.—It will at this stage be unnecessary to give any explanations of how to set out the strings and newels. Each flight is in all respects a straight stair, so that the same set of operations as has been previously described will exactly apply here, and need not, therefore, be repeated. It will be evident, however, that a slight complication arises in dog-legged stairs at the junction of the two strings with the common newel. The joints at this part, in the present example, are fully illustrated by Fig. 89.

The *expansion* of the four surfaces forming the square part of this newel is given by Fig. 90, the face B being that shown in Fig. 89. The face A is shown with the requisite lines for the mortises; C and D, those towards the landing and lower flight respectively, have the necessary housings marked out on them also.

In marking out these housings on the newel it will be better to have it previously mortised and driven on to the strings, the latter having their housings already marked and, preferably, cut out also, these trenches being, of course, on opposite sides. Continue the marks E and F across these opposite faces B and D of the newel, and draw

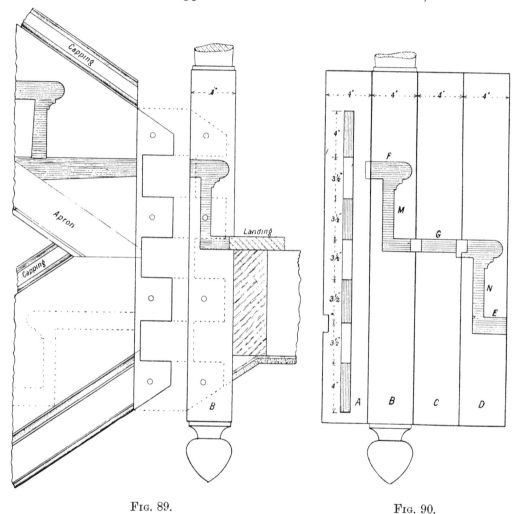

FIG. 89.   FIG. 90.

the housings for the adjacent risers, making their faces M and N in the middle of the width of the post, as previously arranged on the plan. The housing for the landing—extending over the face C, and partially also over those of B and D—can now be drawn, the line G representing its upper surface, being, of course, midway between E and F.

It will be understood that the mortises for the handrails will be marked and cut out of the newels at the same time as those for the strings are being dealt with, the proper height for them being obtained from the elevation.

Taste will partly decide the limits of the turning on the newels, only the squared parts of them should extend at least $1\frac{1}{2}$ inches clear of the rail and capping.

II. CONSTRUCTION OF OPEN NEWEL STAIRS.

Characteristics.—By an easy transition from preceding examples we now come to the consideration of some of the more important details in the construction of what are known as " open newel staircases."

These have the separate flights of which they are composed arranged around a central opening or well, and consequently require more capacious stairways for their reception than those of the form that we have been describing, and this precludes their use in any but public buildings or private dwellings of some pretensions.

The clear space between the flights conduces to a more regular and satisfactory construction than the close arrangement of the "dog-legged" form admits of, and provides for a freer admission of light and a better circulation of air to all parts of the staircase. What is of importance also is, that the *open well* affords a free view of the whole structure, and enables the prominent features of the design to be seen to advantage.

The open newel form of wood staircase was in great favour in this country during what has been called the "Elizabethan period of architecture," and probably at this time reached its highest stage of development —at least as far as that depended on good material, sound construction, and the free and copious use of picturesque ornament. In fact, the staircase formed the most striking and characteristic feature of the stately English mansions of that period. The best examples were characterized by short broad flights with frequent quarter-space landings, and by massive balustrades, so that they were both easy and safe to ascend.

In present day examples of wood stairs of this class the ascent is made mainly by an *advance* and *return* flight, combined with an intermediate platform extending from side to side of the stairway, or, when the well is wide enough to admit of it, a definite cross flight of two or more steps, with two quarter-space landings, would take the place of the single platform. In the former case, regarding the landing as an intermediate partial floor, the construction is obviously reduced to that of two straight stairs, and from the stairbuilder's point of view would be considered as presenting no greater difficulty. It is only when winders are introduced into one or both of the quarter spaces, in order to get up to

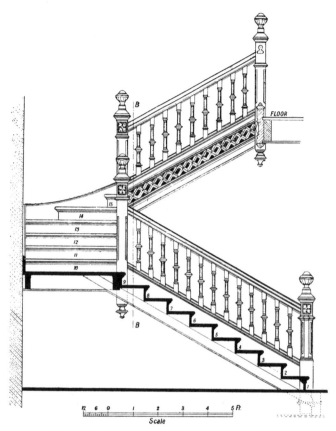

FIG. 91. SECTIONAL ELEVATION ON A A.

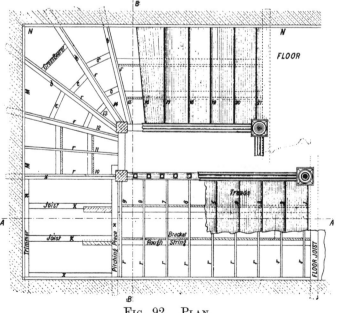

FIG. 92. PLAN.
OPEN NEWELLED STAIR.

the requisite height on a minimum length of stairway, that the resulting construction becomes irregular and complex, and demands some technical skill on the part of the staircase hand.

The example we have adopted for illustration has not been chosen as being the best or most recommendable form of its class, but because it comprehends the main difficulties likely to occur in connection with open newel stairs, and will serve also to show how a fairly satisfactory result may be obtained within the limits of a stairway measuring rather less than 10 feet each way.

General arrangement.—The illustrations consist of the usual plan (Fig. 92) and sectional side elevation (Fig. 91), to which is added a cross sectional elevation (Fig. 93).

From these drawings it will be seen that the advance and return flights are combined with a landing in the first quarter space, winders in the second quarter space, and a cross flight of two steps.

The *balancing* of the three winders in the quarter space with the adjacent fliers, in order to increase the widths of the former at the newel post, should be care-fully noted, as, if the risers had been arranged to radiate from the centre of the post, it would have made the stair at this part awkwardly steep and dangerous. This constitutes a standing objection to the employment of winders in newel stairs which cannot altogether be obviated, how-ever well the steps may be arranged, and when the con-ditions make winders indis-pensable one can only aim at minimizing the defect as far as possible.

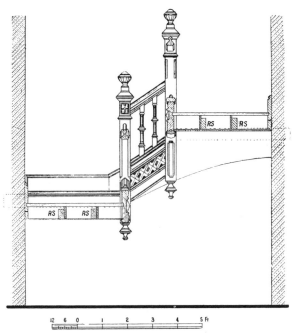

FIG. 93. SECTIONAL ELEVATION ON B B (FIG. 91).

Irregular height of balus-trade at newel due to the winders in quarter space.—Their use also in a case like that before us results in introducing an irregularity into the balustrade which to some extent mars its appearance. Thus, in the example, the introduction of winders causes the handrail and string of the upper flight, and those of the short cross flight, to meet the newel at a very considerable difference of level, as will be seen from an examination of Figs. 91 and 93, the interval between them being necessarily much greater than that on the adjoining post at the quarter space landing. The newel which receives the winders will thus require to be much longer than the others, and will present a somewhat different appearance; in fact, it will often prove a matter of difficulty to apply any specific design to all the newels. When they are of the square form, as in the illustration, there is little trouble in this way, as the rail and string can be brought in almost at any height without altering the character of the newel. With *turned* newels, on the other hand, it may not be easy to make the most of the irregularities, as the square portions that have to be left on them for the reception of the adjacent rails and strings may occupy so much of the length (for example

I

in the long newel, Fig. 93) that there is hardly any part of the body of the post left available for *turning*. Sometimes the one rail may meet the newel post so much higher than the other that a separate square can be formed for each, with a short neck of turning or other ornamentation between them.

Details of supporting framework.—The most direct means of supporting stairs such as that in the illustration, which are required to be completely open below, is by the employment of "cantilevers," called also "pitching pieces," these being rough quarterings, fixed firmly into the wall at one end to carry the outer strings and the newel posts. In arranging the supports, the first consideration should be to obtain a good rigid framework for the landing, so that it may not only efficiently sustain the top end of the lower flight, but also afford a substantial basis for the timbers of the cross flight, which in turn transmit to it part of the thrust of the upper flight.

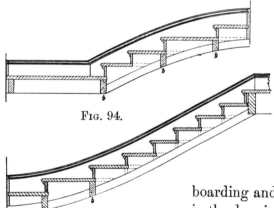

FIG. 94.

FIG. 95.

Framework of landing.— The construction adopted for the landing can be gathered from the plan (Fig. 92), the boarding and adjacent treads being left out in the drawing for this purpose. The several pieces, xx, of which it is composed should be framed together with "tusk tenons" (see Fig. 48), and preparation is made in the wall during the progress of the building for its reception, or preferably it may be built into the wall while the latter is being erected.

The two joists of the platform are so placed that the upper ends of the rough strings, fitted under the lower flight, can be directly attached to them, as seen in Fig. 92, and more clearly in the isometric sketch (Fig. 96). These it will be seen form two rigid ribs, which transmit the pressure due to the load directly on to the back wall and to the floor joist at the stair starting. Additional support is also provided to the overhanging corner of the platform by the combination of the outer string and newels with the bearer x at the start of the cross flight, these constituting a third strong rib.

It will be obvious that the platform is amply supported by these means, even without much assistance from its connection with the walls.

Another method of framing up a landing.—A more usual way of framing up a quarter-space landing is shown by Fig. 97. In this method, besides

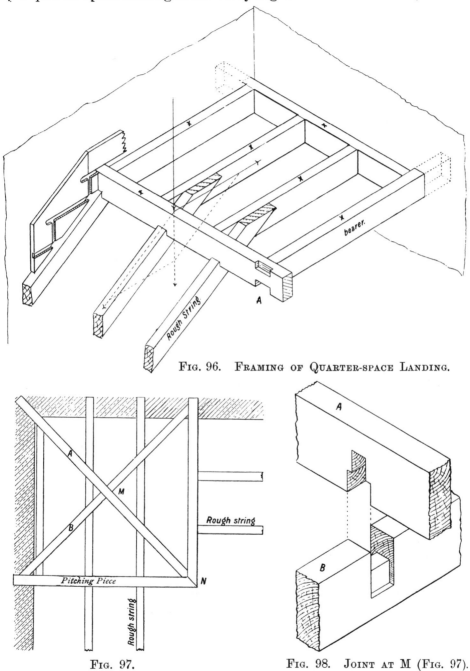

FIG. 96. FRAMING OF QUARTER-SPACE LANDING.

FIG. 97.

FIG. 98. JOINT AT M (FIG. 97).

the support that the various pieces receive from being built into the wall, a diagonal piece, B, is fitted across the corner, with a bearing on the adjacent walls, keeping it as far as possible out from the angle. The outward corner, N, of the landing is supported by another diagonal piece, A, crossing the diagonal B at M, the one being let into the other by the cogged form of joint shown in Fig. 98.

The notches of all these joints should be cut out of those edges of the pieces in which the fibres will be in compression; thus, in the piece B the notch at M is taken out of its upper edge.

Fig. 99 is an isometric sketch showing the connection of the pieces at the overhanging corner N.

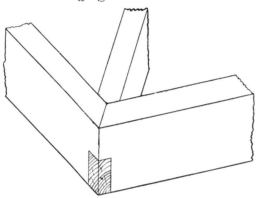

FIG. 99. JOINT AT N (FIG. 97).

Referring again to the plan (Fig. 92), the remaining portion of the stair receives part support from this landing, and part also from the four bearers marked *bb* in the figure. These latter are placed directly under the risers of the winders, and firmly fixed into the wall at one end and to the newel and strings at the other. These bearers are further connected and stiffened by two rows of short carriage pieces marked *cc*, Fig. 92 being disposed partly as a continuation of the carriages under the straight flights. The whole of these rough pieces are trimmed on their under sides to form a regular surface for the plastered soffit.

Sections of the bearers *bb*, taken near the walls, are shown in connection with the elevations of the two wall strings (Figs. 94 and 95).

It may be well to observe here that the stair itself, independently of any auxiliary supports, if it have all its parts properly connected together, will contribute largely towards sustaining itself and the load.

Support derived from spandrel framing.—It is almost unnecessary to state that, if the stair had been represented as being closed in below with spandrel framing, etc., in place of being open, as in the example, a very different arrangement of the supports would be made. For instance, the two intermediate newels might then be continued down to the floor, which would efficiently pillar up the overhanging structure, and this would only have to be associated with the usual stiffening of the steps.

Attachment of newels to joists, etc.—The newel posts are usually bolted directly to the sides of the joists or to the trimmers, as the case may be; but where it is expedient we would recommend that they be likewise framed into them with a cogged joint, as shown by the accompanying sketches (Figs. 100 and 101). This form of joint when fastened with a bolt adds very considerably to the rigidity of the balustrade, and in a fairly good stair, such as the present example is taken to represent, should be adopted, at least at the top and intermediate landings.

Details of strings.—As all the parts of this stair which are exposed to view are presumably of hard wood, it is the most economical method to build up the strings in separate pieces, making the main central portion of rough pine, and facing it up on each side with hard wood.

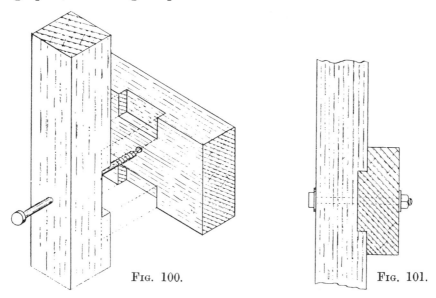

FIG. 100.   FIG. 101.

Fig. 103 shows a section of the outer strings of the stair under consideration built up in this manner. In preparing these strings the plain hard-wood facings towards the stair should be first glued to the pine, then drawn in, the housings cut out, and the ends tenoned and fitted to the newels as described for preceding examples.

The hard-wood mouldings, etc., which ornament the other side of the string, facing the well, can be fitted and fixed after the strings have been permanently attached to the newels.

It will often prove the best plan to only form short stump tenons on the ends of the strings, and secure the joints with one or two "joining" or "bed bolts." This makes a close job, and likewise keeps up the strength of the newel posts.

Bolts should also be used for fastening the handrails to the newels, the former being also housed bodily into the latter about $\frac{3}{8}$ inch.

Fig. 102 represents the lower portion of the newel at the winders, together with a side view of a part of the string of the upper flight, and a vertical section of the cross string taken close to the newel.   The

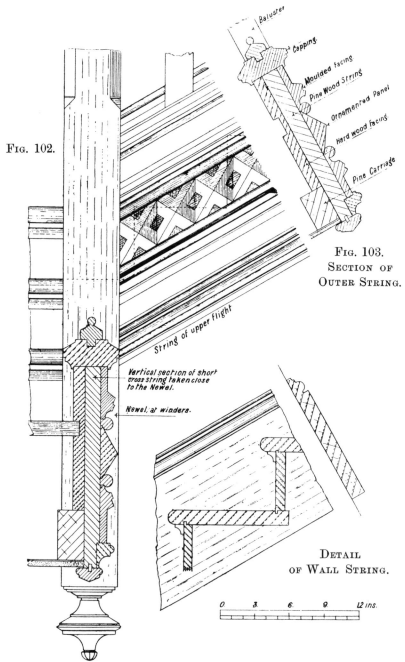

Fig. 102.

Baluster

Capping.

Moulded facing.

Pine Wood String

Ornamented Panel

Hard wood facing.

Pine Carriage

Fig. 103.
Section of
Outer String.

String of upper flight

Vertical section of short
cross string taken close
to the Newel.

Newel at winders.

Detail
of Wall String.

0   3.   6.   9.   12 ins.

figure, besides furnishing enlarged details of the separate parts, serves to show the exact position at which the strings meet this newel.

An enlarged detail of the wall string is added in the same diagram.

CHAPTER VI

CONSTRUCTION OF HALF-TURN GEOMETRICAL STAIRS

General observations.—In the stairs already dealt with, where changes of direction occur, they have been made by means of newels. Those remaining to be treated of in this and the following chapter have their balustrades uninterrupted; that is, their strings and handrails, instead of being framed into a newel at the angle, are continuous throughout their length, the changes of direction being made gradually in curved lines.

One of the principal advantages gained by this form of construction is that the handrail is both very convenient and pleasant to use, the hand encountering no obstacles in passing from one end of the rail to the other, as is the case in newel stairs. One can easily perceive how, especially in steep, confined stairs, objections would naturally arise to the use of newels, at any rate to those in intermediate positions between the top and bottom of the stair; and in this connection it is of some interest to note that, historically, the geometrical staircase—at least in this country—is really a construction of later date than what has been termed the open newel.

The work in connection with the geometrical type of staircase is also more difficult to execute than that of any of the preceding examples, some of the parts being necessarily of " double curvature," but to those that can carry it out on correct principles it proves highly interesting.

I. CONSTRUCTION OF GEOMETRICAL STAIRS WITH WINDERS IN HALF SPACE.—The example we have chosen to illustrate this part of the subject is given by a full detailed plan (Fig. 105), and a sectional elevation (Fig. 104).

The stair, as will be seen from the plan (Fig. 105), is composed of twenty-two successive steps uninterrupted by any intermediate landings, both of the quarter spaces being occupied with winders, an arrangement which, as already pointed out, renders the ascent tedious and somewhat tiresome, but results in economizing the stair space. The stairway in the illustration is rectangular and 10 feet 9 inches wide, with a 21-inch well between the flights, which are thus each 5 feet 4 inches wide.

The wall ends of the steps are supported by housed strings in the usual way, while the outer ends rest on an open bracketed string, which is of course made continuous round the well. The steps receive additional support from the system of rough framework, which is partially shown by the expedient of leaving off the treads 5 to 11 in the plan, although these are shown in place in the sectional elevation. Each of

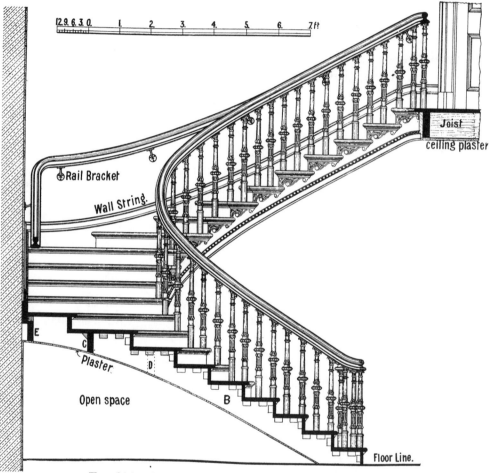

FIG. 104. SECTIONAL ELEVATION ON A A (FIG. 105).

the carriage pieces composing this framework is notched out for the steps, as in a cut string, and fastened to the treads and risers by screws and blocks as shown in the elevation.

The stair starts with a " curtail step," which, in this case, is shown of the same width as the others, its projecting end being made to conform to the outline of the scroll terminal of the handrail.

To make the drawings more explanatory, the handrail round the well, though shown continuous in the elevation, is partly broken away in plan in order to show the position and arrangement of the balusters.

Setting-out the working plan.—Preliminary to laying-off the working plan, which will simply consist of the principal lines shown in Fig. 105, a width rod should be drawn out, as in previous cases, showing by its length the total width of the stairway between the rough walls, and marked out also to furnish such particulars as the width of flights,

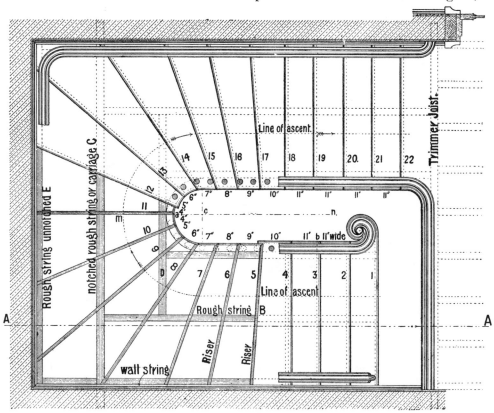

FIG. 105. PLAN.
HALF-TURN GEOMETRICAL STAIR (WINDERS IN HALF SPACE).

width of well, thickness of strings, and position of carriages. It will be assumed that the height from floor to floor will also have been taken on a storey rod.

Having drawn the lines representing the inside of the three enclosing walls, determine the point *c*, the centre of the circular part of the well, which point it will be observed is equidistant from each of the wall lines.

Draw, therefore, a line, *m n* (Fig. 105), midway between the two side walls, and another at the same distance from the back wall and parallel to it; their intersection, *c*, is the centre of the well. From this centre, with radius equal to half the width of the well between the faces of the string obtained from the " width rod," draw the semicircle, and continue it in straight lines beyond the springings parallel to the centre line *m n*.

Section of well string.—At this stage it will be advisable to have arranged a full-sized section of the outer string, as in Fig. 106, showing the projection of the return nosing, thickness of ornamental brackets, and the position of the centre of handrail and balustrade with respect to

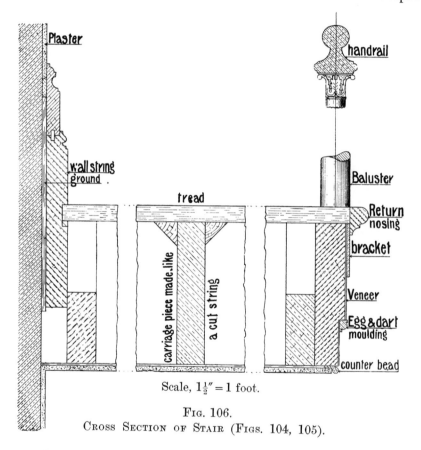

Scale, $1\frac{1}{2}'' = 1$ foot.

FIG. 106.
CROSS SECTION OF STAIR (FIGS. 104, 105).

the face of the string.   These particulars will enable the line representing the centre of handrail to be drawn in plan as well as the other important line, namely, the going line, which should, as previously stated, be chosen about 16 inches from the former.

Division of rods.—Divide the storey rod in the manner previously described to obtain a suitable rise.   In the present case, the height being 11 feet, it divides into 22 rises at 6 inches, a size which we may assume to be well enough adapted to the circumstances.   Now, according to the rules laid down, a 6-inch rise requires a tread 11 inches wide.   Reverting to the plan (Fig. 105), place a riser in the crown of the semicircle, its face coinciding with the middle line, *m n*, of the stair, and making the point *m* where it crosses the line of ascent a starting point, set off from it along the line of ascent towards the bottom of the stair as many equal distances of 11 inches, that is, as many treads as will bring the stair to about the requisite position for starting, so as to be convenient for the surroundings and clear of doors, etc.   In the plan this is supposed to be attained by 10 treads, leaving 11 to be set off for the upper half of the stair.   It will be supposed also that this number of treads lands the stair conveniently at the top.   If not, a re-arrangement of the whole would have to be made, probably by increasing or decreasing the number of steps; but it will be observed that by retaining the same size and number a slight change could be effected by placing the middle of a winder in the crown of the well instead of a riser.

These points now marked on the going line are fixed points through which the lines of the riser faces must pass, and in whatever manner the width of the treads may vary at other parts of the stair they should always be made uniform along this line.

Objections to a radial arrangement of winders.—It should be here observed that the risers in the circular part of the well are not uncommonly, especially in stone stairs of this class, made to converge to the centre of the well, as in Fig. 23, but such an arrangement, although it possesses the advantage in that it keeps the risers strictly normal to the line of ascent, introduces two grave defects, some reference to which has already been made in connection with preceding examples.

First, the radial arrangement of the risers makes the converging ends of the winders, especially in small wells, extremely crowded and narrow, and when one is compelled by any means to use the stair close to the balustrade the insufficient footing afforded proves most inconvenient, and is attended with not a little danger, while the other or divergent ends of the winders are unduly wide.

Second, the great inequality between the widths of the ends of the winders and the fliers in the well causes that part of the continuous string in connection with the winders to have a much steeper pitch than the remaining parts of it which receive the wider-ended fliers; and if the string is made to follow the line of nosings any way closely there will be a sudden and ungraceful bend where the two differently pitched parts join in with each other.

Graduating the widths of steps at the well.—*1st method.*—The defects pointed out above, though they cannot altogether be remedied without introducing other hardly less objectionable features, may be greatly modified by a judicious "balancing" of the steps, as shown in the plan, Fig. 105.

The first method that would probably suggest itself would be to set off all the ends of the steps, both fliers and winders, of equal widths along the centre line of the handrail, keeping only the first and last risers in their normal position, all the others being placed more or less obliquely. An arrangement of this kind would make the well string and handrail of uniform pitch throughout, and no crippled appearance would be presented. Further, all the steps would be of uniform width along any line of ascent parallel to the well string, a result which would not be obtained by any other division of the ends of the steps at the well. The excessive displacement, however, from the normal positions that this would cause in some of the risers precludes such an arrangement from being adopted in practice. In fact, it is most desirable in such an example as that before us to retain several parallel steps both at the top and bottom to give definiteness to the directions of the separate flights.

2nd method.—The more usual way, instead of making the width of the treads absolutely equal to one another all round the well, is to start with a narrow-ended winder at the middle of the curve, and gradually increase the widths of successive steps, according to some law of progression, till the full width of the fliers is reached at about three or four steps past the springings. For example, in the stair illustrated they increase in arithmetical progression from winders Nos. 10 and 11 at the crown, which are 4 inches wide, by a common difference of 1 inch, round to the parallel steps. Nos. 3 and 18 in the advance and return flights respectively (see Fig. 105).

It may be noted that the two narrowest winders at the crown should be made in all cases a little wider than they would be with a radial arrangement of the risers.

The ends of the steps may be arranged thus progressively, either, (1) by a series of trials, commencing as in the example (Fig. 105) at the fourth riser, and regularly decreasing each successive step by an assumed decrement, which would be modified if necessary in subsequent trials till the desired graduation is attained; or, (2) the width of the narrowest step at the crown and the common difference can be found by calculation. Thus, suppose it agreed to make the arithmetical series extend over eight steps, that is from point *a* (Fig. 105) at the crown of the well to point *b* at the third riser from the bottom. This distance in the example when stretched out is 60 inches, and since this has to be occupied by eight steps, therefore the average width $= \dfrac{60}{8}$. But average width also $= \dfrac{\text{1st term of series} + \text{last term}}{2}$. Now the last term of the series is 11 inches, *i.e.*, the width of a flier, and if $x = $ 1st term, we get therefore $\dfrac{x + 11}{2} = \dfrac{60}{8}$. Therefore $x = 4$ inches.

Again, the common difference of the terms is found by subtracting the first from the last term and dividing by the number of terms, minus one. That is, common difference $= \dfrac{11 - 4}{8 - 1} = \dfrac{7}{7} = 1$ inch.

The widths of the ends of the steps are thus 4, 5, 6, 7, 8, 9, 10, 11 inches, which are set off on both sides of the well from the point a (Fig. 105).

If the width x of the narrowest step at the crown of the well found as above should prove to be less than would result from that given by a radial disposition of the risers, the series may be made to extend over more of the steps, so as to increase the first of the series and decrease their " common difference." Thus (taking another step into the series) the nine steps would stretch over **71** inches, and the narrowest by the above calculation would be increased to about $4\frac{3}{4}$ inches, and the " common difference " reduced to $\frac{3}{4}$ inch full.

This method of graduating the ends of the steps round the well in an arithmetical progression gives, as will be seen from the elevation (Fig. 104), and the development (Fig. 110), satisfactory curves to the handrail and string. But as few workmen take readily to calculative processes—at any rate, in the workshop—the two methods that we are now about to explain may appear easier to the majority of artisans, and will be found to give good results.

3rd method.—This consists of first drawing the development of a suitable nosing line either at the outside of the string or at the line representing the centre of the handrail, and then making the widths of the treads conform to it. We will take for illustration the nosing line over the outside of the string, so that the lines of the steps will be drawn as they appear in the development of that surface, and may be made use of for marking out the string.

To do this bend a thin lath round the well over the line representing the outside of the string in plan (Fig. 105), and mark upon it the faces of the first and last risers, Nos. 1 and 22 respectively, as well as the springings, S S, of the semicircle.

Let now the batten be sprung straight, as in Fig. 107, and square up lines from the points S S, and the riser faces 1 and 22. With the pitch-board, P B (Fig. 107), set out two or three of the fliers at the bottom, and by means of the height rod obtain the levels of a few of the top-most fliers, and draw them also as shown by the full lines. On the fliers draw the straight nosing lines *a b* and *c d*, producing them to meet the springings at *b* and *c* respectively, and join *b c*, cutting the centre line at *k*.

The angles at *b* and *c* are then eased off by reverse curves, which may be either arcs of circles, as in the figure, if the centres are conveniently accessible, touching these lines and tangential to each other

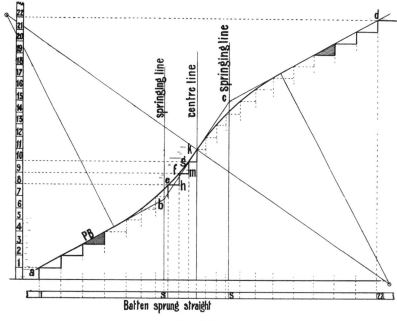

FIG. 107.

at *k*; or easements made in the ways shown respectively by Figs. 62, 63, and 64; or, again, curves pleasing to the eye may be drawn by means of a batten.

The proper widths for the ends of the winders and diminished fliers are now easily determined from this "nosing line."

Draw horizontal lines at the levels of the respective treads to cut the curve, and from these points of intersection draw vertical lines giving the corresponding riser faces, the horizontal distances between which are, of course, the required widths of the treads to be set out round the well.

Thus, for example, in the illustration (Fig. 107), let the level lines at the heights of the treads 8, 9, and 10, intersect the nosing line at the points e, f, and g, respectively, and draw the perpendiculars $f h$ and $g m$, then $e h$ and $f m$ are the widths of the ends of the treads, Nos. 8 and 9. The other widths are found in the same manner.   These widths are set out on the batten, as shown by the dotted lines, which is then re-bent in its former position round the well in the plan (Fig. 105), and the marks transferred to it.   Straight lines drawn from these divisions, and passing through the corresponding points of division previously spaced off on the line of ascent, represent the plans of the several riser faces.

4th method.—Another way of obtaining a suitable graduation of the ends of the steps round the well is shown by Fig. 108.

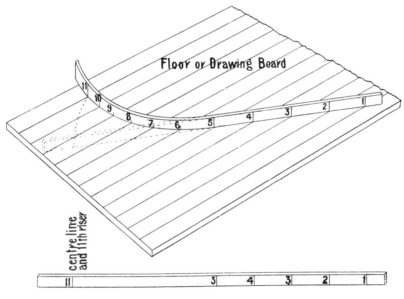

Fig. 108.

A series of parallel straight lines are drawn on the shop floor or on a convenient drawing-board, at equal distances apart, which should not be greater than a width considered appropriate to the narrowest winder. Next obtain with an evenly prepared batten the stretch out of half of the plan length of the outside of the string from riser 1 to 11 (Fig. 105), as in the last method, and space off from one of its ends the number of fliers that are to be left intact, as shown at the lower part of the figure.   Then lay the batten obliquely on the parallel lines with the several points 1, 2, 3, 4, 5, upon successive lines, and, keeping this part of the batten fixed in position, bend round the free end of it in a fair curve until it lies across as many divisions beyond the point 5 as there are to be steps (in this case six), the exact position for the batten being attained when the mark upon it denoting the crown of the well, which is also the 11th riser, lies on its proper parallel line. Mark the batten at the intermediate points, 6, 7, 8, 9, and 10, where it is crossed by the parallels, and re-bend it round the plan of the outside of the well string (Fig. 105) to transfer the divisions to this line as in the previous method.

CONSTRUCTION OF WREATHED STRINGS.—These are built up in various ways; for example, (1) by staving; (2) staving and veneering; (3) grooving and keying; (4) kerfing; (5) by laminating; (6) in solid segments. These methods will now be dealt with in the order given.

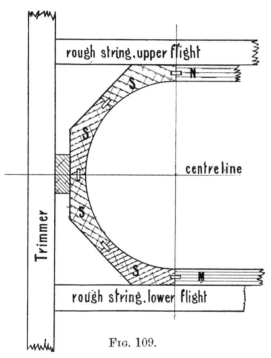

FIG. 109.

1. **Staving.**—In this method the curved part of the string is built up by glueing together, edge to edge, several vertical pieces called "staves," which are worked concave or hollow on one face to agree with the cylindric surface of the well.

The accompanying illustration (Fig. 109) shows the plan of a string made up in this way, the cylindric portion being composed of four staves S, S, S, S, of the same form, having the grain of the wood vertical and the edge joints disposed radially and cross-tongued, the same kind of joint being used to connect them to the straight portions, M and N, of the string.

In putting the staves together, small iron dogs or crampets driven into the end wood may be conveniently employed for bringing up the joints and holding them together till the glue sets.

The construction shown in the figure is adapted for the well of a stair with a half-space landing. When there are winders in the half space the joints of the staves should be made coincident with the faces of the risers, the staves being of the width of the ends of the steps. This plan is convenient and saves material, as the staves can be glued up in a stepped form to roughly form the notches on the upper edge of the string.

The lower ends of the staves when glued together are cut to form a continuous and fair line with the under edges of the adjacent straight portions of the string, the line being drawn on with a flexible mould made from a development of the surface, as explained under the next head.

It may be stated, that this method of staving is only resorted to for small wells, and mostly in the cheaper class of stairs, in which the strings are finished in paint instead of polish or varnish.

It will be apparent that a well string formed in this manner cannot be of itself a strong one, and if adopted should be associated with efficient rough framework to make a reliable structure.

2. **Staving and veneering.**—Figs. 112 and 113 show by a perspective elevation and a plan the well string of the geometrical stair (Figs. 104 and 105), having the curved portion built up by staving and veneering.

In preparing a string in this manner a cylindric surface has first to be built up out of rough scantlings to fit the concave side of the string, and extend some distance beyond the springings. This auxiliary structure is termed in stairbuilding a *cylinder*, although in general it would only represent part of a geometrical cylinder. It is made by nailing rough " cleading " to cross ribs, as shown in the isometric sketch (Fig. 111), which represents the cylinder for the well string of the stair (Figs. 104 and 105), the outside of the " cleading " being planed down accurately to the requisite curved surface.

The veneer has next to be prepared, but preliminary to this a development of the outside surface of the string has to be drawn out on a board. If the second method of graduating the well ends of the steps, as explained in connection with Fig. 107, namely, by means of a pre-arranged " falling line," had been adopted, the required development, as in Fig. 110, would have already been drawn ; but since in the example they are set out in arithmetical progression, this part of the work would be performed at the present stage.

Development of veneer.—The usual way of doing this is to bend a lath, as previously described, round the line representing the plan of the surface to be developed—in this case the outside of the string—and mark accurately upon it the points where the lines of the several riser faces intersect the outside of the string. The two springings of the circle should also be carefully marked on the batten. The batten, when sprung straight, gives by its divisions the total widths of the ends of the steps as they will appear in the development. The development of the line of steps can now be drawn out on the board, as in Fig. 110, by making each step equal to the width found, and joining with it at right angles the proper height of riser obtained from the storey rod. Of course the

L

fliers at top and bottom may be most conveniently drawn out with the pitch-board.

Having completed the line of steps, and drawn on the springings and centre line, trace the nosing line, which is shown dotted in Fig. 110. This latter line forms a guide for drawing the lower edge, which would generally be gauged from it, making the string of equal width throughout,

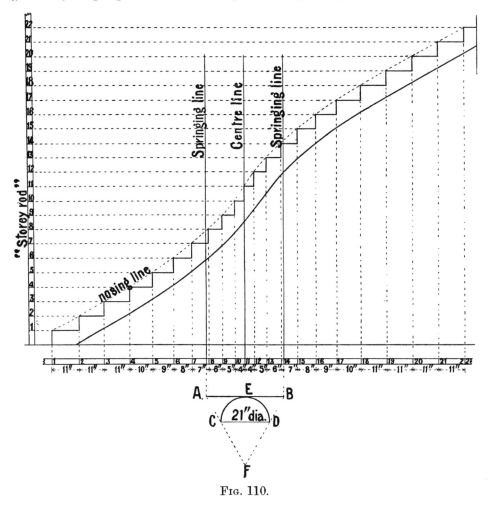

FIG. 110.

excepting in small steep wells, where it may be desirable to make some deviation from this in order to get an easier curve. It should be noted that, when the wreathed portion of the string is of much steeper pitch than the parts above and below it, if the string be made throughout to a development set off to an equal width measured square to the nosing line, it would be found that when bent into the cylindric form the wreathed portion would have the appearance of being too wide for the rest of it, and, therefore, the development of that part of the string should be made a little narrower.   But experience and taste will prove the best guides in these cases.

Instead of using a flexible batten to find the length or stretch out of the semicircle, a geometrical construction is often employed.   This is shown on the lower part of Fig. 110.   Draw a semicircle the size of the well, and using the extremities C and D of the diameter as centres and the length of the diameter as radius, draw two arcs intersecting at F. The point F is then joined to C and D, and these lines produced to inter-

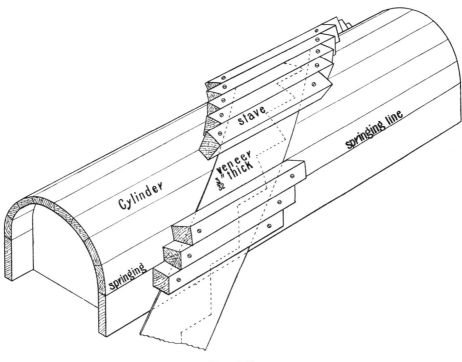

FIG. 111.

sect the tangent A B, drawn parallel to the diameter, in the points A and B.   The length of the line A B is approximately the stretch out of the semicircle.

The stretch out of the semicircle may also be found by multiplying the radius by $3\frac{1}{7}$, or more accurately by $3\cdot1416$.

Preparing and bending veneer.—The veneer for the curved part of the string is now got out long enough to extend a few inches beyond the springing at each end, and carefully taken to a thickness which will depend on the size of the curve.   In the present case, the well being 21 inches diameter, it would probably bend nicely at $\frac{3}{32}$ inch thick.

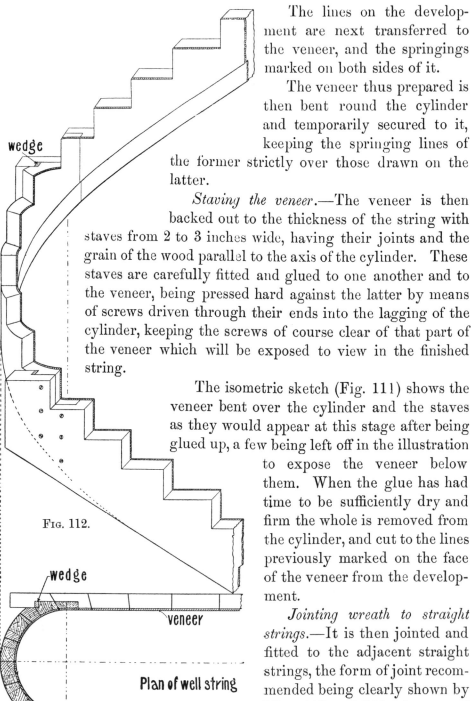

wedge

FIG. 112.

wedge

veneer

Plan of well string

FIG. 113.
DETAILS OF WELL STRING OF STAIR
(FIGS. 104, 105).

The lines on the development are next transferred to the veneer, and the springings marked on both sides of it.

The veneer thus prepared is then bent round the cylinder and temporarily secured to it, keeping the springing lines of the former strictly over those drawn on the latter.

Staving the veneer.—The veneer is then backed out to the thickness of the string with staves from 2 to 3 inches wide, having their joints and the grain of the wood parallel to the axis of the cylinder. These staves are carefully fitted and glued to one another and to the veneer, being pressed hard against the latter by means of screws driven through their ends into the lagging of the cylinder, keeping the screws of course clear of that part of the veneer which will be exposed to view in the finished string.

The isometric sketch (Fig. 111) shows the veneer bent over the cylinder and the staves as they would appear at this stage after being glued up, a few being left off in the illustration to expose the veneer below them. When the glue has had time to be sufficiently dry and firm the whole is removed from the cylinder, and cut to the lines previously marked on the face of the veneer from the development.

Jointing wreath to straight strings.—It is then jointed and fitted to the adjacent straight strings, the form of joint recommended being clearly shown by Figs. 112 and 113, the curved portion being *tabled into* the faces of the straight strings above and below it, being both wedged and well secured with screws. These joints are disposed vertically, and show on the outside of the string as lines parallel to the riser faces, and about 2 inches beyond the springings.

Tongued and groove joints square to the string (not vertical) may also be employed, as in Fig. 114, but fastened with two handrail bolts;

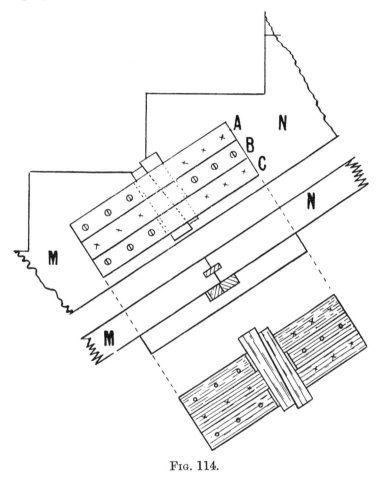

Fig. 114.

or, by the arrangement shown by Fig. 114. In the latter method three separate fish pieces, A, B, and C, are screwed on to the inside of the string across the joint, two of these, A and C, being first screwed to M, one of the two parts of the string to be connected, and the third or middle one B to the other part N, the other ends of the pieces being left unscrewed in the meantime. Previous to their being screwed on, a groove is cut out across the back, down to about half the thickness, for the reception of a pair of wedges. These wedges are driven in from

opposite sides, the one wedge bearing against the middle piece B and
forcing it and the part of the string N to which it is fastened in one
direction, while the other is made to bear on the two outer pieces, A and
C, which being attached to the part M of the string pushes it in the
opposite direction, the result of their united action, therefore, being to
draw up the joint firmly. The fastening is completed by inserting the
rest of the screws marked with the crosses, x x x, in Fig. 114. The
arrangement described is sometimes referred to as the *counter cramp*.

3. **Forming curved strings by grooving and keying.**—Fig. 115
illustrates a plan sometimes resorted to for curved strings. Instead of a
veneer a board from $\frac{3}{4}$ inch to $1\frac{1}{4}$ inch thick, as required, is used, the lines

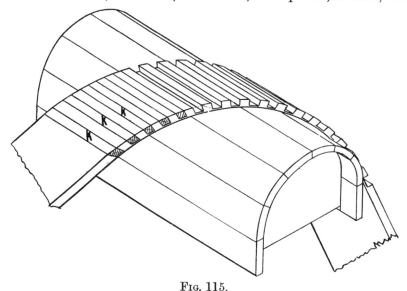

FIG. 115.

of steps, springings, etc., being set out as before on the face side as copied
from the development. A series of trenches about $\frac{1}{2}$ inch wide and
about $\frac{1}{2}$ inch apart are cut out of the back of the board, in the interval
between the springing lines, and in a direction parallel to them, so that
when the strings are in position the trenches would be vertical. These
trenches are taken out down to within $\frac{1}{8}$ inch to $\frac{3}{16}$ inch from the face, so
that the board at this part will bend easily to the curvature of the well.

The string is then bent round the cylinder, and the trenches filled in
with accurately fitted keys (k, k, k, Fig. 115), well glued.

This can now be made up to any required thickness by glueing on
successive thin layers of pine to the back.

In the case of an open string, it can be fixed as a facing to a rough carriage, the latter furnishing the necessary support to the ends of the steps.

It greatly adds to the strength of a string, built up either in this manner or by staving, to glue two or three continuous strips of veneer from 2 inches to 3 inches wide on the back or unexposed side. This binds the several staves well together, and is better than canvas, which is sometimes used for the same purpose.

4. **Saw kerfing**.—This method of building up wreathed strings is chiefly confined to cheap inferior work, and is not so strong as staving. It proves a ready way of building up the bases and rails of curved spandrel framing or similar kinds of work.

A veneer is first marked out and bent round the cylinder precisely as in the second case; but in place of staves it is backed with a board of

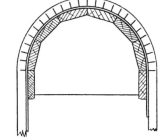

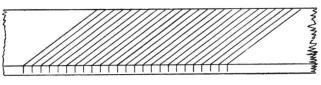

FIG. 116.

FIG. 117.

the required thickness made flexible—so that it also can be bent round the curve—by inserting a series of saw cuts or kerfs parallel to the axis of the cylinder and at equal intervals apart, the spacing of the saw cuts being made so that they are firmly closed when the kerfed piece is bent to the desired curvature. Fig. 116 shows a board kerfed in the way described, while Fig. 117 represents it when bent and glued to the veneer.

The saw cuts are, of course, taken out of the side that is to be concave, or that towards the veneer, and down to a depth leaving only the thickness of a veneer on the other side intact.

To find the requisite spacing between the saw cuts, take a piece of stuff of the same thickness and of the same material as that to be used, and insert one saw cut in it to the proper depth; then, having bent it so as to close firmly the saw cut just made, lay it on to a board and mark the angle that the two ends now

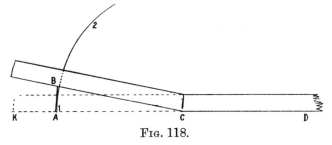

FIG. 118.

make with each other. This angle is shown in Fig. 118 as E C D. Next, using C as a centre, draw an arc of a circle 1 2 with radius equal to the radius of the well plus the thickness of the veneer. The intercepted tangent A B to this arc, between C D produced and E C is the required distance.

The board is then marked out, and the kerfs cut with the *same saw* as was used in the trial piece.

5. **Laminating.**—A laminated string is one that is composed of several thin layers of wood glued together flatwise. The several layers are made to a thickness that will admit of their being easily bent round the well cylinder without fracture.

If the strings are to show in hard wood, the outer layer or veneer will

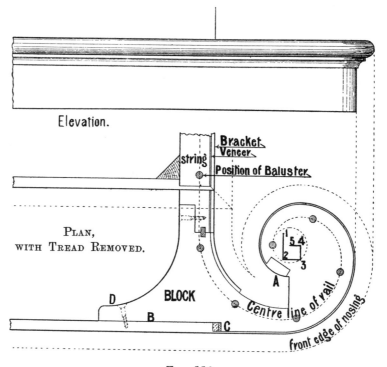

Fig. 119.

be of this material, while the inner ones will generally be of pine or other soft wood which is easily bent.

When the several layers have been prepared they are bent over the cylinder, and fastened down temporarily with cross cleats, 3 or 4 inches apart, made long enough for a screw to be driven through each end into the lagging and quite clear of the string. The whole is then removed from the cylinder, and having been thoroughly heated and glued is re-fastened in its previous position. The glueing should be all done in one operation, and this will generally be possible, except with very long strings, in which cases one half only should be first glued and fastened down, and when this is completed the remaining half similarly operated upon. In both cases the screwing down of the cross bars should be commenced at the middle and proceeded with towards the ends.

6. **Wreathed strings built up in solid segments.**—This method is not generally regarded as being an economical one, and is not often adopted for house stairs. The wreathed strings of ships' stairs, however, especially those exposed to the weather, are often jointed up in the solid, and the lines for getting out strings in this manner will be treated of in the subsequent part of the work dealing exclusively with ships' stairs, and to which the student is referred (see pages 123 and 133).

Construction of curtail step.—An enlarged elevation and plan of the curtail step of the stair under consideration are given by Fig. 119, the tread being removed from the plan to show the several parts of which it is composed, and how it is jointed to the string.

The outline of the projecting end is made to follow the scroll of the handrail under which it stands. When the latter is described geometrically the former is drawn from the same set of centres.

Methods of striking out the curves of scroll terminals for handrails are given by Figs. 282-284, and are equally applicable to drawing out the step illustrated by the adjoining sketches, the centres 1, 2, 3, 4 and 5, from which it is drawn, being shown in the plan (Fig. 119).

The Figs. 120 to 122 are introduced to further elucidate the construction.

A block is made up by glueing together two or more thicknesses of pine, with the grain of each piece crossing that of the next adjoining it at a small angle to prevent warping. When the grain is made to cross at right angles the inequality in the shrinkage may lead to disfigurement of the rounded surface. The block is then cut with the band saw to the required curved outline, etc., shown by the plan.

The riser is prepared as shown by the sketch (Fig. 120). It is made

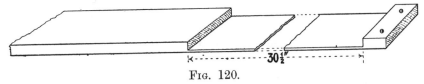

FIG. 120.

long enough to be continued round the curved end of the block, where it is reduced in thickness to that of a veneer, excepting about 2 inches at its extremity, which is left intact to enable this part to be sunk into and fixed to the pine block, as shown at A in Figs. 119, etc. The front of the block at B (Figs. 119-122) is checked out to receive the full thick-

M

ness of the riser, and at the shoulder C sufficent room is left for a pair of suitable wedges.

When the block and riser have been prepared in the manner indicated, the latter is first screwed to the former at A (Figs. 121, 122). The whole veneer is next glued and bent round the curve, pressing it hard up against the block.

This is best accomplished by laying the outer face of the riser on to

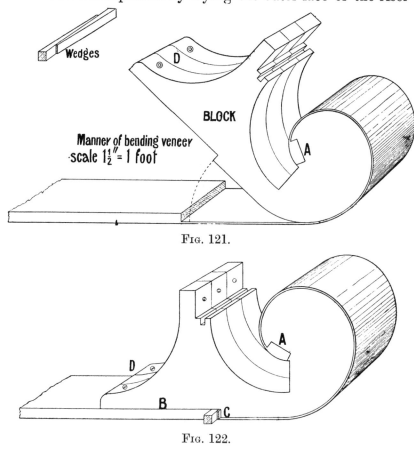

Fig. 121.

Fig. 122.

a flat board on the bench, and rolling the block along, as shown by Fig. 121, till the riser is brought into its sinking at B, as in the next illustration (Fig. 122). The wedges are now glued and driven up, bringing the veneer still closer to the block, and when sufficiently tight the screws are finally inserted at D.

It need scarcely be remarked that it would hardly prove safe to glue it before having had the veneer previously bent into its position and temporarily wedged, to ascertain if it is of the correct length and otherwise properly fitting.

In the example the block is connected to the string by a rebated and tongued and grooved joint fastened with screws, as shown in Fig. 119. The counter-cramp arrangement, as illustrated by Fig. 114, is often employed also for this joint.

Section of string.

12 ins.   6   0   1   2 feet

FIG. 123.   DETAIL OF STAIR (FIGS. 104, 105).

Detail of balustrading.—An enlarged drawing of a portion of the balustrade, scroll step, etc., at the bottom of this stair is shown by Fig. 123, accompanied with sections of the string and handrail.

The design there shown is intended to represent an arrangement with cast-iron balusters throughout, no newel or larger baluster being employed to support the scroll, as is sometimes adopted. The spacing of the group of balusters below the scroll is clearly shown separately set off along the line of centre of handrail in Fig. 119. The spacing of the balusters round the entire well is shown in the plan, Fig. 105, there being two on each of the fliers, the others distributed over the winders so as to maintain as nearly as possible the same spacing from centre to centre as those that occur on the wide-ended fliers.

The lengths of these balusters, which necessarily vary, will be ascertained either from an elevation or from a development made on the

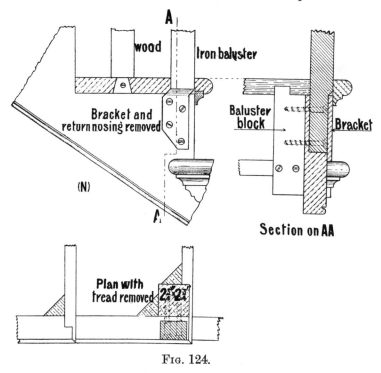

Fig. 124.

centre line of handrail, preferably the latter. In the case before us the variable length is worked into the base of the baluster, the other members being made uniform throughout.

Fastening iron balusters.—There are various expedients employed for connecting iron balusters to the steps and handrails; that shown at A, Fig. 125, illustrates the method more usually adopted of fixing them to the steps, being the same as that already shown for wood balusters in Fig. 71. A dovetail projection is cast on the end of the baluster, which is sunk into the end of the tread, and fastened with a strong screw, all being concealed by the return nosing in the finished stair. Another less frequent method is, in place of the dovetail, to have an iron screw set in the base of the baluster when being cast. Other means sometimes employed are to leave a broad flat base on the baluster in the form of a flange to admit of several screws being driven through it into the tread. Or again, to have iron sockets screwed to the treads which receive the bases of the balusters.

The heads of the balusters are simply screwed to the underside of the rail through the husk or capital, as at A, Fig. 123. Another method is often employed, namely, by attaching them to a flat iron core, the latter being sunk and screwed to the underside of the handrail. This latter method is illustrated by Fig. 152, in the section dealing with ship stairs.

Strengthening wood balustrade. —When light wood balusters are used for stairs with open strings an iron one of the same pattern should be introduced at intervals of every seventh or tenth baluster to provide additional stiffening to the balustrade. This should be done in all good work, and to insure that the iron balusters are properly fixed at the bottom special preparation should be made for them, as shown in Fig. 124, namely, by fitting a block of pine about 3 inches square below the tread in the angle formed by the string and riser, it being well screwed to them and stump-tenoned into the tread, as shown by the section on A-A.

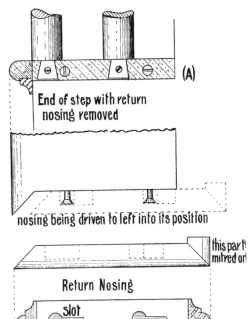

End of step with return nosing removed

nosing being driven to left into its position

this part mitred on

Return Nosing

slot

FIG. 125.

Returned nosings and ornamental brackets.—The returned nosing, and the way of attaching it to the end of the tread by concealed screws, to avoid disfigurement of the polished work, is shown by Fig. 125, being a detail of the stair, Figs. 104, 105.

It will be noticed that the return of the moulding on the end of the nosing at A in the figure is not worked across the end wood, but formed by mitring on a piece of the moulding itself, it being required to project beyond the back of the nosing the thickness of the bracket, as the end of the tread in this arrangement has to be cut flush with the outside of the bracket, and not with that of the string. The ornamental brackets for the curved part of the well should be cut out of the solid, to fit the curvature of the strings, and with the grain of the wood following the inclination of the stair. This will generally prove a better plan and cheaper in the end than attempting to bend them; but in the case of stairs that are to be painted, the curved brackets may be got out with the grain of the wood vertical, and then bent to the shape by pressing them round a hot steam pipe.

Enlarging and diminishing ornamental brackets.—Let A, Fig. 126, be the bracket for the fliers; it is required to reduce it and its members proportionately to suit the end of a winder or of a diminished flier.

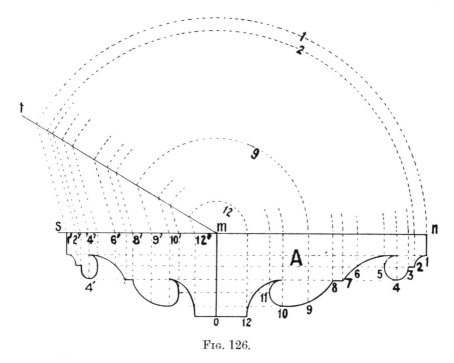

FIG. 126.

Select points on the outline of the pattern bracket A, as 1, 2, . . . 12, and square them over to the edge $m\,n$. Then transfer the divisions on $m\,n$ to a line $m\,t$ drawn through m at any angle with $m\,n$. Next set off $m\,s$, on $n\,m$ produced, equal to the width of the required winder, and divide $m\,s$ proportionately (see Appendix, Problem 3) to $m\,t$ by joining $s\,t$ and drawing parallels to it as shown, giving the divisions 1', 2', . . . 12', Through these points, 1', 2', . . . 12', draw lines parallel to $o\,m$ to intersect corresponding lines parallel to $m\,n$, through the points 1, 2, . . . 12.

The lines and curves traced through these points of intersection, and similar to those of A, give the outline for the diminished bracket.

CHAPTER VII

CONSTRUCTION OF HALF-TURN GEOMETRICAL STAIRS (*continued*).

II. STAIR WITH LANDINGS IN THE QUARTER SPACES.—We shall complete this section of the subject by an illustration of a geometrical staircase (Figs. 127 and 127A) composed of three straight flights associated with two quarter-space landings, and having a *close* ornamented string at the well side.

It will, however, be unnecessary at this stage to enter at any length into the constructive details, as the principles and methods treated of in connection with previous examples will enable the student, if he has followed us thus far, to cope successfully with all *ordinary* cases of wood stairs that he would in common practice be called upon to execute.

Description of the illustration.—The drawings, Figs. 127 and 127A, represent this stair by the usual plan and elevation, the latter showing the lower flight in section.

The bottom and return flights are composed of ten and nine parallel steps respectively, while six steps constitute the cross flight. These flights, together with the two quarter-space landings, reach the required height, namely, 13 feet.

The stair starting is made with a round-ended step built up to accommodate a large octagonal newel, which is placed in the centre of the round end of the step, and receives the string and rail in one of its "canted" faces, these turning in to it with short wreaths standing over an eighth of a circle in plan.

The two *quarter turns* at the landings are made on a curve of 12 inches radius in plan, measured to the centre of rail or string, the turns at the top and bottom of the stair being of the same radius.

The rough carriages and the scantlings that compose the framework of the quarter-space platforms are shown by dotted lines in the plan, the latter being put together similarly to that described for the landing of the open newel stair (illustrated by Figs. 91 and 92).

A *dado frame* is shown in connection with this example fitted round

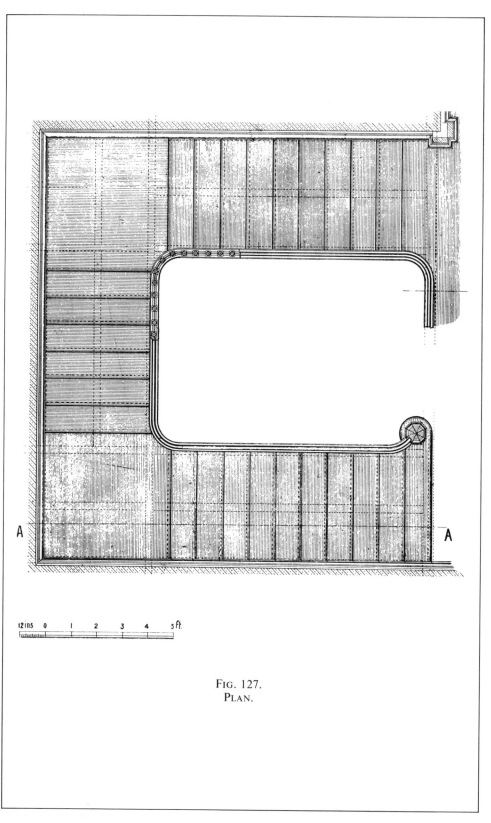

12ins 0 1 2 3 4 5ft.

Fig. 127.
Plan.

Geometrical Stair with Landings in Quarter—spaces.

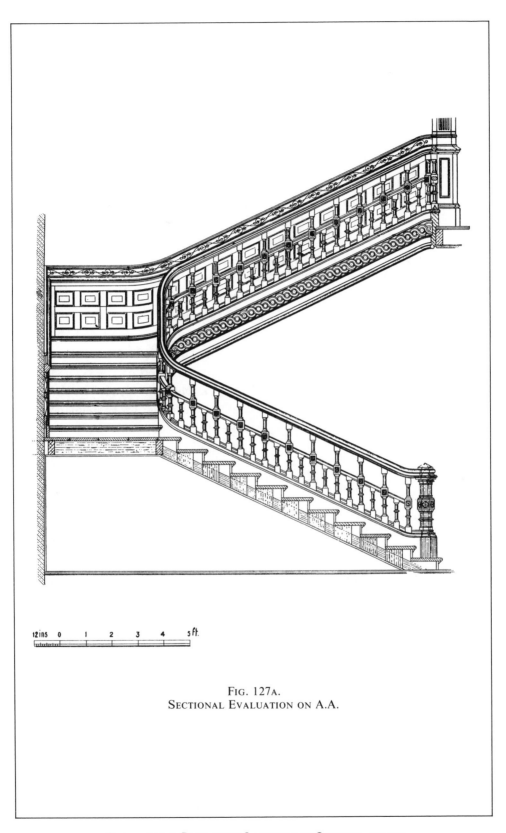

12 ins 0   1   2   3   4   5 ft.

FIG. 127A.
SECTIONAL EVALUATION ON A.A.

GEOMETRICAL STAIR WITH LANDINGS IN QUARTER—SPACES.

the stairway, and extending from the wall string to a little above the height of the handrail.

The elevation further shows the complete balustrade, which it will be seen is fitted with a small intermediate rail, having alternate short balusters below it.

Arrangement of risers at the quarter-space landings.—This is a point that requires attention in setting out the plan of the stair, as, when the radius of the curve has been decided on, the positions of the risers will largely, if not entirely, determine whether the lines of the balustrade will appear easy and graceful or the reverse.

When the student has made some progress in the theory of hand-

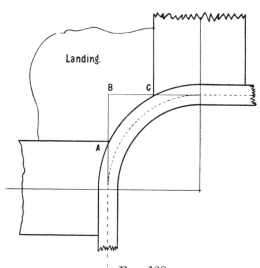

Fig. 128.

railing he will be able to see that there are certain positions in which these risers may be placed that will enable the handrail and the capping of the string, etc., to be easily made, and enable them also to be taken out of the least material. The arrangement alluded to is that adopted in the stair under consideration, and to make it clear an enlarged sketch of that part of the plan is repeated in Fig. 128. Produce the plans of the centre lines of the handrails of the straight flights to meet at B, Fig. 128, and from this point set off the distances B A and B C, each equal to half the width of a tread; A and C are then the positions of the risers in question. It will give the same result if the sum of the distances A B and B C is made equal to the width of a tread, only the landing would not then be placed in a symmetrical position with respect to the two adjacent flights.

When the two risers are disposed in the above manner the *centre lines* of the two straight rails meet when produced in a point above B, so that they are both brought into the same plane; any other arrangement of the risers causing the one centre line to be above the other, at B, and consequent easings of the rail, requiring more material for its production.

In setting out the plans of these stairs a very common way is to endeavour to get the end of the landing at the well equal to the width of a tread measured along the centre line of rail, so that when a development is made on this line it will give a straight nosing line throughout.

This part of the subject will be further referred to in connection with *ships' stairs*, in which these quarter turns are of frequent occurrence.

As regards appearance, both these arrangements of the risers will give satisfactory curves for strings making turns of moderate size, say, above 6 inches radius of centre line. It may be observed, however, that good results can hardly be obtained with a close string that is comparatively thick when it has to wind round a small curve in plan.

CONSTRUCTIVE DETAILS.—Fig. 129 represents an enlarged detail of the newel at the bottom of this stair, with a portion of the balustrade. In the same figure is also given cross sections of the handrail, middle rail, and string.

1. **Round-ended step**.—The round end of the bottom step below the newel would be built in soft wood in the same way as has been illustrated for the curtail step (Figs. 119-122), the riser at the end being reduced to the thickness of a veneer and bent round the block.

2. **Newel post**.—Its cross section is octagonal throughout. The base is made just large enough to take in one of its canted faces, the full width of the capping, which is the widest part of the string. The top of the newel is also made of sufficient size to receive the section of the handrail in the same way. For large newels like that shown, especially when of oak, it is difficult to get for the purpose a single piece of timber *sound* and *well seasoned*. Consequently they are often *built up in parts*. This can be best done by first preparing an octagonal piece of pine about 1 inch less in diameter than the smallest section of the newel, and then making it up to the required design by planting on to its several cants mouldings and facings in suitable sections of the kind of wood specified. In the latter method a good deal of work is involved in forming the joints and mitres, but it has an advantage over the solid newel in that the mouldings may be run by a spindle moulding machine in lengths cut across the grain of the wood. The pine core should be left long enough below the base to extend through the step, so that it may be securely fastened to the floor joist or trimmer.

3. **Well string**.—Close strings for geometrical stairs, unless of the plainest character, necessarily involve much labour in their preparation. Being seen on the stair side as well as on the side towards the well, the operations of veneering, planting, etc., have of course to be performed on both these faces, and besides, they require a moulded capping for the reception of the balusters, which has to be worked out of the solid.

From the sectional drawing of the string (Fig. 129) it will be seen

that the body of it is worked in pine, the stair side being faced over with
a thin veneer, while the well side is made up with planting to produce a
continuous ornamental panel or sinking in the middle of the depth.

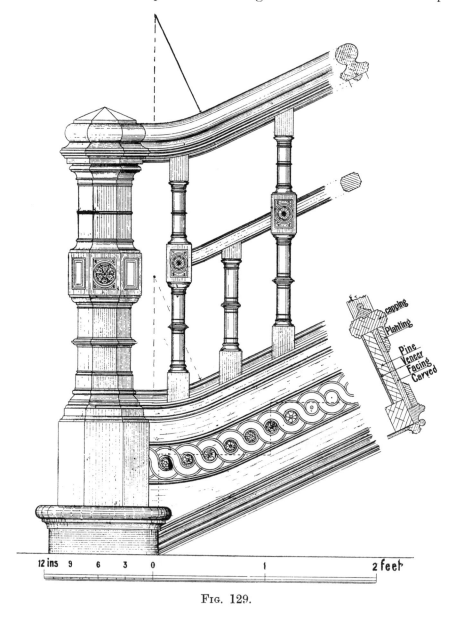

FIG. 129.

These facings may be fixed to the pine when the stair is in course of
erection at the building, as when this is done it allows more freedom in
putting together the constructional parts than when glued on as parts of
the string at the bench.

It will be obvious that for this string the wreathed parts of the outside facings will have to be *cut out of the solid* and worked to their proper curvature, as they would be rather thick for bending. With respect to the pine, or central portion, it may be either cut out of the solid, and jointed and bolted to the straight length above and below it, or built up by any of the methods of staving and kerfing described in the preceding chapter.

Cutting wreathed strings out of the solid.—We shall now show how to get out the wreathed portion of the string or any of its facings from the solid plank, *i.e.*, without having recourse to staving or bending.

To do this economically the grain of the wood is made to follow approximately the pitch of the stair, so that the plank is tilted up at one end to this inclination. For the purpose of *lining off* the plank two moulds are required, one to apply to the edge of the stuff to enable the vertical faces to be cut out to the cylindric form, so that they will stand directly over their circular plans; the other to bend round these curved surfaces, after they have been formed, to mark out the piece for trimming its edges to the requisite falling line. The former is generally called a *face mould*, while the latter is known as a *falling mould*. They are sometimes also called respectively *edge* and *side moulds*.

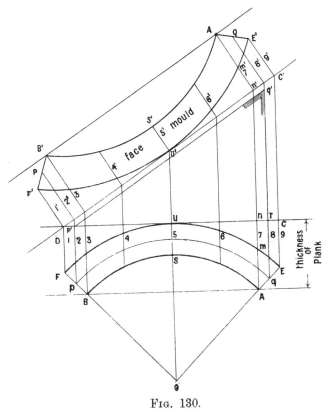

Fig. 130.

Directions for drawing face mould.—1*st, by level ordinates.*—Let the quarter circle A B F E (Fig. 130) be the plan of the wreathed portion of the string of the stair (Fig. 127), which we will suppose is to be jointed to the straight parts at the springings with plain butt joints, cross-tongued and fastened with bolts.

From p and q, the middle points of F B and A E, Fig. 130, draw ordinates $p\,p'$ and $q\,r$ respectively square to C D. Produce $q\,r$, and make $r\,q'$ equal to the difference in levels between the points p and q obtained from the development of the centre falling line. Then the angle that this line $p'\,q'$ makes with the horizontal line C D is the inclination of the plane of the mould.

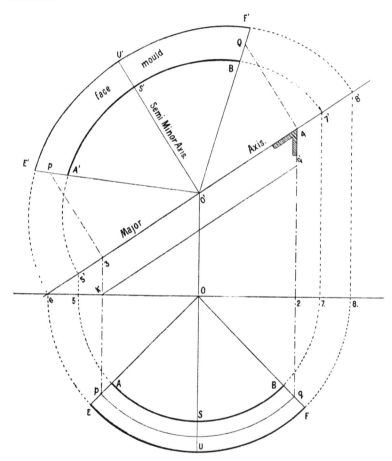

Fig. 131.

From the points F, B, A, E, Fig. 130, draw the ordinates 1, 3, 7, 9 respectively at right angles to C D and also any convenient number of intermediate ordinates, as 4, 5, and 6.

Through D, where ordinate 1 cuts the horizontal line C D, draw D C parallel to $p'\,q'$, and produce all the ordinates, 2, 3, 4, etc., to cut this line as shown. From the points of intersection set out lines at right angles to D C', and make them equal to the corresponding ordinates, 1, 2, 3 . . . 9, drawn across the plan; for example, make $n'\,m'$ A equal to

$n\,m\,\mathrm{A}$ on ordinate 7. The lengths of the other ordinates with their divisions being similarly copied, the joint lines are drawn by joining A E' and B' F', and the curves of the mould traced through the several points by a flexible batten. This mould when held at the proper inclination may be made to stand perpendicularly over the circular plan, the several ordinates at the same time being horizontal. In this connection the student should read Appendix Problem 16.

2nd, by describing ellipses.—As the curves of the mould are portions of ellipses, of which the semi-minor axes are *os* and *ou* (Fig. 130), the respective radii of the plan circles, in place of using ordinates as above the mould may be drawn out by finding the major axes of these curves, and hence describing them either by means of a trammel or by a string, as explained in the Appendix (Problems 13 and 18).

The necessary construction for drawing out the face mould in this manner is shown by Fig. 131, A B F E being the plan as before, and O the centre of the quarter circles. Continue the circular arcs to cut the diameter drawn through O parallel to A B at the points 6 and 5, and through point 6 draw 6 8' parallel to the line of inclination $k'\,q'$, the latter being found as in Fig. 130. Projectors 5 5' and O O' determine O' 5', and O' 6 the semi-major axes of the inner and outer curves of the mould respectively, and O' S' and O' U', set out at right angles to O' 6 and equal to the corresponding plan radii, give the semi-minor axes, so that from these particulars the ellipses may be described. The joint lines A' E' and B F' converge to the centre of the ellipse, so that we have only to find one point, say P and Q for each joint, these points being determined by ordinates, as in the first method (Fig. 130).

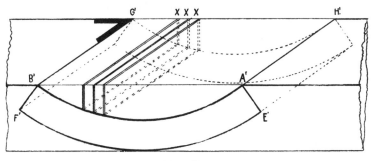

Fig. 132.

Application of face mould to plank.—The adjoining sketch (Fig. 132) shows the face mould applied to one edge of the plank for marking it out. The mould would be similarly placed on the other edge of the plank to draw the lines on it also, but moved along lengthwise of the plank to a position which is determined by the *plumb bevel* applied across the face, as shown at G′ in the sketch (Fig. 132). This bevel is of course the angle represented at *q′* in both Figs. 130 and 131, and is the complement of the *pitch angle*.

The curved surfaces are then formed by cutting away the waste wood to these lines, and working strictly parallel to the bevel lines A′ H′ and B′ G′ (Fig. 132), which in this case are the springings, and are of course vertical when the piece is held up to the proper pitch.

Where there is no machinery, several saw cuts, *x, x,* may be made as shown in Fig. 132, which will enable the interspaces to be easily cleared away to the lines. The concave side would be finished with a "round soled plane" suitable to the curvature. The finishing of the convex side and the forming of the joints will present no difficulty.

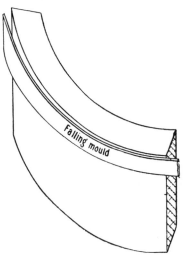
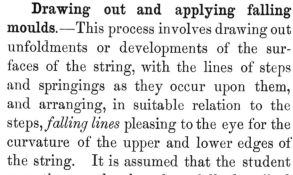
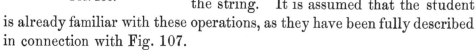

When these operations have been carried out the piece is then ready to be lined off with falling moulds for the edges to be cut.

Drawing out and applying falling moulds.—This process involves drawing out unfoldments or developments of the surfaces of the string, with the lines of steps and springings as they occur upon them, and arranging, in suitable relation to the steps, *falling lines* pleasing to the eye for the curvature of the upper and lower edges of the string. It is assumed that the student

FIG. 133.

is already familiar with these operations, as they have been fully described in connection with Fig. 107.

A thin mould, which may be a veneer or any piece of stuff that will easily bend round the cylindrical surfaces, has its edge accurately formed to the falling line, and the vertical springing lines carefully marked on it. It is then bent round the corresponding curved surface of the piece, and, being adjusted to the proper height, with the springing lines on it coinciding with those marked on the stuff, as represented in the sketch (Fig. 133), a line is drawn round the edge of the mould with a pencil, thus copying the exact falling line from the development on to the surface of the string.

When the string is thick and has to be fitted with a capping it will facilitate the fitting of the latter, and may give better curves, to line off

the concave side also with a falling mould.   The lines for the under edge
can be gauged off the upper.

Before these edges are accurately cut the wreath piece should be
bolted temporarily to the straight lengths, and eased properly into them.

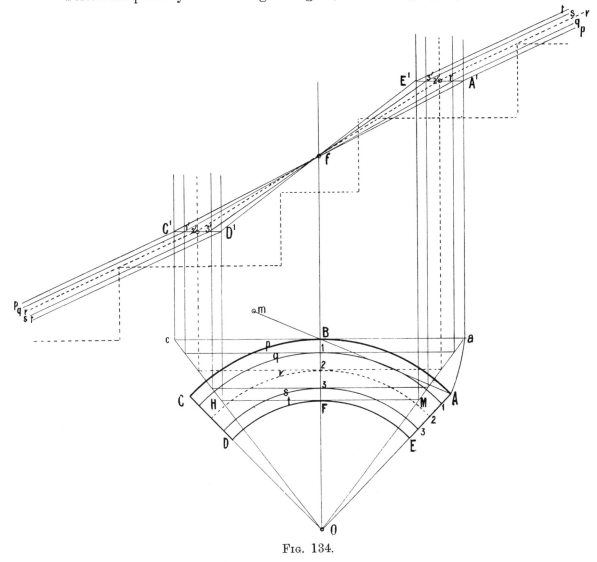

FIG. 134.

All the facings, mouldings, and cappings, in connection with the
wreathed portion of the string, may be marked off and cut out of the
solid in the same way as described above.

Developments.—Fig. 134 shows five falling lines (the easing curves
not being drawn to avoid confusion of lines) for the curved string in the
example, $2'f2'$ being that corresponding to the centre, $1'f1'$ and $3'f3'$ the

outer and inner edges of the string, and C′f A′ and D′f E′ those of the capping. The quarter circles, representing the plans of these, are similarly numbered and lettered. The drawing is introduced principally to show how, when one development has been made, the others may be readily obtained from it, the ordinary practice being, if more than one is required, to make a separate construction for each.

In the diagram there is also shown another method than that given by Fig. 110 of obtaining the stretch out of the arc of a circle along the tangent at one extremity.

We shall first show how to find the stretch out of the quarter circle A B C representing the plan of the *convex* side of the capping.

Draw the tangent $a c$ (Fig. 134), touching the arc at its middle point B. Next draw the chord A B, and produce it to m, making the produced part B m equal to one half A B. Using m as a centre, and m A as radius, draw the arc A a, cutting the tangent at a. Then B a is the stretch out of the arc A B, and B c marked off on the other side of B equal to B a gives $a c$ as the length of the whole arc of the quarter circle A B C.

The stretch out of the other arcs are now easily obtained, being the lengths of the parallel tangents intercepted between O a and O c; thus H M is the stretch out of the arc D F E.

The vertical lines shown in the figure, drawn from the extremities of the separate tangents, represent the respective springings.

The development of the line of steps as they occur on any of the arcs in plan is first drawn. In the illustration (Fig. 134) the dotted lines represent the development of steps on the centre line of the string for the stair (Fig. 127). On this line of steps draw the straight nosing lines above and below the wreath, meeting their appropriate springings at the points marked 2′. Then through these points 2′ and 2′ draw the level lines C′ D′ and A′ E′, and from the points where these intersect the other vertical springing lines draw parallels to the nosing lines, r 2′, already drawn. These lines, $p\,q\,s\,t$, represent the straight parts of the falling lines of the other curves, and are in their correct positions, the same as if separate developments of the steps had been made for each.

The ogee falling lines can now be drawn with a batten to please the eye, beginning preferably with the centre one 2′f 2′, taking care to ease it neatly into the straight at each end. To avoid confusion of lines the curves are not drawn in Fig. 134. It will be observed that they must all cross the centre line at f.

In this manner any number of falling lines belonging to the same

wreath can be quickly laid off in the same drawing, and are likely to prove more exact with respect to one another than if separate drawings were made.

4. **Dado framing.**—We conclude this chapter with an enlarged illustration (Fig. 135) of part of the dado on the slope of the stair represented in Figs. 127 and 127A. A section of the lying pieces and wall string, etc., is drawn across the elevation, and shows the panels fielded with a cavetto moulding stuck on the frame. The dado is finished at the top with a surbase at the height of the handrail, and above it an ornamental carved band.

The chief difficulty in connection with these continuous framed dados is in the arrangement of the eas-
ings at the junction of the level and raked portions, and this piece of the frame should be laid off full size.

FIG. 135. DETAILS OF DADO, ETC., OF
STAIRCASE (FIGS. 127 AND 127A).

CHAPTER VIII

CONSTRUCTION OF STAIRS FOR PASSENGER SHIPS

General observations.—On board ships, stairs are fitted in situations where it is desirable to have easier and more commodious means of communication established between one deck and another than would be obtained by ordinary deck or companion ladders. In merchant vessels they should be used at all parts connected with the passenger accommodation. In vessels of the Royal Navy wood stairs are seldom fitted.

The ship draughtsman or designer in arranging the deck plans of a vessel shows, in a general manner, the kind of stairs to be fitted and their size, while the planning and working out of the details are, as a rule, left entirely in the hands of the foreman joiner and his staff.

In most cases the small amount of space which can be set aside for the stairway, coupled with the curvature given to the decks and other irregularities of form, make staircase work rather more difficult to perform in ships than in houses. From these causes ship stairs are mostly steep, confined, inelegant structures; indeed easy, convenient, and well-planned examples are exceptional, being only met with in the largest and best appointed passenger vessels.

Having examined the principal stairs of a considerable number of typical passenger ships, we found that the easiest pitch was about 30°, with a tread of $10\frac{1}{2}$ inches; and that, again, a pitch of 45°, with a tread of 8 inches, was very common—figures which agree with our own experience of stairbuilding on passenger vessels.

Headroom.—The question of headroom generally constitutes a standing difficulty in the planning out of ship stairs. In the case of vessels with little height between decks, rather less headroom than would be deemed sufficient for house stairs may only be obtained. But it is very desirable that the rules we have laid down in Chapter II should be generally adhered to.

Proportion of tread to rise.—The same rules that are followed in the determination of the proper rise that should correspond to a given tread for house stairs are equally applicable to ship stairs, and have been discussed at length in Chapter II.

Disposition of steps with respect to the decks.—The stair treads should not be placed so as to follow the *sheer*[1] and *camber*[2] of the decks, but kept strictly level, that is, parallel to the water planes of the vessel, while the risers should be vertical. Any departure from this rule should only be made in the case of a stair starting from, or landing at, a position of extreme sheer or camber, when it may be desirable to set the top or bottom step a little off the level, to bring them more nearly into agreement with the deck curvature.

Different forms of ship stairs.—The conditions as to space being much more restricted in ships than in houses, fewer varieties of stairs occur, the height between one deck and another only allowing in general a quarter turn to be made.

The three common forms are:

(1) Straight stairs ; (2) quarter turn, side flight stairs; (3) circular stairs, sketch plans of which are given (Chapter I) by Figs. 6, 15, and 13 respectively.

CONSTRUCTION OF STRAIGHT STAIRS.

These in ships always consist of a single flight, which reaches from deck to deck without an intermediate landing. They are not attended with the same danger from the rolling of the vessel in rough weather as turning stairs, and if made of easy pitch and placed in a fore and aft direction prove safe and otherwise very suitable for the passenger traffic on board ships. On the other hand, they obviously require a greater length of the ship's space than other forms which change their direction in the course of the ascent.

Straight stairs arranged fore and aft are characteristic of vessels of the White Star Line, built by Harland and Wolff, of Belfast, the principal staircases of the SS. " Teutonic " and " Majestic " being most elaborate and tasteful examples of this class.

Description of illustration.—We illustrate by a half plan and two elevations (Figs. 136, 137, 138), and by enlarged details (Figs. 139 to 149), the general arrangement and construction of a stair suitable for the first class accommodation of a large passenger vessel.

The arrangement for two consecutive decks is shown, and consists of straight flights disposed in the fore and aft direction, a single one 7 feet

---

[1] Sheer is the curvature given to the ship's deck in the fore and aft direction.

[2] Camber is the curvature of the deck in the transverse direction.

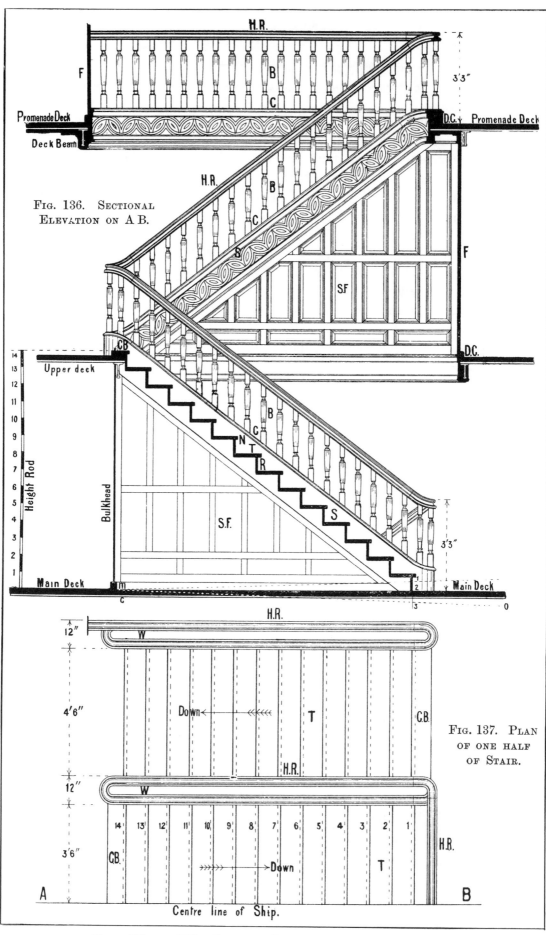

FIG. 136. SECTIONAL ELEVATION ON A.B.

FIG. 137. PLAN OF ONE HALF OF STAIR.

FIGS. 136 AND 137. STRAIGHT STAIRS FOR PASSENGER VESSEL.

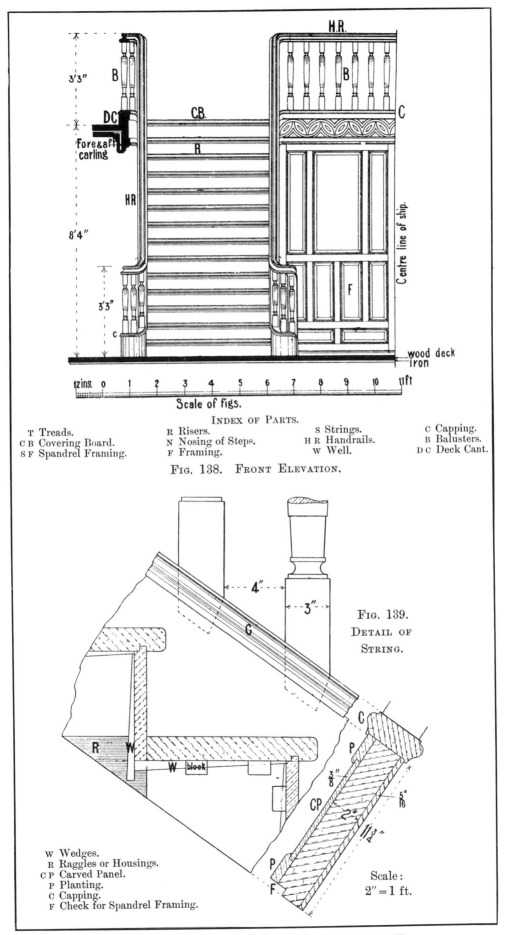

3'3"

B

DC

Fore&aft
carling

C.B.

R

HR

8'4"

3'3"

c

H.R.

B

C

F

Centre line of ship.

wood deck
iron

12ins. 0   1   2   3   4   5   6   7   8   9   10   11ft
Scale of figs.

INDEX OF PARTS.

T Treads.
C B Covering Board.
S F Spandrel Framing.

R Risers.
N Nosing of Steps.
F Framing.

S Strings.
H R Handrails.
W Well.

C Capping.
B Balusters.
D C Deck Cant.

FIG. 138.   FRONT ELEVATION.

4"

3"

FIG. 139.
DETAIL OF
STRING.

C

R   W

W   block

C

P

P

CP

3/8"

5/16"

2"

1 3/4"

P

F

W Wedges.
R Raggles or Housings.
C P Carved Panel.
P Planting.
C Capping.
F Check for Spandrel Framing.

Scale:
2" = 1 ft.

FIGS. 138 AND 139.   STRAIGHT STAIRS FOR PASSENGER VESSEL.

wide in the centre leading from the *main* to the *upper deck* and two narrower flights reaching the *promenade*.

Fig. 137 is the half plan, A B representing the middle line of the vessel, the dotted lines the fronts of the risers, and the full lines the front edges of the treads. Fig. 136 gives the sectional elevation of the lower stair, and an elevation of one of the upper, the other elevation of the latter being given in Fig. 138.

The strings, which are *close* ones, are continuous, no newels being employed; those of the lower stair being continued round small wells and joining into the strings of the upper.

SETTING OUT THE STAIR.—The student should read in this connection the methods described in Chapter III for *taking account of* and *setting out* straight stairs for houses.

1. **Taking dimensions.**—Take, for example, the lower stair, Fig. 137. The exact height that the stair has to rise from the one deck to the other is first ascertained at the ship, measuring with a height rod from the upper surface of the main deck to the top of the "covering board" on the upper deck, as shown to the left of Fig. 136.

Taking sheer into account in the height.—The stair is supposed situated about amidships, where the deck fore and aft may be taken as level. If, on the other hand, it had been placed well forward or aft in the ship, it would be necessary in that case to take into account the rise of the deck due to the sheer on the plan length of the stair. For instance, suppose the dotted line $m\,n$, Fig. 136, to represent the deck line, then on the length $m\,2$ the rise of the deck would be the distance 1 2, which would have to be deducted from the height as obtained above. Of course if the sheer was in the opposite direction with respect to the stair, and $m\,o$ the deck line, the difference in levels 2 3, would in this case have to be added, not subtracted.

The *height* being thus obtained, and presuming that the positions of the first and last risers have been determined, the horizontal distance between their faces, *i.e.*, the going of the stair, is marked on a rod.

2. **Division of rods.**—These two rods, with the going marked on the one and the height on the other, are then divided out for the number and widths of *treads* and *risers* respectively, in exactly the same way as has been already explained for house stairs on pages 24 and 25, remembering that the number of risers is always one more than the number of treads.

It will prove convenient also to "set out" a third rod showing the correct width of the stairs, length of steps, thickness of strings, depth of housings, and any other particulars peculiar to the class of stair, such, for example, as the length of the indiarubber, if any, for covering the treads, and width of end clamps for the rubber.

3. **Marking out the strings.**—A "pitchboard" should now be made, and a detail drawing, as in Fig. 139, to arrange the width of the strings, which having been prepared are marked out for the housings as explained in Chapter III, pages 26-28, and illustrated by Figs. 36 and 39.

DETAILS.—1. **Strings.**—In ships' stairs of any importance the parts exposed to view are usually made of hard wood (teak, oak, or mahogany) and polished.

Although the strings require to have a certain degree of *strength* and *rigidity*, it would prove expensive, as well as add unnecessary weight, to make them of solid hard wood for inside stairs, and the general practice is to make them of pine faced up with "veneers" and "planting" of the kind of hard wood adopted. In the example before us the body of the string, which is given in section by Fig. 139, is represented as a pine plank $11\frac{3}{4}$ inches $\times$ 2 inches, covered on the side next the stair with a $\frac{5}{16}$ inch thick veneer, and on the outside planted and finished with carved panelling.

The upper edge of the string is finished with a moulded hard wood "capping," its width being adapted to the base of the baluster, and into which the string is housed from $\frac{1}{8}$ inch to $\frac{1}{4}$ inch. The rebate F, shown on the lower edge, is for the reception of the spandrel framing fitted below the stairs, which is shown in elevation along with the stair in Fig. 136.

2. **Steps, indiarubber covering.**—In the best class of stairs for passenger traffic the treads should be covered with V-ed indiarubber, in which case they may be made of pine, and each tread finished on the front edge with a brass plate, which is rounded or chamfered to the form of the nosing, and which should project above the wood tread to receive the rubber and prevent it from creeping over the edge of the step.

Two methods of preparing the nosings for the indiarubber are shown in Figs. 140 and 141, the first being considered the more satisfactory.

With *close strings* the indiarubber may extend the full length of the step, and the tread may then be made wholly of pine, which proves quite satisfactory, and is of course lighter than hard wood, lightness being an important consideration in ship construction. But for facility in cleaning the indiarubber, it is frequently stopped short a few inches from the strings. The treads have then to be made entirely of hard wood, or only the exposed ends beyond the rubber may be made of this material, framed to the pine in the form of cross clamps, as shown for stairs with open strings, Figs. 173 and 174.

The risers are of hard wood, and may be made from $\frac{3}{4}$ inch to 1 inch thick. Fig. 141 shows the most usual methods of uniting them to the treads. A rebated and grooved joint is adopted at the upper edge of the riser, as at A in the figure, and a plain joint at its lower edge, the riser running down the back edge of the tread. Both joints should be well fastened with screws, and the upper one should also have several

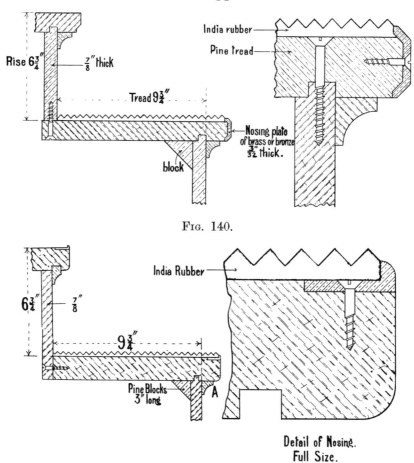

Rise 6$\frac{3}{4}$″ $\frac{7}{8}$″ thick

Tread 9$\frac{3}{4}$″

India rubber

Pine tread

Nosing plate of brass or bronze $\frac{3}{32}$″ thick.

block

FIG. 140.

India Rubber

6$\frac{3}{4}$″ $\frac{7}{8}$″

9$\frac{3}{4}$″

Pine Blocks 3″ long

A

Detail of Nosing.
Full Size.

FIG. 141. SECTION OF STAIR STEPS, SHOWING OTHER ARRANGEMENT OF JOINTS, NOSINGS, INDIARUBBER, ETC.

blocks glued into the inner angle; but it may be well to remark that in ships the same dependence cannot be placed on glue as in the case of house stairs. The other forms of joints illustrated by Fig. 43, Chapter III, may be used, but are not so suitable as the above for ship stairs.

Whenever possible, each tread and its riser should be jointed together, glued, screwed, and blocked at the bench separately, before the stair is put together.

Straight stairs may generally be put together and nearly finished at the shop before being taken to the ship, but of course this will depend upon whether or not they can be without difficulty got into their places through the available openings. The series of operations involved in putting straight stairs together are described on pages 30 and 31, there being nothing in the mode of procedure peculiar to ship stairs.

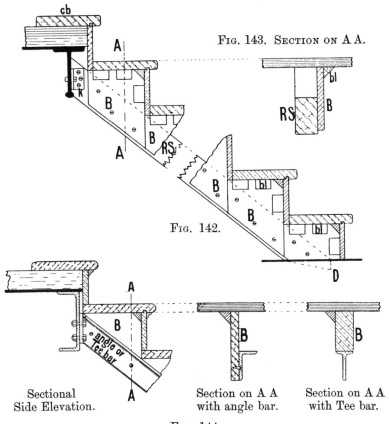

FIG. 143. SECTION ON A A.

FIG. 142.

Sectional Side Elevation.   Section on A A with angle bar.   Section on A A with Tee bar.

FIG. 144.

3. **Rough strings and brackets.**—Details of these are shown by Figs. 142 and 143, the rough string being marked R S, the brackets B, and the blocks *b l*.

It will generally prove the most convenient method to fit up the carriages along with the stair at the ship. The manner of fixing their extremities is shown in Fig. 142, the lower end being let into the deck, with a bevel housing, so as to obtain an abutment at D, while the top of the string is fastened to the beam or carling by a small iron knee shown at K. It may be noted that the outside strings may be fastened to the decks in the same manner as is here illustrated for the rough strings.

P

Angle or T-bar carriages.—Instead of the rough wood scantlings shown in Fig. 142, light steel angle or T bars, well secured to the decks at top and bottom by flanging and bolting them to the beams, may be adopted, and wood brackets fastened to them, as illustrated by Fig. 144.

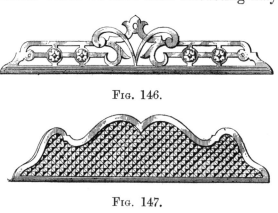

When a stair is not supported by rough strings, as above described, it may be strengthened and stiffened by brackets in the manner shown by Fig. 145. The brackets, B B, are from 1 inch to 2 inches thick, and nailed and blocked to the treads and risers, each being screwed to the one under the preceding step.

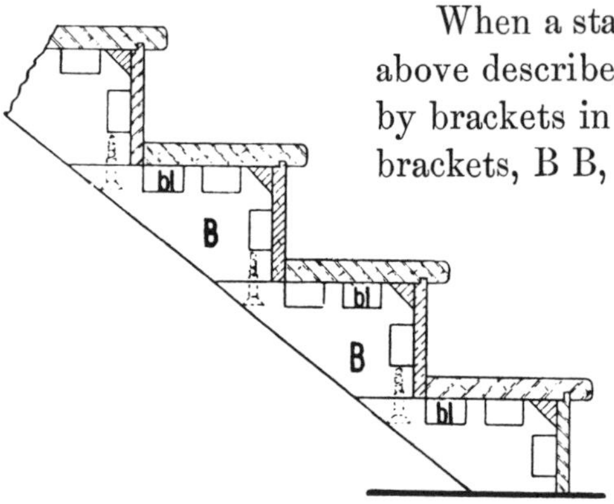

It may be remarked that in stairs which are closed below the strings by spandrel framing the divisional bulkheads required under the stair for lockers, or other purposes, may be arranged to supply also the neces-

FIG. 145. METHOD OF STIFFENING STAIRS OF ORDINARY WIDTH.

sary support to the stair steps, so that in such cases the carriages in the forms which we have been discussing may be dispensed with.

FIG. 146.

FIG. 147.

Step plates.—In common stairs, where no india-rubber is used, ornamental brass step plates are screwed to the treads to preserve them from wear. They are rather objectionable for passenger traffic, and are not unattended with danger from slipping.

Examples of these step plates are given by Figs. 146, 147, and 148, as made by Cruickshank and Co., Denny Ironworks.

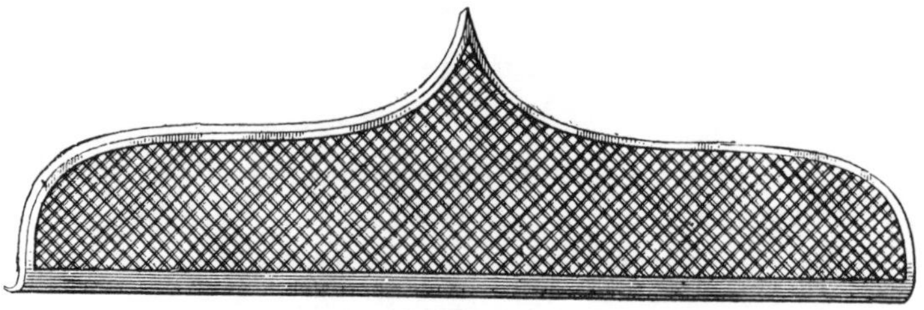

Similar ornamental *toe plates*

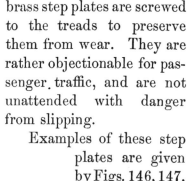

FIG. 148.

are in almost all classes of ship stairs screwed to the faces of the risers to protect them from disfigurement.

Lead covering.—It is a very common practice with some shipping companies to cover their stair steps with sheet lead. Although this has some advantages, for example, in being a non-slipping material, it proves expensive, is heavy, and is not so satisfactory for inside stairs, which are well protected from wet, as indiarubber. Of course if its situation requires the stair to be perfectly water-tight the lead covering must be resorted to.

Balustrade.—Enlarged sketches showing the methods adopted in fixing the balusters to the string and handrail on the incline are given by Figs. 139 and 149. The bases of the balusters are united to the string by mortised and housed joints. The tenons, which are shown

by dotted lines in Fig. 139, extend through the capping, and for a little distance into the pine string, while the housings of the shoulders are about $\frac{1}{4}$ inch deep into the capping.

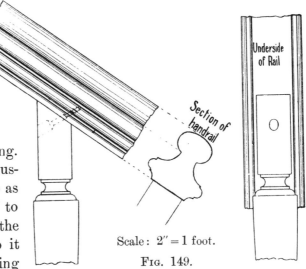

Scale: $2'' = 1$ foot.

FIG. 149.
DETAILS OF HANDRAIL AND FASTENING OF BALUSTERS.

The heads of the balusters are shown (Fig. 149) as being merely splayed off to fit the under-surface of the handrail, and fastened to it by stout screws, this being the common practice. The heads of the screws should be sunk below the surface, and the holes neatly plugged up. Glue should be used both at the top and bottom of these wood balusters. Very frequently a shallow trench, about $\frac{1}{8}$ inch deep, is taken out of the under-side of the handrail, of a width exactly equal to that of the head of the baluster, which not only helps to steady them, but also hides the joint as well. It has one objection, however, namely, that the thin lip is very liable to be split off, unless care is taken, in fitting the balusters.

On the *landings* a somewhat different method is adopted. A round pin, as shown in Fig. 172, is turned on each end of the baluster, and corresponding holes bored to receive them in the rail and covering board or capping. The balusters should also be housed at both ends, $\frac{1}{8}$ inch at the top, and about $\frac{1}{4}$ inch at bottom.

Order of work in fitting up the balustrade.—When the stair has been properly fixed, the positions of the mortises on the incline, and the holes on the landing for the bases of the balusters, are set off on the cappings and cut out. The positions of the holes in the level rails on the landing are set out at the same time and these holes bored.

All the balusters are then driven one by one into the capping, and marked round their bases for the housings, numbering each one to its place as it is removed. Before taking out the balusters on the landings, drive on the rails temporarily, and mark round the heads for the housings in them also.

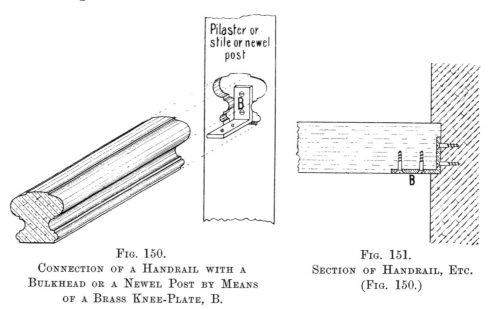

FIG. 150.

CONNECTION OF A HANDRAIL WITH A
BULKHEAD OR A NEWEL POST BY MEANS
OF A BRASS KNEE-PLATE, B.

FIG. 151.

SECTION OF HANDRAIL, ETC.
(FIG. 150.)

The housings being taken out accurately to the markings, and to their correct depths, the balustrade should first be put up on the landings. To do this, drive the balusters singly into their places, glueing thoroughly the holes as well as the pins. When they are all in position, glue the pins at the top and the holes in the rail, and drive on the rail, using struts from the ceiling.

It need hardly be stated that these operations require to be performed very expeditiously, before the glue has had time to chill, otherwise it will prove of little service to the connections.

Where a landing rail terminates in a bulkhead it is housed into and may be fastened to the latter by a brass *knee plate*, as shown in the sketches Figs. 150 and 151. This connection requires attention when putting on the rail finally, as its end cannot enter the housing till it is driven hard up to the shoulders of the balusters.   These handrails on the landings when disposed athwartship should follow the *camber* of the deck.

The rails on the stair are next set up in position, and their butts glued and bolted.

The balusters on the incline are then fitted under the rails, glued, and screwed in one by one, commencing at the bottom of the stair and working upwards.   Care has to be taken that they are fitted so as to stand strictly vertical, their heads not leaning forwards or aft on the stair.

Iron balusters.—These are not unfrequently used in ship stairs, but though they have the advantage in that they can be cast to give a great variety of ornament, are in other respects not so suitable and convenient

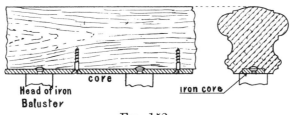

Fig. 152.

as wood balusters.   For example, their weight, and the difficulty experienced in the manipulation of their lengths to suit variations in the height of the handrail so often occurring in ships, as well as the often unsatisfactory methods that have to be resorted to in fixing them, constitute some of the principal objections to their use.

Illustrations of iron balusters are given in Fig. 123, and also in the illustrations of stone stairs, Chapter XX.

When iron balusters are adopted they are very commonly fastened to the handrail by means of a flat wrought-iron bar called a *core*, about $\frac{3}{16}$ inch thick and an inch or more in width.   The core is riveted on to the heads of the balusters, sunk flush with and screwed to the under-side of the handrail (see Fig. 152).

The core is fitted into the groove of the handrail before it is riveted to the balusters.   The iron core under wreaths and easings have to be shaped to suit the twist or curvature by the blacksmith, these portions of the handrail when squared up being taken to him for this purpose.

CHAPTER IX

CONSTRUCTION OF STAIRS FOR PASSENGER SHIPS (*continued*)

SIDE-FLIGHT STAIRS

General remarks.—A stair of this kind consists of one short flight arranged fore and aft, and terminating on a landing, from which branch off two narrower flights, one to the port, the other to the starboard side.

This type is a favourite one for the principal stairs in connection with the saloons of passenger vessels, and when adopted in public buildings are styled "grand staircases." Being symmetrical about the middle line, they are well adapted to the symmetrical arrangement of doors and passages observed on each side of a ship. They also afford the advantages of a landing in the course of the ascent without occupying much of the vessel's length. When well planned and arranged they form convenient staircases, and also, as regards appearance, can be made very satisfactory.

The position of the landing and the length of the flights are of course varied to suit the requirements of the situation, but the single fore and aft flight, which may be placed either at the top or bottom as required, is usually a step or two longer than the athwartship flight, and since it embraces the combined traffic of the other two should be made about twice their width.

The lower ends of the strings and two or more of the bottom steps are often curved outwards, which produces a better effect and gives a more convenient start when the stair is approached from the sides than when simply straight.

Among modern passenger vessels excellent examples of these stairs will be found in the SS. "Campania" and "Lucania" of the Cunard Line, and the "Paris" and "New York" of the American Line.

They may either be constructed with newels at the turnings, or with continuous balustrades wreathed at the turnings, the latter construction being the most common in ships.

I. Construction of Side-flight Stairs, Newelled.

Illustration.—A typical stair of this class is presented by a full plan, Fig. 154, and front elevation, Fig. 153, and a fore and aft sectional elevation on the middle line A M is added in Fig. 155.

The strings of the lower flight are curved outwards from the fourth riser downwards, and some swell outwards is also given to the four bottom steps.

The plans of the curved parts of the strings are made exact octants of a circle, so that their directions at the bottom make angles of 45° with the middle line of the flight, enabling them to spring from the canted faces of the octagonal newels, an arrangement which will prove satisfactory in practice and result in a good finish.

A prominent feature in the design of the stair illustrated is the " swan neck" arrangement of the handrails, a construction adopted to make them meet the newels at the same level. By this means the long squares that have to be formed on the newels for the reception of the handrails, when they abut on them obliquely in the usual way, is avoided, and a more shapely newel can be obtained.

The constructive details of newelled staircases have been fully dealt with in Chapter V, and it will only be necessary for us here to make some observations on peculiarities incidental to the altered situation. We may notice, in the first place, a few points that may present difficulty in obtaining the correct height when the *camber* as well as the *sheer* has to be taken into account.

Modification of height rod for sheer and camber of decks.—The height to be attained by the stair is the difference of level between the points of starting and landing, that is, in Fig. 154 the difference in level between the point X on the top of the covering board C B at the centre line of the flight and the point A on the deck below. To obtain this, measure the height of the upper surface of the one deck above that of the other, and add to it the thickness of the covering board. This will then be the height of the point X from the deck below. From this height deduct Y M, the rise of the deck due to the camber on the width X Y, as obtained from the *beam mould*. Add to or subtract from this result the difference of level of the points A and Y due to sheer—A N in Fig. 154—adding if A is lower than Y, and subtracting if A is higher, which will of course depend respectively on whether A is nearer or farther from amidships than Y.

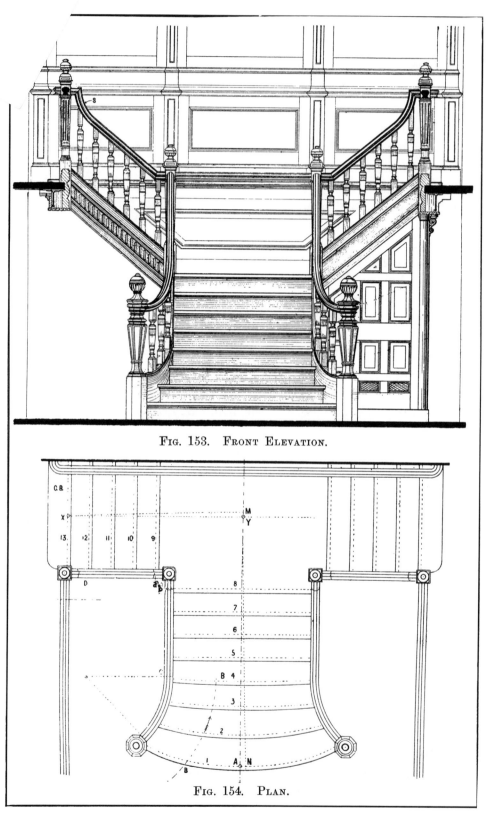

FIG. 153. FRONT ELEVATION.

FIG. 154. PLAN.

FIGS. 153 AND 154. SIDE-FLIGHT STAIR, NEWELLED.

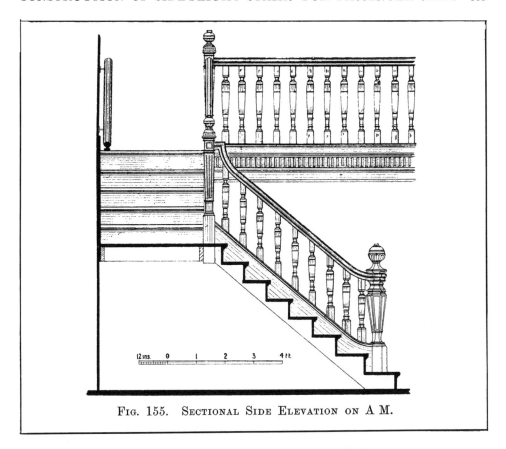

FIG. 155. SECTIONAL SIDE ELEVATION ON A M.

For example, suppose the particulars to be as follows:

Height from the upper side of one deck to that of the other . 8 feet.

Thickness of " covering board "   .   .   .   .   . 2 inches.

Difference of level of X and Y due to camber   .   .   . $\frac{1}{2}$ inch.

Difference of level between Y and A due to the sheer .   . $\frac{3}{8}$ inch.

Then if A be nearer amidships than Y :

Height rod $= 8$ feet $+ 2$ inches $- \frac{1}{2}$ inch $+ \frac{3}{8}$ inch.

$= 8$ feet $1\frac{7}{8}$ inch.

If, again, A be farther from amidships than Y :

Height rod $= 8$ feet $+ 2$ inches $- \frac{1}{2}$ inch $- \frac{3}{8}$ inch.

$= 8$ feet $1\frac{1}{8}$ inch.

The rise of step is then obtained by dividing this height by the requisite number of risers.

In the case of a very wide central flight it would be advisable to take the height from a starting point, B, on the line of travel, which would be from 15 inches to 18 inches from the line of the centre of the handrail, instead of at the centre of the flight as in the example.

Q

Top and bottom risers.—A little extra width has to be left on the first riser so that it may be scribed to fit the camber of the deck, and should be made to the correct rise at the middle line A, Fig. 154, or in wide stairs at the lines of travel B B, and will of course be a little more than this at the newel posts.

The top riser of each side-flight being the proper depth at its centre, is necessarily in excess of the correct rise at one end, and falls short of it at the other, in consequence of the covering board being made to follow the deck with its sheer, while the steps are level.

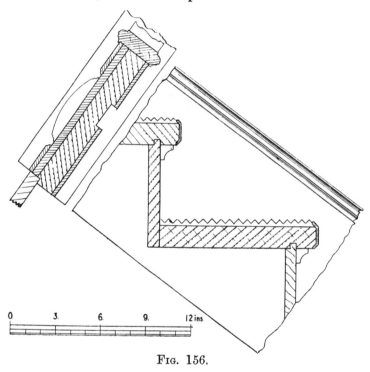

FIG. 156.

It may be remarked that if the width of the flight and the situation of the stair are such as to make the taper on the top riser excessive, the adjoining step may be tilted a little off the level so as to share the inequality between two risers.

Arrangement of steps at the landing.—This is a point that should always receive careful consideration, as some arrangements would detract very much from the appearance of the stair.

The position of the last riser of the lower flight and those of the risers at the startings of the side flights may be varied to suit the circumstances, only it should be kept in view that the strings when meeting in a newel are best placed for appearance when corresponding lines on their outer faces are in the same plane. This is secured as in the example, Figs. 153-155, by making the horizontal distance between risers Nos. 8 and 9, measured on the plan lines of the outside of the strings, equal to the width of a tread. Thus, in Fig. 154, the distance from *a* to *b* measured round the angle is 9 inches, the width of a tread.

Marking off the strings.—This will present no difficulty, as in this case they can be marked out with the pitchboard, as explained in connection with Fig. 36, except the four curved steps at the stair starting,

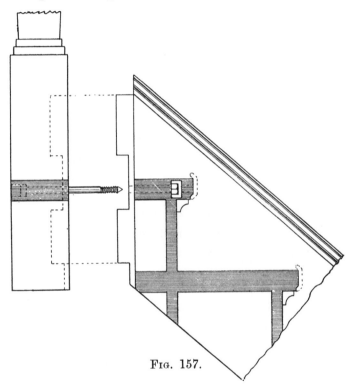

FIG. 157.

where their breadths at the housings have to be measured along the line representing the inside of the string in plan.

Details of steps and strings.—These are given in section by the accompanying Fig. 156, and it will be seen that they are very similar to those of the preceding stair. The curving outwards of the string at the bottom entails some troublesome work in an otherwise easily constructed stair, having either to be built up by some of the methods of staving and veneering, kerfing, etc., or taken out of the solid (see Chapters VI, VII).

The strings are framed into the smaller newel posts, and the joints secured with bolts, the details of one of them being given in Fig. 157.

Fixing newel posts to decks.—The two large octagonal newel posts at the bottom of the stair should be housed about ½ inch into the wood deck and well secured to it by joining bolts. The smaller newel posts at the top should be bolted to the sides of the beams or carlings surrounding the deck opening.

The staircase not being open beneath, but having the spandrels below the strings filled in with framing, the two newels at the junction of the flights may, if desirable, be made long enough to reach the deck. When this is done the strings are very efficiently supported, and the balustrade stiffened in a corresponding degree.

Landing.—A rough framework composed of scantlings 5 inches to 7 inches deep, with a few cross bearers, is prepared along with the stair and securely attached to the athwartship bulkhead at one side and to the newels at the other, when the stair is being erected at the ship.

There is, however, no stereotyped construction for the framework of the landing in a case of this kind, where the divisional bulkheads for the lockers under the stair may be made to furnish very efficient support.

It need hardly be remarked that when a staircase of this kind requires to be entirely open underneath, a strong and rigid construction would have to be made, so that the stair may be in a sense self-supporting; but ship stairs are almost always close, except in the case of one stair standing over another in the same stairway and leading to a higher deck.

Wreathed parts.—The swelling out of the stair in width at the bottom necessitates the formation of wreathed cappings and handrails to stand over the circular plans, requiring for their proper setting out the application of the principles of geometrical handrailing, which is fully treated of in subsequent chapters.

II. Construction of Side-flight Stairs—Geometrical.

Figs. 158 and 159 furnish another illustration of the side-flight class of stair, but unlike the last example, illustrated by Figs. 153-155 the single central fore and aft flight is at the top.

In the drawing, Fig. 159 represents the plan, Fig. 158 a half elevation and section, and Fig. 158A a fore and aft elevation.

The rails and strings, starting from newel posts at the bottom, are continuous to the other deck, where they terminate in exactly similar newels. The stair may therefore be classed as a geometrical one from this feature of continuity of rails and strings, the changes of direction at the landing being effected by wreaths, in place of newels as in the preceding example.

Considerations relating to the arrangement of steps.—The stair, it will be seen, occupies considerable deck space, and would be suitable

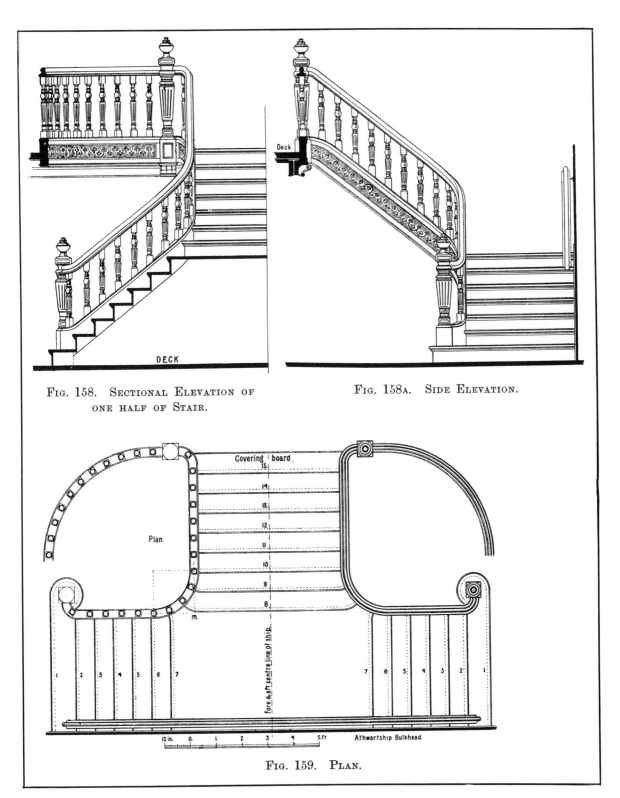

FIG. 158. SECTIONAL ELEVATION OF
ONE HALF OF STAIR.

FIG. 158A. SIDE ELEVATION.

DECK

Deck

Covering board
15.
14.
13.
12.
11.
10.
9.
8.

Plan.

m.

Fore & aft centre line of ship.

1 2 3 4 5 6 7

7 6 5 4 3 2 1

12 in. 0. 1 2 3 4 5 ft   Athwartship Bulkhead.

FIG. 159. PLAN.

SIDE-FLIGHT STAIR—GEOMETRICAL.

only for a large vessel, the extreme width over the bottom steps being
17 feet, rendered necessary from the unusual width (8 feet) of the central
fore and aft flight.

Of course other arrangements of the steps may be made without
changing the width of the flights, but would probably not prove so satisfactory as that given.   For example, a step might be taken out of each
of the side flights and compensated for by adding one to the upper flight.
This, however, would result in either taking more of the vessel's length,
or in curtailing the width of the space at the stair head and lowering the
landing by one step, which might give it the appearance of being too
near the deck.   Or, again, retaining the same arrangement of steps, the
two side flights might be brought closer together, curtailing the landing
in this direction, increasing it in the other by a corresponding displacement of the upper flight.   This change, though not interfering with the
height of the landing, requires, as before, more of the vessel's length.

Whatever arrangement of steps is adopted for any given case it should
be such as will produce graceful curves in the strings and handrails, this
being a primary consideration in all geometrical stairs, and can be tested by
means of a development or stretch out of one or both sides of the string.

A very usual way is to endeavour to get the steps and landing of a
uniform width along the centre line of the string and rail in plan, giving
a straight line development, and for ordinary large *winds*, say above
9 inches in radius; this would prove quite satisfactory as regards appearance.   For "winds" or "turns" of smaller radii this would give
the lines on the concave side of string and rail a crippled appearance,
in consequence of the pitch on that side being much steeper in the
wreath than in the straight lengths that join with it, having to rise to the
same height as the lines at the centre of the rail on a much shorter plan
length of curve.   In the latter case a better result is obtained by setting
off the steps and landing of equal widths upon the plan of the concave
side instead of at the centre line, so that lines on this side of both string
and rail would be approximately helices, and be about straight in
development.

In practice, as we have already had occasion to observe (see page 88),
it is a common arrangement, when the conditions permit, to place the
adjacent flights so as to make the centre lines of the two straight rails
meet when produced, as it simplifies to a great extent the lines for
getting out the wreathed handrail and capping, dispensing with all
easings.   To obtain this it would obviously require the sum of the
distances of the point *m*, Fig. 159—the intersection of the plans of centre

lines of straight rails—from risers Nos. 6 and 10, to be equal to the width of four treads.

The plan in the present example is not set out in accordance with any of the above methods, but so as to make the lines on the outer face of the string lie in a plane; that is, the lines of the straight lengths, if produced, would meet at the angle.

It may be well here, however, to impress upon the beginner that the whole subject of the planning out and making of geometrical stairs is so closely interwoven with that of handrailing as to make it almost necessary, or at any rate a decided advantage, to study the one subject along with the other.

Building up wreathed strings for ship stairs.—1*st method.*— " Staving and veneering " (see pages 73-77) is the method most usually resorted to for inside stairs.

Cylinder.—An isometric sketch of a rough cylinder as usually made in ship joinery for stair work is shown by Fig. 161, adapted to the quarter circle " wind " of the stair illustrated by Figs. 158-159. It simply consists of battens about 1 inch thick, and from 1 inch to 2 inches wide, kept a little apart and nailed to three cross ribs.

The several operations involved should be carried out somewhat as follows: When the cylinder has been nailed together and its surface accurately formed to fit the concave side of string the veneers for both sides of string may then be prepared.

Development.—Preliminary to this a development of the steps on the housing side of the string—in our example the convex—is drawn out on a board. To do this, proceed to bend a thin flexible strip of wood round the curve representing the convex side in plan, marking on the strip the springings and faces of risers as they occur upon that line.

When this batten is sprung straight the distance between the springings is, of course, the stretch out of the curve.

Draw two parallel lines (S D and S A, Fig. 160) on the board at this distance apart to represent the vertical springing lines, which are the divisions between the straight and curved parts of the developed surface. Then draw the riser lines 5, 6 . . . 11 parallel to the springings and at the correct distance from them, as copied from the batten, and also at right angles to them the tread lines at the correct rise apart.

From this development of the line of steps completed to the top and bottom of the stair, if necessary, the length and width of the veneer can be ascertained.

Having then taken the veneer to a suitable thickness so that it will bend easily round the cylinder, set out upon it the tread and riser lines, etc., in the same way as has just been done in the development (Fig. 160), obtaining the direction of the lines with respect to the edge of the veneer from that development, and complete the lines for the housings, using templates as described in connection with Figs. 36 and 37.

Next draw upon the veneer the lines representing the upper and lower edges of the string up to the springings, meeting them as at A and B, Fig. 160. Set off the distance of the upper edge from the nosings of the steps in the wreathed part, and draw a curve, A E B, through the points by a batten, easing it into the straight parts beyond the springings.

To obtain the development of the veneer for the concave or outside of the strings: Find first the distance between the springings by bending a lath either round the curve in plan, as was done for the other side, or round the cylinder, on which the springings will have already been accurately marked.

Of course the lengths of these quarter circles can be readily found from the radii by arithmetic, as follows: Multiply the radius by 3·1416, and divide the product by 2. For example, the radius of concave side is 18 inches; the stretch out of the quarter circle $= 18 \times 3\cdot 1416 \div 2 = 28\cdot 2744$ inches $= 28\frac{1}{4}$ inches fully.

The methods of finding the lengths approximately of circular arcs graphically have already been given (see Figs. 110 and 134). One of these methods (that given by Fig. 110) is shown applied in the plan, Fig. 160, where A B is the quarter-circle arc. Through B draw B D, making an angle of 30° with the tangent B C, and meeting A D at D, then A D is the length of the arc nearly.

The development of the veneer for the concave side can be conveniently shown on the top of the other development (Fig. 160), both coinciding up to the springing at A. Draw the line S b at a distance from S A, the lower springing line, equal to the stretch out just found, namely, about $28\frac{1}{4}$ inches. Through B draw a horizontal line B b, cutting the springing line S b in b, then the dotted line b h through b parallel to B m represents the upper edge of the outside veneer beyond S b, the upper springing line for that side.

Next ease the lines K A and b h into each other with a fair curve, A F b, as shown by the dotted line in the figure, which completes the contour, K F b h, of the upper edge of that veneer. The lower edge, p q, may be gauged from the upper.

This veneer being then roughly taken to the requisite width, the

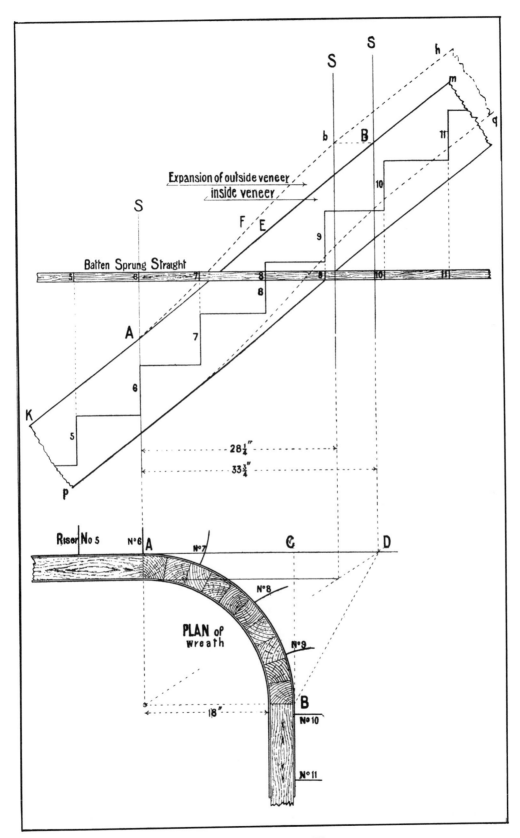

FIG. 160. EXPANSION OF VENEERS.

R

portions of it beyond the springings are glued to two battens (see Fig. 161) to form the straight parts of the string, the ends of the battens nearest the well being previously cut obliquely to the pitch.

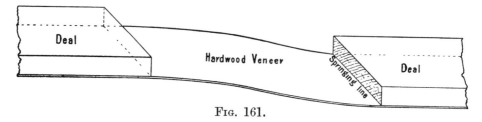

FIG. 161.

When the glue is properly set the whole is laid over the cylinder, as shown in Fig. 162, making the springing lines on the veneer exactly coincide with those marked on the surface of the cylinder, and fastened to it with handscrews.

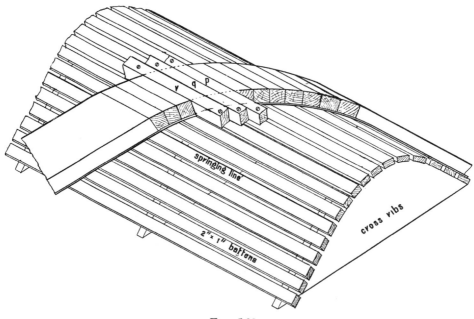

FIG. 162.

The gap between the ends of the battens is then filled in with pine staves, carefully fitted and glued to one another and to the veneer. The staves are pressed hard against the veneer by screws driven through their ends into the lagging of the cylinder, being left long enough for this purpose, as shown by the three staves p, q, r in Fig. 162. The rest of the staves are shown as they would be afterwards trimmed, when the veneer on the back had been laid.

After the glue has had time to become thoroughly dry the staves are carefully planed on the back down to the correct thickness and curvature, and this surface, as well as that of the veneer which is to be laid on it, *toothed* and *sized*.

To lay this veneer it would be best to first glue and fasten it with handscrews to either of the straight lengths up to the springing. Next glue and bend the veneer round the curved part up to the other springing, and press it closely down to the staves by temporarily screwing over it a number of stiff cross bars placed in the same direction as the

staves, noticing to insert the screws into those parts of the veneer which will not be exposed to view in the finished string. These bars may also be screwed to the uncut projecting ends of the staves if necessary. The remaining straight part is then glued and held down with handscrews in the same way as the other which was first operated on.

The whole is allowed to remain on the cylinder till the glue is thoroughly dry.

The edges of the string are then cut to the lines on the veneers, and the narrow

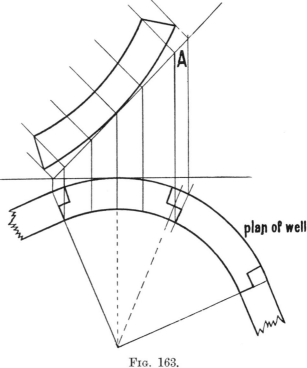

Fig. 163.

strips of planting (if any) on the outside glued on with the aid of handscrews. If the planting prove too stiff to bend properly round the curve, it may be softened by steaming in a steam-chest, which is available in most shipbuilding yards.

Building up wreathed strings.—*2nd method.*—The sketches Figs. 163 and 164 illustrate a method frequently adopted for building up wreathed strings for this class of stair.

The wreath, in place of being staved, is first built up of two or more pieces of yellow pine, or other soft wood shaped to the curvature, and with the grain of the wood running in about the direction of the string.

The pieces are half-lapped to each other and to the ends of the battens forming the straight parts of the string, these joints being glued and fastened with screws.

The two sketches, Figs. 163 and 164, show respectively the manner of drawing out the face mould and of applying it to the edge of the piece, the principle involved in the method employed being the same as that explained in connection with Figs. 130-133, illustrating how to cut wreathed strings out of the solid.

On the pine string thus built up, the veneers, marked out as before, are laid with the aid of handscrews and clamps.

In this method the veneers, being accurately lined off on the edges, do the duty of falling moulds for guiding the trimming of the edges of string.

The method of kerfing, grooving, etc., which we have described for

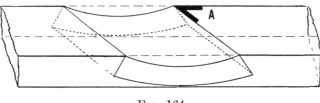

FIG. 164.

geometrical stairs in houses, are seldom resorted to in ships. The small turns at the top and bottom of this stair may be profitably taken out of solid hard-wood cuttings, but may of course be built up by any of the methods just described.

Wreathed cappings.—These are best got out by using the same system of lines as is adopted for the handrails.

Construction of round-ended step.—Fig. 165 is a *section* and *plan*, with the tread removed from the latter, showing the manner of building up the round-ended step below the newels at the startings of the stair in Fig. 159. The method is essentially the same as that illustrated for a curtail step by Figs. 119-122, Chapter VI, to which the student is referred.

Other arrangements of joining rail and string to the newel.—Fig. 166 shows a plan, not unfrequently resorted to in ship stairs, of working the handrail into the newel at the starting, which has the advantage of taking up much less room than the arrangement shown in Fig. 159, where the rail and string are represented as turning into the newel with small quarter-turn wreaths, requiring the round end of the step below the newel to project considerably beyond the stairs. Mouldings of the same contour as those on the rail are turned upon the newel post at the required level, and out of this part a recess is taken to admit the full width of rail, bringing the side of it next to the stair flush with the newel, as shown at B, Fig. 166. This arrangement gives the rail the appearance of being carried round the newel.

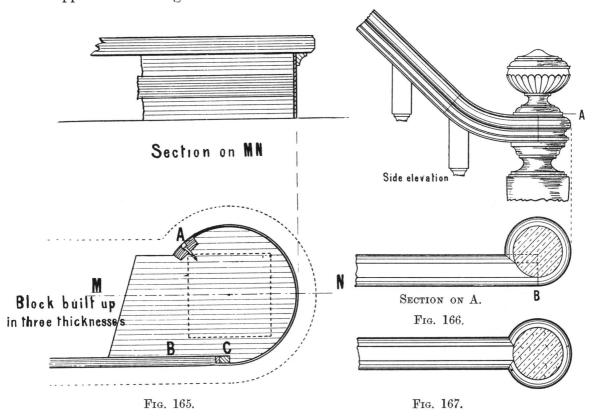

Section on MN

Block built up in three thicknesses

Side elevation

Section on A.

Fig. 166.

Fig. 165.

Fig. 167.

It will be understood that the string would be made to terminate in the base of the newel, in the same manner as the handrail.

The simplest arrangement, however, is that shown in Fig. 167, with the centre of the newel in the same line as the balustrade, and the rail and string butting up against it.

CHAPTER X

CONSTRUCTION OF CIRCULAR STAIRS FOR PASSENGER SHIPS

Remarks.—Under this general head may be included all ship stairs whose plans are of a circular character, and which have the whole or greater part of their steps winders.

They are most commonly of the quarter-circle type, which have the directions of the stair starting and landing at right angles to each other. In ships these are generally termed quarter-circle stairs, and in one form or other are very common.

Since the curved lines of the strings and handrails follow helices more or less closely, these stairs, when open below and favourably situated, present a very graceful, pleasing, and striking appearance, and on this account they are often preferred to stairs of more convenient forms.

Good existing examples, in which these features are well brought out, are the main staircases of the Canadian Pacific Railway Company's steamers " Empresses of India, China, and Japan," and more notably those of the SS. " Ophir," of the Orient Line.

QUARTER-CIRCLE STAIR.—The subject of the illustrations, Figs. 168 and 169, is a winding stair with open strings on both sides, self-supporting, and reaches from the one deck to the other in a quarter of a turn. This example will serve to illustrate the leading features in the construction of the more general class of circular stairs.

The small supplementary sketch, Fig. 170, represents the plan of the stair head, showing the general arrangement of the main stairs suitable for a large passenger vessel, the example being the part of it on one side of the centre line.

All the steps converge to the common centre, except the bottom one, which lies beyond the quarter circle, the springings coinciding with risers No. 2 and 13. The radii to the faces of the strings are 3 feet 6 inches and 8 feet 6 inches, making the stair 5 feet wide. The going line is struck at a distance of 16 inches from the centre line of the

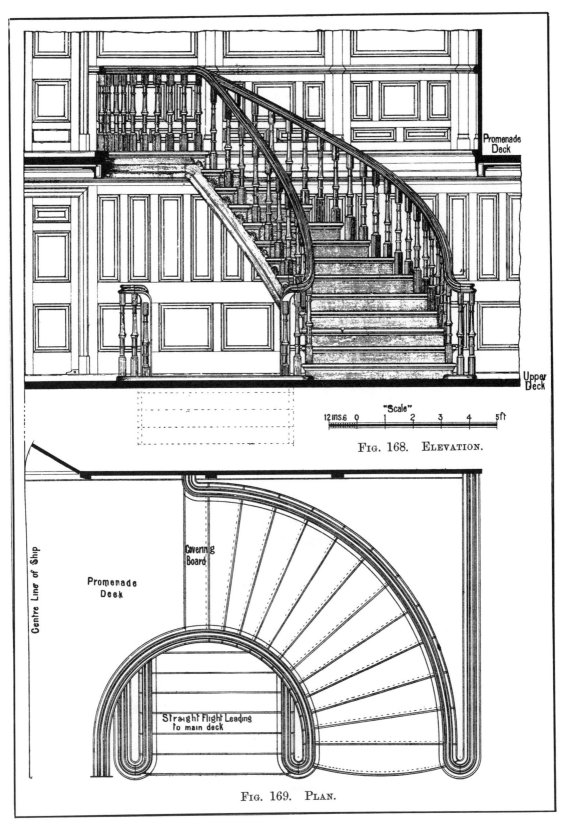

Promenade
Deck

Upper
Deck

"Scale"

12 ins.6   0   1   2   3   4   5 ft

FIG. 168.   ELEVATION.

Centre Line of Ship

Promenade
Deck

Covering
Board

Straight Flight Leading
to main deck

FIG. 169.   PLAN.

FIGS. 168 AND 169.   QUARTER-CIRCLE STAIR,

handrail over the narrow ends of the steps, the treads being spaced off on that going line at the correct width—namely, 9 inches—required for the rise, which is $7\frac{1}{2}$ inches.

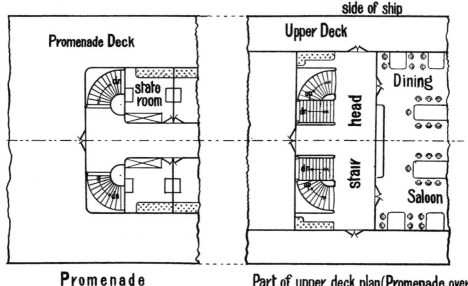

FIG. 170.

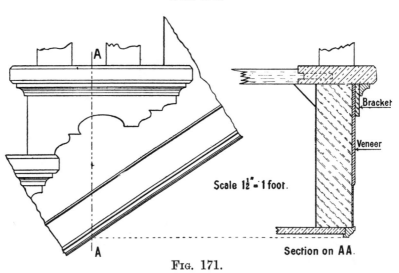

FIG. 171.

Strings.—These in the example are of the open and bracketed type, and would be built up by staving and veneering on prepared cylinders, as already explained in Chapters VI and IX. Of course they have only to be veneered on the outside, and the veneers are partially covered by the ornamental brackets.

Fig. 171 shows a section of the longer string, and a detail of the bracket and return nosing of the steps.

Similar details are shown for the other string in Fig. 172.

Spacing of balusters.—It may be remarked that open strings are not in general very suitable for ship stairs, as with them difficulty is experienced in obtaining a proper *spacing* of the balusters, owing to the narrowness of the steps and other irregularities.

For example, in a stair with 8-inch treads, which is a very common size for the ordinary class of vessels, one baluster on each step gives too wide a spacing (8-inch centres), while, on the other hand, two on a step results in the spacing being too close, unless the balusters be of a small pattern. Of course an arrangement with two balusters on one step and one baluster on the next, alternately, would give a spacing in such a case of nearly

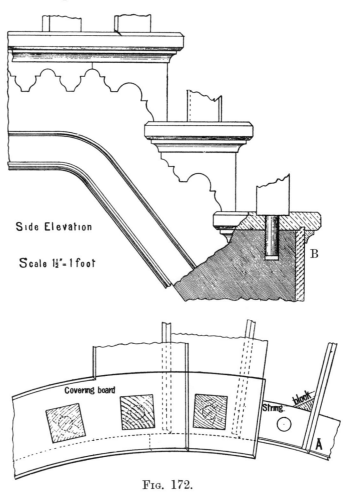

Side Elevation

Scale 1½"=1 foot

Fig. 172.

$5\frac{3}{8}$ inches centres, which would be satisfactory; but this plan is otherwise not very commendable, as it introduces an irregularity in the lengths of the bases of the balusters.

The difficulty alluded to above is not met with in the case of close strings, as with them any desired spacing of balusters can be made independently of the particular arrangement of steps.

In the example before us, however, the arrangement and size of the steps admit of a satisfactory spacing of balusters with the open strings,

S

one being fitted on the narrow end and two on the wide end of each step. The ends of the steps being 6 inches and 12 inches wide give the the same spacing of balusters on both sides of the stair.

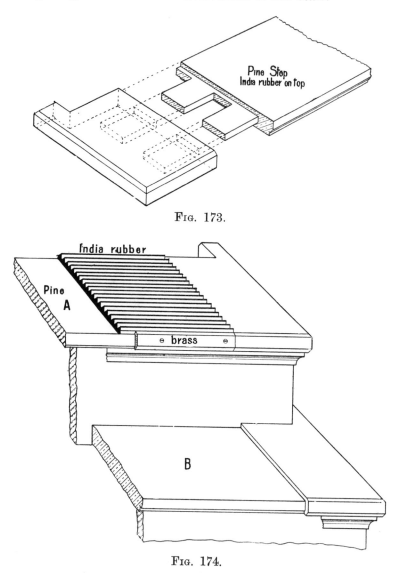

Fig. 173.

Fig. 174.

The details of the steps, which are constructed to receive india-rubber, are given by Figs. 173, 174. The treads are made of pine, and cross-clamped with hard-wood at the ends, the form of the joints being shown by Fig. 173.

The hard-wood clamps, it will be noticed, are made thick enough to stand $\frac{1}{4}$ inch above the pine, to form an abutment to the indiarubber.

The ends of the clamps are also made to project beyond the front edge of the pine tread the thickness of the brass nosing, so as to finish flush with it.   This is clearly shown by the isometric sketch (Fig. 174), the brass and indiarubber being shown broken away on one step marked A in the figure, and completely removed from the other tread, B, below it.

The nosings, which are shown in the example as chamfered—not rounded, as is mostly the case—are returned on the clamp, which projects over the face of the ornamental bracket the same distance as it projects over the face of the riser, to enable the *cavetto moulding* to be returned under it also.

The risers should be jointed to the treads, and screwed and blocked in the same way as ordinarily constructed steps, the risers being previously cut to their proper lengths, and mitred to joint in with the bracket, as at A, Fig. 172.

Both treads and risers are fixed to the strings with screws, and well blocked underneath.

Brackets (ornamental).—These should be cut out of the solid to fit the curvature of the strings, and being of hard-wood, and finished like the string in French polish, they should have the grain of the wood following as nearly as possible that of the veneer on the string. Bending these brackets to the curvature is

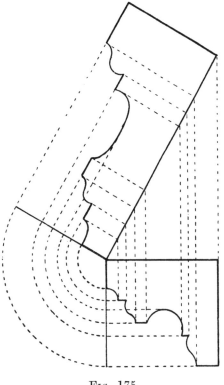

FIG. 175.

not a good plan, except in the case of painted stairs, where the grain of the wood can be disposed vertically.

Fig. 175 illustrates the method of enlarging or diminishing in one direction the stair brackets to suit the different widths of treads, retaining the several members of the ornament in the same proportion.

Fixing balusters.—In the side elevation (Fig. 172) part of one step is broken away at B to show how the wood balusters are fixed to the stair. This is done in the same manner as in the case of a balustrade on a level landing.   A pin about $1\frac{1}{8}$ inch diameter is turned on the end of the baluster, a hole for its reception being bored through the hard-wood clamp forming the end of the tread and extending some distance into the body of the string. In addition, the square base should be housed ¼ inch into the clamp. When well glued this makes a firm connection, and further assists in binding the tread and string together.

Structural parts.—The two strings should be made strong enough in themselves to supply the necessary strength and rigidity to the structure. If they are built up by staving, a good strong veneer of pine should be glued on to their rough unexposed sides, in order to bind the several staves together.

Any system of rough carriages and brackets may be fitted underneath the steps to give local stiffening to them. These may be arranged in short straight lengths; but as the stair in the example is represented as exposed to view on its under-side or soffit, the steps and risers themselves must either be finished on this side with planting to form panels, or the stair lined up below and planted to show a panelled soffit. If the former method is carried out the rough carriages will have to be dispensed with, and the steps and risers made exceptionally thick to compensate for their absence.

OUTSIDE STAIRS (CIRCULAR).—For outside circular stairs the methods we have previously described of building up curved strings, namely, by staving, veneering, etc., are obviously inapplicable, glue being of no practical utility in holding the parts together in situations exposed to the weather.

Under these circumstances the strings have to be cut out of the solid material in segments, *butted* and *bolted* to one another, the number of the segments depending necessarily on the form and size of the strings and the thickness of the planks available for the purpose.

Joints of strings.—When this method of building up the strings is followed, "plumb joints" are probably the most suitable for uniting the several segments, and for circular plans they should lie in radial vertical planes containing the common axis of the cylindric surfaces.

Joint fastenings.—There should be *two bolts* in each joint (see Fig. 180), and also a *cross-tongue* to keep off the byewood; and for very heavy stairs of this kind, which are entirely open below, and without any intermediate supports, the joints may require to be further strengthened. This may be done by screwing either short iron straps across the joints on the lower edge of the string, or iron plates to the inside below the steps.

Directions for lining off and cutting the segments of strings out of plank.—Taking Fig. 177 as the plan of the longer string of a quarter-circle outside stair to be built of teak, we shall describe the several operations involved in making the string.

The method of drawing out the necessary moulds has already been described in its application to small circular wreaths (see Figs. 130-133, and also Fig. 163), but as the example before us would be of more importance from a structural point of view we shall here describe the method in fuller detail.

The number and positions of the joints should be arranged in the full-sized plan of the string, as in Fig. 177, having regard to the thickness of the material at command.

In the present case the quarter-circle string is shown divided into three equal segments, and since the pitch is uniform throughout, it is obvious that the same mould and bevel will serve for each segment.

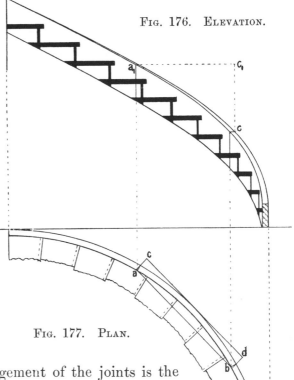

Fig. 176.   Elevation.

Fig. 177.   Plan.

The thickness of the plank required for this arrangement of the joints is the distance between the two parallel lines ab and cd, Fig. 177, while its width will require to be a little more than that of the development—which in this case is straight— of the corresponding part of the string. It need hardly be remarked that if planks of this thickness are not available the quarter circle would then have to be divided into four or more equal segments.

In Fig. 178 A B F E represents the plan of one of the three equal segments in Fig. 177, drawn to a larger scale for clearness.

To mark out the mould, join A B, and draw the tangent C D parallel to it.   Divide A B into any number of parts, and through the points of division, as well as the points E and F, draw the ordinates 1, 2, 3 . . . . . . 12 at right angles to A B or C D.   Produce E C to C_1, making C C equal to the difference in the levels of the points E and F, obtained from a development of the outside of the string. Join C_1 D, and produce the ordinates to cut it as shown ; through the points of intersection draw the ordinates 1, 2, 3, ... 12, at right angles to C_1 D, making them equal in length respectively to their corresponding ordinates in the plan. Then bending a batten to the points thus obtained the curves of the edges of the mould may be drawn.

Application of mould to plank.—Fig. 179 illustrates the position of the mould on the upper edge of the plank, which is represented as being tilted up at one end to about its required inclination. The mould has next to be applied to the lower edge of the stuff, and vertically below its position on the upper, as shown by the dotted lines.

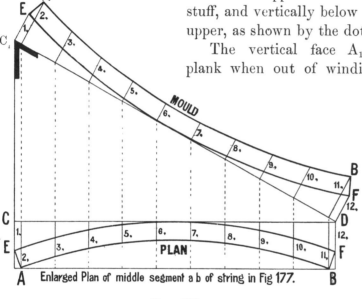

FIG. 178.

The vertical face A_1 B_1 B_2 A_2 of the plank when out of winding forms a guide in one direction for placing the mould, that is, by keeping A_1 B_1 on the mould flush with that face when applied to both edges. The position of the mould in the direction of the length of the plank is determined by applying the *plumb bevel*, which is obtained from the angle C C_1 D, Fig. 178, across the face of the piece, from the points A_1 and B_1, and drawing the plumb lines A_1 A_2 and B_1 B_2 as shown. The extremities A_1 and B_1 of the mould, when it is applied to the under-edge, are placed on the points A_2 and B_2 respectively.

It may be remarked that when the plank is set up to its correct inclination, the bevel lines A_1 A_2, B_1 B_2 will be strictly vertical, and the superfluous wood on both sides of the stuff must be removed by cutting in the direction of lines parallel to them, so that when finished the sides will form cylindric surfaces that will everywhere stand vertically over the plan.

Lining off the edges.—When the curved sides have been accurately formed, the edges are lined off, preferably on the convex side, for trimming.   This is done by applying a thin falling mould made to suit the development of the outside of the string; but for the present case the edge of this mould would be straight, being the development of a true

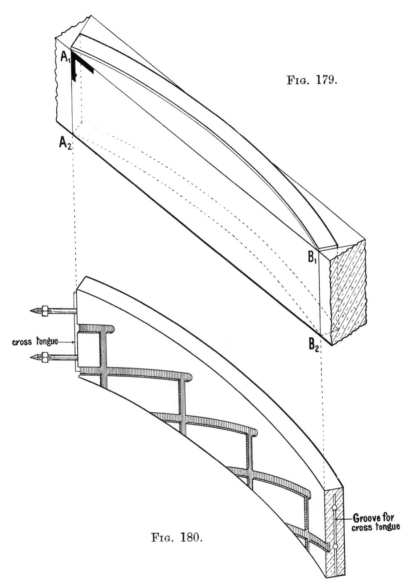

Fig. 179.

Fig. 180.

helix.   The falling mould is bent round the convex side of the piece, making the vertical lines on it coincide with the corresponding vertical lines on the surface of the piece, the joint lines being in the present case the most suitable for this purpose.

CHAPTER XI

Designs for balustrades.—In addition to the various forms of newels and balustrades that have already been given in connection with the several examples illustrating staircase construction, a few more suggested designs are given by Figs. 181-186.

In making up a design, the main features of the newel and balusters are usually made to harmonize with each other, but it is neither necessary nor desirable that for this purpose the baluster be made merely a diminished copy of the newel post; it will be sufficient that some general resemblance between them be presented. Very frequently no similarity of form is observed, the newels showing no feature in common with the baluster, and even in the latter two different designs often alternate with each other in the same stair, and with a good result.

As a rule a better effect is obtained by square than by round balusters; the economical advantages in the production of the latter, however, are so decided that they are employed even in the best staircases.

In some early examples of wood stairs, previous to the introduction of turned balusters, the members of the square balusters were made to follow the slanting lines of the stair, a style which is rarely adopted in modern practice, and indeed has little to recommend it.

A rich variety of design is obtained by combining the square and the round forms in the same baluster.

It may be worth while to observe that sketches representing side views of square newels may prove misleading with respect to their size, as they will appear much larger when viewed diagonalwise, and it will be safer to make other sketches representing them from this point of view, and make corrections or alterations in the designs accordingly.

Design for quarter-turn geometrical stair with pillar newel.— Fig. 187 represents a portion of a stair which may be regarded as an example of some difficulty, both with respect to planning and execution.

The system of lines for the moulds of the handrail on the well side is given in the section of "Practical Handrailing," Figs. 339-346.

The outside balustrade starts from a pillar or column—marked P in the drawing, Fig. 187—which would form a structural part of the

FIG. 181.   FIG. 182.

building or ship, being so placed as to be serviceable also as a newel post for the staircase.

The numerous pillars required for the support of the decks make this arrangement in ships sometimes a necessary one, but when well designed may be made an effective and attractive feature in the stair structure. The rough steel or iron stanchion is inclosed by a wood casing wrought to the approved design. In the example only the lower part of the pillar in connection with the stair is shown. The other side of the stair is shown finished with a framed dado.

T

FIG. 183.

0 3 6 9 · 12   20 inches

FIG. 184.

EXAMPLES OF STAIR STARTINGS WITH COMMODE STEPS.

At this stage of the student's progress the drawing itself will be sufficiently explanatory of the principal details.

Sections of handrails.—In Fig. 188 are given several handrail

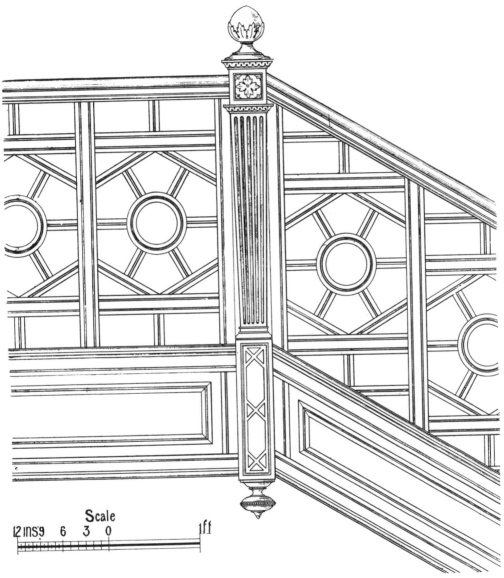

Scale
12 INS 9 6 3 0   1 ft

FIG. 185. FRAMED BALUSTRADE.

sections arranged progressively in somewhat similar groups, beginning with one of the very plainest and simplest form in use, *i.e.*, a continuous surface, and from it the others are shown gradually increasing in size and number and complexity of members.

A few other varieties will be found in connection with the respective examples of stairs given throughout the work.

The scale to which they are drawn is 3 inches = 1 foot.

Elizabethan Stairs.

We may now close this section of our subject with some brief refer-ences to a few historical examples, constructed towards the end of the sixteenth and earlier part of the seventeenth centuries, a period when wood-newelled stairs may be said to have reached their fullest development.

They consisted of short broad flights, with numerous landings, built round a rectangular well-hole with newels at the corners. They were entirely of native oak, elaborately worked and carved, and always conveying an idea of strength and sound substantial workmanship, and the characteristic arrangement of short flights and the frequent landings made them very convenient and easy to ascend.

Their most striking features are the massive solid newels of bold design and the elaborately wrought balustrades. The newels were gener-ally surmounted with vases, miniature statues, or quaint animals, though in some early ex-amples they were carried up to the top and connected by arches. In early specimens, as at Leeds Castle, Kent (see Parker's Glossary), the balustrade below the handrail was filled in with plaster. In later examples this gives place to the characteristically carved balus-trade as we see it at Crewe Hall.

Fig. 186.

The staircase at Crewe Hall (1618-35, see frontispiece,) has been characterized by eminent authorities as one of the finest existing ex-amples of the period. It occupies a space of about 24 feet square from wall to wall, and the height of the storey is 20 feet.

Barry, in his lectures on Elizabethan architecture, says: "The beauty of the staircase at Crewe Hall has always been recognized by artists, and I believe the late Mr. Stanfield once adopted it as the subject of a great picture which he painted for a drop-scene at Drury Lane

12 INS 6 0 1 ft.

FIG. 187. DESIGN FOR GEOMETRICAL STAIR WITH PILLAR NEWEL.

Theatre. With its handsome newels, carved and panelled, surmounted by quaint animals with heraldic cognisances; its richly wrought balustrade, and picturesque arrangement; this staircase is certainly one of the most interesting examples of the skill of the builders of the seventeenth century, both in the art of design and the science of construction."

The staircase at Hatfield (1605-11), is another beautiful example belonging to the reign of James I. It measures 35 by 21 feet, and consists of five flights of steps.

Although of earlier date than the one at Crewe Hall, it has a balustrade more closely resembling those of a later date; square wrought balusters, with small connecting arches at the top, taking the place of the fret-work carving more typical of the period.

The carving and the finials on the newels, the hanging scroll work adorning the lower edges of the strings, the ornamental plaster soffits, and the half balustrade against the wall, are all highly characteristic of the Elizabethan style.

The staircase at Knowle, Kent, may also be noticed as an example of the period, although it shows in its details considerable differences as compared with the preceding, and perhaps a closer approximation to modern examples. The points of difference appear chiefly in the pillared newels, and the round and comparatively slender balusters.

The pointed arch with the double tier of pillars combine to give a lofty and pleasing effect to the design.

The intermediate newels show the distinctive features of the period, and the usual half balustrade against the wall may also be noted.

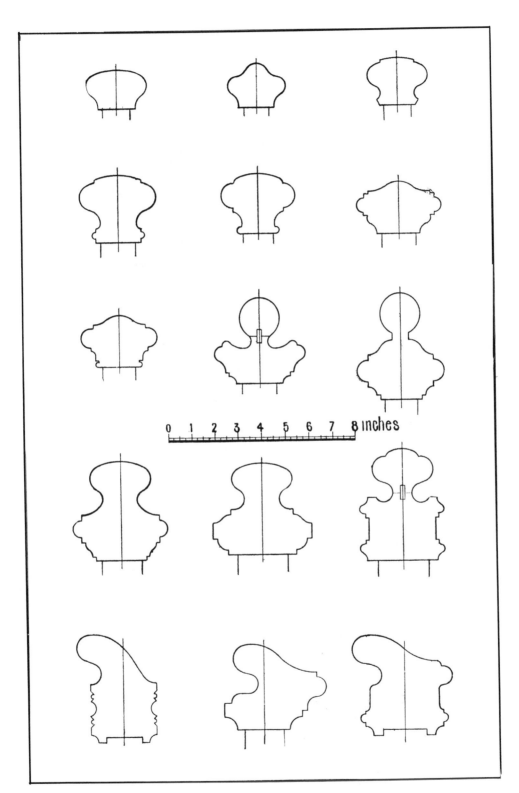

FIG. 188. SECTIONS OF HANDRAILS,

PRINCIPAL STAIRCASE, HATFIELD HOUSE (1605-1611).

STAIRCASE, KNOWLE, KENT.

PART II.—HANDRAILING

THEORETICAL AND PRACTICAL

PART II.—HANDRAILING

THEORETICAL

CHAPTER XII

REMARKS AND DEFINITIONS

The problem of handrailing is the delineation on geometrical principles of a system of lines for obtaining such moulds and bevels as will enable a wreathed handrail solid to be cut out of the plank, jointed and squared with accuracy, and without undue waste of material, so that it may stand over a given plan and conform to a prearranged falling line.

A difficult branch of joinery.—It may not at once be apparent that there should be much difficulty experienced in the accomplishment of this object, but in the trade handrailing is usually regarded, and rightly so, as one of the most difficult branches to acquire. Indeed more has been written on this subject than on any other section of woodwork, and from the time of Peter Nicholson, who is generally credited with being the first to place the subject on a geometrical basis, it has proved a fertile field for discussion among those who are engaged or interested in the art. It is true that in practice many cases of handrailing occur which present even less difficulty than is experienced in some other sections of joinery—where the simplest means are sufficient, and which an ordinary workman, without any special knowledge, would be able to accomplish in a satisfactory manner; but, on the other hand, complex cases arise, particularly in connection with geometrical stairs, where, in order to secure a satisfactory result, with due regard to economy of labour and material, it is necessary that methods of procedure be adopted involving principles which cannot be well understood without a certain amount of systematic study.

A knowledge of geometry necessary to proficiency.—In handrailing the methods employed are based on the principles of descriptive geometry, and it affords one of the best examples of the application of this useful science to practical purposes. Practical geometry, therefore, should be studied by those who aim at making a wreathed handrail, not merely by following mechanically any particular method, but with a thorough understanding of the principles that underlie the various operations.

It is, however, not uncommon to find a workman who, although his knowledge of geometry is of a very limited and fragmentary character, and who employs only the most primitive methods of procedure, is nevertheless able, by long experience in this class of work, and by the aid of a good practised eye, to produce a passable handrail; but being deficient in geometry, he is wanting in one of those fundamental requirements without which he can never feel on sure ground in undertaking cases that arise outside the range of his experience. In fact, sound theory, supplemented by experience and observation, as well as good taste, are combined in an accomplished and successful handrailer.

Practice as well as theory essential.—Since practice as well as theory is essential to proficiency, the student who may have no opportunity of acquiring the necessary practical experience in the workshop should make models to as large a scale as possible of all the typical cases illustrated in the following pages, as well as others that may be suggested by his own observation. By this means he will gain confidence to undertake actual examples when brought face to face with them in the workshop.

Technical Terms.—Various terms are employed in the art of handrailing, some of which it will be necessary to explain at this stage, others can be best explained as they occur.

Wreaths.—Handrails of circular stairs, and the parts of handrails that stand over circular wells, or plans formed by other curves, which at the same time are made to follow the inclination of the stairs, have to be wreathed or twisted, and are termed *wreaths*, to distinguish them from the straight and other parts of the rail.

A ramp is that portion of a handrail which is curved in the vertical direction only, being straight in plan, and occurs where there is a change of inclination of the rail without a change in direction. According to this definition all vertical *easings* might be called *ramps*. The term is sometimes, however, used in a more restricted sense, being applied only to a vertical easing in the rail concave on its upper side, while a vertical easing convex on the upper side is termed a *knee*.

A level easing is that part of a level rail where a change of direction occurs. It will be apparent that a level easing may be cut out of a plank whose thickness is equal to the depth of the rail, and that a ramp may be cut out of a plank whose thickness is equal to the width of the rail.

A swan-neck is a combination of a ramp and a knee. A rail is often formed in this way at its junction with a newel post, and for effect the swan-neck is sometimes worked up to a mitre, as at S, Fig. 153.

A shank is the short straight portion formed on the end of a wreath piece to correspond with the straight rail.

Centre line, or centre falling line.—This is an imaginary line supposed to pass through the centre of the width and depth of the rail throughout its length. The proper arrangement of this line beforehand is of the greatest importance, as it determines the character of the rail, and all lengths are measured and joints arranged upon it.

SYSTEMS OF HANDRAILING.—There are two general systems of handrailing, named according to the form of the squared wreath, namely:

I. The cylindric system (including) $\left\{\begin{array}{l} \text{(1) Bevel cut.} \\ \text{(2) Square cut, or tangent} \\ \qquad \text{method.} \end{array}\right.$

II. System by square or normal sections.

The two divisions of the cylindric system differ mainly in the manner of cutting the solid out of the plank.

Form of the wreath in the cylindric system.—In this system, which is the one usually practised, the squared wreath (that is, the wreath before being moulded) is regarded as forming part of a "right hollow cylinder" (see Fig. 192) whose base coincides with the plan of the wreath. Its vertical sides thus form parts of two parallel cylindrical surfaces apart from each other the *width* of the rail. On the other hand, the rail, in the direction of its depth, is included between two parallel skew or twisted surfaces, the distance between them being equal to the thickness of the rail.

The handrail solid is thus bounded by two kinds of surfaces of very different natures, the vertical sides being quite definite, easily formed and developable, while the surfaces forming the upper and under sides are of a complex character, undevelopable, and do not in general admit of exact definition. The nature of the latter surfaces may be viewed in relation to that of regular helicoidal or screw surfaces, to which they, in many cases, may be said to closely approximate, and which we shall now define.

The helix and helicoidal surface.—If a horizontal straight line be made to revolve uniformly in one direction so as to always intersect a fixed vertical line, and at the same time to rise uniformly, any point on the moving line will trace out a curve called a helix, and the line will generate a helicoidal or screw surface.

As indicated in the annexed sketch, Fig. 189, $Y Y_1$ is the axis, $D P$ the horizontal line, the curve $P P_9$ traced out by P a helix, and $D P P_9 D_9$ a regular helicoidal surface.

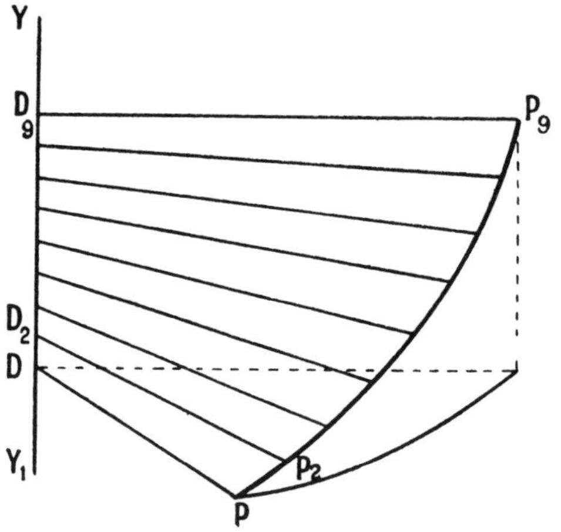

The surface just defined is sometimes termed the "skew screw surface," and an example on a large scale is that which is presented to the eye in the under-surface of a spiral stair, and is a particular case of the more general class of surfaces termed "conoidal."

Now with respect to the mode of generating the upper and under surfaces of a wreath: Let a section of the squared rail, as $A B C D$, Fig. 190, be supposed to move with its centre, O, always coincident with a line representing the centre falling line of the wreath, and in such a way that in each successive position of the section its plane will be perpendicular or normal to the falling line, and at the same time keeping the upper and lower edges, $A B$ and $C D$, horizontal, these two lines would then generate the twisted upper and under surfaces of the wreath solid.

FIG. 189.

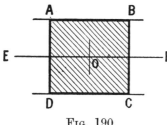

FIG. 190.

It is not often the case that, throughout the length of the wreath, the falling line is of uniform pitch, but varies according to circumstances from point to point. When the pitch is uniform throughout, as, for example, in the handrail of a true spiral stair, the centre falling line is then a true helix, as defined above; and further, the level line $E F$, which passes through the centre of the section, when produced intersects the axis of the cylinder and generates a right helicoidal surface. But at the same time it is important to keep in view that the horizontal lines $A B$ and $C D$, when produced, do not, like $E F$, intersect the axis of the cylinder, but pass at a little distance from it, being tangential to a small cylinder described about the common axis, and consequently the surfaces which these straight lines generate are, as stated above, only approximations to the right helicoidal surface.

It has often been erroneously assumed that the handrail spiral is of the same form as a square screw thread—a solid of which all sections, by radial vertical planes passing through the axis of the screw, are rectangular in form.

It may be remarked, however, that in rails over fairly large wells the difference in form of the true rail and that of the square screw thread would hardly be noticeable, but in wells of small radius, associated with rails of large section and steep pitch, the error in the latter case becomes quite apparent, showing itself in the concave side, being much thinner than that of the convex; and a section normal to the falling line would have the appearance presented by that in the sketch, Fig. 191.

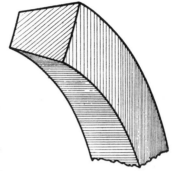

Fig. 191.

Form of the wreath in the system by normal sections.—In this system of handrailing, which is more difficult and less extensively practised than the cylindric method, the squared wreath is of a somewhat different form. Its upper and under surfaces are formed in precisely the same manner as in the previous system, but the sides of the wreath, instead of being simple cylindric surfaces, are made to form parts of skew surfaces which are generated by straight lines inclined to the horizontal at angles which are the complements of those of the tangents to the falling line at the corresponding points. Briefly, in this system the squared wreath conforms to the solid that would be generated by the movement of the circumscribing rectangle of the moulded section of the rail kept normal to the falling line in every position, and its upper and lower edges horizontal as in the first system.

One complete revolution of a wreathed handrail solid fulfilling the conditions of this definition is shown in Fig. 193, with the centre falling line a regular helix, and the normal generating section shown in twelve equidistant positions.

The reader should contrast this example with that in Fig. 192, which represents another wreathed handrail, but delineated in accordance with the first definition, that is, having its vertical sides coinciding with the cylindrical surfaces of the hollow cylinder, whose plan is shown below it.

Referring again to Fig. 193, the broken lines 1 1, $1_1 1_1$, 2 2, $2_1 2_1$, etc., shown in plan and elevation, represent the generatrices of the central skewed surface to which the surfaces of the sides of the wreath are parallel. The curved lines, 1, 2, 3, 4, etc., in the plan, represent sections of this surface by horizontal planes at the levels A B and C D, which are apart from each other the height reached in one convolution of the helix

Each of these generators, 1 1, $1_1 1_1$, 2 2, $2_1 2_1$, etc., it will be seen, being the centre line of the section, touches the helix or centre falling line of the rail, and is in the same vertical plane as the tangent to the helix at the same point and at right angles to it. Therefore the angle that each generator makes with the horizontal plane is the complement of that made by the tangent at the corresponding point, *i.e.*, to the pitch of the rail at that point. Of course in the example (Fig. 193) the pitch is uniform, and consequently the generators are all equally inclined to the horizontal.

It will be instructive to the student to compare this surface with that formed by the tangents to the helix, as these two surfaces are mutually perpendicular. Any section of the latter by a horizontal plane is an involute of the circle forming the plan of the helix, and it has the further characteristic of being a developable surface, and is known as the " developable helicoid."

With these general observations on the nature of the surfaces that form the wreath solid, we may now proceed to consider the elementary principles of the cylindric system.

Elementary Principles of the Cylindric System.

The right cylinder, its sections, etc.—The student at the outset should make himself quite familiar with the definition of a right cylinder, its mode of development with points and lines on its surface, and particularly with its sections, which, when made by planes inclined to the axis, are ellipses, the minor axes of which are equal to the diameter of the cylinder (see Appendix, Problem 38, *et seq.*).

We have already premised that the sides of a wreath in this system are portions of vertical cylindrical surfaces. The intersections of these with the horizontal plane represent the plans of the convex and concave sides of the rail, whilst their intersections with any plane inclined to their common axis are a pair of similar ellipses.

We may now direct attention to Fig. 194, which represents a squared wreath for a quarter of a circle standing in its proper position over its plan A B C D. Let the wreath be included between the two parallel planes represented by the vertical traces E F and G H, then E F G H may be taken to represent the edge of the plank from which the wreath is to be cut, and the planes E F and G H its upper and under sides respectively.

From what has already been said, the intersections of the cylindrical surfaces with the plank would give two pairs of similar elliptic curves, and these if drawn on the surfaces of the plank, as in the upper part of

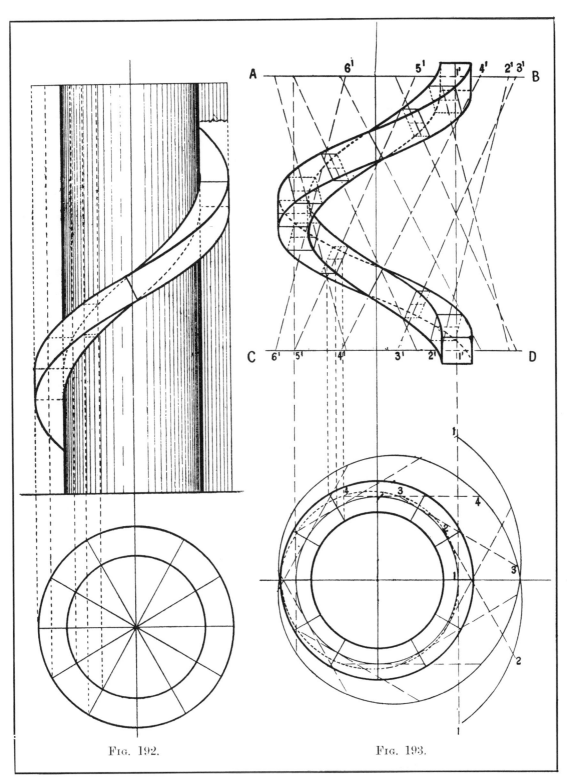

FIG. 192.　　　　　FIG. 193.

DELINEATION OF THE WREATHED SOLID IN THE TWO SYSTEMS OF HANDRAILING.

X

Fig. 194, would of course be the correct lines for sawing out and trimming the vertical sides of the wreath.

Face mould.—These lines are drawn on the surface of the plank by means of a thin mould, termed by handrailers the "face mould," made

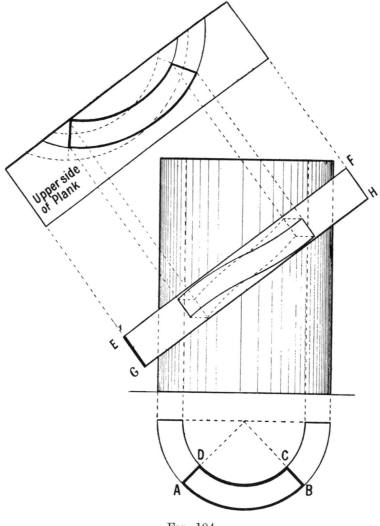

FIG. 194.

with its edges agreeing with the curves of section. Since the sections of a cylinder made by parallel planes inclined to its axis are identical in form, the upper and under surfaces of the plank will have sections with the cylindrical surfaces which exactly agree, and consequently the same mould, properly placed, will answer for both faces of the plank.

It will be seen that the determination of the face mould for a wreath standing over a circular plan resolves into the geometrical problem, viz., *of finding the section of a right cylinder made by a plane inclined to its axis.*

Falling mould.—In the *oblique-cut method*, which was practised antecedent to the *square-cut* or *tangent method*, the wreathed solid was sawn directly out of the plank to the lines marked upon it by means of the face mould, and when cut in this manner the sides would fit the cylinder "off the saw," and the wreath was ready to be taken to a thickness. The twisted surfaces of the wreath were then cut to lines obtained by bending a thin flexible mould, termed a "falling mould," round the convex side, the falling mould being made to the development of that side of the squared rail. Sometimes a falling mould was also used to draw the lines on the concave side. In fact the use of "falling moulds" was characteristic of the oblique method.

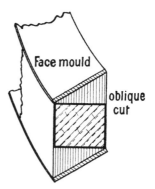

FIG. 195.

In the *square-cut method*, on the other hand, the wreath piece is in the first instance cut square out of the plank, a mode of procedure which avoids the long oblique cut so objectionable in the other method. The vertical sides are then, from a proper adjustment of the face mould, trimmed up to the cylindric form, and the resulting cut in no case need much exceed the thickness of the plank. The sketches Figs. 195, 196, illustrate the difference of the vertical cuts in the two methods.

Centre plane of plank.—The plane passing through the centre of the thickness of the plank, and not those of its upper and under sides, but to

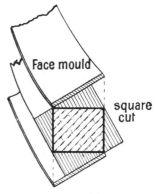

FIG. 196.

which it is parallel, is the one whose position is determined. The face mould is made to the section of the cylinder produced by this plane, and all the necessary lines are obtained with reference to it.

Centre line of plank.—The intersection of the above plane, which is usually termed the " plane of the plank," with the vertical cylindrical surface standing over the centre line of the wreath in plan, and therefore containing the centre falling line, is of course an ellipse also, which, although not necessarily drawn on the face mould, is nevertheless the guiding ellipse in all the operations, and will be referred to as the "centre line of plank " as distinguished from the " centre falling line of wreath."

Since both these lines are on the same cylindric surface their relative positions can, when it is necessary, be shown upon its development. In general they do not coincide, except at a few definite points, as a pre-arranged falling line is usually a curve of *double curvature*, while, on the other hand, the ellipse which represents the centre line of plank is, of course, only a *plane curve*. For example, the centre falling line of the rail of a spiral stair, being of uniform pitch, is a true helix, and no continuous portion of it is contained in any one plane. No plane curve, therefore, such as the ellipse, can be made to perfectly agree with the helix even for the shortest length.

Position of the plane of plank.—From what has been said, the student will be prepared for the statement that of all the planes which could be selected for the lie of the plank, out of which the wreath is to be cut, the best for a prearranged falling line would be that one whose curve of intersection with the central cylindric surface agreed most closely with or showed the least divergence from the given falling line.

To determine the plane fulfilling this condition absolutely is in most cases a tentative process, but since three given points, not in the same straight line, are sufficient data to fix a plane, with experience and judgment three resting points can be selected on the falling line which will determine the position of a plane near enough to the theoretically best plane for all practical purposes. In some simple and straightforward cases of handrailing, and cases where close conformity of rail to stair is not deemed of importance, no centre falling line is previously determined, but the centre line of the plank is made the centre falling line of the finished rail. In fact, the great majority of cases that are met with in practice can be treated in this manner without showing any appreciable defects, and even the centre line of plank often makes a better falling line than one arranged to follow more closely the stairs.

Determination of the plane of plank by the tangent method.—At this stage the student should endeavour to comprehend clearly that all tangents to the plane curve which we have defined as the " centre line of the plank" will lie wholly in " the plane of the plank," and that since any two intersecting lines given in position by their plans and elevations, or by their *traces* [1] on any assumed planes of reference, are sufficient to determine the plane which contains them, any pair of tangents therefore to the curve would fix the plane of the plank. Now the pair of tangents always selected for this purpose are those that correspond to the joints, and of course lie in the vertical tangent planes to the cylinder at the

---

[1] For definition of *trace* see Appendix, Descriptive Geometry.

springings, the traces of which on the horizontal plane are the tangents to the middle line of the rail in plan.

Practical illustration with prism.—This may be illustrated in a practical manner by means of a square prism. Let, for example, the student take a prism such as that shown by Fig. 197, and from any point

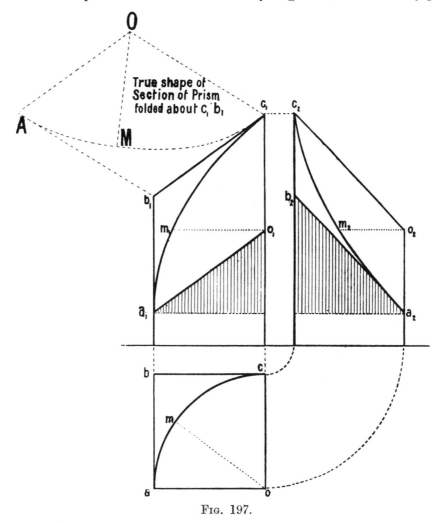

FIG. 197.

b_1 in one of its vertical arrises draw lines $b_1 a_1$ and $b_1 c_1$ across the two adjacent faces at any angle, then evidently *one plane section and one only* can be made passing through these lines. If now such a section $a_1 b_1 c_1 o_1$ be made, and the prism placed as in Fig. 197, with its square base over the plan $a b c o$ and a curve $a_1 m_1 c_1$, that would stand vertically over the quarter circle $a m c$ in the plan, traced on the section. Then the oblique section thus made would fitly represent the " plane of the plank," and the elliptic curve $a_1\,m_1\,c_1$ traced on it the "centre line of plank." Also the lines $a_1\,b_1$ and $b_1\,c_1$ which determine the section, are the tangents to the ellipse at the points a_1 and c_1, and the two faces of the prism containing these lines would represent the two vertical planes tangential to

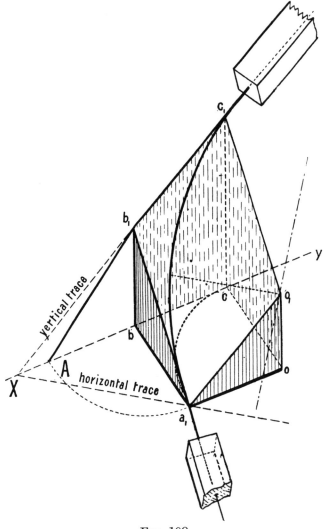

Fig. 198.

the cylinder at the "springings"; and further, the level line, $o_1\,m_1$ is the line of the minor axis of the ellipse. The true shape of the section is shown by O A $b_1\,c_1$ folded about the edge $b_1\,c_1$, A M c_1 being the quarter ellipse.

The same prism and its section is illustrated by an isometric view in Fig. 198, which represents it standing on a horizontal plane taken at the level a_1, the lowest point of the section.   In the same figure is shown the construction for determining the horizontal trace of the plane of section. This line is of great importance in drawing out the face mould, as it gives the *direction of the minor axis*, the latter being always parallel to it.

Figs. 199 and 200 show another section of the same prism, illustrating the simple case, viz., when one of the tangents is horizontal.

Variations that arise in the positions of the tangents.— A wreathed handrail may be required to stand over any prescribed curve in plan and

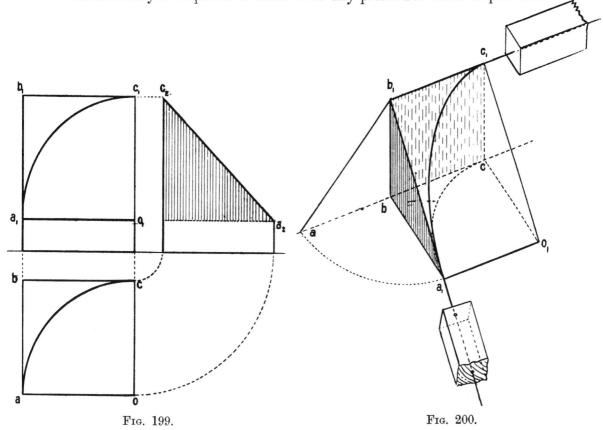

FIG. 199.   FIG. 200.

follow any falling line of either uniform or varying pitch, but most frequently the plan will be part of a circle, and for the present we shall only deal with this curve.

It will be obvious to the reader that the tangents may form with each other, in plan, an angle that may be less than, equal to, or greater than a right angle, according as the plan of the centre line is greater than, equal to, or less than a quarter circle.   Again, with respect to their *pitch* or inclination to the horizontal plane: (1) both tangents may be horizontal, in which case the rail is merely a " level easing; " (2) one tangent level, the other inclined; and (3) both tangents inclined, (*a*) at equal pitches, (*b*) at unequal pitches. These three cases, taken along with the variations of angle between the tangents in plan, as stated above, give

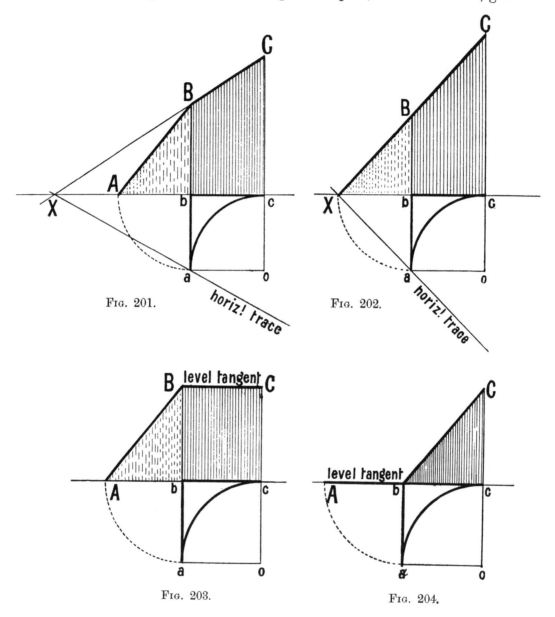

FIG. 201.   FIG. 202.

FIG. 203.   FIG. 204.

rise to *nine* different cases. But it should be pointed out that these need not necessarily require different methods of construction, as we shall see in the next chapter that the system of lines that apply to the general case, namely, *with tangents of unequal pitches and making any angle in plan*, will be equally applicable to all cases, although the diagrams may assume different forms.

The three cases with a quarter-circle plan occur oftenest in practice, and are shown by Figs. 201-203.

To find the traces of the plane of plank.—Let $a\,b$ and $b\,c$, Fig. 201, be the plans of two tangents of unequal pitches, the elevations of which on a vertical plane through $b\,c$ are b B and B C.   Now the upper tangent being in the assumed vertical plane, its elevation, B C, will therefore be coincident with the vertical trace of the oblique plane.   Produce C B to meet the ground line in X, then X is one point in the horizontal trace, and a the lower end of the lower tangent $a\,b$ being in the horizontal plane is therefore another point on the required trace.   Join X a, then X a and X C are the horizontal and vertical traces respectively of the plane containing the tangents.

Figs. 202-204 represent other particular positions of the tangents. The lines $a\,o$ and $a\,b$ in Figs. 203 and 204, it will be seen, are the horizontal traces respectively of the planes of planks.

Development of tangents.—Reverting to Fig. 201, let the triangle formed by the lower tangent, its plan $a\,b$, and elevation b B, be rotated about b B into the vertical plane containing the upper tangent B C, bringing the lower tangent into the position A B as shown, then A B and B C represent the true lengths and inclinations of the tangents, and the drawing is referred to as the *development of tangents*.

CHAPTER XIII

DETERMINATION OF FACE MOULDS AND BEVELS

Geometrical principles.—Before proceeding to describe the methods of drawing out the face mould, it will be necessary to remind the student of the following principles:

1. *The plans of horizontal or level lines are equal in length to the lines themselves.*

2. *Level lines lying on an oblique plane are parallel to one another and to the horizontal trace of the plane.*

3. *Parallel lines have their projections parallel.*

4. *Parallel planes have their intersections with any other plane which cuts them also parallel.*

5. *If a right cylinder, standing with its axis vertical, be cut by any inclined plane, the minor axis of the ellipse which forms the section is always a level line, and equal in length to the diameter of the cylinder, while the major axis is a line of steepest ascent of the plane.*

Methods of drawing out the face mould.—Let the plan of the centre line of rail and the tangents with their development be given, then to draw out the face mould from these particulars different modes of procedure may be adopted. (1) The plane of section or plane of plank may be rotated about its vertical trace into the vertical plane of projection, with the points, lines, etc., on it. (2) The plane may be similarly rotated about its horizontal trace into the horizontal plane. (3) The plane of section may be rotated about a second vertical trace made by it on a vertical plane, containing the axis of the cylinder, and having its ground line at right angles to the horizontal trace. These three methods of rotating the " plane of section," so as to obtain the particulars for drawing out the face mould, are shown in the same diagram by Figs. 205-207 respectively, and for the same quarter circle plan, $a\,m\,c\,o$. The student will find it instructive to draw out the diagram on stiff paper, and this done, beginning, say, at the point X on the ground line, cut with a sharp knife round the figure on the outline X a^1 E e E^1 X^1 a^1 E^{11} X, thus making a complete circuit. Next fold the upper part of the paper about X e,

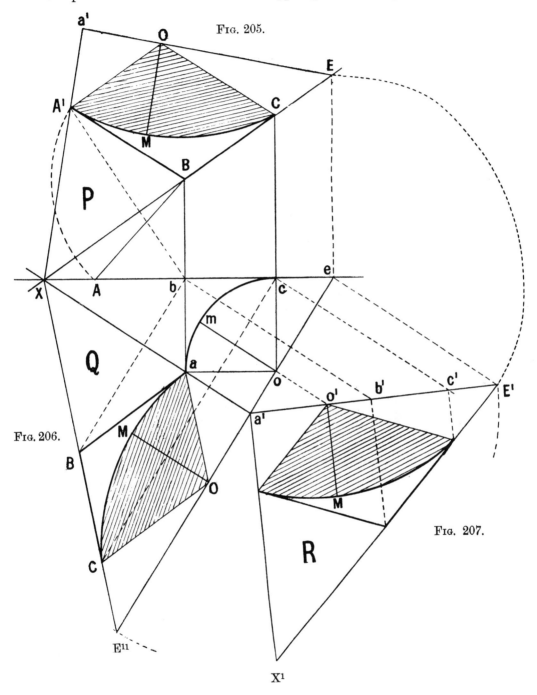

FIG. 205.

FIG. 206.

FIG. 207.

and that to right of $a^1 e$ about $a^1 e$, both through a right angle; then fold
the triangles P, Q and R about X E, X a^1 and a^1 E^1 respectively, which

will coincide with one another when folded so as to stand directly over the plan $X a^1 e$.

We shall now explain in detail the application of each of these three methods to the determination of the face mould.

FIRST METHOD.—This method will be found to be the most convenient in the majority of cases, and has been generally adopted in our practical illustrations in subsequent chapters.

We require to determine :

1. The correct positions of the tangents.

2. The centre of the ellipse and the directions of the two principal axes.

3. The width of the mould on the springing line.

1. **Placing of the tangents.**—Referring to Fig. 209, which represents the general case, *i.e.*, with the tangents A B and B C of unequal pitches, and their plans *a b* and *b c* making any angle with each other, it will be seen that the top tangent, B C, is already in position, being in the vertical trace which in this method is our axis of rotation of the plane. The position of the bottom tangent may be found in several ways. (*a*) With point B—the intersection of the two tangents—as centre, and B A the real length of the bottom tangent as radius, cut the perpendicular drawn from the point a_1 at right angles to the top tangent in the point A_1. Join A_1 B. Then A_1 B and B C represent the tangents in their correct positions on the mould. (*b*) The same result can also be easily obtained by finding the length of the chord, A_1 C, joining the extremities of the tangents. This may be done as shown in Fig. 208, by marking off from *c*, along the ground line X Y, the distance $c A_2$, equal to the plan length, *c a*, of the chord. $C A_2$ is its true length, which, with the two tangents A_1 B and B C, form a triangle that can be readily drawn, since the lengths of its three sides are now ascertained. In the same diagram (Fig. 208) the true length of the chord is found by constructing it into the horizontal plane, as shown by the dotted line $c_1 a$.

2. **To find the centre of the ellipse and the directions of the axes.**— Through *o*, the centre of the plan circle (Fig. 209), draw *o z* parallel to the horizontal trace, cutting the plan of the curve in *m* and the ground line in *z*; then *o z* is the plan of a level line lying on the plane of section which will be equal in length to the line itself, and since *o z* also passes through the centre, *o m* must be the plan of the semi-minor axis of the ellipse as well as the *real length* of this semi-axis.

Again, it is obvious that if the points X and A_1 be joined, this line will represent the horizontal trace of the plane of the plank constructed into the vertical plane, and therefore all *level lines* on the mould will be parallel to X A₁, which may be conveniently termed the *director of level lines.* This will now enable us to place the line O M Z on the mould, as it must be parallel to X A₁. From *z*, therefore, draw the perpendicular *z* Z, cutting X C, the vertical trace of the oblique plane in Z; then draw from Z a line parallel to X A₁, and mark along it from Z the distances Z O, Z M, equal to *z o* and *z m* respectively in the plan; O is the centre of the ellipse, O M the semi-minor axis, and the line at right angles to O M through O represents the major axis.

The lines O A₁ and O C, joining the extremities of the tangents to the centre of the ellipse, are termed the *springing lines,* as they divide the curved from the straight portions of the mould. These springing lines, when the plane of the mould is folded back into its correct position, will stand over the radii *o a* and *o c* in the plan.

In the particular case shown in Fig. 208, where the plans of the tangents are at right angles, the springing lines O A₁ and O C are parallel to the opposite tangents B C and A₁ B. This fact enables us in such cases to readily find the centre of the ellipse. For example, in Fig. 208, through the points A₁ and C, the extremities of the tangents, draw two lines parallel to B C and A₁ B respectively, intersecting in O the centre of the ellipse. The semi-minor axis O M may then be marked off from O, equal to the radius of the circle in plan, on a line, as before, parallel to X A₁ the director of level lines.

When the tangents are of equal pitches the construction is still further simplified, as they are equal to each other as well as to the springing lines, and therefore form a rhombus, and by symmetry the minor axis bisects the angle between the tangents, or, in other words, coincides with a diagonal of the rhombus. (See Practical Handrailing, Fig. 225.)

These particulars enable us to describe the central ellipse of any face mould, but of course it is only the curves representing its *inner* and *outer* edges that in practice really require to be drawn, and to obtain these some further observations are necessary.

Since the minor axis is a level line on the plane of the plank, therefore the upper and under sides of the rail at this part will be parallel to the surface of the plank, or, in other words, the rail at that section has no twist relatively to the surfaces of plank, and the width, consequently, of the mould on the line of the minor axis is equal to the width of the rail.

Therefore, in Figs. 208 and 209, set off on each side of M on the line of the minor axis half the width of the rail at the points 1 and 2,

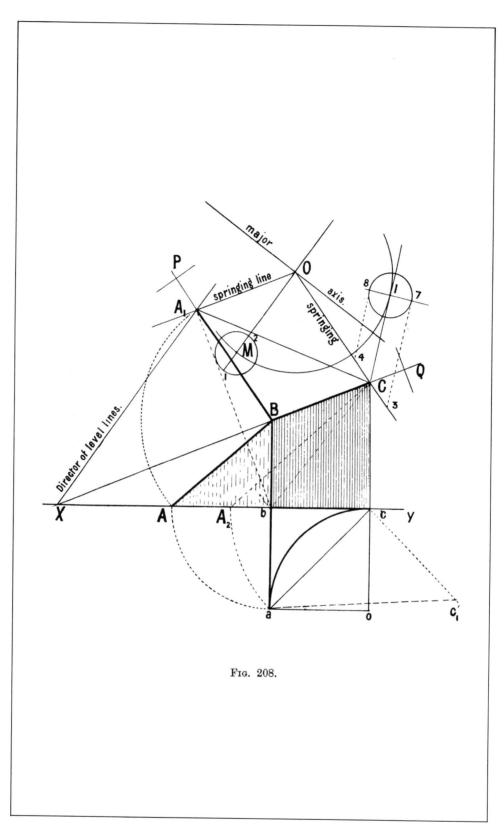

Fig. 208.

Face Mould Diagrams.

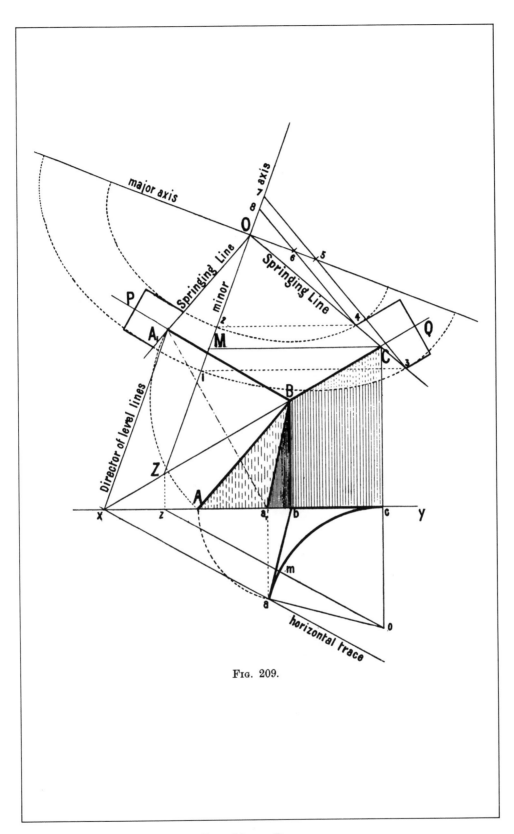

FIG. 209.

FACE MOULD DIAGRAMS.

then O 1 and O 2 are the semi-minor axes of the outer and inner curves respectively.

3. **To find the width of the mould on the springing lines.**—The width of the mould on *one* at least of the springing lines is also required, and this may be obtained in several ways, but probably most simply by joining M C Fig. 209 and drawing through the points 1 and 2 lines parallel to it, cutting the springing line O C in 3 and 4; then 3 4 is the width of the mould on that springing. Another method is shown in Fig. 208. With O as centre, and radius equal to that of the well, draw the arc M *l* as shown, and from C draw C *l* a tangent to it, then parallels to C *l*, and at half the width of the rail on each side of it, give the width 4 3 on the springing line O C.

To describe the curves.—This may now be done by means of the trammel, as shown in Fig. 209. With point 3 as centre, and radius equal to the semi-minor axis O 1 of the outer curve, cut the line of the major axis in 5; join 3 5, and produce it to cut the minor axis in point 7. Then 3 7 is the length of the semi-major axis, and with the division on it at the point 5 represents the trammel, which, when moved round in such a way as to make 5 and 7 always lie on the major and minor axis respectively, the point 3 will describe the outer ellipse. The trammel 4 6 8 is obtained and applied in a similar way to draw the inner curve.[1]

Shanks.—When the wreath joins with straight rails, it is usual to have short shanks formed upon it, so as to avoid having the butt joints at the springings, their lengths being arranged on the development of the tangents. The edges of a shank portion, for example, those of the shank C Q, Fig. 209, are got by drawing lines, through the points 3 and 4 on the springing, parallel to the tangent at that end of the mould, and these lines when drawn will necessarily be tangential to their corresponding curves. The mould may then be completed by drawing at the ends of the shanks the joint lines, which are always square to the tangents, except in some special cases where the easing is formed on the wreath piece.

SECOND METHOD.—In Fig. 210 is exemplified the manner of drawing the face mould by folding the plane about its horizontal trace into the horizontal plane. We leave it as an exercise to the student to follow out the construction therein given. The noteworthy point in this method is in being able at once to draw the major axis, which is at right angles to the horizontal trace of the plane, and passes through the point *o*, the centre of the plan. The elliptic curves, to avoid confusion, are not

---

[1] For methods of drawing the ellipse see Appendix, Problems 13-21.

drawn in the figure, but the lengths of the trammels for this purpose are shown, being found exactly as in the last example.

THIRD METHOD.—Let the plan $a\,m\,c$, Fig. 211, and the development A B C of the tangents be given, and the horizontal trace X a of the oblique plane be found, as already described.

Through o, the centre of the plan circle, draw $X_2\,Y_2$ at right angles to the horizontal trace, intersecting X Y at e, and consider it as the

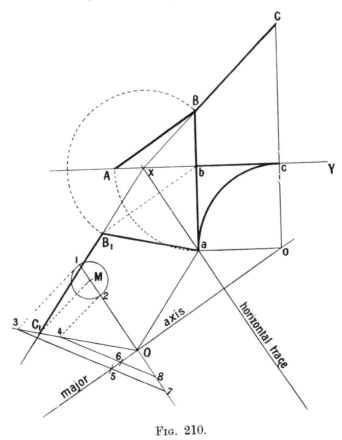

FIG. 210.

ground line of a new vertical plane, which will obviously contain the axis of the cylinder as well as the major axes of the ellipses. From e draw e E and e E_1 at right angles respectively to the old and new ground lines X Y and $X_2\,Y_2$, making e E_1 equal to e E; join a_1 E_1, which is the trace of the oblique plane or plane of section on the new vertical plane; a_1 E_1 is also the line representing the major axes of the ellipses, and about which the plane of section is rotated.

The tangents, etc., are got into position on the plane of section by means of level ordinates. For example, the point B_1, the intersection of the two tangents, is found by drawing through b the line $b\,5$ parallel to the horizontal trace $X\,a$, and continuing it to meet $a_1\,E_1$ in b_1, and $b\,5$ being a level ordinate, its length is set off from b_1 along a line $b_1\,B_1$ perpendicular to $a_1\,E_1$.

The points A_1, C_1, and the semi-minor axis $O\,M$, are found in a similar manner. Then the mould, after its width has been found on one of the springing lines, may be drawn with trammels as already explained; or,

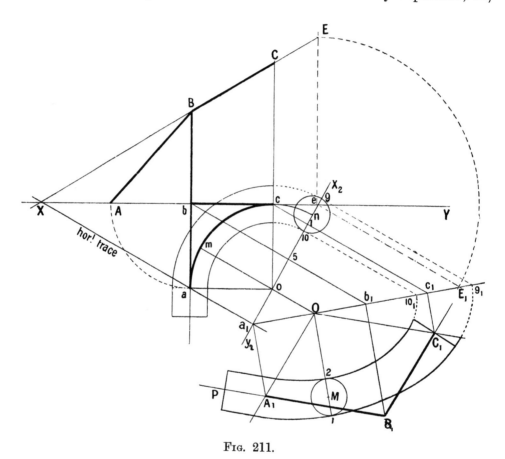

Fig. 211.

instead of finding the width of the mould on the springing, continue the circle representing the middle line of rail in plan to meet $X_2\,Y_2$ in the point n, and set off on each side of it one half the width of rail, and draw the projectors $9\,9_1$, $10\,10_1$; then $O\,10\,10_1$ is the semi-major axis of the inner curve, and $O\,9_1$ that of the outer. The axes of the two ellipses being thus determined, a trammel may be used as before for drawing the curves, or the foci may be found and the curves described by means of a string. (See Appendix, Problem 13.)

Method by ordinates.—When the plan of a wreath is not a part of a circle, the curves of the face mould are not of course ellipses, and cannot therefore be drawn with a trammel nor with a string. In all such cases a number of points have to be found on the curves by means of *ordinates*, and the lines traced through them by the aid of a flexible batten. The construction of the mould by ordinates is often adopted, even when the curves *are* ellipses, especially in connection with large wells, and in these cases this method may prove more expedient than finding the axes and using the trammel. (See Figs. 271, 272.)

Butt joints—A *true* butt joint formed in a wreath should be perpendicular to the falling line element at which the joint occurs, that is, at right angles to the tangent to the curve of the falling line at the joint.

Now in the tangent system the joint plane is not necessarily normal to the falling line, being nearly always made at right angles to the common tangent to the two elliptic curves that represent the centre lines of the planks corresponding to the two wreath pieces connected at that joint. For example, in the handrail of a spiral stair the true butt joint is one with its plane normal to the helix, which in this case is the falling line, and has a less inclination to the horizontal plane than a joint formed by the ordinary tangent method.

For all spiral wreaths standing over the same part of a circle in plan, the angle of inclination of the true butt joint, and that made normal to the plane of plank, are so related that their trigonometrical tangents have a constant ratio to each other.

Thus: Let A represent the angle of inclination of a joint plane normal to the helix, and B that of a joint normal to the ellipse or centre line of plank; then:

For a wreath over a quarter of a circle . . . $\tan A : \tan B = \cdot7854 : 1$
   ,,   ,,   one-eighth ,,   . . . $\tan A : \tan B = \cdot7854 : \cdot8284$
   ,,   ,,   one-sixteenth ,,   . . . $\tan A : \tan B = \cdot7854 : \cdot7956.$

To take an example: Let the pitch of a true spiral wreath for a quarter circle be 40°, then the inclination of the true butt joint plane, being the complement of the angle of pitch, is 50°. We have, therefore, from the above proportion: $\tan B = \dfrac{\tan A}{\cdot7854} = \dfrac{\tan 50°}{\cdot7854} = \dfrac{1\cdot1917}{\cdot7854} = 1\cdot518 = \tan$ of $56\frac{1}{2}°$ nearly. Therefore angle $B = 56\frac{1}{2}°$.

The joint plane, therefore, when formed by the tangent method, would differ from the true butt joint by about $6\frac{1}{2}°$ in the example chosen, namely, with the joints at the quarters and 40° pitch of falling line.

This divergence in a rail 4 inches thick would show itself in the joint, being ·227 inch (nearly ¼ inch) further up the rail on its upper side, and the same distance down the rail on its under side, from what would be the lines of the true butt joint.

If the joints were made at the octants, the divergence would only be about 3°, and the nearer the joints are to each other the less the divergence becomes, as shown by the relation of the trigonometrical tangents given above.

The difference in the angles of inclination between the plane of the true butt joint and that formed at right angles to the tangent can of course be easily shown geometrically. In the accompanying diagram, Fig. 212, A B C represents the development of the equally-pitched tangents A B and B C of the spiral wreath for the quarter circle, and A_1 C the helix or centre falling line developed into the same plane. The latter is got by marking along the ground line A Y from the point c the distance c A_1 equal to the stretch out of the quarter circle a m c, and joining A_1 C, the development of the helix being, of course, a straight line. Through the point C draw lines C T and C R perpendicular to the helix C A_1 and to the tangent C B respectively ; then C T represents the line of the true butt joint, and the steeper line C R the joint normal to the tangent.

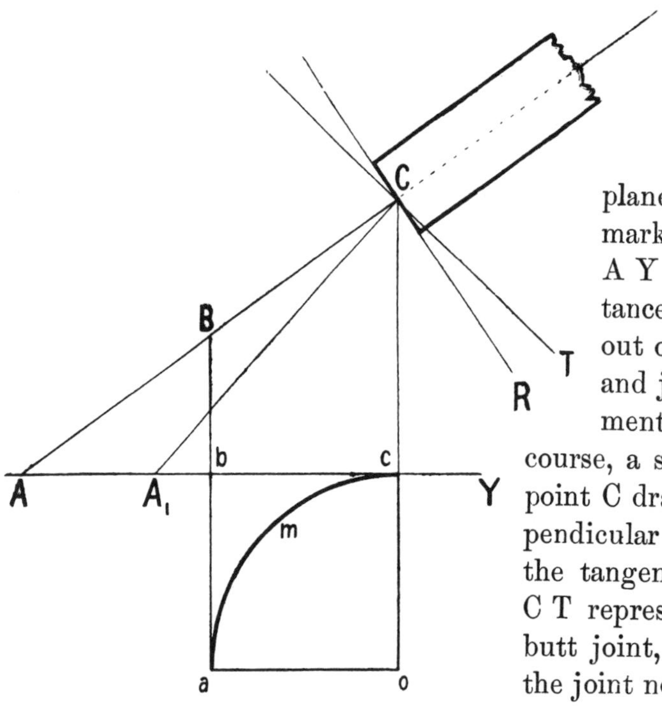

FIG. 212.

It should be understood, however, that if the centre line of plank be taken as the falling line instead of the helix, the joint formed perpendicular to the tangent would appear normal to the falling line element of the rail at the joint; but when this is done, it makes the pitch of the wreath vary slightly from point to point, which is undesirable, as the rail in that case would not conform to the uniformly pitched stair.

In subsequent pages it will be described how true butt joints may be formed, and the wreath made to follow a falling line deviating in any manner from the centre of the plank.

BEVELS FOR BUTT JOINTS.—From the above considerations respecting the directions of the joint planes it will appear that in some cases it may be desirable to make them in planes *not* perpendicular to the tangents, and the problem of bevels must therefore be considered in conformity with this general aspect of the joints in relation to their tangents.

I. **To find the bevels when the joints are not at right angles to the tangents.**—Three angles are required in connection with every butt joint of a wreathed piece, two to form the joint itself, and the third to draw on the surface of the joint when formed to give the proper twist to the rail. (1) There is the angle that the joint line on the face of the plank makes with the corresponding tangent, being the plane angle contained between the two lines made by the plane of the plank cutting the joint plane and the vertical plane containing the tangent. (2) The angle that the plane of the joint makes with the face of the plank. (3) The

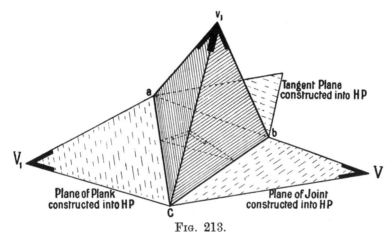

FIG. 213.

angle that has to be drawn across a butt joint after it has been accurately formed, to enable the face mould to be placed in its correct position on each side of the plank, and thereby give the correct twist to the rail. This bevel may be defined as the plane angle contained by the two lines made by the plane of the butt joint cutting the plane of the plank and the vertical plane containing the tangent, and is termed the *twist bevel*.

It is of practical importance to note that when the joint is made normal to the tangent the first two bevels are right angles, and therefore, only the third or twist bevel has to be found; and in particular cases *it* also becomes a right angle.

Handrail pyramid.—It may help the student to form a more definite idea of these bevels, as required in the general case, if he consider that the three planes, namely, (*a*) the plane of the plank, (*b*) the joint plane, and (*c*) the vertical plane containing the tangent, would form the *three faces of a triangular pyramid*, having for its base the triangle formed by

their traces on a horizontal plane, a simple solid which can easily be
realized by the mind. Two of the plane angles at the apex (see Fig.
213) would represent the bevels (1) and (3), and the dihedral angle
between the same two faces the bevel (2) referred to above.

The problem, therefore, of finding the three angles or bevels for any
butt joint is the same as the geometrical one, namely, " *having given the
plan and elevation of a triangular pyramid standing with its base on the
horizontal plane, to find the development or true shape of two of its slanting
faces and the dihedral angle between them.*" The problem, as we shall
see, is rendered easier in the case of the handrail pyramid, since one of

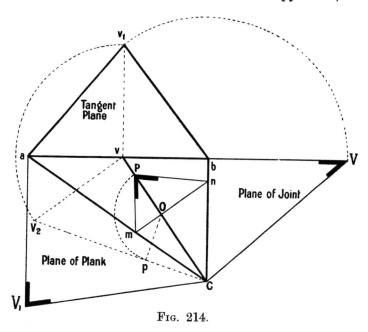

FIG. 214.

its faces, *i.e.*, the plane containing the tangent, is always vertical and
another—the joint plane—at right angles to it.

In Fig. 214 let *a b c v* be the plan of the pyramid—point *v* being the
plan of its vertex—having the face *a v b* vertical and the sloping face *b v c*
at right angles to it; and let *a v₁ b* be its elevation on a vertical plane
through *a b*, *i.e.*, the plane of the face *a v b*. Then the vertical face *a v b*
may be taken to represent the *vertical tangent plane*, the two sloping faces
a v c and *c v b* *the planes of plank* and *joint* respectively.

First, to find the true shape of the sloping faces of the pyramid we may
fold them into the horizontal plane about *a c* and *b c* respectively. Now
the true lengths of the two slant edges *a v* and *b v* are obviously given
by their elevations *a v₁* and *b v₁*, and in order to draw the triangles, there-

fore, we have only to find the true length of cv. Set off from b to the right the length b V along the ground line equal to bv_1 and join c V, then c V is the true length of the edge cv, and c V b is the *true shape* of that face of the pyramid, while the angle b V c represents the *twist bevel*.

Next with a and c as centres, and av_1 and c V respectively as radii, describe arcs intersecting in V_1; a V_1 c is the true shape of that face, and the angle a V_1 c gives the bevel that would be applied to the tangent to draw the joint line on the face mould.

Second, to find the dihedral angle between the two sloping faces. Through any point o in cv draw a line at right angles to it, cutting ac and bc in m and n respectively; construct cv into the horizontal plane as at c V_2, and draw op perpendicular to it; make o P equal to op, and join P n and P m, then m P n is the angle required, and represents the bevel between the face of the plank and the plane of the joint.

If the above problem be thoroughly understood, the student will have no difficulty in finding the bevels for a butt joint making *any* inclination whatever with its tangent.

General method of finding the three bevels.—In Fig. 215 is shown the above construction applied to the most general case, namely, *when the tangents are unequally pitched and make any angle with each other in plan, while the planes of both joints are not normal to their tangents.*

The construction for finding the bevels for the *upper* butt joint is shown at (A), Fig. 215, and that for the *lower* at (B), the same letters being used as in Fig. 214 to denote corresponding lines and angles, and this will enable the student to follow out the construction with little explanation. For the bevels in the diagram (A) for the upper joint, any convenient point a may be chosen on the line of the upper tangent B C through which a ground line, ax, may be drawn. Any other point v_1 may also be chosen on B C, and the line v_1b drawn through it parallel to the assumed joint line rs. Next through the point a draw ac parallel to the horizontal trace of the oblique plane, and through b draw bc at right angles to the ground line, ax, intersecting ac at c; from v_1 drop a line v_1v perpendicular to the ground line ax and join cv. Then $abcv$ is the plan of the pyramid, av_1b its elevation, and the three bevels at V, V_1, and P found as in Fig. 214.

With respect to the bevels at (B) for the lower joint, any point a is chosen in the plan line of the lower tangent and av_1 drawn to the pitch of that tangent. Through any point v_1 in av_1 draw a line v_1b, making an angle with av_1 equal to the inclination of the joint line tu to the lower tangent A B. As before, through point a draw ac parallel to the horizontal trace, and bc at right angles to ab, cutting ac at c; let fall the perpendicular v_1v and join cv, then $abcv$ is the plan and av_1b the elevation of the pyramid. The rest of the construction for the three bevels is the same as in the preceding cases.

It is almost unnecessary to remark that when the tangents are of equal pitches, and also the joint planes, the bevels at both ends of the wreath are identical.

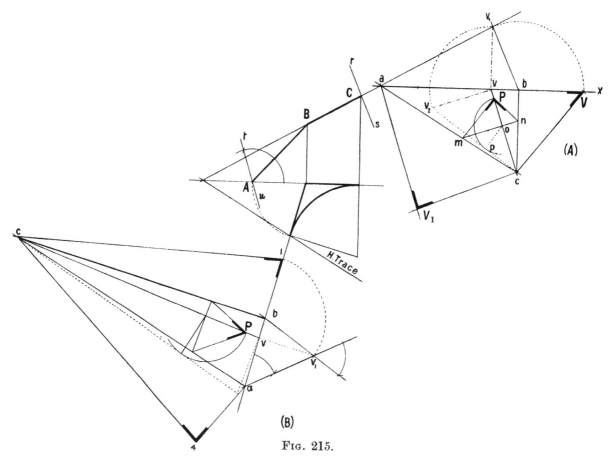

FIG. 215.

II. **To find the bevels when the joints are at right angles to the tangents.**—When the joints are arranged in this way, it very much simplifies the problem of handrailing, and is one of the practical advantages attending the strictly tangent system, because the joints being cut square to the face of the plank, and also square to the tangents, *only the twist bevel* has to be determined for each joint.

Though the general method above, in Fig. 215, for finding the twist bevel is strictly applicable in all cases, a somewhat different definition of this angle may be given when the joint plane is normal to the tangent, and in practice the construction can often be shortened by utilizing lines already on the drawing for other purposes.   In this case the twist bevel becomes the *dihedral or measuring angle between the plane of the plank and the vertical plane containing the tangent,* a definition which is not applicable in the general case, and the geometrical problem of finding this angle may be stated thus: "*To determine the inclination of an oblique plane to the vertical plane of projection.*"   (See Appendix, Prob. 29.)

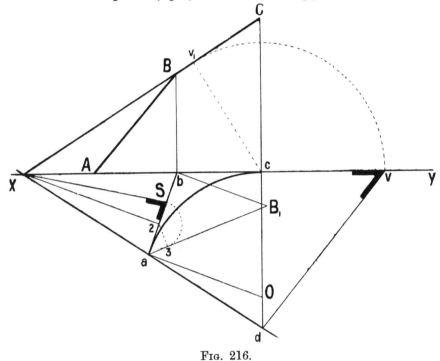

FIG. 216.

In Fig. 216 the bevels for the two ends of a wreath whose tangents form *any* angle in plan are found at V and S, and the student will see that, though the lines are differently placed in this diagram, the construction in no way differs from that given for finding the corresponding bevels in the general case, Fig. 215. If the construction were completed so as to discover the other two bevels for each joint, they would be, as above stated, both right angles. It will, however, be advantageous to describe in some detail the construction here shown, **as it is the one that occurs most frequently in practice.**

To find the bevel for the upper joint of wreath.—From any point *d* on the horizontal trace, X *a*, Fig. 216, draw a line perpendicular to X Y— since *d c* is already drawn, it may be utilized for this purpose—and from

c draw $c\,v_1$ perpendicular to the upper tangent B C; with c as centre and $c\,v_1$ as radius describe the arc, cutting the ground line in V and join d V, then the angle d V c is the twist bevel required.

To find the bevel for the lower joint.—Draw $b\,B_1$ at right angles to $b\,a$, making it equal to b B, and join $a\,B_1$; this line is the elevation of the lower tangent on a vertical plane, whose ground line is $a\,b$. As before, take any point on the horizontal trace, X a, as X, and draw X 2 at right angles to $a\,b$; from 2 draw 2 3 perpendicular to $a\,B_1$, and with 2 as centre and 2 3 as radius describe an arc cutting $a\,b$ in S; join S X, then the angle X S a is the bevel for the lower joint.

Obviously, the work is reduced to that of finding *one bevel* when the two tangents are of equal pitches, and also when one tangent is horizontal and the two tangents forming a right angle in plan. In the former case both bevels are identical, and in the latter the bevel at the inclined end of the wreath becomes a right angle.

Another method of finding the twist bevels.—An easy and comprehensive way of obtaining the twist bevel at a joint, or at any other section of a wreath when formed at right angles to the tangents at the points, is shown by Fig. 217, a method which will be found very accurate, and has the further advantage of giving all these bevels with reference to a common line.

The construction depends on the principle that *if perpendiculars are drawn from a common point to two intersecting planes the angle contained by the two perpendiculars is the supplement of the dihedral angle between the two planes.* Hence, instead of finding the angle between the two planes which gives the twist bevel, we may find the angle contained between two lines perpendicular to them and drawn from a common point.

In Fig. 217 $o\,a$ and $o\,c$, the two radii of the plan circle, are necessarily lines at right angles to the vertical tangent planes at the lower and upper joints respectively. Then if we suppose a line drawn through o perpendicular to the oblique plane, its plan, $o\,p$, will be at right angles to the horizontal trace of that plane, and the *real angles* made by this perpendicular with $o\,c$ and $o\,a$ will be the bevels of the upper and lower joints respectively, since these angles represent the supplement of the angles which the oblique plane makes with the two tangent planes.

As a practical illustration of the above the student should place the point of his pencil on the centre, o, of the quarter circle in plan and hold it in a direction perpendicular to the oblique plane or plane of the plank; the angle formed by the pencil thus placed with any radius, such as $a\,o$ or $o\,c$, is the twist bevel at that section.

Hence *the construction for finding the bevels* by this principle consists of folding into one plane the radii $o\,a$ and $o\,c$ together with the common perpendicular o P, so as to show the real angles between them.   To do this, through o, Fig. 217, draw $p\,e$ at right angles to the horizontal trace, X a, and from e set up perpendiculars e E and e E$_1$, making e E$_1$ equal to e E and join p E$_1$.   Then E$_1$ $p\,e$ is the angle of pitch of the plank. From o draw o P at right angles to p E$_1$, then o P represents the common

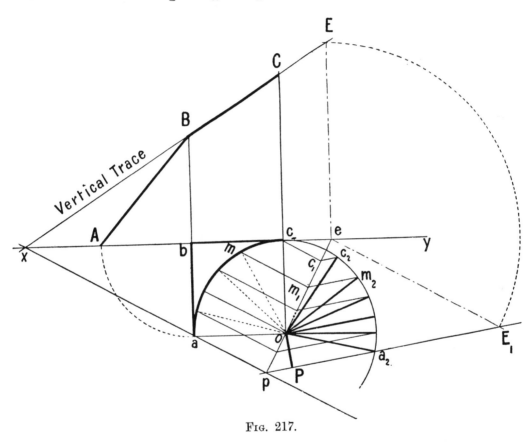

FIG. 217.

perpendicular constructed into the horizontal plane; and now to bring the two radii $o\,a$ and $o\,c$ into their new positions with respect to o P, draw $c\,c_1$ parallel to the horizontal trace, and $c_1\,c_2$ parallel to the pitch line p E$_1$ cutting the plan circle in c_2; join $o\,c_2$, then $c_2\,o$ P is the obtuse bevel for the upper joint.   Again, let a_2 be the point where the pitch line p E$_1$ cuts the plan circle; join $a_2\,o$, then $a_2\,o$ P is the bevel for the lower joint.

The twist bevel at any other section in the wreath can be obtained in the same way as we have shown for the joints.   For example, to find the bevel at section m, draw $m\,m_1$ and $m_1\,m_2$ parallel respectively to the

A A

horizontal trace X a, and to the pitch line p E$_1$, join m_2 o, then m_2 o P is the twist bevel required.

Remark.—The method just given of obtaining the twist bevel at any section will be found very satisfactory, both as regards quickness and accuracy, and can be very readily applied when the face mould is got out, as in Fig. 211, where the line representing the pitch of the plank is already drawn for the purpose of constructing the mould. It is also particularly well adapted for the system of handrailing by *normal sections*, in which the twist bevel has to be found at a number of intermediate points in the wreath as well as at the joints. Further, if it were required to solve the converse problem, viz., to determine the position of the section that corresponded to a given angle of twist, the above construction made in the reverse order would obviously discover the point in question. Thus, set off P o m_2 (Fig. 217) equal to the given angle and draw m_2 m_1 and m_1 m, respectively, parallel to the pitch line p E$_1$ and horizontal trace X a ; then m is the point in the wreath required.

Diagrams of the twelve principal cases of tangents and bevels, arranged progressively.—These are shown by Figs. 218 and 219. Cases I. to VI. illustrate the variations of construction with one of the two tangents horizontal, while cases VII. to XII. similarly show the variations that arise when both tangents are inclined. In each diagram all the necessary lines are found for drawing the face mould, and the bevels for the joints are also found.

These will furnish a series of progressive examples which the student should draw to a larger scale, and complete the curves of the moulds as previously explained.

All the cases (I. to XII.) show the plane of the mould folded about the upper tangent, in the manner already shown in Figs. 208 and 209, and it will only be necessary to make a few observations to render intelligible the method here illustrated of finding the bevels, as it has not been previously given, and being most convenient for this method of rotation of the plane, is the one we have mostly used in the examples of practical handrailing by the "cylindric system."

To determine the twist bevel by the method shown in the several cases. The lower tangent being got into position, and the centre of the ellipse found, from the latter point let fall a perpendicular on each of the tangents. From the feet of these perpendiculars draw tangents to the well circle described from the centre of the ellipse, the angles which the tangents to this circle (which may be called the auxiliary circle of the central ellipse) make with the perpendiculars are the twist bevels required at the respective ends of the wreath.

Case XII. as here shown calls for some remark, as the joints, unlike the rest of the cases, are not at right angles to the tangents, so that *three* bevels are required for each end of the wreath.

The construction employed in the other cases is, we shall see, included in this more general one. The elevations of the centre of the ellipse are first found on the two vertical tangent planes, as at H^1 and H^{11}. Parallels to the joint lines through H^1 and H^{11} give points E and F, their intersections with the tangents, which, being joined to H_2, the centre of the ellipse, give lines H_2 F and H_2 E^1, that are parallel respectively to the upper and lower joint lines on the mould. In other words, the angles which these lines make with their respective tangents are the bevels to apply across the latter to draw the joint lines at the ends of the wreath.

Again, tangents drawn from the points F and E_1 to the auxiliary circle, as in the other cases (I to XI), determine the angles m F H_2 and n E_1 H_2, which are the respective twist bevels.

The bevel to apply across the thickness of the plank, that is, the dihedral angle that the plane of the joint makes with the plane of the plank, can now be easily found by the following construction :—Take any point 2^1 on the minor axis and draw 2^1 3^1, 2^1 4^1, respectively, at right angles to H_2 E_1 and H_2 F. Make H 3, H 2 and H 4 in the plan, respectively, equal to H_2 3^1, H_2 2^1 and H_2 4^1; then 2 3 and 2 4 will be the bases of two triangles, as shown constructed on the face mould diagram, namely, 2^1 3^{11} t and 2^1 4^{11} r, having t 3^1 and t 2^1, r 4^1 and r 2^1 for their other sides respectively, which give the bevels required, as shown at t and r.

Other methods of determining the bevels are given in the chapters on Practical Handrailing that follow, but as they are referable to the same principles as we have already discussed need not be described here.

Another method of describing the curves of the face mould. General principle of the trammel.—The usual, and probably the most convenient, method of drawing the curves of the face mould, is that which we have adopted in the illustrative examples and explained in connection with Fig. 209, namely, *to find the major and minor axes of the ellipses, and draw the curves with trammels guided on these axes.*

It will, however, be seen that this mode of procedure is only a particular case of a general principle. For example, the trammel need not be confined to the two principal axes of the ellipse, as *any* pair of lines passing through its centre may be taken as guiding lines, and to which an appropriate trammel corresponds; but such trammel may not have its

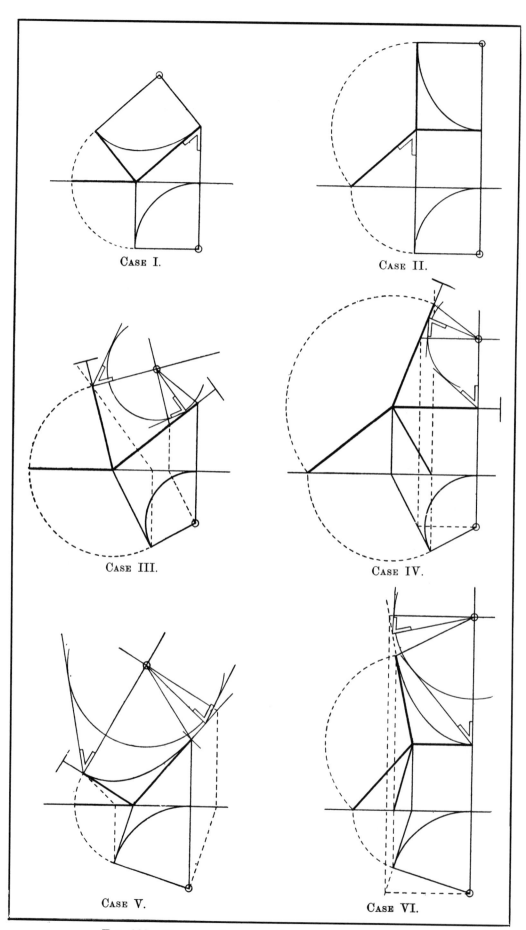

FIG. 218. VARIOUS CASES OF TANGENTS (ONE LEVEL).

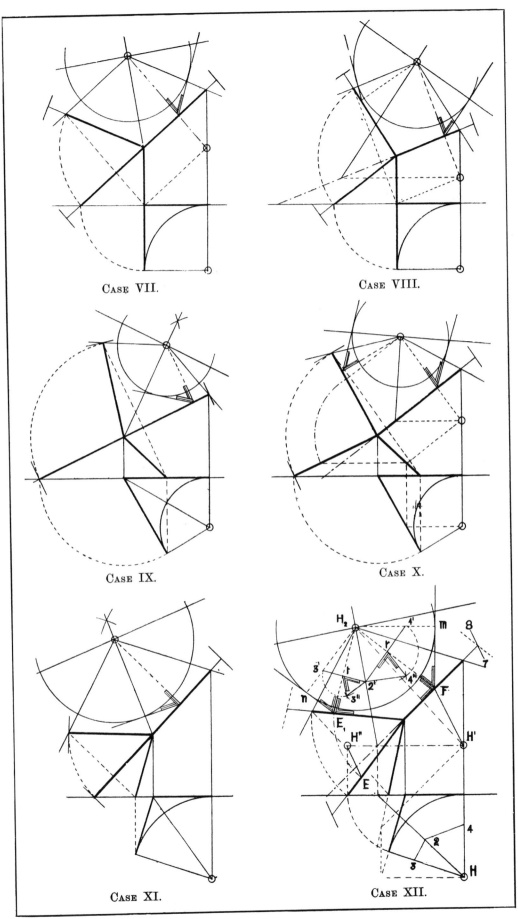

FIG. 219. VARIOUS CASES OF PITCHED TANGENTS.

three points on the same straight line; in fact, the straight trammel is only a particular case of what may be called the *triangular trammel*, the essential of a trammel for describing an ellipse being simply three points rigidly connected—two guiding points, and a third a tracing point.

Fig. 220 is introduced to show how the curves of the face mould may be described by a straight trammel guided on one of the springing lines and another line which can be easily determined.

The mould, as will be seen, is for a quarter-circle wreath, the diagram being arranged as in Fig. 208.

Before proceeding to get the necessary trammels we have to find the width of the mould on at least one of the springings. In the present case the width 3 4 on the springing line O C, Fig. 220, is found by first determining the twist bevel at that end. Thus, from the point G, where the joint line produced cuts the springing A_1 O, an arc is struck with a radius equal to that of the well, a tangent to which from Q gives L Q G, the twist bevel. Two parallel lines to Q L at half the width of the rail on each side of it give the points 11 and 12, and again, parallels to the tangent B C through the latter points obtain the required points 3 and 4 on the springing, O C. The bevel, and consequently width of mould, at the other end is similarly found. By this construction the twist bevel and width of mould on the springing are found together, which is some little advantage as compared with the other methods already given.

To find the trammels.—Through C, Fig. 220, draw C F perpendicular to the tangent B C, and produce F C to E, making C E equal in length to the tangent B C, and join E to O the centre of the ellipse. Then E C F would be the trammel for describing the central ellipse of the mould, C being the tracing point, and the ends F and E those that would be guided along the springing O A_1 and the line E O respectively. Of course this central ellipse is not drawn in practice; but we have now only to draw through the points 3 and 4, lines parallel to E F, to obtain 5 3 7 and 6 4 8, the trammels for the convex and concave edges of the mould respectively.

The dotted line $5^1 3^1 7^1$ shows the position of the former trammel when tracing the curve at the point 3^1. It is obvious that when the tracing point 3^1 reaches 13, the extremity 7^1 will have landed at O, and the trammel itself will be coincident with the springing line O A_1.

Again, by setting out the length of the tangent B C on the other side of C at e_1, and joining e_1 to O, cutting 6 4 and 5 3 in 15 and 14 respectively, we get other two shorter trammels, 6 15 4, and 5 14 3, that will similarly trace out the same ellipses, 3 and 4 being, as before, the tracing points, and 5 6, and 14 15, the points that have to be guided on the springing O G and the line O e_1 respectively.   The longer trammels previously found are much to be preferred, as in the case of the shorter trammels the two guiding lines form so acute an angle with each other as to make accuracy in drawing the curves not easily attainable.

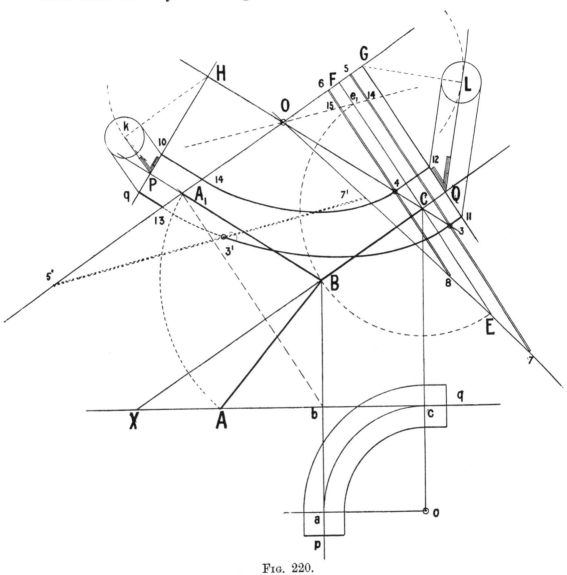

FIG. 220.

It will be apparent that this method of obtaining the curves is just as easy and straightforward as the ordinary one, and is quite general in its application, as by a slight modification in the construction it may be employed also in cases where the tangents are not, as here, at right angles in plan.

Further considerations respecting the trammelling of the ellipses of the face mould.—We will now ask the reader to turn to Fig. 221, which is simply a copy of the principal lines in the preceding figure, in which it is shown that any number of other trammels may be found that will describe the same ellipses.

Bisect O E, the guiding line for the trammel E F, at m. With m as centre describe the circle passing through the points O, F and E, as shown by a dotted line. Now any chord of this circle passing through C (see Appendix, Problem 21) may be selected as a trammel to draw the central ellipse, each chord or trammel having necessarily its appropriate guiding lines, which pass through O the centre of the ellipse, and its extremities. As there is obviously an *unlimited* number of different chords that can be drawn in this circle passing through C, there is therefore also an *unlimited* number of trammels which will describe the same ellipse.

Similarly, if the line O E_1 be bisected at m_1, and the smaller circle drawn passing through O, F and E_1, then any line drawn from C cutting this circle may be taken as a trammel for drawing the same ellipse, C being the tracing point. We have thus another distinct set of trammels, unlimited in number, also at our disposal.

We shall first notice the properties of that chord of each circle which passes through the centre, and which is consequently a diameter. Let these cut the larger circle in the points r and s and the smaller in r^1 and s^1. Then the points s and s^1, r and r^1, are severally in the same straight line with O, which may now be drawn. Now these lines O r and O s are the guiding lines for the longer trammel r C s and shorter one $r^1 s^1$ C, and the angle which they include at O, being in a semicircle, is therefore a right angle. The importance of these two lines lies in this, that they represent the major and minor axes of the ellipse, so that there is here an independent construction for finding the direction of these axes. As a test of accuracy O r should by this construction turn out to be parallel to the level line A_1 X, as used in Fig. 208. It will be further observed that C r and C r^1 are each equal to the semi-major axis, while C s and C s^1 are each equal to the semi-minor.

Finally, we may notice the peculiarity of the chord $t u$ at right angles to $r s$. Since it is perpendicular to the diameter, it is bisected at C, so that $t u$ is an *equal-ended trammel* for describing the ellipse on its appropriate guiding lines O t and O u. Of the whole sheaf of trammels this is the easiest one to use, as it cannot be wrongly applied, since it can be turned end for end. It may be noted also that its half-length C t or C u is a mean proportional to C r the semi-major and C s the semi-minor axes of the ellipse, and is equal in length to the two tangents from C to the smaller circle. These two tangents, with the chord joining their points of contact, form an isosceles triangle, which is the counterpart of the trammel $t\,u$. (See Appendix, Problem 21.)

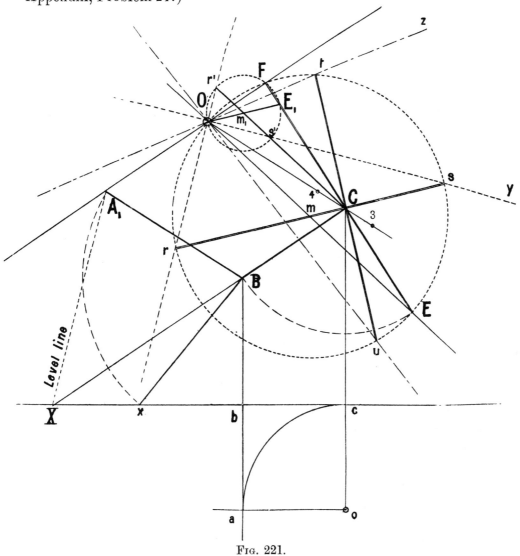

FIG. 221.

Parallel lines to these different trammels through the points 3 and 4, Fig. 221, and terminated by other corresponding guiding lines, would give the trammels for the outer and inner edges of the mould respectively, precisely as in Fig. 220.

Triangular trammel.—We may now briefly allude to the still more general aspect of the problem of describing the ellipse as presented in

Fig. 221, *i.e.*, by departing from the straight line trammel and adopting the triangular form.

In Fig. 221, any triangle having its vertex at C and its base a chord of either circle may be used as a trammel, the guiding lines being those that pass through the centre of the ellipse and the extremities of the chord. Thus, for example, in Fig. 221 take the triangle $s \, C \, t$, and suppose the points s and t guided along the lines O y and O z respectively, the point C would trace out the central ellipse. And similarly for any other triangle chosen in either circle.

This principle is further illustrated in the Appendix, Problem 21.

Application of the triangular trammel to draw the mould from the springing lines.—The triangular trammels for doing this are easily determined for quarter-circle wreaths where the springing lines on the face mould are parallel to the opposite tangents. The construction however for finding them becomes rather complicated for ready application in the workshop when the tangents and springings do not together form a parallelogram.

Fig. 222 is again the same case of a wreath as that in Fig. 220, and in the figure two sets of trammels are obtained for describing the same ellipses.

In this case, as in Fig. 220, the widths of the mould on the springing lines are first obtained by means of the twist bevels.

To find the trammels: From C, Fig. 222, draw a perpendicular, C s, to the opposite springing A_1 O produced; from C and on each side of it set off along the springing O C the distances C m and C m^1, each equal to P H the perpendicular distance between the lower tangent A^1 B and its opposite springing, O C, and join $m \, s$ and $m^1 \, s$, both shown by dotted lines in the figure; these form two triangles, m C s and m^1 C s, each of which is a triangular trammel that would trace out the central ellipse of the mould, C being the tracing point, the points m and s of the one triangle and m^1 and s of the other being moved along the springing lines.

Next draw E u and D t parallel to C s; then from the two points u and t draw the lines $u \, r$ and $t \, n$ parallel to $s \, m$, and also $u \, r^1$ and $t \, n^1$ parallel to $s \, m^1$. This gives four triangles, two of which, $n \, t$ D and $n^1 \, t$ D (shaded differently in the figure), will trace the outer ellipse of the mould, and the other two smaller triangles, $r \, u$ E and $r^1 \, u$ E, the inner curve.

Fixing our attention more particularly on the two shaded triangles $n \, t$ D and $n^1 \, t$ D, it will be seen that they are in their correct position when tracing the point D of the curve, D being the common vertex of the two triangles, and the extremities of the bases n and t and n^1 and t lying on each springing line. We may choose the darkly-shaded triangle to trace out the curve, as, having the longer base, it can be moved on the springings with greater accuracy. It is shown again on the left of the

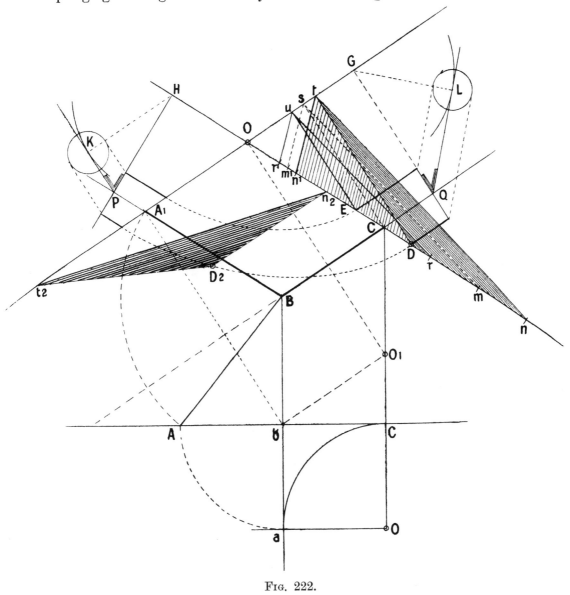

Fig. 222.

figure in the position, $n_2\,D_2\,t_2$, which it would occupy when tracing the ellipse at D_2.

It need hardly be mentioned that in practice a close triangle like that shown is not necessarily required. A straight lath like that used for an ordinary straight trammel may be taken, the length of the base of the triangle, as $n_2\,t_2$, to be guided on the springings, and any piece nailed across it to include the tracing point D_2 will form a convenient trammel.

It should be noted particularly, (1) that with tangents of equal pitches, and therefore of equal lengths, as in Fig. 224, these triangular trammels take the isosceles form, and (2) that in the case of one of the tangents being level and at right angles to the other in plan (see Fig. 254) the triangles merge into straight lines and become the ordinary trammels used for describing the ellipses on the major and minor axes.

HANDRAILING :—PRACTICAL

CHAPTER XIV

THE WAY TO MAKE A QUARTER-CIRCLE WREATH

Position of handrail on the stair.—The handrail should be placed as near the side of the stair as practicable, its exact position being arranged and shown in plan along with the strings and other details on the general working plan of the stair. Of course when the stair has "close strings" the position of the rail is fixed, the latter having to stand directly over the former, when balusters are fitted. This is partly the case also in stairs with "open strings," but the design of the balusters, and the method of fixing them at the bottom, are also determining factors in fixing the position of the rail, as the base of the baluster should not stand beyond the face of the string; and when wood ones are fitted it is usual to bring the outside of the base in line with that of the string or bracket. In stone stairs the balusters are sometimes fixed to the ends of the steps, so that the handrail stands farther out than when the balusters are let into the tops of the steps.

When a rail runs alongside of a wall or of a bulkhead there should be from $1\frac{1}{4}$ to $1\frac{1}{2}$ inches clear space between it and the most projecting part, so that the hand may move along the rail with freedom.

Height of handrail.—On the stair slope the height measured from the tread to the upper surface of the rail on a plumb line over the faces of the risers varies from 2 feet 6 inches in small houses to 2 feet 9 inches, or even 2 feet 10 inches, in the large stairs of public buildings, a very common height for ordinary houses being 2 feet 7 inches. On a level landing the rail should be half a riser or more higher than on the stair, being 2 feet 10 inches to about 3 feet 2 inches.

In ships, in consequence of the rolling and unsteadiness in a sea-way, stair balustrades should be made a little higher than in houses. The height of the rail should not be less than 3 feet measured vertically from the middle of the width of the tread to top of the handrail, or 3 feet minus one half the rise at the nosings in line with the faces of the risers. As in houses, the rails on the landings should always be made a few inches higher than those on the incline, a very common height being 3 feet 3 inches from the deck to the upper side of rail.

As a general rule the same height should be maintained throughout the length of a stair, both over fliers and winders, except at parts where there are sudden changes in the pitch; when it may become necessary to raise or lower the rail a little in order to avoid abrupt and unpleasing curves.

But although uniformity of height of rail on the stair is the general rule, in many cases that occur regard should be had not only to the degree of steepness of the stair at the winders as compared with that at the fliers, but also to the oblique position in which the risers have sometimes to be placed with respect to the direction of the line of ascent. For example, in the case of small wells with winders, the rail, if preserved at a uniform height throughout, would appear to be closer to the stair round the curve than at other parts, and would in fact be nearer to the nosings of the steps measured square to the falling line. This, of course, becomes more and more noticeable as the pitch increases, and not only results in giving a bad appearance to the rail, but also the protection that the balustrade affords from falling over the sides of the stair is correspondingly reduced.

To remedy in some measure these defects the rail should be raised a few inches higher over the winders than the standard height over the fliers.

Again, in the case of excessive obliquity of risers, in passing up or down the stairs one is kept farther from the rail at some parts than at others, and the height should be varied accordingly. For an example of this see " Elliptic Stair," Figs. 292-294.

It would be of little use to lay down more definite rules with respect to these points, as the raising or lowering of the rail from the specified height, either for the purpose of easing or for the reasons just given, will be determined largely in each case by the judgment and taste of the workman, who will be able to take all the circumstances into consideration.

Drawings required.—A set of lines for getting out a wreath on the cylindric-tangent method may comprise: 1st. *The plan,* which shows the centre line of rail, position of joints and tangents, and also the arrangement of the risers. 2nd. *The development of the tangents* and sections of the steps. 3rd. *The face-mould diagram.* 4th. *Construction for determining the bevels.* In some cases also it may be desirable to make a development of the vertical surface containing the centre falling line of the rail.

These drawings need not necessarily be detached, and in the practical illustrations that follow they are placed in relation to one another, as far as is expedient, according to the system adopted in ordinary projection.

Quarter-circle wreath for a stair with a landing in the quarter space, and with straight flights above and below.—The example (Figs. 223-225) shows how to get out a quarter-circle wreath when the risers are so arranged in the well that the centre lines of the two straight rails meet when produced, and may be taken as the tangents to the wreath. Each tangent being simply the continuation of the centre line of the straight rail, no easing is required, which makes this case the simplest one that can occur with inclined tangents, and for this reason we have chosen it as the first practical illustration.

Plan.—In Fig. 223 $a\,m\,c$ is the centre line of rail, the radius being 15 inches, and $a\,b$ and $b\,c$ the tangents to the quarter circle; $o\,a$ and $o\,c$ the two radii at the points of contact, forming with the tangents the square $a\,b\,c\,o$.

The tread is taken at 9 inches and the rise $7\frac{1}{2}$ inches. The distance of each of the two risers, 5 and 8, from b, the point of intersection of the two tangents, is made equal to a tread and a half, *i.e.*, $13\frac{1}{2}$ inches, which brings the centre lines of the two straight rails to the same height over the point b, and which will then form a straight line when developed.

The object of having the risers 6 and 7 curved towards the ends is to give the landing some breadth at the well, an expedient that has often to be adopted in ships, but is seldom resorted to in house stairs.

Development of tangents.—The next operation after the plan has been arranged is to draw the development of the sections of the steps made by the vertical tangent planes. The purpose of this development of the steps is to enable the positions of the tangents with respect to the straight rails and easings to be arranged, and their real lengths ascertained. In the present example this part of the work can be entirely dispensed with, as the pitches of both tangents are already fixed—being the same as that of the straight rails—and consequently their real lengths can be easily ascertained.

To draw then the development of tangents (Fig. 224): Through c the springing and b the point of intersection of the tangents in plan (Fig. 223) draw the vertical lines $c\,C$ and $b\,B$, and on the left of $b\,B$ draw the other springing line at a distance from it equal to the plan length $a\,b$.

Draw an indefinite line, $v\,w$ (Fig. 224), at the pitch of the straight rail, got by the pitchboard, cutting the springing lines in A and C and the central vertical line B a_1 in the point B; also through A draw the horizontal line A Y; then A B and B C are the real lengths of the two tangents, and B a_1 and B C their elevations.

Position of joints.—With respect to the joints, it may be observed that they should always be formed a few inches outside of the springings, and short shanks worked on the wreath piece; because if made just at the springing, the joint, not being plumb, but at right angles to the pitch, would bring that part of the straight rail below the centre of the lower joint, and that above the centre of the upper, into the cylinder. In the example, mark off A P and C Q, Fig. 224, equal to (say) 4 inches; through P and Q draw the joint lines perpendicular to the tangents.

Face mould.—With centre B and radius B A, Fig. 225, describe an arc cutting the line drawn through a_1 perpendicular to the tangent B C in the point A_1. Join A_1 B and produce it to P_1, making $A_1 P_1$ equal to A P on the development, and through P_1 draw the joint line at right angles to it. The other joint line at Q being already drawn, the face mould, as far as the tangents and joints are concerned, is now determined.

Next, through the points A_1 and C draw the springing lines A_1 O and C O parallel respectively to their opposite tangents B C and B A_1, intersecting each other at O, which point is the centre of the ellipse.

Join B O and produce it as shown, then B O is the line of the minor axis of the ellipse, and a second line drawn at right angles to it through O will give the line of the major axis. With O as centre and radius equal to that of the centre line, $a m c$, in plan, draw an arc, H m N, cutting the line of the minor axis in m, and on each side of m set off m 1 and m 2 equal to half the width of the rail; then O 1 and O 2 are respectively the semi-minor axes of the outer and inner ellipses of the face mould. We have now to find the width of the mould on one of the springings, and this may be done by joining m C and drawing parallels to it through 1 and 2, cutting the springing in the points 3 and 4, which gives the width 3 4 required. From the two tangents being of equal pitch, the two halves of the mould are exactly alike, so that the width 3 4 can be set off on the other springing, and the shanks then drawn at both ends parallel to the tangents as shown.

To be able to describe the two ellipses forming the edges of the mould we have to find the lengths of their semi-major axes. With centres 3 and 4, Fig. 225, and radii equal to O 1 and O 2, the semi-minor axes cut the line of the major axis at the points 5 and 6 respectively. Join 3 5 and 4 6, and produce them to meet the minor axis at 7 and 8. Then 3 7 and 4 8 are the lengths of the semi-major axes required, and the curves to

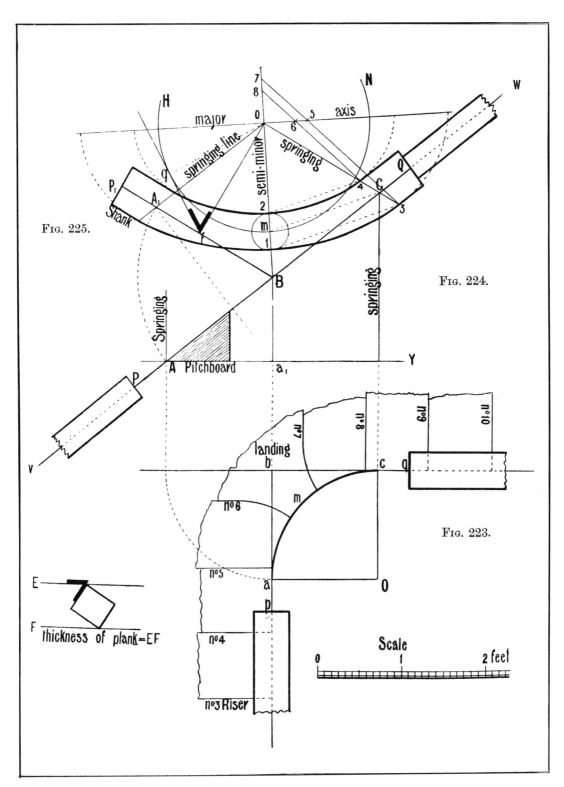

FIG. 225.

FIG. 224.

FIG. 223.

QUARTER-CIRCLE WREATH (LANDING IN QUARTER SPACE).

C C

complete the face mould may now be drawn, either by the trammel or
by a string.   (See Appendix, Problems 13 and 18.)

In Fig. 226 the lines of the face mould are shown transferred to a
thin board from which the mould is supposed to be cut, the edge of the
board representing the line of the major axis. In order to guide the end

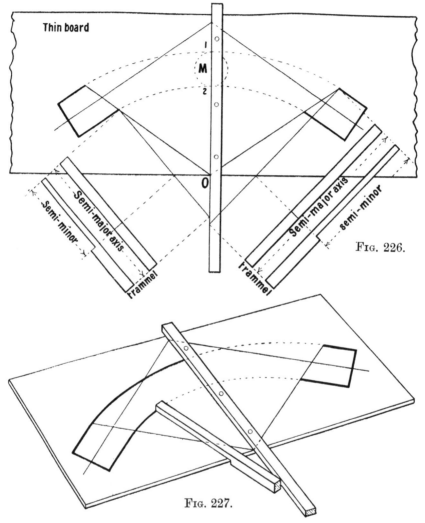

Fig. 226.

Fig. 227.

of the trammel along the line of the minor axis a small straightedge is
fastened temporarily to the board, with its edge coinciding with the axis
line O M. An isometric view of the same is given by Fig. 227, which shows
one of the trammels as it would be used in drawing the ellipse for the
concave edge of the mould. In drawing the curves of the other half of
the mould the straightedge has of course to be shifted to the left-hand
side of the line of the minor axis O M.

Twist bevels.—The method shown for determining these bevels on the face-mould diagram the student will find both simple and easily remembered, and is the one adopted in the most of our illustrations. The method has been already illustrated in the diagrams of the twelve cases, Figs. 218 and 219.

From O, the centre of the ellipse (Fig. 225), draw Of perpendicular to the tangent A_1 B, and from f draw a line touching the auxiliary circle H m N at q, then Ofq is the bevel for the joint at P_1, the lower end of the wreath.

The bevel for the upper joint would be found in precisely the same way—by drawing a perpendicular through O to the upper tangent B C; but in this case, the tangents being of equal pitch, the one bevel serves for both ends of the wreath. Several other methods for determining the twist bevel are given in the previous chapter, and the principles upon which any construction depends there stated.

Thickness of plank.— The next step, when the twist bevel has been found, is to ascertain the thickness of plank required. An approximation to this is given by the diameter of the circle circumscribing the section of the moulded rail. Fig. 228 shows how to find the minimum thickness of plank, and also the thickness required for the complete squared wreath.

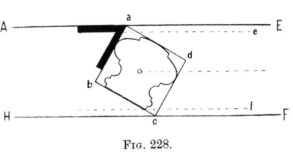

FIG. 228.

Take the section of the moulded rail (Fig. 228), and draw its circumscribing rectangle, $a\,b\,c\,d$, as shown, and through a draw A E, making an angle, A a b, equal to the twist bevel; then the distance between A E and a parallel, H F, to it, drawn through c is the thickness required for the squared wreath with its arrises complete. The minimum thickness would be the distance, ef, between the two dotted lines.

For a beginner it is better to use the thickness of plank required to take out the squared wreath, otherwise he would experience difficulty in getting it properly squared and moulded. After making a few wreaths he will be able to work with a somewhat less thickness of plank, having small corners awanting on the squared wreath. It is not advisable even for experienced handrailers to work a wreath out of the minimum thickness, as the saving in material may not compensate for the extra labour required in moulding it, and the finished rail is not likely to prove so satisfactory a job as when some additional thickness beyond the minimum is allowed.

DIRECTIONS FOR CARRYING OUT THE PRACTICAL BENCH WORK IN CONNECTION WITH A WREATH.—Figs. 229 to 236 illustrate in eight successive stages the formation of a wreath from the rough plank to the condition of being accurately squared and ready for moulding.

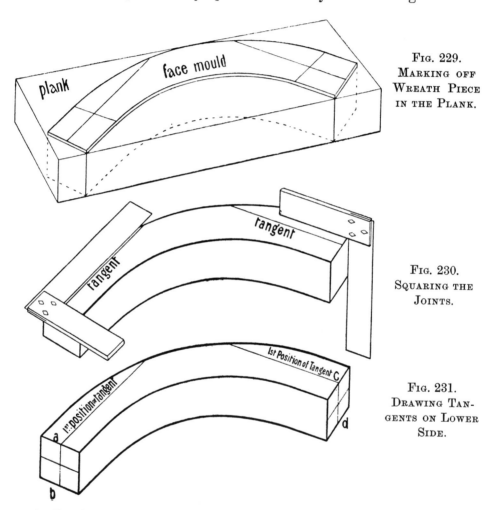

FIG. 229. MARKING OFF WREATH PIECE IN THE PLANK.

FIG. 230. SQUARING THE JOINTS.

FIG. 231. DRAWING TANGENTS ON LOWER SIDE.

1. Cutting the wreath out of the plank.—Apply the face mould to the plank as shown by Fig. 229, and mark out all round. Cut it out with a " band saw " square to the face of the plank, leaving the lines a little full at the middle or minor axis, where there is no twist, and, if it is required to take out the full squared rail, gradually increasing this width towards the springings. The width of stuff at the latter sections is obtained in the same way as the thickness of the plank; thus, in the present case the width is the distance between two vertical lines drawn through *b* and *d*, Fig. 228, which is also shown clearly on the ends of the wreath piece, Fig. 234.

2. **Forming the joints.**—Plane the upper side of the wreath piece out of winding, and it will be better also to have it taken to a uniform thickness. This can of course be done by "planing machines" in shops where they are available.

Lay the face mould again on to the *upper side* of the piece and in the same position as before. Mark the joints accurately to the mould with a cutting knife, and copy at the same time the two tangents on to the face of the piece. Cut the joints accurately to the lines and strictly square to the face of the piece, testing at the same time whether they are also at right angles to the tangents by applying the stock of the square to the joint and the blade in the direction of the tangent, as shown to the left in Fig. 230. When the joints have been completed the tangents should be drawn on the *under side* in exactly the same position as those on the upper surface, this being ensured by squaring down a line on each joint from the extremities of the face tangents, as *a b* and *c d*, Fig. 231, and then drawing through the points *b* and *d* square to the joints.

3. **Application of bevels.**—The twist bevel has now to be applied in the manner shown by Fig. 232, and a line drawn through the centre of each joint. The centre of the joint represents the intersection of the imaginary *centre line of plank* with the *joint plane*, and is of course the middle point of the thickness of the stuff on the line *a b* or *c d*, Fig. 231. The student should carefully note that the twist bevels are applied with the stock on the face or upper surface of the wreath piece, and also that for the upper joint the stock is always towards the well, and for the lower joint in the opposite direction. This he will be able to verify by holding up the wreath with the tangents at about their required pitch, when, if the bevel stock has been rightly applied, the bevel lines should lie in vertical planes at right angles to the joint planes, since they are the intersections of the vertical planes containing the tangent with the joint planes.

4. **New positions of the tangents.**—In order to draw the lines on the stuff for cutting the sides of the wreath to the cylindric form, the face mould has to be laid upon it in new positions, which are determined by drawing another pair of tangents on each side of the wreath piece from the extremities of the bevel lines on the joints and parallel to the tangents first drawn. In Fig. 233 the full lines *e g* and *m n* represent the new tangents on the face side drawn parallel to the old ones, which

latter are here shown by the dotted lines *a f* and *c h*, and which, to avoid mistakes, may now be erased, as they are of no further use.

Care should be taken by the operator to draw the new tangents strictly parallel to the old ones, which should be done by marking off the distance *f g* equal to *a e* by means of a pair of compasses. This will prove a safer method than that of drawing them with a square applied to the butt joint.

It should be here observed, that at either end of the wreath the two *new tangents* (the one on the upper, the other on the under side of the plank) and the *bevel line* drawn on the corresponding joint *lie in the same plane*, which becomes a vertical plane when the wreath is set up to its proper pitch. This plane contains also the imaginary tangent to the " centre line of plank," and is the tangent plane to the cylindric surface containing the centre line of rail.

The above observations may be otherwise expressed thus: The vertical planes containing the tangents to the centre line of rail cut the joints in the bevel lines drawn across them, and their intersections with the upper and under sides of the plank are the tangents in their new positions. The student may therefore distinguish three so-called tangents, in connection with each joint, parallel to one another and in the same vertical plane, one on each surface of the plank, and one imaginary lying exactly midway between the other two and passing through the centre of the joint, being the one that is used in drawing the face mould.

5. **Application of the face mould.**—This is illustrated by Fig. 234. Lay the mould on the upper side of the wreath piece, so that the tangents on the former may stand over the new tangents drawn on the latter. This is easily done by first reconciling (say) the upper tangent on the mould with that on the stuff, and then sliding the mould along, still maintaining these lines in agreement till the lower tangents also coincide.

As the tangents on the stuff are for the most part hidden by the mould, for easy adjustment, one or two holes may be bored in the latter in order that some parts of the lines under it may be seen.

When the mould has been accurately placed in the position indicated, the upper side of the wreath is marked out to it, and the springing lines, as well as the level line representing the minor axis, also transferred to the stuff.

The mould is then applied to the under side in precisely the same manner, and the same lines marked on it also.

The piece is now properly lined off for wreathing.

6. **Taking the wreath to a width.**—For this purpose secure the piece in the bench vice in a convenient position, with, first, the concave

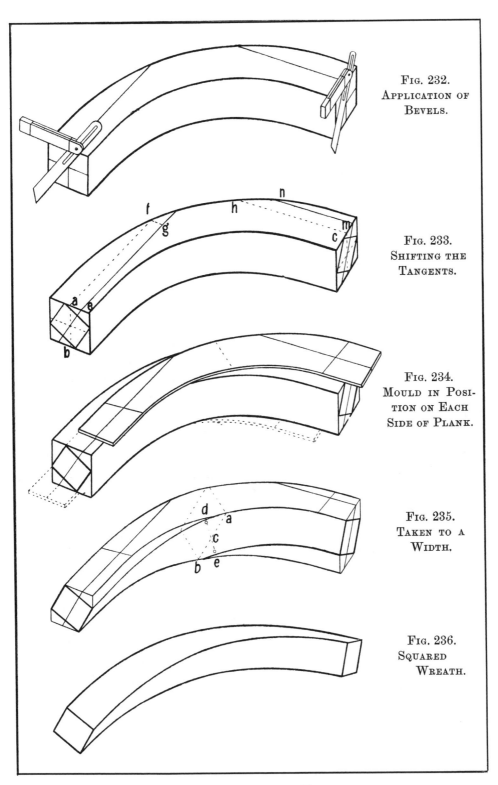

FIG. 232.
APPLICATION OF
BEVELS.

FIG. 233.
SHIFTING THE
TANGENTS.

FIG. 234.
MOULD IN POSI-
TION ON EACH
SIDE OF PLANK.

FIG. 235.
TAKEN TO A
WIDTH.

FIG. 236.
SQUARED
WREATH.

FORMING THE SQUARED WREATH.

side uppermost, and cut away the superfluous wood down to the lines, working *not square* across the piece, but everywhere as near as possible *parallel to the axis of the cylinder*, that is, parallel to lines joining points on one side to their corresponding points on the other; for example, from one springing line to the corresponding one on the other side. The material is roughly cleared away by means of gouges or with a stiff bow saw, and finished to the lines with a compass plane, which should fit the concave side of the wreath in plan, testing at the same time the surface by a straightedge applied parallel to such lines throughout the length of the wreath as we have indicated.

The piece is then turned over and the convex side cut to the lines in the same manner, and finished with an ordinary smoothing plane.

It will be seen in Fig. 234 that the mould, owing to the piece being cut square out of the plank, projects at some parts, and for this reason it is necessary to sprig it temporarily in its position on the surface of the plank to take the place of the absent lines in guiding the cutting. As fallen wood gives trouble to beginners, they will find it advantageous to use two moulds, one sprigged on to each face, to supply the lines that are awanting, clearing away the projecting material between them so that the surface will agree at every part with a straightedge applied from mould to mould in the specified direction.

The wreath will now be in the condition shown by Fig. 235, and if held up into position its sides would accurately fit their corresponding cylinders, and is ready to be taken to the proper thickness.

7. **Taking the wreath to its thickness.**—It is not usual in the square-cut method to draw definite and continuous lines on the wreath for forming its upper and under surfaces. Of course a falling mould could be made and applied to the convex side, as was the practice in the oblique-cut method, but for a wreath of ordinary length it would prove almost superfluous, as these surfaces, with a little experience, can be made sufficiently accurate for all practical purposes from the guidance obtained by the definite sections at the joints and springings, and also at the minor axis. We would not, however, advocate dispensing entirely with falling moulds without putting something in their place, as in forming long wreaths there is unavoidably, even to those of wide experience, a certain amount of indefiniteness and guess-work, unless some intermediate points on the arrises are found to serve as guidance.

Reverting to Fig. 235, find c, the middle point of the plumb line ab at the minor axis, and through c draw de square off the face of the piece. Mark off on this line from c the distances cd and ce equal to half the thickness of the rail; the points c and d (shown by small circles) are on the arrises of the wreath, and similar points being found on the convex side, the four points determine the square section of the rail at that part.

Begin by working off the superfluous wood from the shanks nearly up to the springings, and next at the middle section; then work from the latter towards the ends, making the surfaces gradually twist into those of the shanks, taking care that the arrises are made into *fair lines*.

This being roughly accomplished for both upper and under sides, the wreath should be bolted to the straight rails, the "bye-wood" cleared off at the joints, and any irregularities that appear on its upper surface, when viewed in connection with the straight rails, eased off. The wreath should then be unscrewed, and the under side completed to lines obtained by gauging off the upper side, and it will then have the appearance presented by Fig. 236, the piece being now ready for moulding.

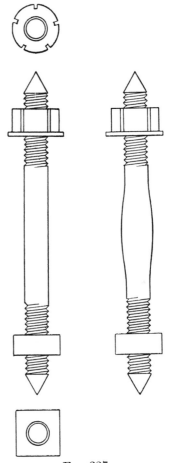

Joint fastenings.—Two kinds of bolts are in use for handrail joints. These are illustrated by Fig. 237, the swelled form being preferable, as this can be made tight in its hole at the joint. With respect to the position of the bolts, they will naturally be placed in the centre of the section; but to keep up as far as possible the strength of the rail, it may be placed a little nearer the under side, as in Fig. 240, so that the holes for the nuts will not have to be cut so deep in the rails as when the bolt holes are in the centre.

FIG. 237.

The bolt should be always accompanied by two or more dowels from $\frac{5}{16}$ inch to $\frac{3}{8}$ inch or larger, according to the size of the rail. These add strength to the joint and keep off the bye-wood.

Marking the joints.—The centres of the holes for the reception of the bolts and dowels are first carefully marked on a thin section of the rail or on a template, which is then applied to the joints, and the centres pricked through on to the stuff.

The same template may be conveniently used for marking the outline of the moulded rail on those joints which connect the wreath with the straight rail. On the other hand, in the case of joints between two wreath pieces the squared-up section will not in general be quite rectangular when eased into each other, as described in a previous paragraph, so that the moulded section will be correspondingly distorted, and cannot be marked out accurately with the template. This observation would not apply to wreaths squared up on the system by normal sections (see Chapters XVIII and XIX), as by definition the template would accurately apply at all joints and sections throughout the wreath.

Moulding the wreath.— In working the moulding on a wreath piece, square rebates should be first made in some such way as illustrated by Fig. 240. These will be advantageously sunk at the flat lists of the mouldings when they occur as in the sketch. When this has been accurately done, the curved portions of the moulding are worked out roughly with *gouges, chisels,* etc., and then finished with small *thumb planes, rounds* and *hollows,* etc., made purposely. *Saw gauges* and *routers* may also in some cases be profitably employed.

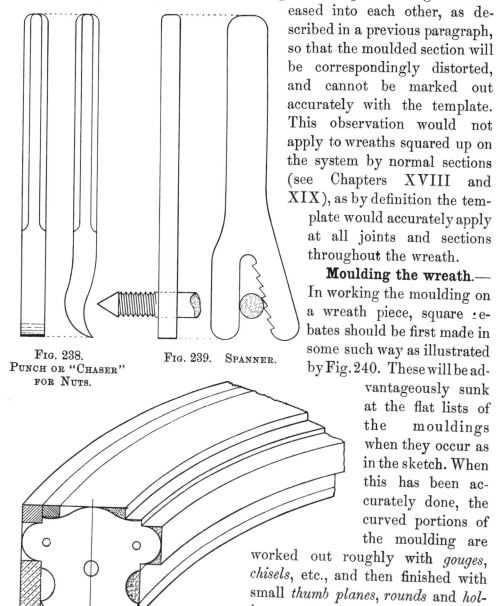

FIG. 238.
PUNCH OR "CHASER"
FOR NUTS.

FIG. 239.   SPANNER.

FIG. 240.

Much experience and taste is required to properly mould and finish a wreath, and this is only possible of attainment when the preliminary rebates and sinkings have been accurately made.

CHAPTER XV

THE student will be supposed to have thoroughly mastered the previous example, as in this and the following illustrations, to avoid repetition, only such additional remarks will be made as may appear to be necessary to elucidate the variations in construction which occur in the different cases.

In all the illustrations, as far as possible, the same letters have been used to denote similar points, lines, etc., and this it is hoped may assist the student in following out the constructions in the diagrams.

Development of tangents (Fig. 242).—In the case before us the number and arrangement of the risers, as shown in plan (Fig. 241), are such that, unlike the previous example, the centre lines of the two straight rails *do not* meet when produced, or in other words these lines do not lie in one plane. This difficulty is met by altering the pitch of a part of one or both straight rails at their junction with the wreath, so as to make the centre lines thus altered in direction meet when produced and form, as before, the tangents to the wreath. The change of pitch is of course made gradually in a curved line, and is referred to as an *easing* in the straight rail.

Before these easings can be arranged and the tangents determined, a development of the sections of the steps made by the tangent planes should be drawn. This is shown in Fig. 242, and in the workshop is generally drawn on a board by means of a steel square, in the same way as already described for setting out a stair string.

In the diagram for the section of steps made by the plane of the upper tangent the faces of the risers 7, 8, 9, etc., are obtained by projecting them up from the points 7, 8, 9, etc., where they intersect the tangent and centre line of straight rail in plan. For the section of steps by the plane of the lower tangent the faces of the risers are obtained by drawing the vertical lines 6, 5, 4, etc., at their proper distances from the centre line, B b, given by the distances of the points 6, 5, 4, etc., from the point b in plan. The horizontal lines representing the treads may then be drawn, commencing, for example, at the lower step, and marking off the height of the next riser, and so on till the line of the upper tread is reached.

Draw a portion of the straight rail at each end resting on the fliers, 2, 3, and 10, 11, as shown, and also their centre lines W Q and V u.

It has now to be settled whether easing should be made at one or at both joints. *It is better, if possible, to dispense with an easing at the top joint,* as this may not only save a little work and material, but may also, in some cases, conduce to a better appearance of the rail as a whole. But obviously when this course is adopted the easing at the bottom is accentuated, and care has to be taken that this does not become a defect; and further, that the rail is not by this means raised too high above the steps towards the middle of the wreath.

In the example in question the easing is formed *at the lower joint only.*

Produce therefore W Q, the centre line of the upper rail, to cut the springing in C and the central line in B. This determines the upper tangent B C.

Next take a point, u, in the centre line of the lower straight rail about three-quarters the width of a tread from the lower springing, and join u B, cutting the former in A; then A B is the lower tangent.

Mark off suitable lengths of shanks, A P and C Q, and draw the joint lines at P and Q *square to the tangents.*

Easing.—To draw the easing curves, set off $u\,r$ equal to u P; the intersection of the perpendicular to the straight rail through r with the joint line produced gives the centre to strike the curves.

Face mould.—Through A draw the ground line X Y, and produce the upper tangent, C B, to meet it in the point X. The point A_1 may be found, as in Fig. 225, by drawing a perpendicular through a^1 to the upper tangent, intersecting the arc A A_1 in A_1, or by the construction shown in the figure, namely, by finding the real length of the chord A_1 C, which forms a triangle with the two tangents. This is done by setting off from Y the distance Y A_2, equal to the chord $a\,c$ in plan, and joining A_2 C; then using C as centre and C A_2 as radius, draw the arc A_2 A, cutting the arc A A_1 in A_1, and join A_1 B.

The centre, O, of the ellipse is found as before, by drawing the springing lines parallel to the opposite tangents.

By joining X A_1 a level line is obtained on the plane of the mould, and a parallel to it through O is the line of the minor axis. A line at

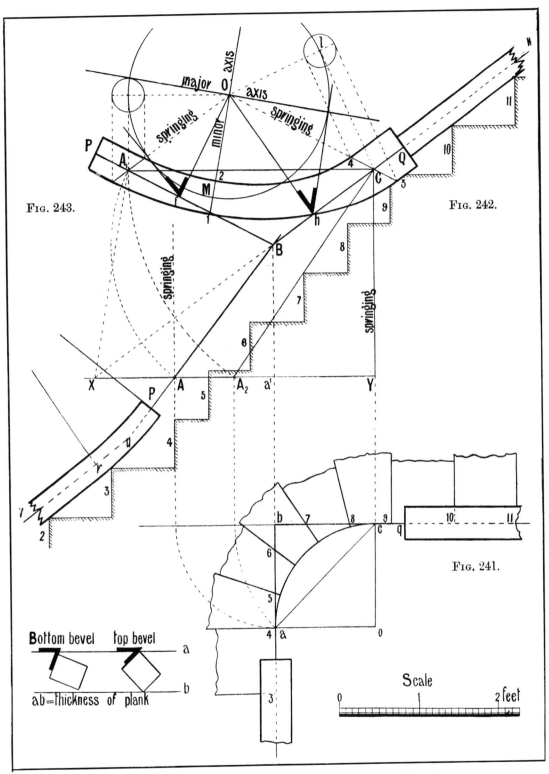

FIG. 243.

FIG. 242.

FIG. 241.

Bottom bevel   top bevel
ab=Thickness of plank

Scale
0   2 feet

QUARTER-CIRCLE WREATH (WINDERS IN QUARTER SPACE).

right angles to the latter through O is of course the line of the major axis.

The only other point we have to notice in connection with the face mould is the method shown of obtaining its *breadth* on the springing lines. Taking, for example, the upper springing; from C draw a line, C *l*, touching the auxiliary circle at *l*, and with *l* as centre strike the small circle with its diameter equal to the width of the rail, then draw the two lines as shown parallel to C *l*, cutting the springing line in the points 3 and 4, which gives the width required.

The twist bevel for each joint is found exactly as shown in the last example (Fig. 225), that is, by drawing lines to touch the auxiliary circle from the feet of the perpendiculars let fall from O on to the joint tangents.

Wreath for Plan less than Quarter Circle, with Winders at the Turn (Straight Flights above and below).

In Figs. 244 to 248 are illustrated two methods of obtaining the face mould and bevels for this case, in which the tangents are of unequal pitches, and their plans form an obtuse angle with each other, the most general position of tangents that can occur. The reader should compare this practical example with that illustrated in theoretical handrailing, Fig. 209.

The plan.—Fig. 244 shows the tangents *a b* and *b c* drawn to the centre line of rail at *a* and *c*, *o* the centre of the plan circle, and *o a* and *o c* the two radii at the springings.

Development.—Fig. 245 shows the development of the steps, together with the tangents and springing lines as in the last example (Fig. 242), the only easing required being, as in the preceding case, formed on the lower straight rail.

Face mould.—Fig. 246 shows the mould obtained, as in the previous examples, by the rotation of its plane about the line of the upper tangent, but from the altered conditions some points in the construction require explanation.

The tangent A_1 B is got into its position on the mould by finding the true length of the chord *a c*, as in Fig. 242, and by joining A_1 X the level line, to which the minor axis is parallel, is obtained. Since the springing lines are not in this case parallel to the opposite tangents these lines cannot be employed for finding the centre of the ellipse, and therefore another construction has to be adopted for determining this point.

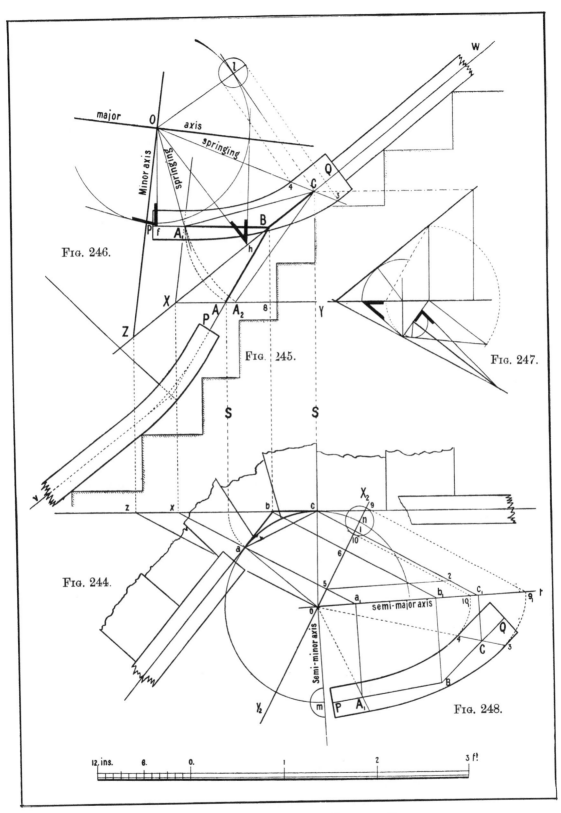

FIG. 246.

FIG. 245.

FIG. 247.

FIG. 244.

FIG. 248.

WREATH FOR PLAN LESS THAN QUARTER CIRCLE.

To find the centre of the ellipse.—From X, Fig. 246, let fall the projector X x on to the plan, cb, of the upper tangent produced, cutting it in x, and join ax, then ax is the direction of the plans of level lines on the plane of the mould, and therefore parallel to the plan of the minor axis. Through o therefore, Fig. 244, draw the plan of the minor axis parallel to ax, and produce it to meet the plan, cb, of the upper tangent produced in z. Draw the projector zZ intersecting the upper tangent produced in Z, and through Z draw Z O parallel to X A_1, making Z O equal to the line zo in the plan; then O is the centre of the ellipse, and O Z the line of the minor axis. A line drawn through O at right angles to O Z is the line of the major axis.

To the geometrical student other methods will readily suggest themselves for finding in this case the centre of the ellipse.

By joining O A_1 and O C the springing lines are obtained, and for the remaining part of the construction for completing the mould, as well as that for finding the bevels, the reader is referred to the previous illustrations.

Face mould by another construction.—The method we have been describing, and have generally adopted in our illustrations, of obtaining the face mould by folding its plane about the upper tangent will be found very convenient of application in all cases; but when the tangents are *not at right angles to each other in plan*, as in the case before us, some appearance of complexity, unless the principles are well understood, is given to the diagram by the construction for finding the centre of the ellipse, and the other method, shown in the same diagram, Fig. 248, may seem to the student to be the simpler of the two. Both methods, however, are merely variations of the same geometrical problem, the projections being made only on different ground lines. The construction has been explained along with the others in the chapters on " Theoretical Handrailing " (see Figs. 207 and 211).

The development of the tangents being obtained (Fig. 245), commence by drawing a level line, X Y, through A. Transfer the distance X 8, Fig. 246, to the plan, Fig. 244, at bx, and join xa, then xa is the trace of the oblique plane at the level X Y, and gives the direction of the plans of level lines on the plane of the mould.

Through o (the centre of the plan circle) draw the new ground line X_2Y_2 at right angles to the trace xa. Produce xa to meet X_2Y_2 in the point 5, and draw the lines b 6, c 1, parallel to it. Set up the height 1 2, equal to Y C, Fig. 245, and join 5 2, which gives with X_2Y_2 the pitch of the plank, *i.e.*, the inclination of the plane to the horizontal. The mould might then be constructed on the line 5 2, but in this case it will be better to do so on the line $o\,9_1$, drawn parallel to 5 2, through o. Then $o\,9_1$ will be the line of the major axis, and $o\,m$ drawn at right angles to it the semi-minor.

To obtain the tangents, joints, etc., on the mould diagram, Fig. 248, let $a_1\,b_1\,c_1$ be the points where the projectors from 5, 6, and 1 cut $o\,9_1$. Draw the ordinates $a_1\,A_1$, $b_1\,B$, $c_1\,C$ at right angles to $o\,9_1$, making them respectively equal to the level ordinates $5\,a$, $6\,b$, and $1\,c$ in plan. Join $A_1\,B$ and $B\,C$, and produce them making the shanks $A_1\,P$ and $C\,Q$ equal to their lengths in the development, Fig. 245. Draw the joint lines through P and Q at right angles to the tangents, and draw also the springing lines $O\,A_1$ and $O\,C$. The width at either of the springings can be obtained as in Fig. 246, and the mould drawn as before. Or otherwise the lengths $o\,9_1$ and $o\,10_1$ of the semi-major axes of the curves may be determined, as here shown, Fig. 248, by marking off half the width of the rail on the ground line $X_2\,Y_2$ on each side of n, and drawing the projectors $9\,9_1$ and $10\,10_1$ shown by dotted lines.

Bevels.—Fig. 247 is a supplementary diagram showing how the twist bevels are most usually obtained. The principles involved in the construction have been fully explained in Chapter XIII (see Fig. 216). To follow out the diagram the student has only to remember that the twist bevel for any joint, normal to the tangent, is simply the dihedral angle that the oblique plane, *i.e.*, the plane of the plank, makes with the vertical plane containing the tangent to the joint in question.

HANDRAIL OVER QUARTER-CIRCLE PLAN, WITH LANDING IN QUARTER SPACE (WREATH IN TWO PIECES).

Arrangement of risers.—The risers about the well in our first example, Fig. 223, were so placed that the centre lines of the straight rails when produced would meet, and therefore lie in the same plane, an arrangement which, though it results in a simple set of lines, is not conducive to a good appearance of the wreath on its concave side when the rail is wide and the radius of the well small.

In such cases the risers may be arranged as in Fig. 249, in which the widths of the steps and landing are made equal on the plan line of the concave side of the rail. This results in making the falling line of that side of the rail when developed a straight line throughout, and the centre lines of the straight rails would not meet when produced.

Advantages and disadvantages of forming such a wreath in two pieces.—If the wreath is to conform closely to this falling line it obviously precludes any easings from being formed on the straight rails, and therefore the preceding methods would not be admissible. One of two courses may then be adopted: either (1) to make the wreath in *one* piece and form its own easings, *i.e.*, causing the centre line of rail to deviate from centre line of plank; or, (2) to form the wreath in *two* pieces with a joint in the middle of the quarter.

The former method introduces some complexity, and will be taken up later on (see Chapter XVII).

The latter course is the one adopted in the diagram, and is the more economical of the two, but has one objection, that unless long shanks are formed the rail presents a somewhat patchy appearance, the three joints being so close together.

By making the wreath in *two pieces* we are enabled to get each half into a plane containing the corresponding straight rail, and further, the shortness of each wreathed portion causes the centre line of the plank to deviate very little from the desired falling line.

Cross tangent.—To effect this a *third tangent* has to be introduced with its extremities resting on the centre lines of the two straight rails produced, and a joint made at right angles to it at the point of contact with the cylinder.

In Fig. 249 *b d* is the plan of the line referred to, touching the plan circle at *a*, and intersecting the other two tangents—which are the continuations of the centre lines of the straight rails—at the points *b* and *d*. Then *a d* and *d e* are the plans of the two tangents for the lower part of the wreath, and *a b* and *b c* those for the upper.

The development of the sections of the steps is shown in Fig. 250, the riser lines being set out as they occur on the tangents *c b*, *b d*, and *d e* in the plan. The vertical lines *e*, *d*, *a*, *b*, *c* (Fig. 250), representing the springings, etc., are drawn in position, the distances between them being the same as those between the points *e*, *d*, *a*, *b*, *c* in plan (Fig. 249).

Next, to obtain the tangents in their proper positions on this development, draw the portions of the straight rails resting on the fliers with their centre lines *v* P and *w* Q as shown, and produce them to meet the vertical lines *d* and *b* in the points E and B. Join E B, then A E, D E, and A B, B C, are the tangents for the lower and upper parts of the wreath respectively.

The construction lines of the face mould for the upper part of the wreath is shown in Fig. 250, being copied and the mould completed in

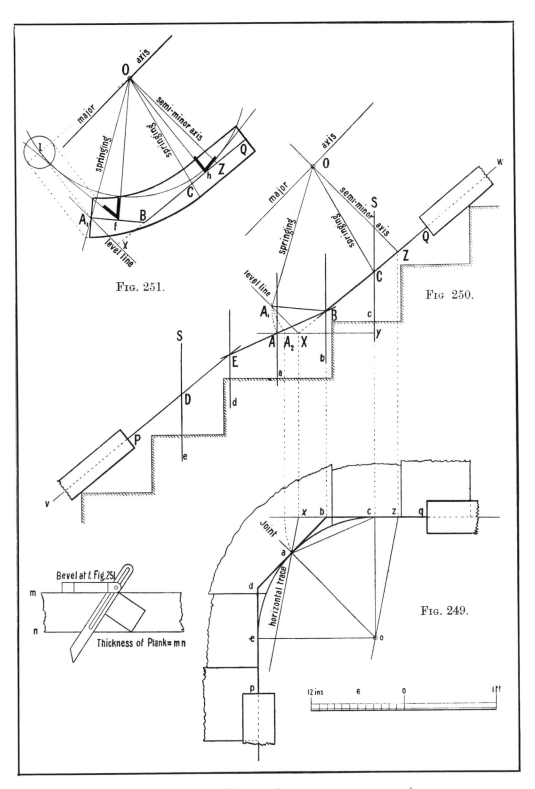

Fig. 251.

Fig 250.

Fig. 249.

Bevel at f. Fig.251.

Thickness of Plank = mn

12 ins   6   0   1 ft

QUARTER-CIRCLE WREATH (FORMED IN TWO PIECES).

Fig. 251. The method in no way differs from that of the last example, only, as some of the lines fall in different positions, it will be as well here to follow out the main points in the diagram.

The horizontal line, A Y, is first drawn through A, Fig. 250, then Y A$_2$ is set off equal to the length of the chord $a c$ in plan, Fig. 249. With B and C as centres, and radii B A and C A$_2$ respectively, draw the arcs intersecting at A$_1$, and join A$_1$ B, which gives the tangent A$_1$ B in position on the plane of the mould. There being no shank at this end, the joint line is drawn through A$_1$, Fig. 251, at right angles to the tangent A$_1$ B. The joint at the other end is placed so as to give a good long shank, C Q, to avoid the patchy appearance referred to above.

Produce the upper tangent C B, Fig. 250, to meet A Y in X, then X A$_1$ is a level line on the mould, and the minor axis is, of course, parallel to this line.

To find the centre of the ellipse, let fall the projector X x, and join $x\,a$, Fig. 249, which is the plan of a level line, and $o\,z$ drawn parallel to it is the plan of the minor axis. Draw the projector z Z, and through Z draw Z O, Fig. 250, parallel to X A$_1$, making it equal to $z\,o$ in the plan, Fig. 249. This gives O the centre of the ellipse and O Z the semi-minor axis. The major axis is of course at right angles to the latter. The rest of the construction for completing the face mould, Fig. 251, will not require any explanation, and the usual method for obtaining the bevels is shown in the same figure.

From the equality of the pitches of the corresponding tangents and the symmetry of the arrangements in plan it will be at once seen that the two halves of the wreath are identical, and therefore that the same mould and bevels will answer for both ends.

CONSTRUCTION OF WREATHS FOR SEMICIRCULAR PLANS.

I. SMALL WELL (STRAIGHT FLIGHTS OF EQUAL PITCH).

Plan (Fig. 255).—We have here our first example of a rail over a plan which is an exact semicircle. The illustration is for a *ship's* stair, similar to that shown by Figs. 136-138, but the remarks are equally applicable to similar cases of house stairs.

As it would prove impracticable to take the whole wreathed rail out of one piece, it is usual to joint two quarter-circle wreaths together to make up the complete semicircle. We have already seen in the last

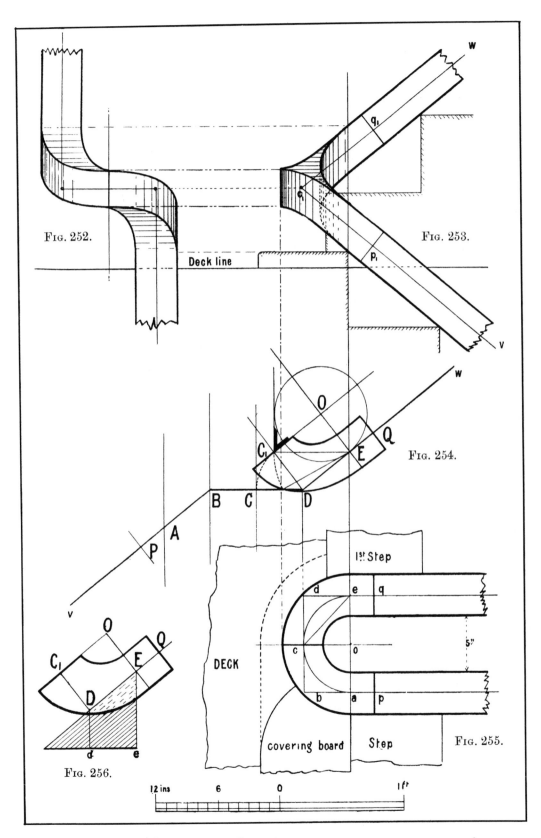

Fig. 252.

Fig. 253.

Deck line

Fig. 254.

O

Q

C₁

E

B   C   D

P A

v

O   Q

C₁   E

D

Fig. 256.

d   e

DECK

covering board   Step

1st Step

d   e   q

c   o

5″

b   a   p

Fig. 255.

12 ins   6   0   1 ft

Wreath for Semicircular Plan (straight flights of equal pitch).

example how to get out a wreath in two pieces, and a similar mode of procedure has to be adopted in the present case. In the plan, Fig. 255, the middle joint is shown at c, and $b\,d$, its corresponding tangent, laid across the other two tangents $a\,b$ and $e\,d$. The latter are simply continuations of the centre lines of the equally-pitched straight rails, which are in parallel vertical planes, but inclined in opposite directions.

The inclination of the cross tangent $b\,d$, Fig. 255, will depend on the position of the two flights of stairs with respect to the well, that is, on the position of the riser at *landing*, and the riser at *starting*. In the example before us these risers are arranged to make the cross tangent a level line, and thereby make the butt joint at c *plumb*, which so simplifies the whole construction that the lines for this pair of wreaths might be obtained from the pitchboard alone (see Cases I. and II., Fig. 218).

Position of risers.—We may now show how to answer the following question. *Given the radius of centre line of well and the pitch of the stairs, to determine the position of the risers so as to make the cross tangent a level one and to bring the rail to a specified height above the deck or floor.*

To do this, commence by drawing a side elevation of the centre lines of the straight rails as in Fig. 253, by squaring up a line from c in plan, and from any point c_1 on it, setting out the centre lines $c_1\,w$ and $c_1\,v$ with the pitchboard. Draw parallel lines on each side of them to represent the upper and under sides of the rail.

Next draw the deck line in such a position as will bring the rail to the specified height above it, usually a little higher than the height of the rail measured at the middle of the width of a flier. Mark off the thickness of the covering board, and where its upper side cuts the underside of the rail gives the position of the face of the top riser of lower flight. The riser starting for the upper flight is obtained by drawing a line parallel to the deck and at the height of a riser above it. This line represents the upper side of the first step, and where it intersects the under side of the rail is the position of the first riser. The positions of the risers are then obtained in the plan, Fig. 255, by squaring down from the elevation.

We have completed the side elevation, Fig. 253, and added another view in Fig. 252. These complete elevations, it should be remarked, though unnecessary for the purpose of getting out the moulds, etc., are introduced to give the beginner an idea of what should be the form of the wreath when squared and jointed up.

Face mould.—In Fig. 254 are shown the tangents unfolded in the usual way, and the general method of obtaining the face mould, as given in previous examples applied to this case. It will be found (1) that the tangents $C_1 D$ and $D E$ on the mould are at right angles; (2) that the twist bevel for the joint at C is the angle of the upper corner of the pitch board; (3) that the bevel at Q is a right angle, and therefore there is no twist at that end of the wreath; (4) that the semi-major and semi-minor axes are the same length respectively as the inclined and level tangents; and (5) that the mould embraces exactly one quadrant of an ellipse, the springing lines coinciding with the axes.

By knowing the above particulars the mould can be got out very quickly by the aid of the pitchboard, as shown in Fig. 256, the true length of the inclined tangent, $D E$, being the only particular that remains to be determined. This is found by marking off its plan length, $e d$, Fig. 255, along the lower edge of the pitchboard, as at $e d$, Fig. 256, and squaring up from d to the hypotenuse, $D E$ being then the true length required.

It need hardly be remarked that the lower wreath is the counterpart of the upper, so that one face mould serves for both.

II. SMALL WELL (STRAIGHT FLIGHTS OF UNEQUAL PITCHES).

Figs. 257-260 furnish another example of a wreath for a semicircular well, but, unlike the preceding case, the straight flights are of *unequal pitches*, and the risers arranged so as to give some *inclination to the cross tangent*.

This arrangement may be adopted when it is desirable to have the rail running on to the deck as short a distance as possible, which would be rendered necessary in situations where there is a narrow passage or landing at the stair head.

Suppose the radius of the well given, and the position of the lower stair fixed so as to bring the top riser well forward into the curve as shown. The section of the lower stair can then be drawn, and the rail resting on the arrises, as shown in Fig. 258. Square up from point c in plan a line to cut the centre line of lower straight rail, $v b_1$, in the point b_1, and mark off c_1 at the required height of the centre of rail above the deck line, making $c_1 d^1$ equal to $c_1 b_1$. Next draw $d^1 w$ at the pitch of the upper stair, and mark off on each side of it the upper and under sides of the straight rail.

The position of the upper stair with respect to the well can now be obtained, as in the last example, by drawing a line parallel to the deck at the height of a step above it; the intersection of this line with the under side of the upper rail gives the position of the first riser, which may then be drawn in plan by squaring down from the position just found in elevation.

On the other hand, it should be observed that the inclination of the cross tangent may be assumed instead of the position of the lower flight, so that the positions of both flights would have to be determined in the same manner as was shown in the last example, Figs. 253 and 255. Again, if the size of the well and the positions of both flights of stairs are fixed beforehand without reference to the rail (which is oftener the case than otherwise in ships), the cross tangent $b\,d$, when laid on to the centre lines of the straight rails, may make the joint c either too high or too low, so that the tangent $b\,d$ would have to be moved up or down accordingly, and "easings" formed either on the wreath itself or on the straight rails. This latter would require a development of the section of the steps on the lines of the tangents to be made, and the easings referred to arranged on one or both of the straight rails, in the same way as we have already shown for the quarter-circle wreath in Fig. 242.

Face moulds.—In the example the pitch of the lower stair is steeper than that of the upper, and consequently a separate face mould as well as bevels have to be found for each wreath. These are shown in Fig. 259. The lower mould being in a new position, its construction may require a word of explanation. The triangle $A\,B\,C_1$ is drawn, as in former illustrations, after having found the length of the chord $C_1\,A$, and the wreath being a quarter circle, the centre O of the ellipse is found by drawing springing lines through A and C_1 parallel to the opposite tangents. The semi-minor axis O M is drawn parallel to the level line $X\,C_1$, the latter being found by producing the lower tangent A B upwards, to cut the ground line through C at the point X, and joining $X\,C_1$.

It may be well to note that, in all cases where there is a joint in the curve, when taking the wreath to a thickness a little extra stuff should be left on at that joint, so that the twisted surfaces of the one part of the wreath may be eased into those of the other.

III. Construction of Wreath for a Semicircular Plan, Rail Rising from Level to Rake.

Plan.—Let Fig. 264 represent the suggested plan of the rail, $a\,c\,e$ its centre line. Draw the tangents $a\,b$, $b\,d$, $d\,e$, circumscribing the semicircle, the tangent $a\,b$ being the centre line of the level rail produced, and $e\,d$ that of the inclined rail. Assuming a small inclination for the cross tangent $b\,d$, we have to determine the position of the stair with respect to the well.

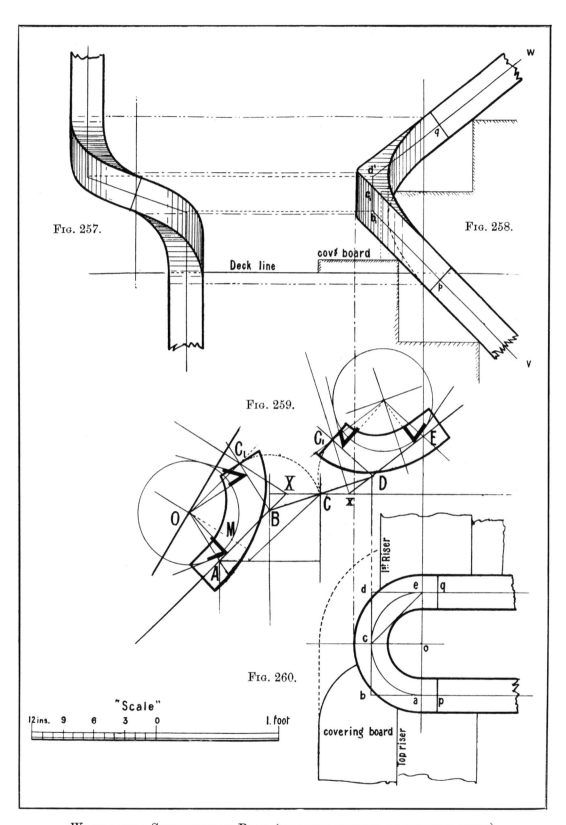

Fig. 257.

Fig. 258.

w

q

d'

c'

b'

cov⁵ board

Deck line

p

v

Fig. 259.

C₁

X

D

O

M

B

C

x

C₁

E

A

1⁵ᵗ Riser

d

e

q

c

o

b

a

p

Fig. 260.

"Scale"

12 ins. 9   6   3   0   1. foot

covering board

Top riser

WREATH FOR SEMICIRCULAR PLAN (STRAIGHT FLIGHTS OF UNEQUAL PITCH).

F F

Development of tangents.—Commence by drawing the floor line (Fig. 263) as shown, and set up the vertical lines a, b, c, d, e at the same distances apart as they are in the plan, Fig. 264.

Next draw a portion of the level rail so as to be a few inches higher than that on the rake measured at the middle of a tread, and produce its centre line v P, to cut the two vertical lines a and b at A and B. From the latter point draw the cross tangent B D at the assumed inclination, and through D draw the line D w at the pitch of the stair, cutting the springing at E. This completes the development, A B and B C being the tangents for the lower wreath, and C D and D E those of the upper.

To get the positions of risers: Produce the under side of the straight rail on the rake, as shown by the dotted line, Fig. 263; then the point T, where it cuts a horizontal line representing the upper surface of the first step, is the position of the first riser, which may then be squared down to obtain its position in the plan, Fig. 264.

If the position of the stair with respect to the well had been fixed beforehand, the inclination of the cross tangent could not of course be assumed, and an indiscriminate arrangement might result in even giving an inclination to it in the wrong direction, or, in other words, bringing the point D to a lower level than B, a thing to be avoided.

Face moulds.—These are shown in the detached diagrams, Figs. 261 and 262. Their construction should now present no difficulty, particularly that of the lower wreath, which represents the very simplest case that can occur. For the latter, since one of the tangents is horizontal, we have only to draw the rectangle A B C O, Fig. 262, with its sides equal to the tangents A B and B C in the development, Fig. 263; then O is the centre, O A and O C the semi-major and semi-minor axes respectively, of the central ellipse. Set off on each side of C half the width of the rail, then parallels to C A through 1 and 2, cutting A O in the points 3 and 4, give the width of the mould on each axis. This completes the data required to draw the mould. The twist bevel at C in this case becomes a right angle, and that at the other end is obtained by the general method, but could be taken from the pitch of the cross tangent B D, being the angle that it makes with the vertical lines, Fig. 263.

The upper mould, Fig. 261 is simply an illustration of the general case with unequally pitched tangents (see Figs. 242 and 243).

IV. Wreath for Large Semicircular Plan.

In Figs. 265-269 are shown the necessary lines for getting out the wreathed handrail round the well of the geometrical staircase illustrated by Figs. 104 and 105, Chapter VI.

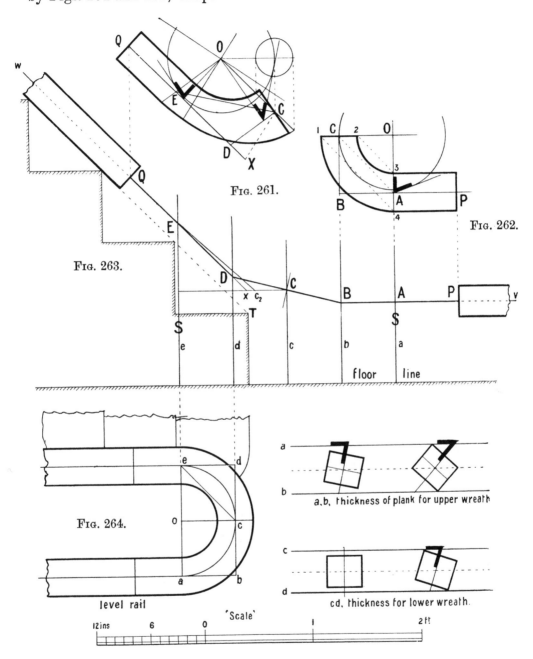

Fig. 261.

Fig. 262.

Fig. 263.

Fig. 264.

level rail

a.b, thickness of plank for upper wreath

cd, thickness for lower wreath.

floor line

'Scale'

12ins   6   0   1   2ft

For this case a development of the falling line, $v\,w$ (Fig. 267), is first drawn, taken along the centre line of handrail. The stretch out of the curve $a\,c\,e$, which is the same as $a\,c\,e$, Fig. 265, is obtained as was shown

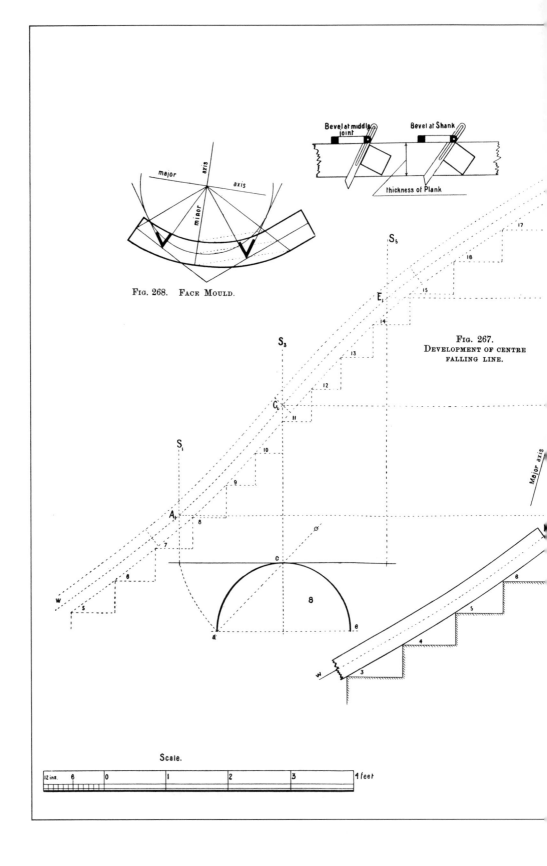

major axis

minor axis

axis

FIG. 268. FACE MOULD.

Bevel at middle joint

Bevel at Shank

thickness of Plank

S₅

E₁

FIG. 267.
DEVELOPMENT OF CENTRE
FALLING LINE.

17

16

15

14

13

S₃

12

11

C₁

10

S₁

9

A₁

8

ø

7

c

6

8

e

w

d

5

Major axis

6

5

4

w

3

Scale.

12 ins. 6 0 1 2 3 4 feet

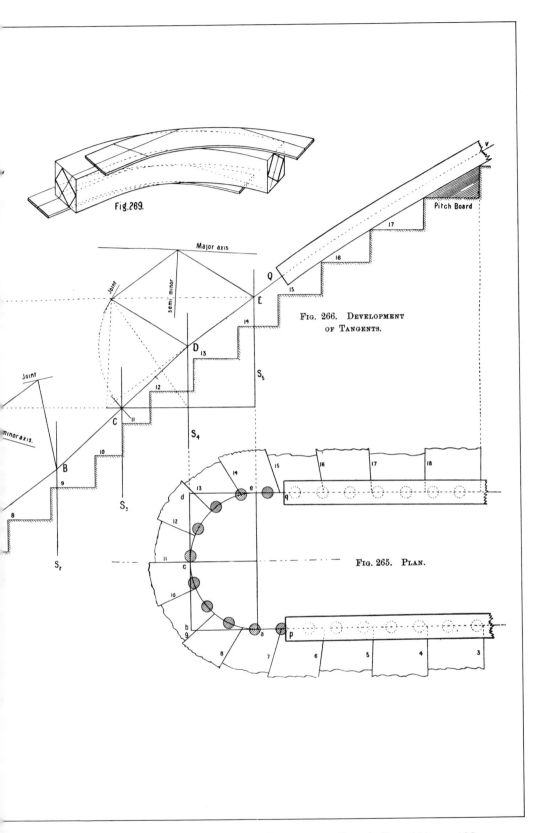

Fig. 269.

Major axis

Joint

semi minor

Joint

Q

E

D 13

C 11

B

9

8

minor axis.

S_2

S_3

S_4

S_5

Pitch Board

v

17

16

15

14

12

10

Fig. 266. Development
of Tangents.

Fig. 265. Plan.

18   17   16   15   14   13

d   e   q

c

b   a   p

12   11   10   9   8   7   6   5   4   3

WREATH OVER LARGE SEMICIRCULAR PLAN (FOR GEOMETRICAL STAIR), FIGS. 104 AND 105.

by Fig. 60, and is the horizontal distance between S_1 and S_5. The points A_1, C_1, and E_1, where this centre falling line intersects the two springings $S_1 S_5$, and the vertical line S_3 at the crown c of the semicircle, are levelled over to intersect the corresponding springings, etc., at A, C, and E, in the usual tangent development (Fig. 266).

The tangents are then arranged in the latter figure to pass through the points A, C, and E, making A B and D E touch the centre line, $v w$, at P and Q, where the joints are formed.

This insures the rail being at the proper height at the three principal points, A, C, and E.

The result of the plan arrangement of steps, which has been fully discussed in Chapter VI, is to make the two tangents A B and D E have the same pitch, so that one face mould will do for both wreaths.

Only the construction lines of the face mould are given in Fig. 266, the mould being shown completed in Fig. 268.

The isometric sketch, Fig. 269, shows the application of the mould to draw the lines on the two surfaces of the wreath piece, and another sketch to the left shows the bevels applied to determine the thickness of plank required.

CHAPTER XVI

THE plan of the example chosen to illustrate this case is given by Fig. 272. The wreath in question lies between the joints e and c, including a portion, ef, of the main rail, whose plan is part of a circle, and a quadrant, fc, of the small well, the wreath reaching the level at the joint c. To obtain this the tangent, dv, at the lower joint, e, has to reach the height of the level tangent, dcb, at the point d, which is the best arrangement for such a case, the positions of the steps and the well being so adjusted to each other as to produce this result.

This is a very good instance of the necessity of the stair and rail being arranged together if the best result is to be obtained.

Mould determined by level ordinates.—The plan of the wreath being made up of arcs of different circles, it is convenient to get out the mould by means of level ordinates.

Commence by drawing a ground line, xy, Figs. 271 and 272, at right angles to the level tangent, bd, and produce bd to cut the former in g. Also through e draw ee_1 parallel to bd. Set up a line, gd_1, at right angles to xy, making it equal to the difference in levels of the points e and d given by G D on the development (Fig. 270), and join e_1d_1, then e_1d_1 represents the pitch line of the plane of the mould. Next draw the level ordinates, 1, 2, 3, 4, etc., parallel to bd at convenient equal intervals apart, and produce them to meet the inclined line e_1d_1. Then from the points of intersection on e_1d_1, square out the ordinates $1_1, 2_1, 3_1 \ldots 9_1$, as shown, making them equal respectively to their corresponding lengths in plan; for example, taking the ordinate 6, mark off m_1n_1 and m_1p_1 equal to mn and mp in the plan. Mark off similarly all the other ordinates, and draw fair curves through the points thus obtained by means of a flexible batten. This gives the edges of the mould.

To obtain the joint lines on the mould, mark off on the ordinate 2_1 the distances d_1D_1 and d_1C_1 equal to gd and gc in the plan, and on

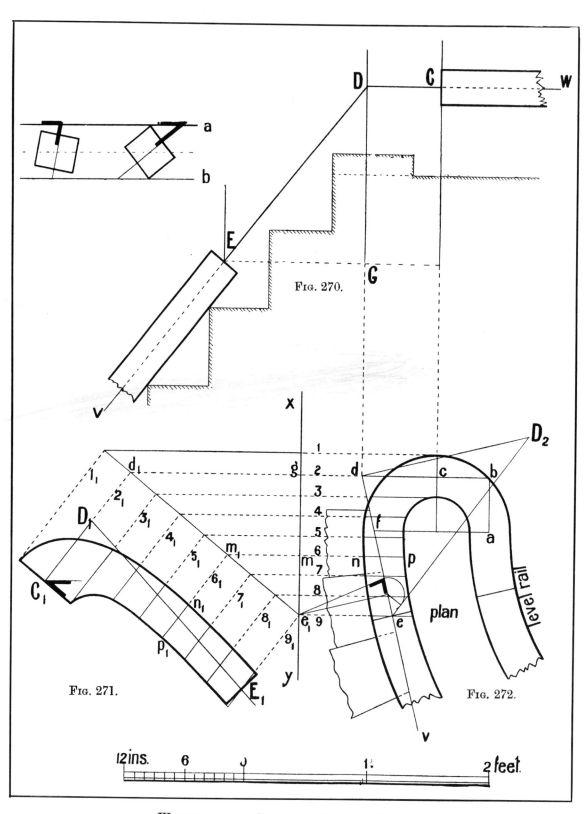

a

b

D   C   W

Fig. 270.

G

V

x

D₂

1₁   d₁   g   1   d   c   b
          2₁   2
          3₁   3
D₁   4₁   4   f
          5₁   m₁   5   a
          6₁   6
          n₁   7₁   7   m   n   p
C₁   8₁   8
                9₁   e₁   9   e   plan   level rail
          p₁
Fig. 271.   E₁   y   Fig. 272.

v

12 ins.   6   9   1'   2 feet.

WREATH AT THE TOP OF A CIRCULAR STAIR.

ordinate 9_1 the distance $e_1 E_1$ equal to $e\,e_1$. Join $E_1 D_1$, then $E_1 D_1$ and $D_1 C_1$ are the tangents, and lines through C_1 and E_1 at right angles to them respectively give the joint lines on the mould.

Bevels.—The twist bevel for the butt joint at c is given by $e_1 d_1 g$, that is, the angle that the pitch line makes with the vertical. This bevel is shown at C_1. The twist bevel at joint e is obtained as in Fig. 216.

WREATHED TERMINALS.

These are formed at the extremities of rails where they are made to turn into a wall or newel post, or in ships into a bulkhead.

The annexed Figs. 273 to 281, illustrate examples of these turns both for the top and bottom of a stair.

In the cases shown an *easing* is formed at one or both ends; or, in other words, the centre line of rail is made to deviate from the centre of plank, and this is the usual practice. They may also be got out as in Fig. 256, but are not so satisfactory in appearance as when carried farther on to the landing, and therefore a greater part of the rail on the level, as in the illustrations.

Commence by drawing the top steps, as shown in Fig. 273, and also a portion of the straight rail resting on them. Next draw the section of the rail, 1, 2, 3, e, at the proper height and distance on to the landing. In ships the bulkhead framing would be arranged so that the end of the rail might be firmly housed into the middle of a stile. Ease the section into the lines of the straight rail, and fix the position of the joint fg. Join ef, and draw a line parallel to it, touching the curve on the upper side of the rail. These lines represent the surfaces of the plank. From this elevation, the plan Fig. 274 is drawn, if required, showing its distance from the wall or bulkhead.

The construction of the face mould will be easily understood from the diagram, Fig. 273. The isometric sketches, Figs. 276 and 277, show how to apply the mould, as well as the bevels, to the piece. Fig. 273 shows how to obtain the terminal from the *least material*, but they are often got out as in Fig. 275, where the upper surface of the plank is made co-incident with that of the straight rail. This latter is a simpler method, and the mould and bevels may be got by the aid of the pitchboard only, as in Fig. 256. It requires a little more material than the method of Fig. 273, but gets the grain of the wood to run with that of the straight rail. Figs. 279 and 280 show the application of the bevels and face mould for this latter method.

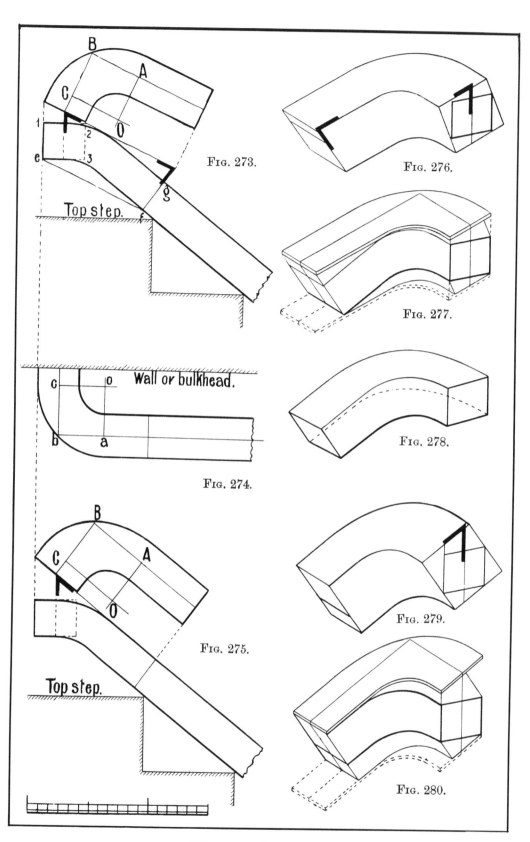

Fig. 273.

Fig. 276.

Fig. 277.

Top step.

Wall or bulkhead.

Fig. 274.

Fig. 278.

Fig. 275.

Fig. 279.

Top step.

Fig. 280.

WREATHED TERMINALS.

A terminal suitable for the lower end of a rail is shown in Fig. 281, which it will be seen is just a *top turn*, as in Fig. 273, inverted.

Scroll Terminals.

Remarks.—The lines of a scroll should be such that their curvature varies continuously from point to point, according to some regular law, and, therefore, no two successive elements of the curve can be drawn strictly from one centre. It follows that the geometrical methods given for drawing scrolls by means of *arcs of circles* can only give a more or less close approximation to a true spiral curve, as when this is done the changes of curvature take place only at a few definite points in the convolution instead of doing so at every point throughout its length.

For stair scrolls the usual method is to draw the curves in quadrants, so that the changes of curvature at the points where the circular arcs join is considerable, and can, in fact, be easily detected by a practised eye.

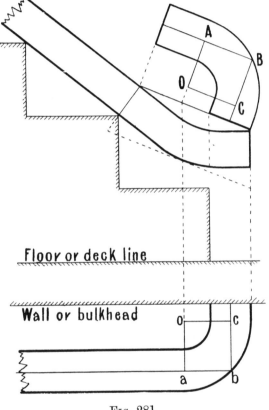

Fig. 281.

When scrolls are cut out in this manner the curves should be eased into one another at the points of changes of curvature, and especially at their junction with a straight rail. The best outline can be obtained by finding definite points on the true spiral, and tracing the curve through them by means of a tapering flexible batten, but this occasions too much trouble in the workshop for ordinary cases, which can be even very well drawn *freehand* without the aid of geometrical construction, and gives satisfactory results.

1. **To describe a handrail scroll when its extreme width is given.**—This is shown by Figs. 282 and 283. Divide the given width A Y into

G G

11 equal parts, numbering them 1, 2, 3, etc., from A, and using point 6 as
the first centre, draw the first quadrant A B. The radius of the quadrant
B C is equal to 5 divisions of the width A Y, which, being set off along
B 6 from the point B, gives the required centre, r.

The radius for the third quadrant C D is a third proportional to the
two preceding radii; and again, the radius of the fourth quadrant is a

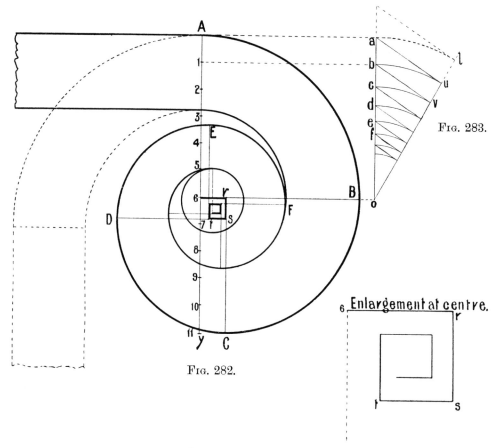

FIG. 283.

Enlargement at centre.

FIG. 282.

third proportional to the radii of the second and third, and so on for the
subsequent quadrants.

In this method, therefore, the radii of successive quadrants form a continued proportion, of which the two first are given, being respectively equal
to 6 and 5 of the equal divisions, and the others may be found by calculation,
or by the well-known geometrical construction shown in Fig. 283. Draw
two lines, $o\,a$ and $o\,l$, at any angle with each other, and make $o\,a$ and $o\,b$
equal to 6 and 5 respectively of the equal divisions on A Y. With o as
centre and $o\,b$ as radius, describe an arc cutting $o\,l$ in u; join $a\,u$, and
through b draw $b\,v$ parallel to it. Again, with o as centre, and $o\,v$ as

radius, draw $v\,c$, then $o\,c$ is a third proportional to $o\,a$ and $o\,b$, and is the radius for the third quadrant C D, which, being set off from C along C r, gives s the centre, and the quadrant is then struck from this point.

Similarly $o\,d$ is a third proportional to $o\,b$ and $o\,c$, and is the radius for the fourth quadrant D E, and so on till the desired limit is reached. The curve of the inner side of the rail is struck from the same centres, and in the example coalesces at the point F with the other.

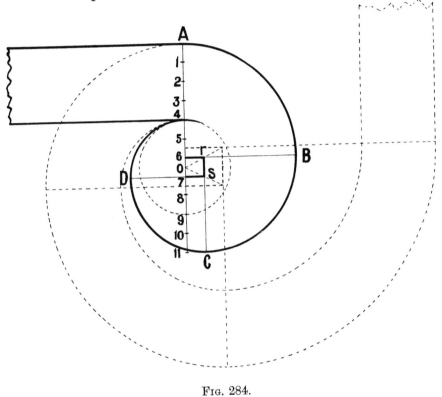

FIG. 284.

Any number of convolutions can of course be added on, as shown by the dotted lines, Fig. 282.

2. **To describe a scroll when the width of the rail only is given.—** Take the width of the rail to be A 4, Fig. 284, and divide it into 4 equal parts, and continue the same divisions on the line produced, making in all 11 of such divisions. Then A 11 is the width of a scroll which will terminate at the point 4 in one convolution.

On the division 6 7, from A, draw the square shown by the thick lines. The angular points 6, r, s, 7, furnish the centres for drawing the scroll. Having produced the sides of this square as in the figure, with point 6 as centre, and radius 6 A, describe the first quadrant A B of the scroll. Next, with r as centre, and radius r B, describe B C the second quadrant. The remaining quadrants, C D and D A, are similarly described from the centres s and 7 respectively.

The scroll may be enlarged to any extent, as shown by the dotted lines, by using as centres the angular points of a second square made with its sides double the lengths of those of the first square, and situated as

FIG. 285.

FIG. 286.

shown by the dotted lines in the figure.

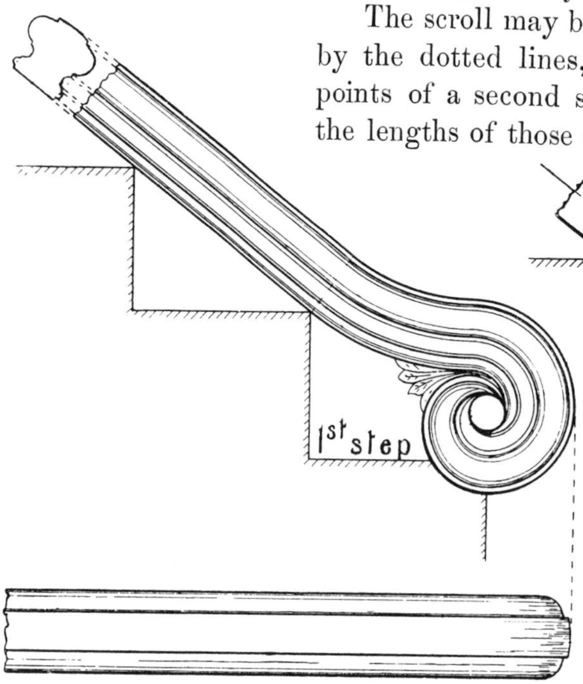

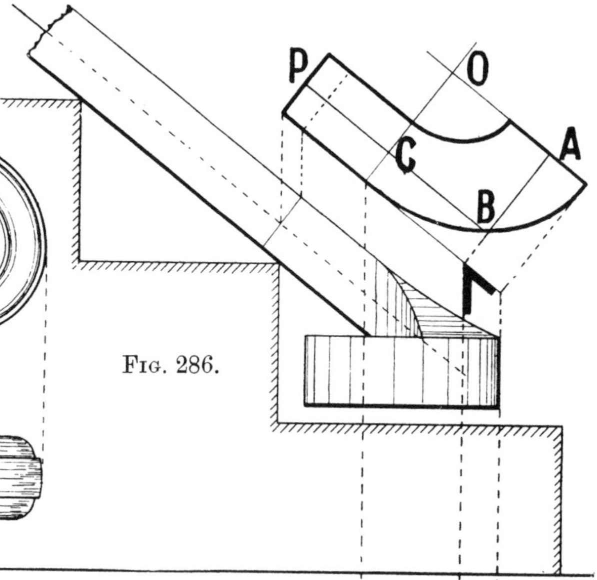

An example of a **hanging scroll** is given in Fig. 285. These are often used to terminate straight rails running alongside of walls instead of wreathed terminals.

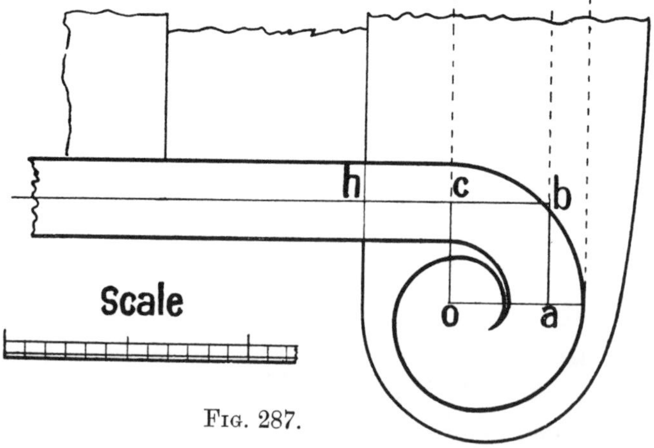

Face moulds for scrolls and scroll shanks.—Figs. 286 and 287 represent, respectively, the elevation

Scale

FIG. 287.

and plan of a scroll in the squared up condition, arranged as a terminal for a straight rail, and standing over a bull-nose step.

The scroll is *on the level* up to the point a, where a joint is made, and the first quadrant $a\,c$, or scroll shank, rising up from a to the straight rail, forms a quarter-circle wreath. For this wreath the tangent ab is level, and the centre line of the straight rail produced meets it in b, and forms the inclined tangent bc. The face mould is shown, along with the elevation, in Fig. 286, and its construction will present no difficulty, being the simplest case that can occur.

By getting out the shank in a separate piece some saving of material is effected, compared with making the scroll and shank in one, as is done in Fig. 288; but if the joints are conspicuous a somewhat patched-up appearance may result.

In shipyards it is usual to form them in one piece, as there is always a good command of suitable cuttings. Fig. 288 shows how this may be done. An elevation is made as in the foregoing, and two parallel lines, ab and cd, drawn to represent the faces of the plank. The face mould is drawn by means of ordinates obtained from the plan, which is the same as Fig. 287. In the arrangement shown by the elevation the shank is simply an easing, and not wreathed as in the last example, and occurs when more of the scroll is made level.

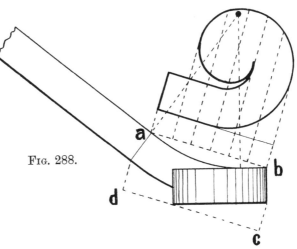

Fig. 288.

Complete Set of Wreaths for Quarter-circle Stair.

Fig. 290 is the complete plan of a quarter-circle stair, and Figs. 289 and 291 show the usual tangent developments, together with all the requisite moulds and bevels for getting out the handrails, which consist of eight separate wreatns. The drawings embody only such principles and methods as have been already illustrated in previous pages, and no detailed description, therefore, will be necessary.

In the plan, Fig. 290, the quadrant extends from the third to the topmost riser. The radius to the centre line of outer rail is taken at $5\frac{1}{2}$ feet, and the inner radius 2 feet. The handrails start from newel posts at the bottom, and finish into level rails at the top, each of the long wreaths covering exactly an octant.

Figs. 289 and 291 are the developments of the sections of the steps

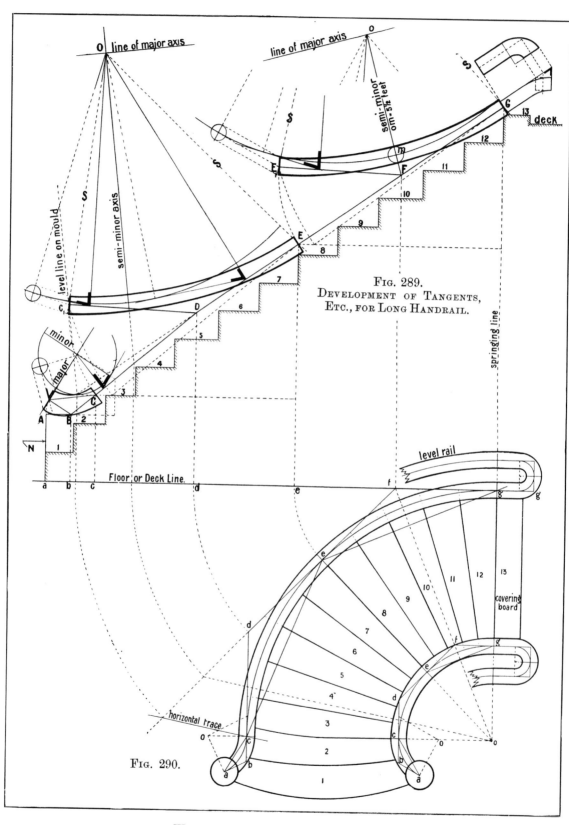

O line of major axis

line of major axis

o

line of major axis

semi-minor 0m=5½ feet

S

G 13 deck

12

F m

11

E

10

9

8 E

7

6

5

4

3

2

Fig. 289.

Development of Tangents, Etc., for Long Handrail.

level line on mould

semi-minor axis

S

S

S

D

c₁

minor

major

C

A B

N

1

springing line

Floor or Deck Line.

a   b   c   d   e   f   level rail

g   g′

e

d

c

10

11

12

13

8

9

covering board

7

6

5

f

4

g

3

e

d

horizontal trace

c

2

o   o   c   d

o   o

b   b

a   a

1

Fig. 290.

Wreaths for Quarter-circle Stair.

made as usual by the
tangent planes, and on
them are arranged the
tangents, so as to make
the rail conform as
closely as possible with
the stair. The tangents
in Fig. 291 are made in
one straight line, B G,
from top to bottom—
which makes the two
wreaths alike — while
those in Fig. 289 form
a straight line from G
to D.

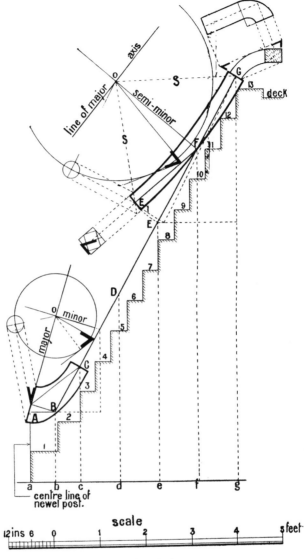

FIG. 291.

WREATHED HANDRAILS
FOR ELLIPTIC STAIRS.

The cases of wreaths
previously considered
have had this in com-
mon, viz., that their
plans have been parts of
circles, and consequently
the curves of the face
moulds have been cor-
responding portions of
ellipses which, from their
well-known properties,
could in general be con-
veniently drawn by means of a trammel or a string.

In Figs. 292-294 we have an example of a rail where the plan of its
centre line is itself an ellipse, which results in making the curves of the
edges of the face mould not ellipses, but merely approximations to these
curves, and consequently cannot be drawn with the trammel. This will
be seen, by considering that the curves representing the plans of the sides
of the rail are not themselves ellipses, but only curves drawn equidistant
from the centre ellipse, and that, therefore, the sections of the vertical
surfaces standing over these lines cannot possibly be ellipses either.

In all such cases the face moulds have to be determined by the method of ordinates.

Fig. 293 is the suggested plan of the stair and rail. The latter is composed of the elliptic quadrant, whose centre is *o*, and axes shown by the chain lines, a scroll at the bottom, and a straight portion at the top leading on to a level landing.

With regard to the arrangement of the steps, it is scarcely necessary at this stage to observe that the treads are set out at a uniform width, proportional to the given rise, along a line about 18 inches from the rail, and "balanced" so that their widths at the ends will produce good falling lines in the strings and handrails. To ascertain if the arrangement is satisfactory recourse may be had to a development of the steps on the centre line of rail in plan, as in Fig. 267.

When the risers have been arranged to give a satisfactory falling line at the inner rail, it will be found that towards the middle of the height they will be considerably displaced from their natural position, *i.e.*, normal to the line of ascent. This constitutes an objection to elliptic stairs, which cannot be obviated without sacrificing the appearance of the rails and strings. One result of this great obliquity of the risers is that the rail, when made to the proper height above the steps, will feel too low where excessive obliquity occurs; for example, when a person ascending stairs like that in the diagram had reached, say, the third step from the bottom, the rail at his level being farther forward, he would naturally be grasping it at a point which corresponds to a lower level than the one he has reached. To meet in some measure this objection, it is usual to raise the rail at these steps a few inches, as shown in the elevation, Fig. 294.

Arrangement of joints and tangents.—The best position for the lowest joint will be at the point *a*, Fig. 293, where the wreath comes on to the level. The top joint at *e* is placed so as to give a good length of shank to the small quarter-circle wreath, *e f g*, which brings the rail to the level on the upper floor. One other joint between these two will be found sufficient in the present case, and should be placed at about the position *c* shown in the figure, which, though it makes the lower wreath *c a* appear a little short, avoids unduly cross wood, which would be introduced into this wreath if the joint was made higher up.

Draw tangents to the curve of the centre line of rail at the points *a* and *c*, and the joint lines at right angles to them, then *a b* and *b c* are the tangents for the bottom wreath, and *c d* and *d e* those for the long wreath.

A development (Fig. 292) of the sections of the steps as they occur on the plans of the tangents is now drawn, as in preceding examples, and the pitches of the tangents adjusted to bring the rail to the desired height, remembering that it has to be raised a few inches in the middle portion of the stair for the reason above stated.

In this and similar cases, as the fixing of the pitches of the tangents is somewhat indefinite, some guidance is required. In the drawing, the heights of the tangents at the joints are taken from the elevation of the rail, Fig. 294 ; but, of course, to draw this elevation takes up considerable time, and though it is useful in giving an idea beforehand of what the rail is to be like from that point of view, would not be drawn in the workshop. The more straightforward course is to draw a development of the steps on the centre line of the rail, and on it arrange a suitable falling line, from which the heights of the tangents at the points where the joints occur are ascertained, as in Fig. 267.

After the tangents have been drawn in development from these data, it is easy to show at any point the vertical deviation of the falling line from the centre plane of plank. If the divergence prove considerable, it may be well to try other pitches of the tangents, to see if a closer approximation could be obtained.

To draw the face moulds.—Through C, Fig. 292, draw the ground line X Y, and proceed to obtain the triangle $C_1 D E$, as in previous examples, by finding the real length of the chord $C_1 E$, and draw the joint lines square to the tangents.

We have next to find the direction of level lines on the mould and on the plan. Produce the upper tangent E D, Fig. 292, to meet the ground line at level C in the point X, and join $X C_1$; this line is then a level one when the mould is held in its correct position over the plan. From X let fall the projector $X x$ on to the plan of the upper tangent $e d$ produced, and join $x c$; this obtains the same level line in the plan.

A series of level lines or ordinates at any convenient distances apart are then drawn across the plan of the rail parallel to the level line $x c$, and intersecting the tangent in the points $1, 2, d$, etc. To determine these level ordinates on the mould: take for example the ordinate $1 m n$ in the plan (Fig. 293); draw the vertical projector $1 1^1$ meeting the tangent E X (Fig. 292) in 1^1, and through this point draw the ordinate $1^1 m_1 n_1$ parallel to $X C_1$, making $1^1 m_1$ and $1^1 n_1$ equal to $1 m$ and $1 n$ respectively in Fig. 293. The rest of the ordinates having been found in the same manner, the curves of the mould are drawn by bending a batten to the points so obtained.

The construction of the mould for the bottom wreath is a simple matter, since one of the tangents $a b$ is horizontal, which at once gives

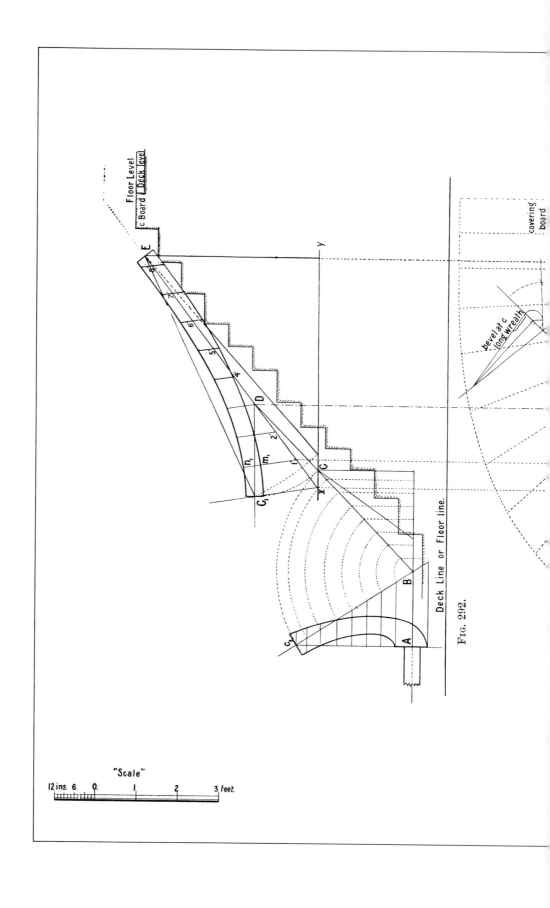

Floor Level
c. Board | Deck level

Deck Line or Floor line.

Fig. 292.

bevel at c
long wreath

covering board

"Scale"

12 ins. 6. 0. 1 2 3 feet.

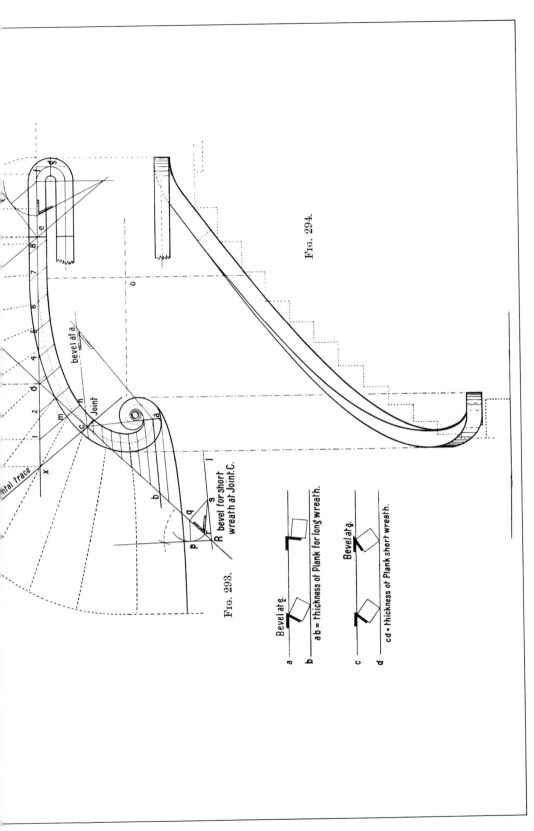

bevel at a

Joint

bevel at a.

R bevel for short
wreath at Joint.C.

FIG. 293.

FIG. 294.

Bevel at a.

a b = thickness of Plank for long wreath.

Bevel at a.

c d = thickness of Plank short wreath.

WREATHED HANDRAIL FOR ELLIPTIC STAIR.

the direction of level ordinates ; and further, the chord $a\,c$ happens to lie in the plane of the joint at a.

This mould is shown rotated about the level tangent A B, Fig. 292, and the triangle A B C_2 drawn, as before, by finding the real length of the chord A C_2. The student will easily follow out the construction for determining the level ordinates on the mould, this being only a matter of dividing B C_2 proportionally to the divisions on its plan, $b\,c$, Fig. 293.

A very common way of drawing the ordinates is to make use of the chord in place of the tangent, dividing it into the same number of equal parts both on the plan and on the mould, and setting of the lengths of the ordinates from it.

Bevels.—Since the joints are at right angles to the tangents, the twist bevel, as in previous cases, is the angle that the plane of the plank makes with the vertical plane containing the tangent at that end of the wreath; but the particular method that we have previously employed for circular plans is inadmissible in this case, and the more general method, Fig. 216, which should now be quite familiar to the student, has to be adopted. For example, to find the bevel for the upper end of the lower wreath $a\,c$; assume any point R on the plan produced of the tangent at c, and through R draw a line R l parallel to the level lines $a\,b$, etc., on that wreath; from the same point set out a line R p at the pitch of that tangent, as obtained from the development, Fig. 292. Take any convenient point q on R b, and draw lines $q\,p$ and $q\,s$ at right angles to R p and R b respectively; make $q\,r$ equal to $q\,p$, then $q\,r\,s$ is the twist bevel required. These directions will apply equally well to the constructions shown for the other bevels.

The varying curvature of the ellipse, continually increasing as it does towards the extremities of the major axis, joins in very fitly with a scroll terminal, the curvature of which is also continually increasing towards its pole.

CHAPTER XVII

COMPLEX CASES OF WREATHS. (EASINGS FORMED ON THE WREATH PIECES)

We have now to illustrate a series of cases which present a greater degree of difficulty than any that we have hitherto considered.

It will have been noticed by the student that all the preceding examples, with one or two exceptions, have either shown arrangements where no easings were required, or where necessary they have been formed on the straight rail.

It has already been stated that easings may be formed on the wreath piece by slight modifications of the ordinary tangent method. When a choice can be made between the two arrangements, the former will generally prove the more economical; but, as we shall see, the latter allows a closer adjustment of the rail to the stair, or to a particular length or arrangement of balusters.

Wreath for Semicircular Plan (Rail rising from Level to Rake).

Plan.—Taking Fig. 301 to represent the suggested plan showing the desired arrangement of steps and balusters, we have to obtain the necessary lines for a wreath to continue the handrail round the semicircle in two pieces, with the joint at the crown c.

Development of centre falling line.—In the first place, draw a development of the steps along the centre line of handrail, and upon them arrange a suitable falling line to join in with the straight rails in easy curves. This development of steps and the centre falling line are shown by dotted lines in Fig. 297, together with the vertical springing lines, S_1, S_2, S_3, corresponding respectively to the points a, c, e in the plan.

Development of tangents.—We next require the development of the vertical planes containing the tangents, so that the tangents may be placed in proper relation to the previously arranged centre falling line, M G F H. This may be done in a separate diagram, as in Fig. 266, but may more advantageously be laid upon the development of the centre line just drawn. The line E 5, which is the highest springing, is made common to both developments, so that the lines to the right of it, being beyond the cylinder, belong to both drawings. The divisional lines for the tangents of the lower wreath are A 1, B 2, C 3, and C 3, D 4, E 5 those of the upper.

Adjustment of the plane of plank to come nearest the falling line.—We have now to get the tangents into such a position as will enable the wreath to be taken out of as thin planks as possible. This in general can only be arrived at by a tentative process, requiring experience to do it expeditiously. The aim, of course, with certain restrictions to be stated presently, is to get the plane of the plank to reconcile as nearly as possible with the centre falling line. The principal points in the procedure may here be described in a general manner.

Resting points for plane.—Three points are judiciously chosen on the falling line as resting points for a trial plane, and either the intersection of this plane with the vertical cylindric surface containing the falling line drawn along with the development of the latter, or the vertical trace of this assumed plane, is found on a vertical plane at right angles to the assumed plane, and on which the centre falling line is also projected. The former process would show the vertical divergence of the centre line of plank from the centre falling line of rail, while the latter would show the divergence of the falling line from the assumed plane of plank in a direction square to its surface.

This process would be repeated with other trial planes, and for rails of ordinary form that plane which gives the least divergence selected. If the resting points are well chosen in the first instance, and an edge view of the trial plane taken as in the examples (Figs. 310 and 314), and then a re-adjustment of the vertical trace made to give equal deflection above and below it, the plane in this new position will be a sufficiently near approximation to the best plane for all practical purposes.

Selection of the resting points.—No rule of any practical value can be laid down for the selection of the preliminary resting points. A cursory examination of the nature of the falling line beforehand will enable one with a little experience to form a rough picture mentally what parts would fall above and what below the plane. One of the three points may generally be taken about the middle of the wreath, and the other two at or near its ends.

Amount of twist and form of rail section should be taken into account in the determination of the best plane.—Another factor which should be considered in fixing the plane of the plank, and which in certain cases would entail a slight departure from the directions just laid down, is the shape of the rail section taken along with the amount of twist. Referring to the sketch (Fig. 295), in which the straight line $a b$ represents the edge view or vertical trace of the plane of the plank, and the waved line the projection of the supposed falling line: if the section of the rail is circular, or nearly circular, the deflections $A a$ and $B b$ at the ends should be equal to the greatest deflections $E e$ and $F f$ of the loops. If, on the other hand, the contour of the moulded rail is such as to come near to its circumscribing rectangle or square, the deflections $A a$ and $B b$ should be less than those of the loops, where presumably there is less twist; and in this case the dotted straight line (Fig. 295) would give a more economical position for the plane than the one which equalizes the deflection.

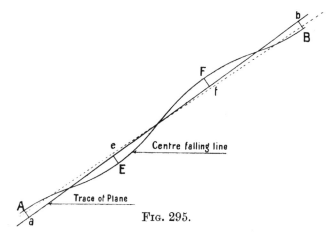

FIG. 295.

The reason will be apparent when it is considered that the rotation of the section of a nearly round rail for the twist may not bring any of the members nearer the surfaces of the plank than others were before rotation, while a section of rectangular form, on being rotated from the upright, or position of no twist, to the angle required, will bring those members at two opposite corners of the section nearer the faces of the plank, so that in the latter case, with a thin plank, only a slight displacement of the section can be made without pushing the corners of the rail beyond its surfaces.

This also explains why the straightforward method oftenest adopted by handrailers, of making the centres of the joint sections in the centre of the plank, may give a satisfactory result, because it is generally at the joints where there is the greatest twist.

Turning again to the development of tangents (Fig. 297), it will be seen that a simple arrangement is obtained without, in this case, employing the above more exact though rather difficult method, the upper tangent and common crown tangent being taken in one straight line, the lower tangent, A B, only requiring to be thrown on to a different pitch from the others. The points in the " falling line " brought into the plane of the plank of the upper wreath are H, E, and F, and the points, F, M, and a third which would occur a little above G, into the plane of the lower.

Face moulds and bevels.—The face moulds are shown drawn out in the usual manner adopted in preceding examples, and call for no explanation here. The principal lines, tangents, springings, etc., are got into position in Fig. 297, and for greater clearness copied on to the detached diagrams (Figs. 296 and 300), which show the moulds completed for the upper and lower wreaths respectively.

Attention may now be directed to the manner of finding the required bevels, and first those for the top joint at Q. This joint, not being at right angles to the tangent, brings us face to face with the general case already noticed (see pages 171-174), where three distinct bevels are required, viz.: (1) that giving the inclination of the joint line to the tangent on the face mould, (2) the bevel that the joint plane makes with the surface of the plank, and (3) the twist bevel.

Two methods are shown in the diagram for obtaining these bevels, one in Fig. 298, which is the most usual, and has been fully explained and illustrated by Figs. 213-215, the other at Q in Fig. 297, in immediate connection with the joint.

To find Bevel No. 1.—From the point l (Fig. 297), where a line drawn through c^1 parallel to the tangent cuts the joint line Q T, draw l L_2 at right angles to the tangent, cutting the springing line C_1 O produced at the point L_2, and join L_2 Q. The angle L_2 Q E gives bevel No. 1, as will be easily seen, because Q D C_1 L_2 is part of the plane of the plank folded about the upper tangent Q E D, the line L_2 Q being its intersection with the plane of the joint.

To find Bevel No. 2.—With centre Q, and radius Q L_2 (Fig. 297), draw the arc L_2 L, cutting the line, l L, drawn perpendicular to the joint line Q T, at L. Join Q L, then L Q l is the bevel No. 2.

Otherwise.—In this case, since the line c^1 l must contain the elevation of the centre of the ellipse, l L will prove equal to the radius of the well, so that the same result would be arrived at by setting out, in the first instance, l L equal to the radius of the well, and joining L Q, giving the bevel No. 2 as before. Then, by drawing the arc L L_2, cutting the line l L_2 perpendicular to the tangent at the point L_2, and joining L_2 Q, would have given bevel No. 1 also, without producing the springing C_1 O.

It need hardly be noted that it is only *convenient* to take the line, $c^1 l$, containing the centre of ellipse; any other line lying in the plane of the plank and parallel to the tangent D E, which is also the vertical trace, would obtain the desired result.

To find Bevel No. 3.—Produce the perpendicular, L l (Fig. 297), to cut the tangent D E Q at R, and from l let fall a perpendicular, $l t$, on to Q L, then, by making l T equal to $l t$, and joining T R, gives the angle R T Q which is the bevel No. 3 required.

Bevels for middle joint.—The common joint between the two wreaths at c, being at right angles to the tangent, only the twist bevels are required at that joint, the other two bevels being right angles. The construction in the present case for finding these twist bevels is shown in connection with the joint lines on the face moulds (Figs. 296 and 300), and will be readily understood, as the principle is the same as that adopted in the majority of preceding examples, there being only a slight variation in the construction. In this case the joint line itself on the face mould is used as the perpendicular on the tangent, and the intersection of this line with the opposite springing is taken as the centre of the circular arc. In previous cases the perpendicular to the tangent was drawn through the centre of the ellipse. Briefly, at C_1 (Figs. 296 and 300), produce the joint lines to cut the opposite springings, A_1 O and E O, at 8. With 8 as centre, and radius equal to that of the well circle, describe the arcs as shown, tangents to which drawn from C_1 give the required bevels.

Bevels for plumb joint at P.—Here, as at Q, the joint plane is not at right angles to the tangent, the latter not being horizontal, so that strictly speaking three bevels would be required. But the fact of the plane of the joint being vertical simplifies the construction, (1) because the joint line on the face mould is parallel to the springing line; (2) since the wreath stands over a right angle in plan, the angle that the upper tangent, B C, makes with the vertical is the twist bevel, that tangent being parallel to the joint line; and (3) the bevel that the joint makes with the plank is not required, because the joint line on the face mould, when applied to the upper and under sides of the wreath piece, is in the vertical plane of the joint in both positions, and therefore the joint line can be drawn on each side of the plank by means of the face mould.

Thickness of plank.—This should be determined by that section at which there is the greatest twist and also displacement of the centre of the section from the centre line of plank. In the upper wreath the twist is, of course, greatest at the joints, and in this case is the same for both;

but as there is no displacement of the centre of the joint from the centre plane of plank at the lower end of the wreath, while there is about 1 inch at the upper, the latter joint should therefore be used for determining the thickness of stuff.

The necessary construction is shown to the right of Fig. 298. We assume that, for convenience in moulding, nearly the full squared section will be required.

Draw a section of the squared rail, Fig. 298, and its middle line, $a\,b$. Mark on the latter the centre, c, of the section, then set off $c\,c_1$ equal to the displacement of the point Q from the centre line of rail as shown in the development (Fig. 297). Draw $f\,g$, making the angle, $m\,f\,g$, equal to the twist bevel marked No. 2, and so as just to cut off a slight corner from the section, and then at the same distance on the other side of c_1 draw $m\,h$ parallel to $f\,g$. The perpendicular distance, $h\,g$, between the parallels $m\,h$ and $f\,g$, would be the thickness required if the joint had been square to the face of the plank. In this instance, as the plane of the joint is inclined to the surface of the plank, $g\,h$ would give an excess of material. By applying the bevel No. 3 (*i.e.*, the angle of joint plane with face of plank) to the line $g\,h$, as shown in the figure, the perpendicular distance between the two parallels $g\,n$ and $h\,k$ is the true thickness of the plank.

The construction for finding the thickness of stuff for the lower wreath is shown by Fig. 299, and is the same as that just described, only since the bevel through the plank for the plumb joint has not been determined (not being required to form the joint itself), the additional lines in the figure answer the purpose of that bevel.

Another method of forming oblique joints is often adopted, and though rather unscientific, has some practical advantages, especially when the joint is at the end of a fairly long shank, as it bridges over the difficulties met with in obtaining and applying the two extra bevels required by the more exact method explained above.

The joints are formed in the first instance square to the tangent and face of plank, as if for a square joint, of course placed so as to leave sufficient material to form the joint finally. The twist bevel corresponding to a square joint is then found and applied to this provisionally made joint, and the wreath squared up with these particulars in the usual manner, and the vertical springing lines accurately marked on its sides. The lines for cutting the true joint on the shank is then obtained, either by laying the shank on to its proper position on the development with the springing lines coinciding, and marking them by means of a set square from the joint line on the board, or, since wreaths of this nature

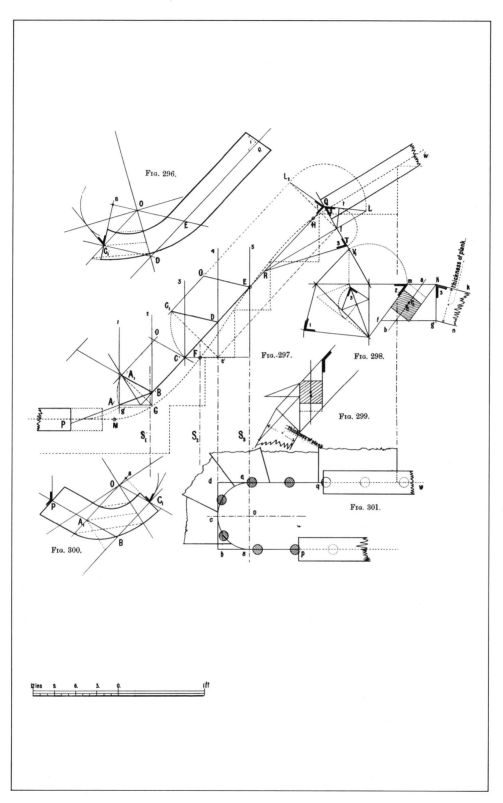

Fig. 296.

Fig. 297.

Fig. 298.

Fig. 299.

Fig. 301.

Fig. 300.

WREATH FOR SEMICIRCULAR PLAN, RAIL RISING
FROM LEVEL TO RAKE (EASINGS FORMED ON WREATH).

are often trimmed up with a side or falling mould made and applied to the convex side, the joint line may be marked upon the falling mould, and copied on to the edge of shank, and the line squared over to the concave side.

Of course this method could not be applied with any approach to accuracy in cases where there are no shanks, which may sometimes occur, as, for instance, at a centre joint between two wreath pieces when they have not a common tangent (see Figs. 339 to 346).

Wreath for Semicircular Plan (Rising from Rake to Level).

The example, Figs. 302-304, presents simply an inversion of the preceding case, the wreath joining with a level rail at the top, the size of the well and arrangement of steps round the curve being the same.

Having set out the development of the steps (Fig. 302) corresponding to the centre line of rail in plan, and the centre falling line of rail W E T G R, and having drawn also the springing lines S_1, S_2, and S_3, and the divisional vertical lines A 1, B 2, etc., of the tangent planes, proceed to level the point G where the falling line intersects the lower springing line S_1 over to the corresponding springing line A 1, in the tangent development, meeting it in g.   Similarly level over the point T to t.

Next copy the falling line, joints, etc., below G on to the tangent development. This is easily done, it being obvious that all the points have merely to be shifted to the left a distance equal to G g.

To place the tangents in position it will be convenient to begin with the lower one, p B, by drawing it as shown, making the deflection of the falling line about equal on each side of it as far as the springing A 1. This gives a slight displacement of the section of the rail from the centre of plank at the springing A 1, and about an equal amount, $p\,r$, at the lower joint.   Taking this as the best position for the lower tangent, the point B, the lower end of the crown tangent, is thereby fixed. Now it would be the most straightforward plan to draw the latter through the point t so as to make no deflection at the middle joint c; but this would incline the upper tangent, D Q, rather far from the horizontal, hence the crown tangent, B D, is raised at its upper end, so as to pass through the point C a little above t, to agree with the most suitable position for the top tangent, which will have been previously drawn in the position D E Q, making the deflection on each side of the shank E Q about equal.

This arrangement of the tangents would prove a satisfactory one for

II

the present case, and as an exercise the student may satisfy himself by following out the general directions on pages 236-237, namely, taking an edge view of each plane along with the projection of the falling line, which will show the actual divergence at each section of the centre of rail from centre of plank.

It need hardly be stated that under the stress and strain experienced in a workshop all the little saving in material that could be effected by an altered arrangement would not compensate for the time spent in applying these tests.

Lines for face mould.—All the lines for completing the face mould are shown in the diagram, Fig. 302, only the elliptic curves are left out to avoid complexity in the drawing. The student will readily recognize that the means here employed for obtaining these lines, as well as those for the bevels for the square joint at C between the wreaths, are precisely the same as that adopted for other cases already discussed.

The lowest joint, p, not being square to the tangents, three bevels are again required. The construction here employed for obtaining these is a little different from the two methods given by Figs. 297 and 298 for the top joint in the last example. Of course there is nothing in the case before us that calls for different treatment, only a slight variation of method sometimes results in giving the student a clear view of a point that may have been to him obscure by another construction.

First, *to find the direction of the joint line $M P_2$ on the face mould*, project C, Fig. 302, on to the vertical line B 2 at C_2, and through C_2 draw $C_2 m$ parallel to the lower tangent B A p, to cut the joint line produced in m, then $C_2 m$ is the elevation of the springing line $C O_1$ on the vertical plane containing the tangent B A p, and the actual line of which $C_2 m$ is the projection, being parallel to that plane, $C_2 m$ will be its real length, and as it would appear when drawn on the plane of the face mould. Hence produce the springing line $C O_1$ on the face-mould diagram to M, making C M equal $C_2 m$, and join $M P_2$, which is the joint line required.

The *twist bevel* to apply on the plane of the joint may now be easily found. With M as centre, Fig. 302, and radius equal to that of the well, strike the arc 6 7, then the angle that $M P_2$ makes with $P_2 N$, the tangent from P_2 to the arc, is the required bevel.

For the bevel which the joint at p makes with the face of plank, a construction is here shown by first ascertaining the thickness of the plank which dispenses with finding this bevel in a formal manner. The latter is here determined by taking a normal section of the rail across the tangent on the shank at the part where there is the greatest deflection, as at (A),

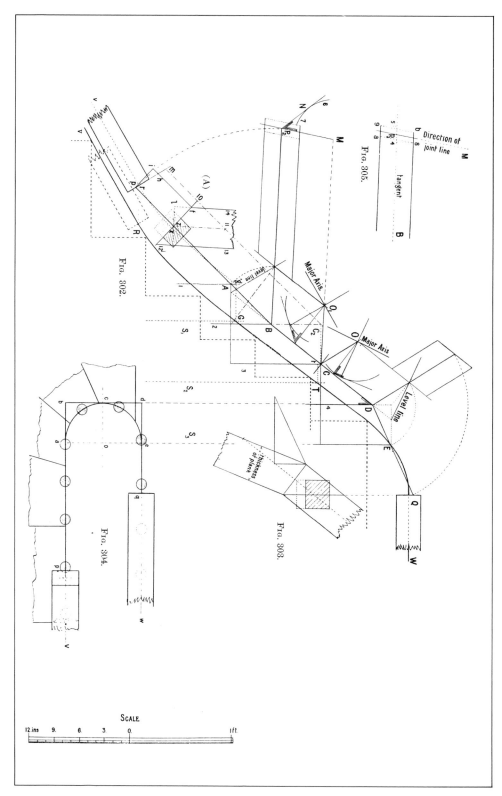

FIGS. 302-305. WREATH FOR SEMICIRCULAR PLAN, RAIL RISING

FROM RAKE TO LEVEL (EASINGS FORMED ON WREATH).

Fig. 302. At the point 10, where the line of section through x, the centre of the section, cuts $C_2\, m$, set out 10 11 equal to the radius of well ; the line joining 11 z will represent the centre line of the plank on the section. Draw the lines 12 13, and 14 l parallel to 11 z, and equidistant from it, so that 12 13 cuts off a slight corner from the square section of rail. The perpendicular distance between these parallels is the thickness of the plank required.

Referring now to the detached sketch, Fig. 305, which is merely the tangent and joint line of the face mould repeated for clearness, set off on each side of B p_2 a distance equal to $f\,l$ at (A), Fig. 302, and draw the parallels $b\,8$ and $9\,a$ as shown. These lines represent the actual positions of tangents when the mould is adjusted on the wreath piece to give the proper twist to the rail. Set off along the tangent, Fig. 305, the distances $p_2\,4$, $p_2\,5$, equal to $i\,h$ at (A), Fig. 302, and draw $4\,8$ and $5\,9$ perpendicular to the tangent. Through points 8 and 9 draw $8\,a$ and $9\,b$ respectively parallel to the joint line M p_2 ; then $8\,a$ represents the joint line as it would be drawn on the upper side of plank, and $9\,b$ that on the under. In marking out the joint on the wreath piece, the line p_2 M is accurately drawn, say, on the upper side of wreath, and squared over and drawn also on the under side. In the present case a parallel line in advance of p_2 M, a distance equal to that between it and either of the lines $9\,b$ or $a\,8$ in Fig. 305, will be the cutting line for the joint on the under side of wreath, while that on the upper side will be back from p M an equal distance. These joint lines now on the upper and under sides may be joined across the edge (see Fig. 306), which will provide cutting lines for the joint on all four sides of the piece. The joint, in the first instance, is usually cut off square to the farthest outline, and afterwards cut accurately to the bevel.

When the oblique joint has thus been formed, the twist bevel is drawn across it, passing (as in other cases) through the centre of the section of plank, giving the distance to

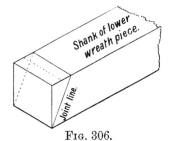

FIG. 306.

shift the tangents to readjust the " face mould " for drawing out the lines for cutting the sides of the wreath. It need hardly be added that the twist bevel M p_2 N would not be the correct one to apply to the square joint. We may observe further, that since the distance to shift the tangents to their new positions on each side of the plank is given by $f\,l$ at (A), Fig. 302, and used in the construction, Fig. 305, the determination of the twist bevel is here unnecessary.

The top joint at Q, Fig. 302, being plumb, the same remarks respecting the bevels as were made (page 239) in connection with the lowest joint in the last example are equally applicable here. The twist bevel for this joint is shown at D, Fig. 302, it being the inclination that the lower tangent D C makes with the vertical.

Fig. 303 is the construction for obtaining the thickness of the plank for the upper wreath, and may be compared with Fig. 299.

Example of a Wreath formed in One Piece standing over a Plan Greater than a Quarter Circle.

In this case, which is illustrated by Figs. 307-310, the wreath starts from the level, where it joins with a newel, is continued round a part of a circle subtending an angle of about 145°, and worked into a straight rail at the top.

The plane of the plank is taken to lie on a level tangent, $a\,b$ (Fig. 310), at the newel, and is inclined so as to conform to a previously arranged centre falling line, 1, 2, 3, 4, etc., Fig. 309. An elevation, $1'$, $2'$, $3'$, etc., of this falling line is made on a ground line, $x\,y$ (A) (Fig. 310), at right angles to $a\,b$, the level tangent and horizontal trace of the plane, and the vertical trace $y\,q^1$ of the required plane is drawn on this vertical plane so as to come nearest the points of the falling line. The position chosen, $y\,q^1$, gives a slight displacement of the centre of plank from the falling line at the joint Q.

Set up $r\,Q$ in the development (Fig. 309) equal to the height of q^1 above $x\,y$, the ground line at (A), Fig. 310, and join Q B, which is then the true length of the top tangent, the point B being projected up from b in the plan, Fig. 310.

The plane of the face mould, with the principal lines upon it, is shown rotated about Q B, as in other examples. The lower tangent being a line of level in the plane, $a\,b$ (Fig. 310) is its true length, and $a^1\,B$ (Fig. 309) its elevation. Through a^1 therefore draw $a^1\,A$ at right angles to Q B (Fig. 309), and with B as centre, and $a\,b$ (Fig. 310) as radius, cut $a^1\,A$ at A, then the line A B is the level tangent in position on the rotated plane, and A K drawn at right angles to A B is the line of the major axis. The centre, O, of the ellipse is at a distance from A equal to $y\,o''$ (A) Fig. 310. The centre, O, may also be found by drawing a line through o^1, the elevation of the centre, at right angles to Q B, which will intersect the major axis in O as shown. It need hardly be stated

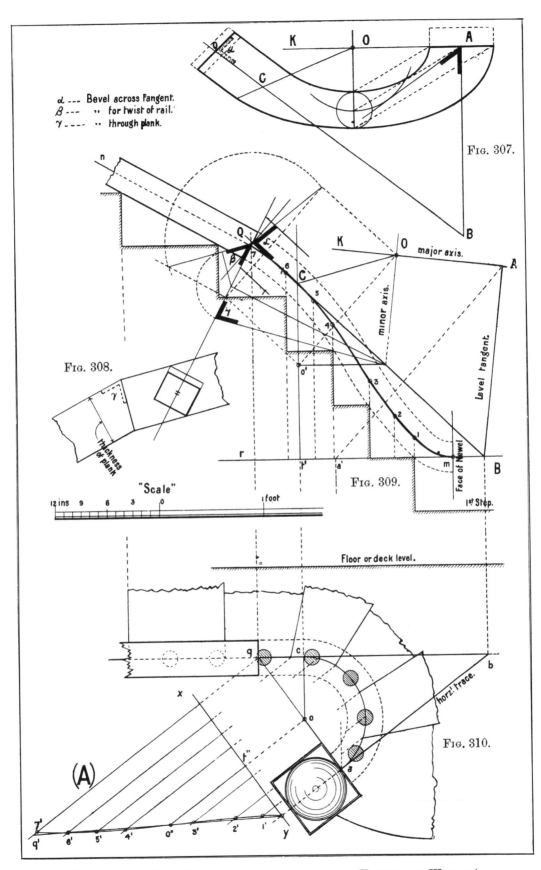

α --- Bevel across tangent.
β ---   ,,   for twist of rail.
γ ---   ,,   through plank.

FIG. 307.

FIG. 308.

FIG. 309.

"Scale"

12 ins   9   6   3   0   1 foot

Floor or deck level.

FIG. 310.

(A)

WREATH FOR PLAN LARGER THAN A SEMICIRCLE (EASINGS ON WREATH).

that the height $o^1 t^1$ is obtained from the elevation (A), Fig. 310, being equal to $o'' t''$.

Join C O, which is one of the springing lines on the mould, O A, part of the major axis, being the other.

These lines are copied in Fig. 307, where the face mould is shown completed, and also the usual construction shown for the twist bevel at the lower end of wreath; but, as will be seen, the bevel marked at A, Fig. 307, is the complement of the twist angle, which angle in this case is identical with the pitch of plane of plank, viz., the angle $x y q^1$ at (A), Fig. 310. The *twist bevel* is of course the angle $x q^1 y$, Fig. 310 (A). The dotted projection shown on the face mould beyond O A is the extra length required for housing the rail into the newel.

The three bevels requisite for the joint at the upper end of this wreath are found at Q, Fig. 309, and the thickness of the plank determined by the construction, Fig. 308, the methods employed being respectively the same as those in Figs. 297 and 298.

WREATH FOR STAIR STARTING.   PLAN AN OCTANT OF A CIRCLE.

The plan, Fig. 315, represents the newel and wreath at the bottom of the stair, illustrated by Figs. 153-155. The radius of the centre line of the plan circle, $a \, n \, m$, in this case is 3 feet. This large radius makes it rather inconvenient to draw out the elliptic curves of the mould by means of trammels, so that the method by level ordinates is here adopted, the same as in Figs. 271, 272, and also in the elliptic stair, Figs. 292-294.

The case before us would be rendered much easier by making the lower tangent, A B, level, as is done in the preceding case; but to furnish the student with a more advanced exercise another arrangement has been adopted, with the lower tangent inclined, which enables the wreath to be taken out of a somewhat thinner plank.

The development of the centre line and that of the tangents are again placed on the same diagram (Fig. 312). The resting points on the falling line (Fig. 312) selected for the *trial plane* are 1^1 at a little distance from the newel, the second point, m^1, where the falling line intersects the vertical springing line C k, and the third, n^1, at a level exactly midway between those of m^1 and 1^1. The third point, n^1, is got by squaring over 1^1 to k, and bisecting $m^1 k$ in l^1, then drawing a level line through l^1, cutting the falling line in n^1.

In the plan, Fig. 315, the chord joining 1 m is bisected at l and this point joined to n, which corresponds to n^1 in the development (Fig. 312);

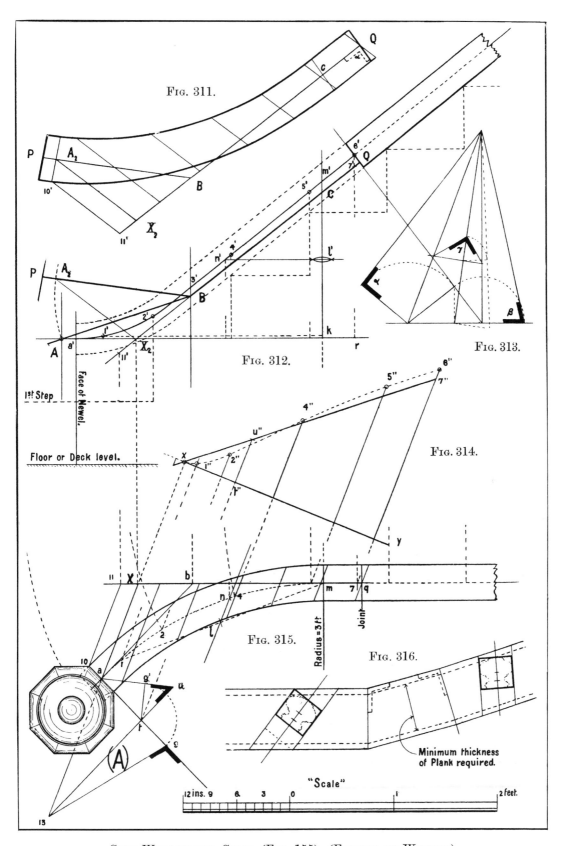

Fig. 311.

Fig. 312.

Fig. 313.

Fig. 314.

Fig. 315.

Fig. 316.

1st Step

Face of Newel.

Floor or Deck level.

Radius=3ft.

Joint

Minimum thickness
of Plank required.

"Scale"

12 ins. 9   6.   3   0   1   2 feet.

SIDE WREATH FOR STAIR (FIG. 155), (EASINGS ON WREATH).

$l\,n$ is then the direction of level lines on this plane, which is all that is required at present.

An elevation, $1''$, $2''$ . . . $6''$, of the falling line is now made (Fig. 314) on a ground line, $x\,y$, at right angles to the level line, $n\,l$, and $x\,7''$ drawn representing the edge view or vertical trace of the required plane, so as to make the falling line have the minimum of deflection from it.

The rest of the construction should now present no new difficulties to the student, and will only be briefly referred to.

The plans of the tangents are $a\,b$ and $b\,q$, Fig. 315, and X is the point in the upper tangent, $q\,b$, produced, at the same level as a. To get the tangents into their position in Fig. 312, project the point X referred to on to the level line $A\,r$ at X_2, and mark off on the vertical line $6^1\,r\,a$ a distance, $6^1\,7^1$, equal to $6''\,7''$ in Fig. 314. Join $7^1\,X_2$, intersecting the upper springing $m^1\,k$ at C, and the divisional line between the two tangent planes at B; then C B is the upper tangent, and by joining B to A gives the lower.

The face mould is then drawn out at Fig. 311. It will only require to be noted respecting the ordinates for obtaining the curves of the mould that the one through q at the upper joint, and 10 11 at the lower end of wreath, are first drawn in the plan, Fig. 315, and then got into position in Fig. 311, being drawn parallel to the director of level lines $X_2\,A_2$. The space along the tangent between these extreme ordinates in both figures is then divided into six equal parts, and the intermediate ordinates drawn through the points of division. The points on the plan ordinates, where they are intersected by the curves, are now transferred to those on the mould (Fig. 311), using the upper tangent, Q B, as a common base line, and the curves drawn through the points by means of a batten.

Remarks respecting joints and bevels.—The lower end of the wreath where it meets the newel being a plumb section, the line of this section on the face mould is the springing, *i.e.*, would pass through the centre of the ellipse; but as this point has not been determined in the construction, the line is drawn from A_2 (Fig. 311) through the point $10'$, the extremity of the ordinate $10^1\,11^1$, which has been introduced for this purpose.

Again, the tangents not being at right angles in plan, an independent construction for the twist bevel and for the bevel through the plank has to be made for the above section. This is shown at (A), Fig. 315. Draw any line, as $13\,u$, at right angles to $10\,a$, produced, intersecting it at t, and cutting X a, produced, at 13. Now regarding t as the plan of a point lying in the plane of the plank, its height above the level of a may be found by squaring up a projector on to the end view of the plane of plank in Fig. 314. Make therefore $t\,u$, Fig. 315 (A), equal to $t''u''$ (Fig. 314), and join $u\,a$, then $a\,u\,t$ is the angle of the twist bevel required. The length of the perpendicular $t\,9^1$ to $a\,u$ laid along $a\,t$ gives point 9, which, joined to 13, obtains the bevel through the plank.

The three bevels required for the top joint are marked a, β, and γ in Fig. 313, and are found by the general construction explained in connection with Fig. 215. It will be seen that the two angles, a and γ, turn out to be extremely nearly right angles, which might have been inferred from the upper tangent, C B, Fig. 312, being almost parallel to the centre line of the straight rail.

These bevels are applied at Fig. 316 to determine the thickness of plank, in the same way as in previous examples in this chapter.

CHAPTER XVIII

SYSTEM OF HANDRAILING BY NORMAL SECTIONS

GENERAL REMARKS.—In Chapter XII, page 151, the form of the wreath solid in the system we are about to consider, was defined as conforming to that of the solid which would be generated by moving a section of the rail along the centre falling line, and kept normal to this line in each successive position. We will now proceed to explain how to get out a wreath in accordance with the above definition by a system of lines, which we venture to hope will prove of interest as well as of practical utility, not only to beginners in the art, but in some measure also to experienced handrailers.

As we have already taken up considerable space in endeavouring to give a full and comprehensive exposition of the tangent system, only a limited number of examples are here introduced, but these will be sufficient to illustrate all that is essential in the method.

The practical advantages attending the system by normal sections are (1) that the wreath can be more expeditiously squared, and (2) from its form it is much easier to mould. In fact, a wreath for an ordinary sized well can, with a little care, be almost completely moulded with a spindle moulding machine.

Objections to the system.—On the other hand, it is attended by some very decided disadvantages, and is limited in its application, since it cannot with satisfactory results be adopted for very small wells, which occur so frequently in practice, especially in ship stairs. (1) A wreath of this form does not join in very well with straight rails, as the straight lined arrises of the latter are not tangential to the corresponding curved lines on the wreath, only the single lines on each side at the middle of the depth—which are the lines of contact of the vertical cylindrical surfaces standing over the plan—being so. This defect always appears prominently in the face mould at the junction of shank and curved part (see Fig. 332). (2) The centre line of the under surface of the wreath does not stand vertically over the centre line of the plan, but always slightly towards the convex side; and this causes a corresponding displacement of the heads of the balusters round the well, the amount of deviation increasing with the depth and pitch of the rail and as the radius of the well decreases. This follows at once from the nature of the skew surfaces of the vertical sides of the squared wreath, the generators being inclined to the horizontal, and only touching the cylinder at their middle points, deviating from it towards the upper and under sides (see Fig. 193). Under ordinary conditions of pitch, etc., however, the displacement of the balusters is only from $\frac{1}{16}$ inch to $\frac{3}{16}$ inch. Its exact amount for any given case can easily be found beforehand either by construction or by calculation. (3) It may also be reasonably urged that since the hand-rail, together with the stair string and balusters, constitute the balus-trade, the rail and string should harmonize and be generated in the same way. But no one would think of making a wreathed string in the same manner as the rail by this method, i.e., rectangular sections normal to the falling line, seeing that it forms a base for the balusters, which are disposed vertically, and straight lines on its surface should be vertical also, otherwise the combination of baluster and string would present a crippled appearance.

The same crippled effect would be produced if we were to suppose a *very* deep rail formed by this method to be placed on the top of the balusters; but as the thickness of the handrail is usually comparatively small, and being always moulded, the defect—apparent in the squared solid—is not much observed in the finished wreath.

Application of the System to a Simple Case of a Quarter-circle Wreath.

Figs. 317 to 319 illustrate what may be termed a simple case, the centre falling line of rail coinciding with the centre of plank, and the two tangents of equal pitch. The centre falling line is, therefore, an ellipse, and the section at any point will be normal to the tangent to the ellipse at that point, i.e., square to the face of the plank.

Having laid down the plan, $a\,m\,c$, of the centre line of rail (Fig. 317), and obtained the development of the tangents A B and B C and the horizontal trace, A a, of the oblique plane, as in the cylindric system, proceed first to draw through o, the centre of the plan circle, the lines $X_1\,a^1$ and $o\,m$ at right angles and parallel respectively to the trace A a.

Position of sections.—Next select the points where it is desirable to have the normal sections. One of the sections should always be taken at each springing, as at a and c, since that section is either a joint or is the division between the wreath proper and the straight rail. A third may be taken at m, as there is no twist at that part of the wreath, and in this case two intermediate sections at the points l and n, midway between m and the springings, will be found sufficient to determine the shape of the wreath.

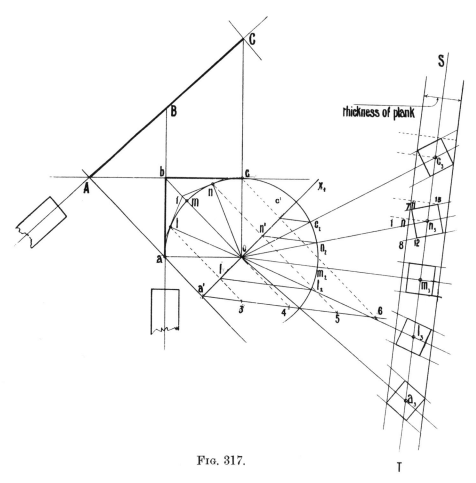

FIG. 317.

Draw the radial lines $o\,l$ and $o\,n$, and the tangents $l\,1$ and $n\,1$ at their extremities.

Using $X_1\,a^1$ as a ground line, set up $a^1\,6$ at an angle with it equal to the pitch of the plank. To do this make $c^1\,6$ equal to $c\,C$ and join $a^1\,6$. This line $a^1\,6$ is the trace of the plane of the plank on the vertical plane, whose ground line is $X_1\,a^1$. Next, from the points of section l, m, n, c draw lines parallel to the trace $A\,a$, cutting the ground line $X_1\,a^1$ in the points l^1, o, n^1, c^1, and the pitch line $a^1\,6$ at the points 3, 4, 5, 6.

Diagram of sections and bevels.—To obtain the bevels at each section, and at the joints, we shall employ the method illustrated by Fig. 217 (page 177). Draw therefore through the points l^1, o, n^1, c^1 parallels to the pitch line a^1 6, cutting the plan circle in l_2, m_2, n_2, c_2. Join each of these points to the centre o, and produce these lines as shown to cut any convenient line, S T (Fig. 317), drawn at right angles to a^1 6 in the points a_3, l_3, m_3, n_3, c_3; then the angle that each of the radial lines makes with S T is the twist bevel at the corresponding section. Draw, therefore, at each of the points a_3, l_3, etc., the rectangular section of the rail as shown, then two lines parallel to S T, touching and including the sections, will represent the two edges of the plank containing the squared wreath. It may be observed that sections equidistant from section m on each side of it have the same bevel.

Marking out face moulds.— It is now a simple matter to draw the face moulds. Two are required in this system, one for each side of the plank.

Take a thin board with one edge shot straight, as $a^1$6, Fig. 318, and lay its straight edge on to the pitch line a^1 6

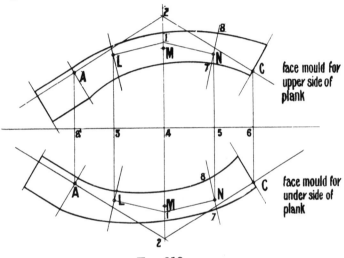

FIG. 318.

(Fig. 317); draw lines square across it from the points a^1, 3, 4, 5, 6. Then measure off from the edge of the board along these lines the distances a^1 A, 3 L, etc., equal respectively to the corresponding level ordinates, $a\,a^1$, $l\,l^1$, etc., in the plan, Fig. 317; then A, L, M, N, C (Fig. 318), are points on the ellipse or centre line of plank.

We have next to draw the section lines on the two moulds, these being, of course, normals to the ellipse at the points A, L, etc., just found. They may be obtained directly, but it is more convenient to first determine the tangents to the curve at the corresponding points, and then to draw the normals at right angles to them.

In Fig. 318, therefore, set off along the middle ordinate, 4 M, the distances, 4 1, 4 2, equal respectively to o 1 and $o\,b$ in the plan, Fig. 317, and join 2 A, 2 C, 1 L, and 1 N. These are the tangents at the several points, and normals are then drawn at right angles to them, as shown.

Set off half the width of rail on each side of M (Fig. 318) on the middle ordinate, which gives the width of the mould there, as in the cylindric system.

The lines on each mould up to this point are exactly alike. We have now to set off the widths at the other sections, and will take as an example that at N on both moulds. Referring to the section n_3 (Fig. 317), draw through its centre a line $n_3 n$, at right angles to S T, and from N (Fig. 318), on the upper mould set off N 7 and N 8, equal to n 7 and n 8 in Fig. 317, and again on the lower mould mark off the same distances, but on opposite sides from that on the other mould. The widths are similarly set off at the other sections on both moulds, and the curves traced through the points by means of a batten. The edges of the shank are, of course, drawn parallel to the tangent A 2, and the joint line at right angles to it, as in the other system.

The two moulds may be drawn out simultaneously as we have described, or one (say the upper) may be made first, and the other obtained from it. This may be done by laying the upper mould on to the stuff and pricking through with a bradawl the points A, L, M, N, C, and the tangents and normals, as they are the same for both moulds; the widths also at the respective sections are identical, but are set off on opposite sides from the fixed points.

Directions for squaring the wreath :

1. Take the plank to the thickness, as given by Fig. 317.

2. Lay either of the moulds on to the plank, and transfer the joint tangents, marking also from it the joint lines and the width at the section M, where there is no twist.

3. Remove the mould, and mark off on the section lines at A and C on each side of these points half the width as given on the same sections (Fig. 317); for example, the distance between the two dotted lines at c_3. Spring a batten through these three points for the curved portion, and draw the edges of the shank parallel to the tangent.

4. Cut the piece square out of the plank to these lines, and form the joints accurately, in this case square to the face and to the corresponding tangent.

5. Square over the tangents, and draw them on the other side of the piece. Fasten temporarily the proper mould on to each face, keeping them flush with the joints, and their tangents coinciding with those on the plank.

6. Clear away the superfluous stuff on both sides to the moulds with gouges or with a bow saw, cutting in the direction of the sections, and finish with a round plane, when, if properly done, a straight edge should touch both face moulds and the piece across the section lines. Having drawn the section lines across the sides thus formed, the wreath will now have the appearance shown by Fig. 319.

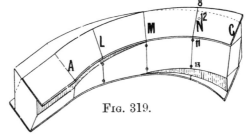

FIG. 319.

7. Before removing the moulds (Fig. 319) measure down from the face of the plank along the section lines the distances of the arrises as they are given by the corresponding sections, Fig. 317. Take, for example, section N: make the distance of the point 11 from the upper surface of the plank, Fig. 319, equal to 7 11 in Fig. 317, and 8 12 on the convex side equal to 8 12, Fig. 317. The points at the other section, A, L, M, C, being similarly marked off, the upper surface of the wreath is cut to the lines traced through the points so obtained. The under side of the wreath may be cut to lines gauged from the upper side.

In place of marking two moulds, as indicated above, it will be found a rather quicker way merely to draw the section lines with the points on the central ellipse, such as A, L, M, N, C, on *one* mould, and having its edges trimmed only for cutting the piece square out of the plank, not for giving the twist lines, these latter being marked on the plank itself with a flexible batten.

WREATHS FOR SEMICIRCULAR WELLS CONNECTING TWO STRAIGHT FLIGHTS, WITH LANDING IN THE HALF SPACE.

Case I. Crown tangent horizontal.—This case is the subject of the illustrations, Figs. 320-325, which show a very simple plan arrangement.

Before proceeding to this and the following examples the student should have thoroughly mastered the last example, Figs. 317-319, which really embraces the essential points in this system of handrailing by normal sections. If he has done this it will prove an easy task to follow out, step by step, the slight modifications that are made in the diagrams to suit the varied conditions of the different cases, otherwise he will not

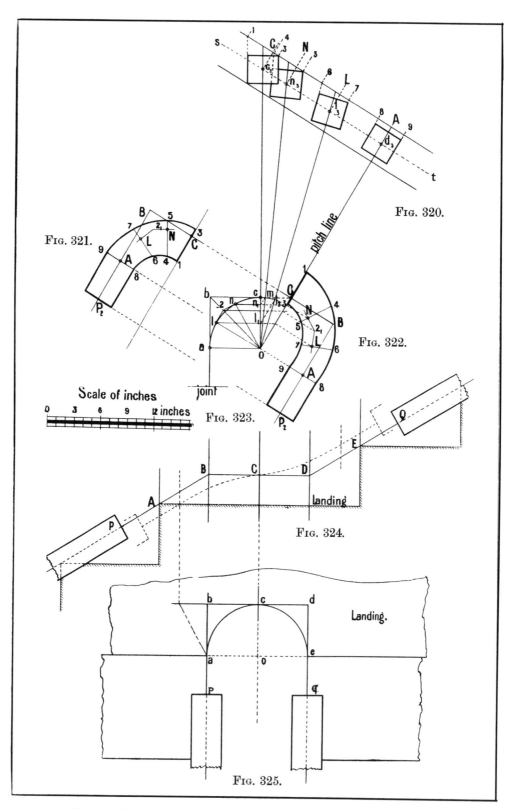

FIG. 320.

FIG. 321.

FIG. 322.

Scale of inches

0   3   6   9   12 inches

FIG. 323.

FIG. 324.

Landing.

FIG. 325.

SMALL WELL, LANDING IN HALF SPACE, RISERS AT SPRINGINGS.

be able to follow out satisfactorily the explanations now to be given, which are necessarily made as short as possible.

It will be seen by the plan, Fig. 325, that the risers of the landing are placed at the springings. The radius is taken equal to half the width of a tread, which results in making a level cross tangent, *b c d*, at the crown. The centre line of plank is taken as the centre falling line of the wreath.

The two straight flights are of equal pitch, so that one set of moulds and bevels will apply to both quarters of the wreath.

In Fig. 323 we have a copy of the plan of the centre line and tangents of the lower wreath. The construction for obtaining the points on the face mould is that by level ordinates (see Fig. 211), the major axis of the ellipse being the base line. Thus *o c* (Fig. 323) is taken as the ground line of a vertical plane at right angles to level lines in the plane, which here are parallel to the level tangent *b c*, the line *o c* corresponding to $X_1 a^1$ in the preceding example (Fig. 317).

Draw, therefore, *o* C, Fig. 323, making an angle with *o c* equal to the pitch of the straight rail as got from the pitchboard or from the development of tangents (Fig. 324); *o* C is then the semi-major axis of the ellipse, and the line of the plumb joint at *c*.

The method for finding the bevels at each section is the same as that given by Fig. 317, the centre line *s t* (Fig. 320) being drawn at any convenient distance from *o*, and strictly at right angles to the pitch line *o* C. Fig. 322 is the mould for the upper side, and Fig. 321 that for the under side of plank.

The student should also again carefully note that in drawing both face moulds the widths of the sections are taken from Fig. 320; thus at section L the distances L 6 and L 7, Fig. 320, are transferred to the corresponding sections on the moulds, Figs. 321 and 322.

Case II. Crown tangent inclined.—In this illustration (Fig. 326) we have a much larger well than that in the previous example, and the landing risers at some distance along the curve from the springings. The arrangement results in giving an inclination to the crown tangent, presenting a case of a wreath with unequally pitched tangents.

The explanations given for the fundamental example apply exactly to the present case, and need not be repeated. The uniform system of lettering adopted will enable the student to trace out similar points in each diagram.

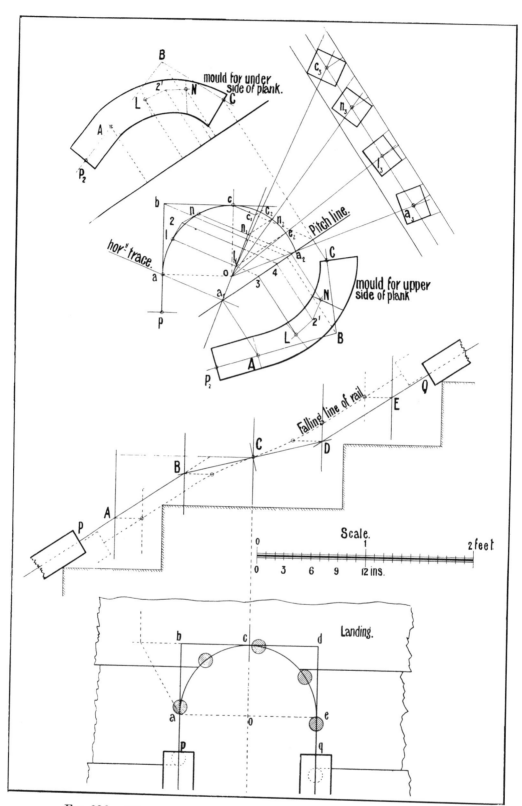

FIG. 326. WREATH FOR LARGE WELL, CROWN TANGENT INCLINED.

QUARTER-CIRCLE WREATH FOR STAIR WITH STRAIGHT FLIGHTS ABOVE
AND BELOW. EASINGS FORMED ON WREATH PIECE.

We now take leave of the straightforward cases, where the centres of
the sections have all been taken in the centre of plank, and come to consider the application of the system to a few examples in which the centres
of the sections are made to coincide with a falling line arranged to suit
the stair instead of the plank.

It will be convenient to commence with a quarter-circle wreath
joining in with two straight rails (as illustrated by Figs. 327-332). In
practice it probably would not be advisable to make so long easings,
which require long shanks, as are here adopted, because the long ogee
form of wreath, though giving a good falling line, would unavoidably
require a thick plank, but the exaggeration provides a clearer diagram
for illustration.

Fig. 328 is the plan. The development of the steps along the centre
line of rail is shown in Fig. 327, being unfolded to the left about the
vertical springing line $c\,C$. The vertical lines $b\,B$ and $A\,D$ on the same
figure are the usual lines for the development along the tangents.

The dotted line touching the nosings represents the under side of
rail, and the full line the centre falling line.

We have first to select three resting points on this falling line to
determine a plane for the lie of the plank from which the falling line will
show the least deviation. This requires judgment and experience, as no
definite rule can be laid down for a falling line like the present, whose
curvature does not follow any definite law. In the example these points
are chosen at R_1, R_2, and R_3, the highest and lowest, R_3 and R_1, being
taken on the shanks about half-way between the springings and joints,
while R_2 is taken at a level midway between these two heights (compare
Fig. 312). The positions of these points are now found on the plan
(Fig. 328) at r_1, r_2, and r_3. By joining the highest and lowest points,
viz., r_1 and r_3 and finding a point on this line at the same level as the
intermediate one r_2, gives us the direction of the lines of level on the
plane. The middle point, g, between r_1 and r_3, Fig. 328, is the one
required in this case. Draw the horizontal trace $r_1\,z$ parallel to $g\,r_2$, and
also the projector $Z\,z$ to meet the level line drawn through R_1 at the point
Z in Fig. 327. Join $R_3\,Z$, Fig. 327, which is the vertical trace of the
plane passing through the three points R_1, R_2, R_3, and $B\,C$ is the upper

tangent. Mark off the distance 12 13 along the base line, Z Z, from 12, Fig. 327, making it equal to $b\,r_1$ in plan, and join B 13, cutting the springing line A D in A; then A B is the lower tangent in development.

In Fig. 327 the thin line v L $R_3\,w$ is the development of the inter-section of the oblique plane with the vertical cylindric surface containing centre line of rail, and shows the vertical deviation of the falling line above or below the centre line of plank. The manner of finding this line will be easily seen from the diagram. The point L, Fig. 327, will serve as an example. Through any selected point l (Fig. 328) draw the plan of a level line, $l\,t$, in the plane of the plank, and square up from t to meet the vertical trace, $R_3\,Z$, of the plane in T; draw then T L, cutting the vertical line in development corresponding to the point l in plan in L; then L is a point in the intersection, and L 3 the amount of vertical deviation of the centre falling line from the plane of the plank at that section.

The plan and development of tangents, to avoid confusion of lines, are copied in Figs. 330 and 329 of the diagram.

It will be easily seen from Fig. 327 that the joints at P and Q are very far from being in planes at right angles to the tangents. All the inter-mediate sections, however, for forming the wreath may be taken at right angles to the centre line of plank, as in the preceding examples. These will then not be strictly normal to the falling line at all sections, as re-quired by the definition, but no appreciable distortion of the wreath will result from so taking them, and it much simplifies the whole problem.

The above assumption enables us to find the twist bevel at each section a, l, n, k, c, exactly as in the preceding examples, the construction being shown in Figs. 330 and 331 (see also Fig. 217).

In drawing the sections of the rail in Fig. 331, however, some of them have to be displaced to a point above or below the centre line of plank $s\,t$. Take, for example, the section A, Fig. 331, at the lower springing. This section has to be pushed down the bevel line from the centre of plank a distance equal to that given by 8 9, Fig. 327. Again, the amount of displacement of section L is approximately given by 4 3 in Fig. 327. The amount of displacement of each intermediate section between the springings given by the short perpendicular is not absolutely accurate, but it may be found exactly, as in Fig. 330. For illustration, take again the section L. Set up from l_1 in Fig. 330 the height $l_1\,3$ equal to that of the point 3 above X Y in Fig. 327; then the perpendicular 3 4 on to $a_1\,7$, the pitch line of plank, is the exact displacement of centre of section below that of the centre plane of the plank, and will, of course, in Fig. 331, be measured square to st, and not along the bevel line, as would be done when the distance 4 3 is taken from Fig. 327.

In order to get accurately the thickness of the plank, sections may be drawn parallel to those at the springings at the joints P and Q, which would have, therefore, the same twist bevel as those at the springings, and the amount of displacement of the centres along the bevel lines may be obtained from Fig. 329. These two sections, be it observed, are not required, in the same way as the others, in order to draw the face moulds, as they are not the joint sections, but only to get the thickness of the plank.

Face moulds.—With respect to the two face moulds, which are shown the one over the other in Fig. 332, it will only be necessary to draw attention (1) to the displacement requiring to be made in some of the intermediate section lines owing to the falling line and centre of plank not being coincident; and (2) to the method of obtaining the joint lines, which are not in this case necessarily square to the tangents. In other respects the work of getting out the moulds is identical with that described in the preceding examples illustrating this system.

1. *Shifting the section lines on the moulds.*—It will be seen from Figs. 327 and 331 of the illustration that all the section lines on the mould, with the exception of those at M and N, have to be displaced before the width of the mould on them can be set off accurately. We will take the section at A as an illustration. In Fig. 332 the normal through A corresponds to a section passing through the point A on the centre line of the plank, v A R_2 w, Fig. 327, but the section is required to pass through the point 9 on the centre falling line vertically below A, so that the displacement of that section along the tangent is given by A 8, Fig. 327, the line 9 8 in the same figure being drawn through 9 at right angles to A v, the tangent and centre line of plank. In Fig. 332, therefore, set off from the line A A along the tangent towards P the distance A 8, equal to A 8, Fig. 327, and draw the dotted line 8 8 parallel to A A; on the line 8 8 set off the widths of the moulds taken from section A, Fig. 331, in the same manner as in the preceding examples.

The displacement of the normals at sections L, K, C are obtained similarly from Fig. 327; but it may be worth while observing that the distance L 4, for example, at section L, Fig. 327, being measured along the curve in place of along the tangent, is not theoretically accurate. For so small a portion of the curve, however, no appreciable error is introduced, as the curve and tangent may be taken to agree for so short a length.

The distances may be obtained accurately by drawing the tangents to the curve at the points L, etc., in Fig. 327. Of course, A 8 at section A is strictly accurate, A 8 being a portion of the tangent at A.

2. *Joint lines.*—Measure off the length of the shanks A P and C Q on the moulds equal respectively to A P and C Q, Fig. 329. The bevels for the joints can be found by the general method given in Fig. 215, but all the particulars that are required can be readily obtained as shown in Fig. 329.

Referring then to this figure: through b, which it will be seen is the elevation of the extremity a of the lower tangent as well as the plan of B, draw a line parallel to the upper tangent B C, cutting the vertical line c C in O_1, and the joint line through Q produced in the point 13. The line $b\,O_1$ is therefore the elevation of the springing line $a\,o$, and O_1 the elevation of the centre of the ellipse. From O_2, the point on the other springing at the same level as O_1, draw $O_2\,12$ parallel to the lower tangent A B, cutting the joint line at P produced in 12.

Reverting now to Fig. 332: from the centre O draw the two lines O 12 and O 13 parallel respectively to the tangents P B and B Q, and mark off O 12 and O 13 respectively equal to $O_2\,12$ and $O_1\,13$, Fig. 329. Join 12 P and 13 Q, which give the directions of the joint lines.

The directions of these joint lines may also be found by drawing $O_1\,14$ and $O_2\,15$ (Fig. 329) parallel respectively to the joint lines at Q and P, and then making B 14 and B 15 (Fig. 332) equal to the corresponding lines B 14 and B 15 in Fig. 329. Then parallels at the joints to O 14 and O 15, Fig. 332, give the lines required.

Next take half the length of the oblique line 16 18 at section C, (Fig. 331) and set it off on each side of C (Fig. 329) on a line, 16 18, perpendicular to the tangent B C. Through the points 16 and 18 (Fig. 329), draw parallels to the tangent B Q, cutting the joint line in 17 and 19.

Then, in Fig. 332, draw the dotted lines 16 17 and 18 19 on the middle of the shanks of the upper and lower moulds, and make the lines 16 17 and 18 19 equal to the same lengths in Fig. 329. Then 17 and 19 are points in the joint lines, and parallels to Q 13 through these points give the true joint lines on the moulds.

A similar mode of procedure at the lower joint completes the moulds.

The case here chosen is one of considerable complexity, arising from the obliquity of the joints with respect to the plane of the plank and the necessary shifting of the sections. With regard to the latter, it should be remarked that the method here given succeeds in bringing the centres of all the sections on to the given falling line at their specified positions, and unless attention is given to this the sections will to some extent be pushed out of the well.

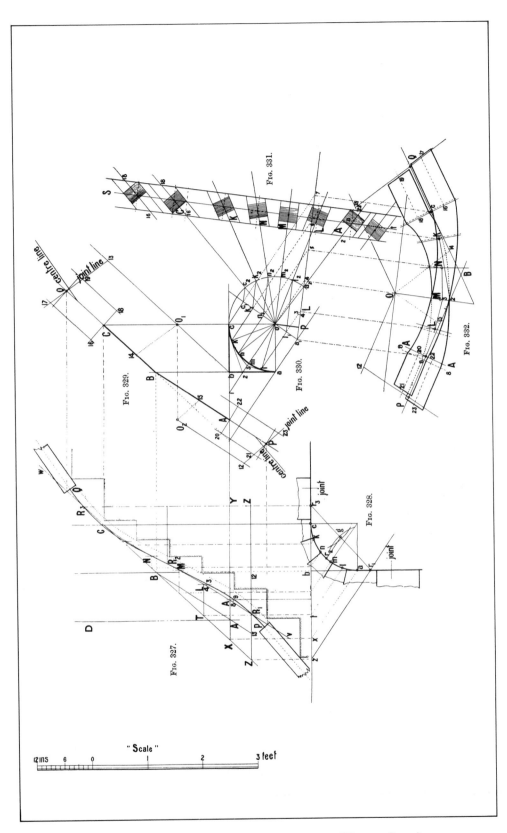

QUARTER-CIRCLE WREATH (EASINGS FORMED ON WREATH PIECE).

CHAPTER XIX

FURTHER CONSIDERATIONS RESPECTING THE SYSTEM BY NORMAL SECTIONS

General remarks as to the direction of intermediate sections.—It will be remembered that in the last example all the intermediate sections between the joints were taken in planes normal to the central ellipse, and therefore were at right angles to the surfaces of the plank, instead of being, as required by the definition, normal to the falling line.

If it is desired to work with all the sections normal to the falling line—a proceeding which involves much labour, and from a practical point of view would hardly be recommendable—each section has to be treated as if it were a true butt joint requiring three bevels.

A separate drawing necessary for each section when treated as a true butt joint.—Further, we have seen that in this system, for each selected section a section of the rail has to be drawn and its appropriate twist bevel applied to obtain the lines where the section is terminated by the upper and under surfaces of the plank, and the definite points on them at which the lines defining the width of the rail intersect them. These intersections with the surfaces of the plank necessarily appear parallel on the section thus drawn; and when the section is inclined to the surface of the plank the distance apart of these lines will be a little in excess of the thickness of the plank, and this distance will of course vary according to the degree of inclination.

The first section that should be set out in this manner is the one which may be expected to have the greatest twist and also the greatest deflection of centre of rail from centre of plank, as it may be reasonably concluded that the thickness of plank sufficient for that section would prove ample for all the others.

The several sections regulated by the plumb depth of plank.—In passing on to draw the remaining sections some constant line is obviously required in the construction, so as to make them all correspond to a common thickness of plank, and for this purpose, in the examples that follow, use is made of the *plumb depth of the plank*, which is, of course, equal at all points.

General method of treating the sections. Explanatory diagram.— To make the next two examples more intelligible and easier to follow out, an explanatory diagram (Fig. 333) representing one normal section— with all particulars in connection with it that are required for application to the plank—is here introduced and drawn to a large scale. The method employed is to represent all the particulars required by folding the section of rail, plank, etc., into the vertical plane containing the tangent at that section.

The explanatory notes on the diagram will enable those who have made some progress in the subject to follow out the construction without much reference to the detailed description that follows.

Turning then to Fig. 333, draw any vertical line A O, and mark on it two points, D and C, to represent respectively the positions of the centre of rail and centre of plank as they occur at any given section, and also a third point, O, at the level of the centre of the ellipse. The vertical divergence, C D, of centre of rail from centre of plank, will be found as in Fig. 327, or from an end view of the plane and projection of the falling line, as in Fig. 314. Through C and D (Fig. 333) draw two parallel lines, C F and D E, at the pitch of the tangent corresponding to the section, and through O draw O F E at the angle that the joint section makes with the horizontal (as got from the development of the centre falling line), cutting the two parallels just drawn in E and F.

Through D draw D 8 parallel to O E, cutting F C produced at 8; then C 8 is the distance that the section has to be moved parallel to itself up the tangent to make it pass through the point D on the falling line, as explained in the preceding example. Construct a section of the rail with its centre at E and O E as its middle line, and set out O M at right angles to O F and equal to the radius of the well. Join M F, and draw the lines G K and P Q parallel to and at equal distances on each side of it, the line K G cutting off as much of the corner of the section of the rail as can be spared and allow it to be properly moulded.

Through G and P draw G A and P B parallel to the tangent line C X, cutting the vertical line A O in A and B. A B is then the *plumb depth* through the plank referred to above, and, being equal at all points of the plank, may be used as a starting line for the construction of other sections of the wreath, so that the pair of parallel lines representing the upper and under surfaces of the plank, such as K G and Q P, would have to accommodate themselves to it and not to the section of the rail.

The real thickness of the plank is obtained by drawing through C a line inclined to the horizontal at the angle of pitch of the plank, and then parallels to this line through A and B include its thickness.

Construction for bevels.—Next, from F draw F T perpendicular to F G, intersecting the line K G representing the upper surface of the

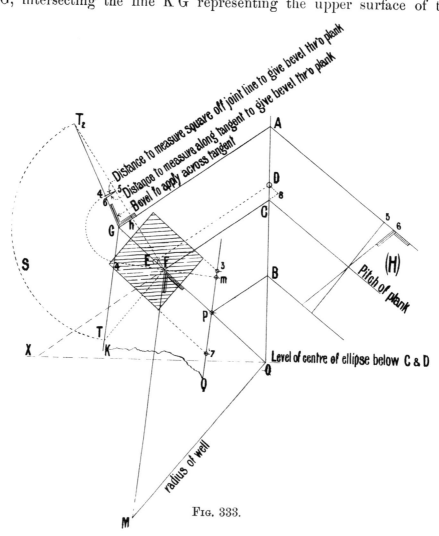

FIG. 333.

plank at T; then F T is a level line on the section when the wreath is in position. With G as centre, and G T as radius, draw the arc T S T₂, cutting the perpendicular F T₂ drawn from F to the tangent lines at T₂, and join T₂ G. The angle T₂ G A is the bevel to apply across the tangent to give the direction of the section on the surface of the plank.

Application of particulars to draw face mould.—In Fig. 334 this bevel is applied to give the section line on the plank at C, which point has been displaced along the tangent from C_1, its original position, a distance, C_1 C, equal to C 8 (Fig. 333). The section would cut the surfaces of the plank in such parallel lines to V W which is drawn through C, as 1 2 and 3 7 (Fig. 334), the former being on the upper side of plank, the latter on the lower. The distance of these lines 1 2 and 3 7 from V W can easily be found on the diagram (Fig. 333) without formally determining the dihedral bevel, *i.e.*, angle that section makes with face of plank, and then applying it across the plank's edge, as is shown at (H) (Fig. 333). Thus, from F (Fig. 333) draw F 4 at right angles to K G, the line of the upper surface of the plank. Lay the distance G 4 along the line $G T_2$

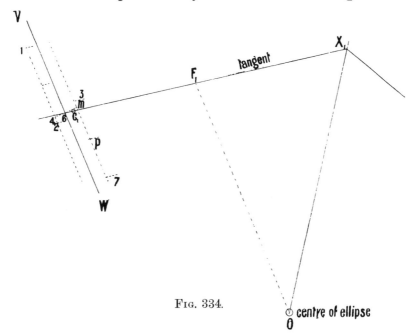

FIG. 334.

from G; then 4 5, drawn at right angles to $G T_2$, is the *perpendicular* distance of the lines 1 2 and 3 7 from V W (Fig. 334). We may observe also that if a line is drawn through 5 parallel to the tangent F C and cutting $G T_2$ in 6, then 5 6 will be the distance in Fig. 334 to measure *along* the tangent on each side of V W to give the positions of 1 2 and 3 7, as before.

The direction of the line V W drawn through C in Fig. 334 may also be found by making $C F_1$ equal to 8 F in Fig. 333 and joining F_1 to O, the centre of the ellipse on the face mould; then the joint line V W is parallel to $O F_1$.

When the positions of the lines 1 2, 3 7 have been determined, we have then to set off the widths of the moulds on them. To do this draw (in Fig. 334) a perpendicular to V W through C, cutting 3 7 and 1 2 at m and

4 respectively. Then the line $m\,4$ just drawn is the projection on the plane of the plank of the line $m\,4$ in Fig. 333. Now from m (Fig. 334) on the joint line of the lower mould set off the distances $m\,3$, $m\,p$, $m\,7$, equal to $m\,3$, $m\,p$, $m\,7$ in Fig. 333, and for the upper mould set off the same distances along the joint line, measuring from 4, but on opposite sides.

LINES FOR A SPIRAL WREATH.

Characteristics of this form of wreath.—The nature and symmetry of the lines of a truly spiral wreath make it instructive to deal with it in this system by normal sections as a special case.

When the falling line of wreath is made to deviate in any manner from the centre of the plank, it will, in general, have no known properties, and normal sections to it would present varying degrees of inclination, both to the plane of the plank and to the horizontal; but in the particular case, viz., of a spiral falling line, though the sections normal to it make different angles with the plane of the plank, they have all the same inclination to the horizontal plane.

It should be observed, however, that though the sections present this regularity, the example we are about to consider will show that the inclinations of the sections normal to the ellipse, or centre line of plank, do not differ so much from those normal to the spiral, or helix, as to make it desirable in practice to use the latter sections in place of the former for getting out and shaping the wreath other than at the joints.

Observations.—We may note (1) that for any portion of a true spiral wreath the tangents at the joints will have equal pitches, so that the direction of level lines on the plane of plank is parallel to the radius of the well at the middle point of the wreath. And that without any previous construction, such as we had to employ in connection with the example, Figs. 327 and 328, a ground line can at once be drawn at right angles to this radius in order to take an end view of the plane along with the projection of the "falling line," as at (A), Fig. 310. (2) That from symmetry the plane of the plank should always pass through the middle point of the falling line of the wreath piece, and the other two resting points at equal distances on each side of it. (3) That, therefore, a diagram representing the expansion of the tangent planes is not required. (4) That the same mould turned end for end answers for both the upper and under sides of plank.

Directions for drawing out the diagram.—Let Fig. 337 be the plan of a portion of a spiral wreath, the length taken embracing exactly one quarter of a circle.

The centre line in plan is first divided into any number of equal parts (in this case six) at the points k, l, m, n, r, the middle point being m.

Having drawn the tangents at the joints and at the several intermediate sections, draw the radius O m, and through O draw the ground line $x\,y$ at right angles to it.

Set up on this ground line an elevation of the several equidistant points on the falling line whose plans are coincident with the points a, k, l, m, n, r, c, and as $x\,y$ is at the level of O m, one-half of this elevation will appear above $x\,y$ and the other half below, and as the several points are at equal distances apart along a true helix they will appear in elevation at successive equidistant levels. The elevation of the curve is shown by the dotted line passing through the points 1, 2, 3, etc.

The straight line $v\,t$, representing an edge view of the plane of the plank, is then drawn through O so as to make the deflections of the falling line at the joints a^1 and c^1 a little less than it is at the inner loops, where there is much less twist.

We have now two sets of points shown in elevation, one set, 1, 2, 3, etc., on the falling line or helix, and the other, $a^1\,k^1$, etc., vertically above or below them on $v\,t$. The latter set of points being situated on the central ellipse are those that are projected on to the plane of the mould (Fig. 335) at A, K, L, M, etc., and to which the tangents, drawn in plan (Fig. 337), correspond. Thus the distances a^1 A, k^1 K, etc., of the points A, K . . . C, from $v\,t$, are respectively equal to the distances $a_2\,a$, $k_2\,k$ of the same points in plan from $x\,y$. The distances O F, O G, O B (Fig. 335) are similarly set off on O M produced, and the tangents A B, B C, G K, G R, F L and F N, drawn.

The remaining particulars required for completing the face mould are given for the three sections C, R, N at Fig. 336, and these by symmetry will apply to the corresponding sections at A, K, L on the lower half of wreath. The method adopted has been already described in full detail (Figs. 333, 334).

Since the same construction is applied at each of the three sections, we will here only refer to one of them, say that at C. Take B C, the length of the tangent at the joint C on the face-mould diagram (Fig. 335), and with the point c^1 (Fig. 336) as centre, cut the ground line X Y at B_2, and join $B_2\,c^1$. The angle $c^1\,B_2$ O is the pitch of this tangent, and the line c B_2 corresponds to C F X (Fig. 333). From C_2, where the projector $c\,c^1$ cuts the ground line, draw C_2 D inclined to X Y at the angle that each

section makes with the horizontal, being, of course, equal to the complement of the angle of pitch of the helix, *i.e.*, the complement of the angle
that the *straight line development of the helix* (not shown in the figure)
makes with the horizontal. The line C_2 D corresponds to O F (Fig. 333).

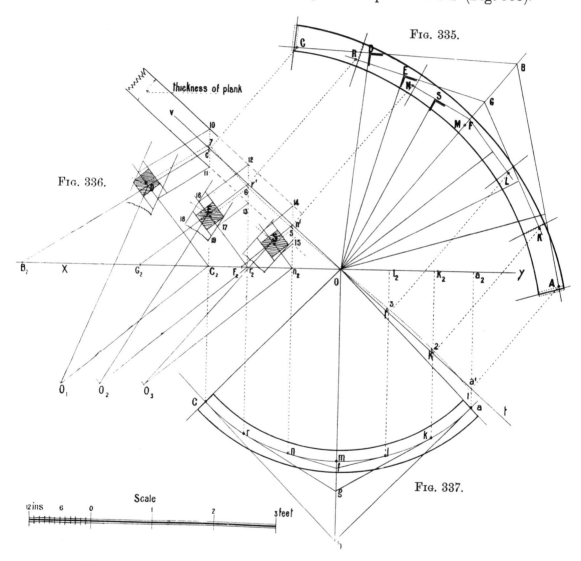

FIG. 335.

FIG. 336.

FIG. 337.

Scale

12ins   6   0   1   2   3feet

Transfer the distance B_2 D (Fig. 336) to B D (Fig. 335), and in the
latter figure join D to O, the centre of the ellipse; then B D O is the
angle that the joint line at C makes with the tangent B C, which joint
line would, of course, simply be drawn parallel to D O. Similarly the
bevels at E and S give the directions of the intermediate section lines at
R and N.

Again, in Fig. 336, by drawing $c_2 O_1$ at right angles to c_2 D, and equal to O m, the radius of centre line of rail in plan, and joining O_1 D, determine the angle O_1 D c_2, which represents the twist bevel at this section.

For completing the construction of the section at this joint the student should refer to Fig. 334, and he should be careful also to note that 10 11 (Fig. 336) is the *plumb depth of the plank*, and corresponds to A B in the figure referred to. In the diagram (Fig. 336), since the straight line v t represents the centre line of plank, parallels to it through the points 10 and 11 give, in this case, the real thickness of plank. Let the parallel lines be produced intersecting the verticals through the other section points r^1, n^1 in 12, 13 and 14, 15 respectively. Then, when drawing out the other sections—that at r^1 for example—begin by drawing parallels to r^1 G_2 (Fig. 336) through the points 12 and 13, cutting the section line E r_2 at 16 and 17, and through the latter points draw the parallel lines to E O_2, viz., 16 18 and 17 19. The next section at n^1 is similarly proceeded with. It will be seen that this proves a convenient way of making each section as drawn conform to a common thickness of plank.

Referring again to Fig. 335, the face-mould diagram, the reader will observe that the section lines are not drawn through the points, A, K, L, N, R, C, which lie on the central ellipse, but occupy altered positions up or down the corresponding tangents in consequence of the sections having to pass through the correct points 1, 2, 3, etc., on the falling line, or helix, which are vertically above or below the former points. The correct positions are shown by the full lines drawn across the mould, while the dotted lines on each side of them mark the positions of the section lines on the surfaces of the plank. The requisite distances of these lines from the specific points A, K . . . C on the ellipse are, owing to the small scale of the drawing, only indistinctly shown in Fig. 336, but they are represented to a larger scale in Fig. 338, being indicated in the latter figure by C^1 8, r_1 q, and n^1 13 for the sections at C, R, N respectively, Fig. 335.

Practical lessons afforded by the example.—One lesson may be learned from this example of a spiral wreath, namely, that—since at the intermediate sections both the angles that the section lines make with the tangent, and the angles that the sections make with the surfaces of the plank, differ so little from right angles—they may be taken square to the tangent and plane of plank without resulting in any appreciable error in the form of the wreath solid; and further, that little difference would result by making these sections pass through the points on the ellipse instead of the selected points on the falling line.

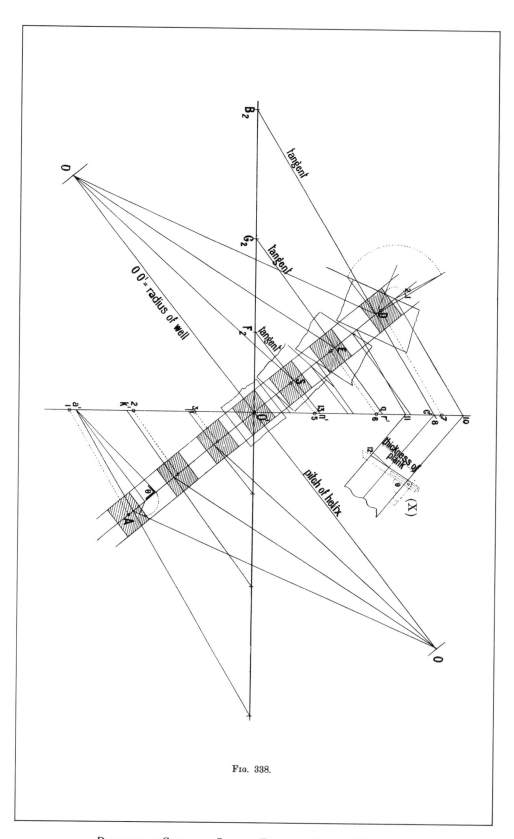

Fig. 338.

DIAGRAM OF SECTIONS, BEVELS, ETC., FOR SPIRAL WREATH.

We may conclude generally that, unless in special cases and examples where great accuracy is required, it would prove a waste of labour to adopt in practice the somewhat complex though exact construction for each section which we have just been describing, though, of course, the exact method has to be rigorously applied at the *joint sections*.

It is well, however, to keep in mind that an approximate method cannot usually be applied intelligently without a clear knowledge of the strictly accurate construction from which it is derived.

Enlarged diagram of bevels for spiral wreath.—The diagram (Fig. 338) may prove of some interest to students of handrailing as showing how the symmetrical character of a spiral wreath permits of all the information, such as bevels, etc., being clearly arranged in one diagram.

The drawing applies to the spiral wreath, Figs. 335, 336, 337, and being to a larger scale some of the particulars are more clearly seen.

The section points on the falling line, and those on centre of plank, are here arranged on a common vertical line, 1 10, at their appropriate levels, and from the fact that all the sectional planes have the same inclination to the horizontal, these sections can all be set off on a common centre line, D O¹ A.

The construction at section D, giving the lines that serve in lieu of the bevel through the plank, is the same as that already given by Fig. 333, while at the lowest joint A the ordinary method of finding this bevel, which is marked θ, is shown. The application of this bevel, θ, to the edge of the plank is shown at (X) (Fig. 338) for obtaining the same particulars as are determined by the other method at section D; thus, the deflection 1 2 of the bevel from the square line at (X) is equal to 1 2 at section D. The one method may serve as a check on the other.

The thickness of plank as shown at (X) (Fig. 338) is of course obtained by drawing through the points 10 and 11 the parallels inclined to the horizontal at the angle of pitch of plank. Note also that the distance 10 11 is the *plumb depth* of plank.

LINES FOR A SEMICIRCULAR WREATH (RISING FROM LEVEL TO RAKE).

Remarks.—This drawing, Figs. 339-346, shows the application of the system by normal sections to the case of the wreath of the geometrical stair with pillar-newel, illustrated by Fig. 187, the plan, Fig. 340, being copied from that example.

There are no constructions employed in the diagram before us with which the reader has not already been made familiar in connection with

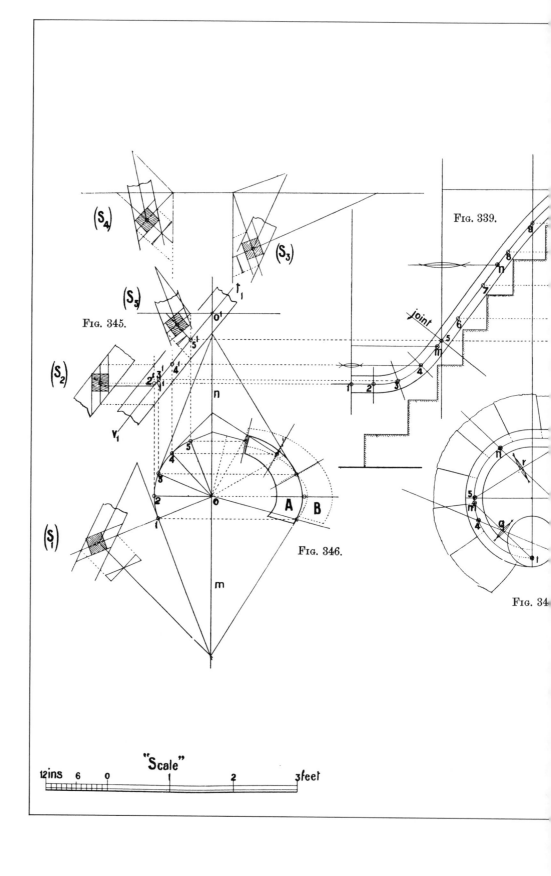

(S_4)

(S_3)

(S_5)

Fig. 345.

(S_2)

(S_1)

t_1

o^1

v_1

n

5
4
3
2
1

o

A B

m

Fig. 346.

Fig. 339.

joint

Fig. 34

"Scale"

12ins 6 0   1   2   3feet

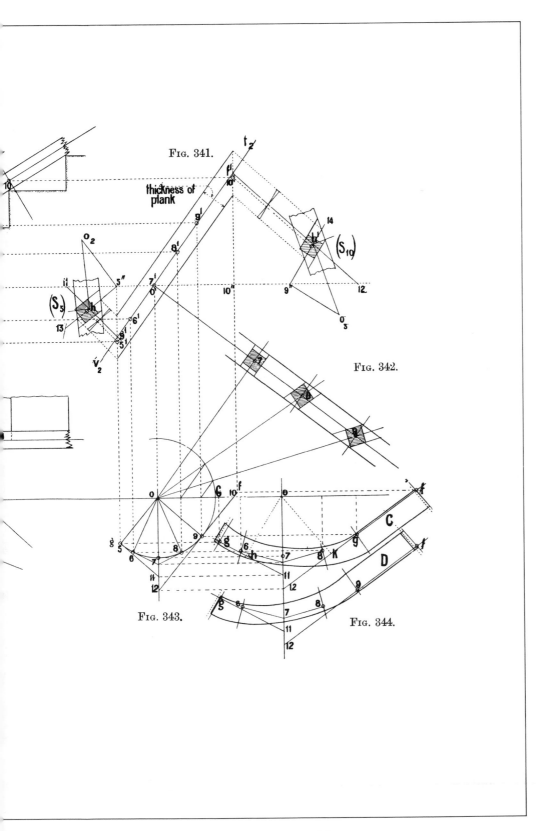

FIG. 341.

thickness of plank

FIG. 342.

FIG. 343.

FIG. 344.

COMPLEX CASE OF A SEMICIRCULAR WREATH.

previous cases, only the positions occupied by some of the figures in relation to the others in the diagram are a little different.

Position of middle joint.—A joint is made in the wreath at the crown, making two exact quarter-circle wreaths, the lower one starting from the level at the newel.

Determination of the plane of plank.—We proceed first to find a trial plane for each wreath in the same way as was done in Figs. 327 and 328. The construction lines for this purpose are shown in the plan (Fig. 340) and the development (Fig. 339), $4\,q$ in the plan being a level line on the trial plane of lower wreath, and $n\,r$ a level line on the upper.

The plans are then re-arranged, being turned round until these level lines are at right angles to the ground line through the centre of well; that of the upper wreath being placed at Fig. 343 on the right, and of the lower at Fig. 346 on the left.

The definite points, 1, 2 . . . 9, at which it is desirable to have the sections, are arranged on these two plans, and transferred to their proper positions on the development of the falling line (Fig. 339). These points, 1 . . . 10, are levelled over on to the vertical projectors from the corresponding points on the two plans, giving their elevations $5^1, 6^1, 7^1, 8^1, 9^1, 10^1$ (Fig. 341) on the right, and 1^1 . . . 5^1 (Fig. 345) on the left. It will be seen that in each elevation just obtained the several points lie very nearly on a straight line, thus showing that the trial planes have been well chosen.

In Fig. 341 we have drawn the trace of the plane or pitch line of plank $v_2\,t_2$, to reconcile as nearly as possible with the four intermediate points 6^1, 7^1, 8^1, 9^1, making small deflections at the joints 5^1 and 10^1. This makes the case as simple as is possible, by allowing us to treat the intermediate points as lying in the plane of the plank. Similar remarks apply to the pitch line of plank $v_1\,t_1$ (Fig. 345).

Intermediate sections and joints.—In the upper wreath all the intermediate sections are taken at right angles to the tangents and to the surface of plank, instead of normal to the falling line, so that only the twist bevel has to be found for each, while in the lower wreath all the intermediate sections are made strictly normal to the falling line, and, therefore, each section of the latter has to be dealt with by the general method, involving constructions for finding three bevels.

At (S_5) and (S_{10}) (Fig. 341) are shown the requisite construction for the two joint sections of the upper wreath. The horizontal dotted line through 7^1 is the line of level of the centre of the ellipse, and the vertical lines through the joint points meet it in $5''$ and $10''$. Setting off the distance

$5''$ 11, equal to 5 11, the plan length of the tangent (Fig. 343), and joining g^1 11, gives the full length and the pitch of that tangent, and must, of course, come out exactly equal to g 11 obtained in Fig. 344. The joint line $5''$ 13 is drawn across the tangent line g^1 11 just found, making with the horizontal an angle equal to the pitch of that joint section, as given at 5 in the development (Fig. 339). The line $5''$ O_2 is then set out at right angles to the joint line $5''$ 13, and equal to the radius of the well, and O_2 joined to point h; then O_2 h $5''$ is the angle of twist of the section, and the rest of the working at this section is identical with that given in Fig. 333. To find the angle that this joint section makes with the tangent on the face mould we have only to make g h on the tangent g 11 (Fig. 344) equal to g^1 h at (S_5), and join h with o, the centre of the ellipse; then a parallel to h o gives the direction of the joint at g.

Similar remarks will apply to the construction shown at (S_{10}) (Fig. 341) for the top joint of this wreath. Thus, $10''$ 12 is set off equal to 10 12, the plan length of the tangent (Fig. 343), 12 f^1 being then its true length and set at its correct pitch. A mistake may easily occur here, as by similarity the joint line might be wrongly drawn through the point $10''$ in place of the correct point $9''$, the latter being the projection of the centre of the ellipse on the vertical plane containing the tangent at the joint. The difference arises from the joint section being in this case outside of the curve along the shank. The position of $9''$ is got by setting off $10''$ $9''$ equal to 10 9 (Fig. 343). As with the other joint, the distance f^1 h^1 is transferred to f k (Fig. 344), and k being joined to o, the centre of the ellipse, gives o k as the direction of the joint line at f on the face mould.

Face mould diagram (upper wreath).—The face moulds for this wreath are shown laid down alongside of the plan, the two being kept a little apart from each other for clearness, that marked C being the mould for the upper, and that marked D for the under side of plank. These moulds are easily drawn out, since the intermediate sections are at right angles to the tangents, and their centres also in the centre of the plank, the necessary bevels being found by the usual method at Fig. 342, noting that the thickness of plank is taken as determined in Fig. 341, and that section 6 is not shown in Fig. 342 with the others, because, being symmetrical with section 8, it has the same bevel, and consequently the same width of mould.

Lower wreath.—We leave the construction in connection with the lower wreath to be followed out by the reader, only remarking that in this instance (in the mould diagram, Fig. 346) the plane of the plank is folded

N N

into the horizontal plane about $m\,n$, the line of the minor axis, and seeing that the section at the lower end is plumb, the direction of this joint line on the moulds is parallel to the springing O 1; and further, that section 2 being also plumb and situated on the major axis simplifies the work at that section.

An Exact Method by Ordinary Projection applied to the case of a Quarter-circle Wreath.

We may fitly close this course of handrailing by an illustration of a method of getting out the face moulds for a wreath of similar form to that shown in Figs. 327 and 328, by which all the sections are taken strictly normal to the falling line.

We shall first explain in general terms the mode of procedure, then describe more particularly the method as applied to one section of the rail, and leave the reader to follow out the similar details at the remaining sections as presented in the drawing.

1. The direction of level lines, on the plane that reconciles most closely with the given falling line, is determined as in Fig. 327.

2. An elevation (Fig. 349) is made of the several normal sections on a plane at right angles to the level lines, the elevations of the sections being kept at the same level at which they occur in the development (Fig. 347).

3. Two parallel lines, A B and C D (Fig. 349), are drawn, embracing the elevations of the sections, the space between them thus representing the square edge of the plank, the upper and under surfaces of which are at right angles to the vertical plane of projection, so that all points and lines on these surfaces have their elevations on the lines A B and C D.

4. The face moulds are then determined from this plan and elevation by folding the upper and under surfaces of the plank about their vertical traces, A B and C D respectively, into the plane of the elevation.

More detailed description of the method.—Fig. 347 is a development of the centre falling line of rail. The three points on the falling line chosen for determining the plane of the plank are 1, 2, and m at a level half way between 1 and 2. The chord 1 2 is bisected in the plan, Fig. 348, at the point 3, and the points m and 3 joined, which line in this case incidentally passes through the centre, o. This line $m\,n$ determines the direction of level lines on the surfaces of the plank.

A new plan, Fig. 350, is next drawn on a ground line, X Y, at right angles to *m n*, and for clearness the centre, *o*, is kept a little away from X Y.

The object now to be attained is from this plan to determine an elevation of the several normal sections as they would appear when looking on to the edge of the plank. The full construction is shown in connection with the lower joint section, *f*.

A vertical projector from *f*, Fig. 350, and a horizontal projector from *f*, Fig. 347, determine by their intersection the point f^1, the elevation of the centre of the joint section. To obtain the line $4^1 f^1$, *i.e.*, the elevation of the centre line of the joint, produce the joint line at *f*, Fig. 347, to meet the level line, Z Z, through *m* at the point *q*, and let fall the perpendicular *f p* on Z Z, thus forming the shaded triangle, *f p q*, the line *p q* being the plan length of *f q*, on the horizontal plane through Z Z; the plan of the line *f q* will lie on the tangent, *t f*, produced, Fig. 350 : set off, therefore, on the tangent *t f*, Fig. 350, the distance *f* 4, equal to *p q*, Fig. 347, then a projector from 4 discovers the point 4^1 on Z Z, which point, joined to f^1, gives the elevation $4^1 f^1$ of the line required.

It will be seen that parallels to $f^1 4^1$ and horizontals from the extremities of the joint line in development, Fig. 347, complete the elevation of the joint section at f^1; the former lines being drawn through the points of intersection of the projectors from the ends of the section line in plan and the horizontal line $f f^1$.

The elevations of all the other sections are obtained in the same manner, the plan lengths of such lines as *f q* being found at the common level Z Z, by producing the section lines, Fig. 347, to meet Z Z, and drawing perpendiculars to it from the centres of the sections, thus forming a right angled triangle for each section.

When the elevations of all the sections have been drawn in the manner described they are enclosed by the two parallel straight lines, A B and C D, drawn close to the corners of the sections on each side, the space between them representing the edge of the plank against the vertical plane, and if lines were traced through the corresponding corners of the several sections, a complete elevation of the wreath solid would be obtained as it would lie in the body of the plank.

We have now to find the traces of the plane of each normal section on the surfaces of the plank. This is done by first finding the vertical traces of these planes on the edge of the plank. The vertical traces of any two lines lying on the section are of course sufficient to determine the vertical trace of the plane of that section. The two lines most con-

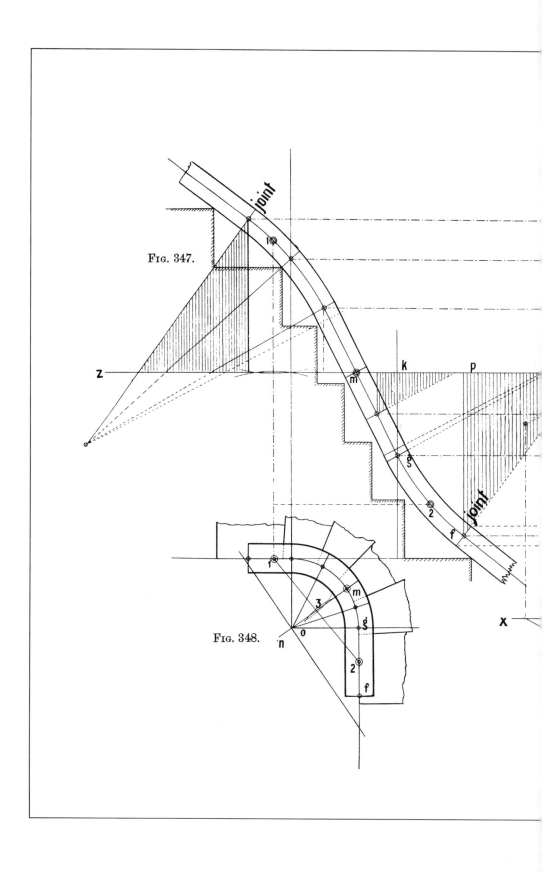

FIG. 347.

FIG. 348.

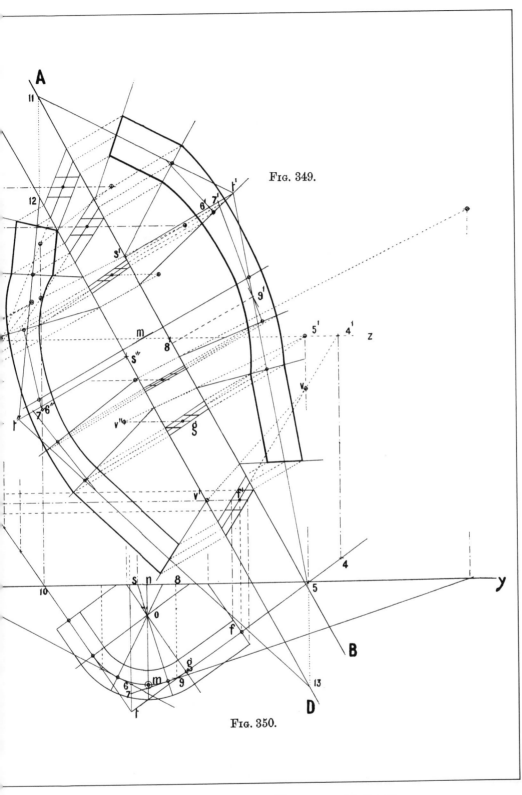

Fig. 349.

Fig. 350.

ILLUSTRATION OF A QUARTER-CIRCLE WREATH, SHOWING THE
FACE MOULDS DETERMINED BY THE ORDINARY METHODS OF PROJECTION.

venient for this purpose are the horizontal line passing through the centre of the section and the other centre line at right angles to it. Both these lines have already been drawn to obtain the elevation of the section. For the section at f^1, Fig. 349, the vertical trace of the horizontal line ff^1 is v^1, and v that of the other line $f^1\,4^1$, these points being projected from the intersections of the plans of these lines with the ground line X Y. For example, the plan of $f^1\,4^1$ is cut by X Y at the point 5, and therefore the vertical trace of the line is the point v on $f^1\,4^1$ vertically above the point 5. The line $v\,v^1$ is therefore the vertical trace of the plane of the joint at f. The vertical traces of the planes of the other sections are determined in a similar manner.

We may now suppose the upper and under surfaces of the plank folded about their vertical traces, A B and C D, respectively, into the vertical plane, bringing with them all the lines of the joints and sections as they would appear on these surfaces, which will enable the two face moulds to be drawn. Several methods of doing this will suggest themselves to the geometrical student; but probably the easiest way is to draw upon the unfolded surfaces, or what may now be called the planes of the moulds, the intersections of the several vertical planes that stand over the plan tangents with these plank surfaces. Take, for example, the two joint tangents $t\,10$ and $t\,5$. Set up vertical projectors from the points 10, t and 5; these cut the edge of the plank at 11 12 and $S^1\,S^{11}$ and 5 13; then through S^1 and S^{11} draw $S^1\,t^1$ and $S^{11}\,t^{11}$ at right angles to A B or C D, making them equal to the ordinate $S\,t$ in plan, Fig. 350; then joining t^1 to the points 11 and 5, and t^{11} to 12 and 13, give the required lines on the upper and lower mould respectively. These lines do duty for the joint sections, as well as those at the springings. It will be seen by inspection of Fig. 349 that the section lines on the moulds are now obtained by first drawing perpendiculars to A B or C D from the points where the centre lines of the sections cut the surfaces A B or C D of the plank, to intersect the tangents at the sections, such as $t^1\,5$ and $t^1\,11$ just drawn. The lines joining these points of intersection with the points where the vertical traces such as $v\,v^1$ of the planes of the several sections intersect A B and C D, are the precise section lines on the moulds.

The width of the mould on these section lines is then obtained by drawing similar perpendiculars from the lines of the sides of the sections.

Considerations of symmetry, etc., will enable the work to be much shortened. For example, when the widths of the moulds at the joint sections are determined, the widths at the springings are, obviously, also found by drawing the shank lines, which are parallel to the tangents, to cut the section lines at the springings. Further, it will be obvious that when the widths have been determined on the several section lines of, say, the upper mould, these answer also for the lower mould at the corresponding sections. The curves of the edges of the moulds are of course drawn in with a flexible batten.

It need hardly be stated that the two moulds, when laid on to the surfaces of the plank for lining it off, have to be placed in the relative positions shown on the diagram.

When the sides of the wreath have been trimmed accurately to the moulds, and the lines of the sections as they occur on these curved surfaces drawn in the manner described on pages 254 and 255, the square distance of each corner of the several sections from the surface of the plank are set off with a gauge, these distances being, of course, obtained as measured from the lines A B or C D in Fig. 349.

PART III.—STONE STAIRS

PART III.—STONE STAIRS

CHAPTER XX

GENERAL DETAILS OF CONSTRUCTION

Preliminary remarks.—In previous chapters we have seen that in modern stairs constructed of wood the steps are made up of two distinct parts, the "tread" and the "riser," these being joined together in various ways, and supported by wood strings.

The physical characteristics of stone are not favourable to this mode of construction, and the steps of stone stairs are generally made of solid blocks, and instead of strings are directly supported by the walls, into which they are firmly built at one or at both ends.

It will thus be seen that the primary points in the construction of stone stairs are more direct and simple than in those made of wood, but the heavy character of the stone steps obviously requires the supporting walls to be solidly and substantially built.

It may be of interest to note that in the very earliest methods of construction employed for wood stairs in this country the steps, like those, of stone stairs, were made of solid blocks of wood, and built into the wall in the same manner, a practice which to some extent prevails on the Continent at the present day, and from the point of view of fireproofness has much to recommend it.

Before proceeding to the consideration of details it will be convenient to draw attention to the various methods of supporting the steps, as the differences arising in this respect may be regarded as roughly dividing stone stairs into three groups.

Group I.—Stairs in which both ends of the steps are supported by solid walls.—This is the simplest and most direct method that can be adopted, the steps being inclosed between two parallel walls, the width of the stair apart, into which their ends are built.

Stairs of the above construction can obviously have any form of plan, and when consisting of short straight flights with intermediate landings prove very convenient, and are well adapted for schools and similar public buildings, where large crowds have to be provided with safe and convenient outlets.

In the case of turning stairs built on this principle, one of the walls may take the form of a central pier about which the several flights of steps are arranged, the pier being rectangular or circular, according to the plan of the stair, *i.e.*, whether it is composed of straight flights with quarter or half space landings, or of a series of winding steps. This central pier is termed the newel, and in some notable examples of large mediæval staircases it was hollow and formed the enclosing walls of a secondary spiral stair, which was thus constructed within and independent of the principal one. As a characteristic ancient example we may cite the celebrated double winding staircase in the Chateau de Chambord in the Valley of the Loire, and as modern examples in which this principle is adopted the eight staircases at the sides of the central hall in the Law Courts, designed by the late G. E. Street.[1]

Group II.—Stairs having the steps built into a wall at one end, and supported at the other.—In these one side of the stair is open and fitted with a balustrade, the steps at this end being supported in various ways, most usually by a light wall built underneath, or by raking iron girders. Where architectural effect is desired, raking arches supported on pillars or columns may be used for the same purpose.

Stone stairs of this construction, when encompassing a well, were designated *open newel staircases*,[2] as distinguished from those with a close central newel noticed above, and historically the one construction naturally followed out of the other.

Group III.—Stairs with the steps fixed at one end, the other being free.—In this construction, which is that of the *geometrical staircase*,[3] and which in turn followed historically that of the "open newel," the steps are securely built into the wall at one end, the other end being left entirely without support except what each receives from its connection with the one next below it, the bearing surfaces of the joints of adjacent

[1] See "Building News," September 21, 1883.

[2] The invention of the open newel staircase has been ascribed to Niccola Pisano, one of the greatest of the early Italian sculptors and architects (1206-78), who introduced this form of staircase in the campanile of San Nicolo, Pisa.

[3] The "geometrical" form of staircase, according to Palladio, was invented by the notable Luigi Cornaro. The well-known geometrical staircase in St. Paul's Cathedral by Sir Christopher Wren is said to have been the first example of the kind erected in this country.

steps being formed so as to transmit the pressure from one step to the
other to a secure abutment at the floor or landing.

It will be obvious that this principle of construction with overhanging steps is not so well adapted for very wide stairs as those in
Groups I. and II.

FORMS OF STEPS.   (1.) **Square steps.**—In the more unimportant
classes of stone stairs the steps are simply rectangular in cross-section

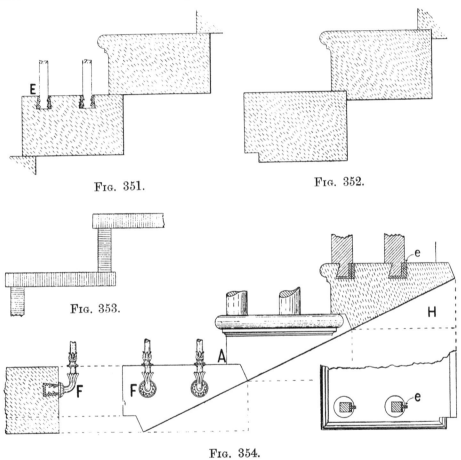

FIG. 351.   FIG. 352.

FIG. 353.

FIG. 354.

(see Figs. 351, 352), and "dressed" only on the two faces which form the
tread and rise, the back and underside being left more or less rough.
They are, however, sometimes used in the best class of stairs, and when
exposed underneath are suitably finished and ornamented.

(2.) **Spandrel steps.**—The portions of the steps built into the wall
are always left rectangular, as at H, Fig. 354, in order that they may rest
on a level bed; but for lightness, as well as to increase the headroom,
and give a better appearance to the stair, the undersides of the steps

beyond the walls are cut away to the slope of the stair (see Fig. 354) to form a raking soffit, which may be finished plain, or panelled and moulded, as required. Steps when worked to this form are termed *spandrel steps*, sometimes also *feather-edged steps*.

(3.) **Built-up steps.**—For back stairs, cellar stairs, etc., the steps are occasionally made of thin slabs in two parts, after the manner of wood stairs, as shown by Fig. 353.

Forms of joints between the steps.—Square steps fixed into a wall at each end are usually made of a thickness equal to the rise, so that one step simply rests on tne next below it, as in Fig. 351, the width of the step being made so as to give an inch or more of an overlap. In this case the steps being fixed at both ends are sufficiently prevented from sliding over one another. When, however, the stair is very wide, a greater thickness of step may be required for strength than that given by the rise, which necessitates a rebate being formed, as in Fig. 352.

A rebate is sometimes used also for the joint between overhanging steps of rectangular section; but more usually this connection is made with the joggled form of joint, which is invariably employed for spandrel steps. This latter joint (see A, Fig. 354) is formed of two plane surfaces, one of which is horizontal, as in the simple rebate, the other perpendicular to the soffit of the stair. This avoids the acute angle that would be formed on spandrel steps by adopting the ordinary rebate, provides a bearing surface normal to the resolved pressure occurring in the direction of the stair, and effectively prevents any slipping of the parts in contact.

The thickness, measured from the interior angles of the steps to the soffit as at A, Fig. 354, should be proportioned to the length of the steps projecting from the wall, a safe rule being to allow $2\frac{1}{2}$ inches for a step 4 feet long, and to add $\frac{1}{2}$ inch for each additional foot of length beyond 4 feet. Thus a step 5 feet long would require 3 inches.

It is easily seen that the principle of support employed in the geometrical staircase is consistent with a stable combination. The bottom step being laid on a solid bed on the floor, and sunk into it is prevented from sliding outwards, and will remain stable for any position of a load placed upon it. The next and successive steps have only two adjacent edges, namely, the front and end at the wall, that receive direct vertical support. Any vertical pressure therefore acting on the unsupported corner would tend to make the step tilt; but this is prevented by its end being built into the wall, so that the effect of a load placed on the step would simply be to increase the pressure on the next below it at the bearing surfaces of the joggled joint, which in turn would be transmitted to the next lower one, and so on to the secure foundation step at the bottom of the stair.

Length of bearing in the walls.—In stairs in which the steps are supported at both ends by a wall, a bearing of 6 inches at each end will prove ample; while in the case of hanging steps it is necessary that they be tailed into the wall at least 9 inches.

Fixing the steps in the walls.—As a rule stone stairs should not be erected till the enclosing walls of the stairway have been built and allowed a sufficient time to settle down and arrive at their bearings. In the case of stairs with steps supported at both ends it is obviously more expedient to lay the steps as the walls are being built, and this is very frequently done. The former, however, is the safer plan, since it avoids any risk of damage to the structure from unequal settlement of the walls, and of injury to the finished steps incidental to building operations at an early stage of the work.

When the former method is adopted, the indents or raglets made in the walls for the reception of the ends of the steps are built up in a temporary manner with bricks, bedded in sand, so as to be easily removed when the steps are being fixed.

The steps should be pinned into the walls with pieces of slate, tile, hoop iron, etc., along with cement. As overhanging steps act to some extent as loaded levers tending to crush and displace the wall, care should be taken to secure good solid masonry in the vicinity of the indents, and from 1 foot to 18 inches of the wall immediately above and below the line of the stair should be built in strong cement mortar to insure greater solidity. It is, of course, equally important that the work of pinning-in overhanging steps should be carefully performed, and all the interstices filled up with solid material, otherwise they are liable to work loose when subjected to heavy and continuous traffic. A pair of iron folding wedges driven in above each of the nosings prove very effective in securing the steps at the wall.

When a step has been fixed in its proper position and levelled, the overhanging end should be temporarily supported by wood struts, or other means, till the cement is thoroughly set.

Landings.—The stones used in the landings are usually of the same thickness as the steps, and are similarly fixed into the walls.

When two or more stones are required to form a landing the joints between them should be joggled, as shown at M, Fig. 358. They are sometimes also plain jointed, and slate or copper dowels inserted at intervals.

With landings of large area, composed of several stones jointed together in the way indicated, it may be necessary to provide additional support other than that afforded by their insertion in the walls, and for this purpose iron girders, brackets, or arches are employed as may be found most expedient and suitable for the situation.   Direct support by iron columns for stone landings, even in situations where they would not otherwise prove an inconvenience, is not to be recommended, as the variations in length due to expansion and contraction of the metal may have the effect of eventually loosening and even cracking the stones.

An intermediate landing on which one flight terminates and another starts in the same direction, when fixed to the wall at one end only, should also have additional support from below in the shape of brackets, etc.   This, in general, will be necessary in order that the landing may form a basis of sufficient strength to take the thrust of the upper flight, since the introduction of the platform causes a break in the continuity of the structure.

Balustrades.—The large and imposing stair structures suitable for public buildings of a palatial character, and outside stairs leading up to terraces, etc., have their balustrades worked wholly in stone, which gives the desired result of great solidity and durability.   Stone stairs of a less pretentious character are fitted with ornamental cast or plain wrought iron balusters supporting wood handrails.

Securing iron balusters to stone steps.—The bases of iron balusters are usually let into the upper sides of the steps, but not infrequently they are fixed into the ends, as at F, Fig. 354, when they are termed *bracket balusters*, a practice adopted probably from a French source.   In either case holes are made in the stone steps at the proper distances apart for the reception of the balusters, the holes being slightly undercut or widened towards the bottom.

Cast iron balusters are provided with dovetail projections beyond the shoulders for insertion in the stone (see Fig. 354), but generally if wrought iron is used the part inserted may simply have a few rags formed on it, as shown at E, Fig. 351.   The balusters are carefully set in place and plumbed.   The hole in the stone being made a little larger than the iron leaves a space to be filled in with molten lead, which when solidified secures the necessary rigidity.   The part at the side of the baluster marked *e* in plan and section, Fig. 354, is where the lead would be poured in.   In place of lead, Portland cement or sulphur with sand are often used for the same purpose.

Stones only of the best quality are suitable for stair steps.   They should be taken from a good quarry and be well seasoned. They should be strong, durable, and of a uniform structure, free from shells and flaws of all kinds.

FIREPROOF STAIRS.—In high buildings where, in the event of fire breaking out, many lives would be endangered, it becomes important in the highest degree that the stairs, since they in general afford the only means of egress from the upper stories, should be constructed of such materials as will best resist the action of fire.

Experience has shown that the best fire-resisting materials are brick, concrete, burnt clay, plaster, and terra-cotta.

Stone is a bad material for fireproof construction, as when exposed to great heat it cracks, and gives way suddenly. Sandstones will resist the action of fire longer than limestones, as the softer varieties of the latter, when subjected to intense heat, become calcined and rapidly disintegrate; while granite, under the same conditions, or even when only subjected to a moderate heat, breaks up into small pieces.

It is found that the steps of stone stairs are very apt to break off suddenly at the wall line. This is due to the part embedded in the wall not expanding to the same extent as that exposed to the action of the fire. In fact, steps of solid hard wood, built into the wall in the same manner, are found to be more reliable than ordinary stone steps; and firemen affirm that they are exposed to less danger in availing themselves of wood stairs in order to reach positions of vantage to extinguish the fire than when compelled to use stone stairs as usually built, as the former gives at least some warning of collapse, the latter none. Of course, wood stairs with steps built up in the ordinary way, *i.e.*, with comparatively thin treads and risers, are in this form highly inflammable, and are rapidly destroyed; but when these are of hard wood (oak or teak), not less than 2 inches thick, they stand out against the action of fire remarkably well.

In buildings, therefore, of the character mentioned above, *i.e.*, warehouses, large hotels, theatres, etc., where the maximum of safety is aimed at, stone steps should not be used for the staircases, unless they are protected and supported underneath by some form of fireproof construction. When for other reasons it is desired to use granite or marble, two kinds of stone which collapse under only a moderate heat, the protection and support referred to may be supplied by raking brick arches supported on brick piers, or some construction of concrete which will stand up and afford a means of escape even after the marble steps have been partially destroyed.

Ironwork of any kind, such as raking iron girders employed for supporting the steps, should be well protected by being encased in fire-clay blocks or embedded in concrete.

Concrete stairs.—Portland cement concrete has proved to be one of the best fire-resisting materials, and of late years has been extensively used in the construction of fireproof stairs. It can be conveniently moulded to any required form, and with tension bars embedded in the steps makes a strong and reliable stair.

The operations in connection with their erection are also of a comparatively simple character. A strong, close platform, to act as a centre, is made to the shape of the underside of the stair, to support and form a bed for the concrete till it is thoroughly set. The concrete is moulded to the form of the steps by riser moulds, which are simply plain deal boards of a width equal to the height of the rise, and fixed in position edgewise so as to enclose the fronts of the steps. When the stair has an open end the moulds are, of course, returned round that end of the steps also. If the treads have projecting nosings the reverse pattern of these are worked on the upper edges of the riser moulds.

Raglets are left in the walls for the reception of the concrete steps in the same way as for stone steps.

The exposed surfaces are finished in finer stuff than that used for the body of the step, and to effect a satisfactory amalgamation of the two the riser and nosing should be filled in first against the mould with the requisite amount of neat cement, and the body of the step with the rough concrete immediately after, and the surface of the tread at once finished. Smooth treads prove a source of danger, and to obviate this some fine hard facing spar may be sprinkled on them and pressed into the soft concrete with a roller; or, again, small channels or " flutings " may be rolled into the surface before the concrete has set, to answer the same purpose.

For concrete stairs of not more than 3 feet wide it will not be necessary to have the concrete assisted by any ironwork. But in wider stairs an *iron angle* or *tee bar* should be embedded lengthwise in each step. When these bars are used in stairs with overhanging steps they are pinned into the wall in the manner of cantilevers, and the concrete filled in round about them. Further strengthening of the structure may be effected by connecting these bars at their free end by a scantling of *bar iron* running in the direction of the stair. The raking bar is bolted or riveted to the horizontal bars, the free ends of the latter being turned up square for this purpose.

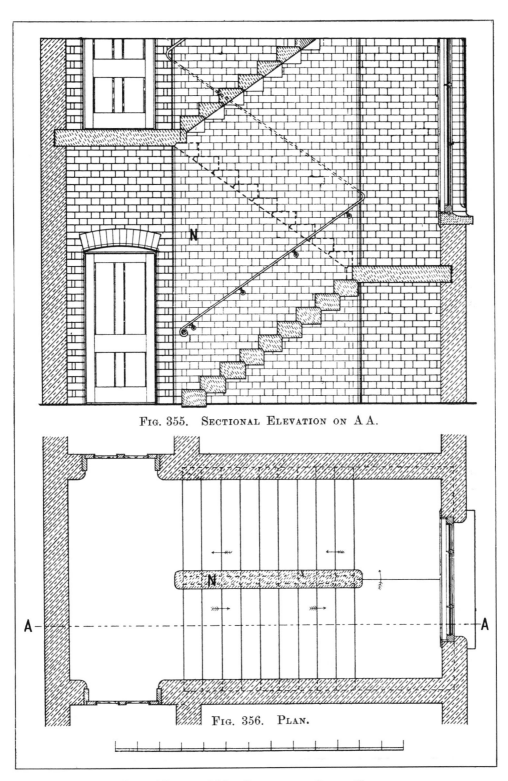

FIG. 355. SECTIONAL ELEVATION ON A A.

FIG. 356. PLAN.

FIGS. 355 AND 356. STAIR WITH SOLID NEWEL.

P P

Illustrations of Stone Stairs.

We may now draw attention to the illustrations of stone staircases (Figs. 355 to 358). After the general remarks already made on the subject, together with the general details of stone steps given on page 283, the drawings will be found sufficiently explanatory of the arrangement and construction employed in each case, and it will not be necessary to add enlarged details of the principal parts.

I. Stairs with return flights (solid newel).—In the example, Figs. 355 and 356, the arrangement shown is that of alternate forward and return flights with half-space landings, these being disposed around a central brick pier or newel (N), which directly supports one end of the steps, and also provides support for the centre of the half-space landing.

The steps of the lowest flight are of rectangular section, while those of the upper flights are splayed off on their under sides to the rake of the stair, thus forming spandrel steps, the square seatings of which at the walls are shown in section in the third flight. Joggle joints, as in Fig. 354, are employed between the steps to avoid the acute angle that would otherwise be formed at the soffit by a rectangular rebate joint.

The joint between the two stones composing the landing may be formed as shown at M (Fig. 358).

The dimensions would be taken, and the rods divided, as explained in the beginning of Chapter III, pages 22-25, to obtain a correct proportion of tread and rise.

The form of stair illustrated is very suitable for dwelling-houses built on the system of flats. They are often constructed having blocks of concrete for steps and landings, and are thereby rendered practically fireproof.

II. Geometrical staircase.—Figs. 357 and 358 illustrate a large stone staircase consisting of three flights, with a quarter and a half-space landing, disposed about a rectangular well-hole, the steps being pinned 9 inches into the wall and having their connecting joints of the usual form. The front edge of the half-space landing is shown additionally supported by a girder extending across the width of the stairway, and resting on the walls at both ends. A section of the landing through the joint is given at M in the plan Fig. 358, the joggle form being adopted. At N in the plan, Fig. 358, is shown a horizontal section of one of the steps.

In this example the soffit of each step is shown moulded to an ogee form, as given in the sectional part of the elevation. A stepped plaster

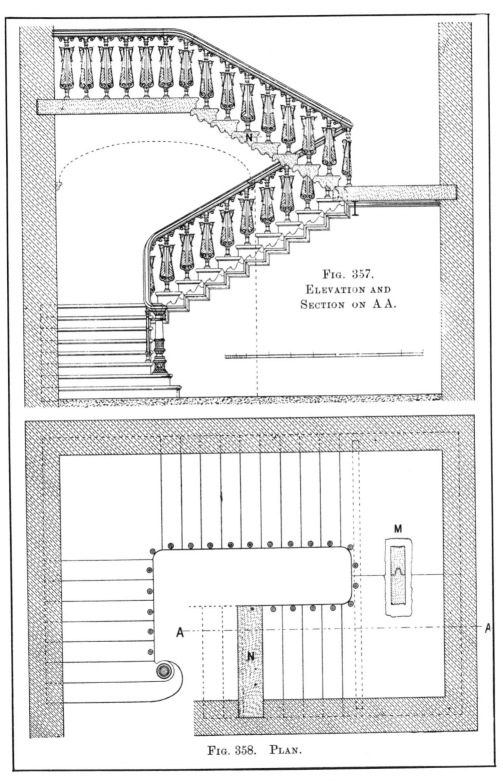

FIG. 357.
ELEVATION AND
SECTION ON A A.

FIG. 358. PLAN.

FIGS. 357 AND 358. GEOMETRICAL STAIRCASE.

moulding, shown also in the elevation, Fig. 357, is worked below the ends of the steps at the wall, the square seatings being made to project beyond the wall surface for this purpose.

The entrance to the stairway in the front wall is shown in the elevation, Fig. 357, by the dotted lines, the opening being 9 feet wide, and spanned by an elliptic arch carrying the ends of the steps and landing.

In setting out the plan attention should be given to the proper placing of the two risers at the quarter-space landing. In the illustration the end of this landing is set off as in Fig. 128, so as to make an easy handrail. Very often, however, architects with similar examples arrange the landing so that it may have the same width each way as the adjacent flights, thus bringing the two risers, in plan, into line with the ends of the steps; of course, reducing the landing abutting on the well to a point. The latter arrangement, though requiring less plan space than the former, produces an ugly ramp in the handrail, and this defect is hardly compensated for by its bridging over the difficulty that occurs with spandrel steps, when set out as in the illustration, in getting the quoin end of the landing to appear uniform with those of the steps. Of course, the difficulty alluded to would not arise if steps of rectangular section were used.

After a correct mould has been made to the section of the steps (and this is only a matter of neat drawing), the stonecutting in this, as in the preceding example, is of a comparatively straightforward character.

CHAPTER XXI

CONSTRUCTION OF SPIRAL AND ELLIPTIC STAIRS

Remarks on winding or spiral staircases.—Considerable historic interest attaches to this form of staircase. Though there are elements of complexity in their construction as compared with straight stairs, yet there is little doubt that they were in use at a very early period. As an example of interest we may mention the spiral staircase in the historic column of Trajan, the steps of which (185 in number) are hewn out of solid circular blocks of marble, 12 feet in diameter and 5 feet in height; the newel being three-sevenths of the diameter of the stair.

The spiral staircase was a distinctive feature of Gothic architecture, the circular form being peculiarly well adapted to the architectural requirements of later mediæval times, and some remarkable examples exist, particularly in France, which show that it received a striking development and elaboration at the hands of the architects, or rather of the master masons, of that period; and this form of staircase was regarded with so much favour that it was adhered to in that country even after the transition to Renaissance architecture had become quite general. In those Gothic examples, whatever outline the external walls assumed the plan of the stair internally was almost invariably circular, and designed on the usual principle of a central cylinder or newel with radiating steps, the general sizes being in proportion to the scale of the building; but they were generally enclosed in circular turrets, which were disposed so as to add picturesqueness to the exterior elevations of the building. Smaller service stairs could be constructed in the characteristically thick walls.

In the earliest examples the steps were composed of several stones, and supported by raking vaulting. In the best examples the large central newels formed the favourite point for ornamentation, being in some instances richly shafted, and decorated with carved arabesques. The newel thus ornamented, and with a boldly moulded handrail winding round it in graceful helical curves worked in the solid stones of the newel itself, produced a striking and pleasing effect. In later examples the newel was carried up to form an abutment for the elaborately moulded ribs of a groined roof, a most effective form of construction.[1]

I. Spiral stair with solid newel formed by ends of steps.—Figs. 359 and 360 illustrate a typical winding stair, built on a circular plan, having a solid central newel. The characteristic feature of the construction is that the end of each step is wrought so as to form a segment of the newel (see sketch, Fig. 361). The broad ends of the steps are, of course, built into the enclosing wall, so that both ends of the steps receive direct vertical support.

The combination is manifestly of a character to produce a very strong stair, but, as we shall see, certain objectionable features are associated with the construction that preclude the use of this type for any but secondary stairs, where the principal consideration is to reach a specified height on the smallest plan space. They are principally used in turrets, and are eminently suitable for these situations.

It will be apparent that practically the diameter of the newel, when thus formed on the steps themselves, is limited, and consequently the ends of the steps where they radiate from it will be inconveniently narrow if only an ordinary width of tread is to be secured at the line one would naturally take in mounting the stair. The number of steps of a given width that can be set out along this circle is fixed, so that if the staircase exceeds one revolution in reaching the desired height the difficulty of obtaining sufficient head-room presents itself unless the steps are made inconveniently high. In the example there are fourteen steps in one turn, having a rise of $6\frac{1}{2}$ inches, so that if more than one convolution is made, as shown in the figure, the *vertical* head-room is only about 6 feet 8 inches, which is rather confined for ordinary traffic, and a rise of, say, 8 inches would not be found inconveniently steep, and would provide much more freedom in the matter of head-room. A little additional head-room is also gained, as shown in the illustration, by making the soffit of the stair a helicoidal surface, instead of leaving the steps rectangular, a form which might be otherwise suitable.

Disposition of the steps in plan.—The arrangement shown in the plan (Fig. 360) makes the planes of the rises radiate from the axis of the newel, the lines of which are shown dotted. But they are often placed otherwise; for instance, when no projecting nosings are formed on the steps the planes of the rises may in that case be placed so as to be tangential to the surface of the newel; or an alternative arrangement

See "Staircases, Historical and Artistic," by T. Marwick.

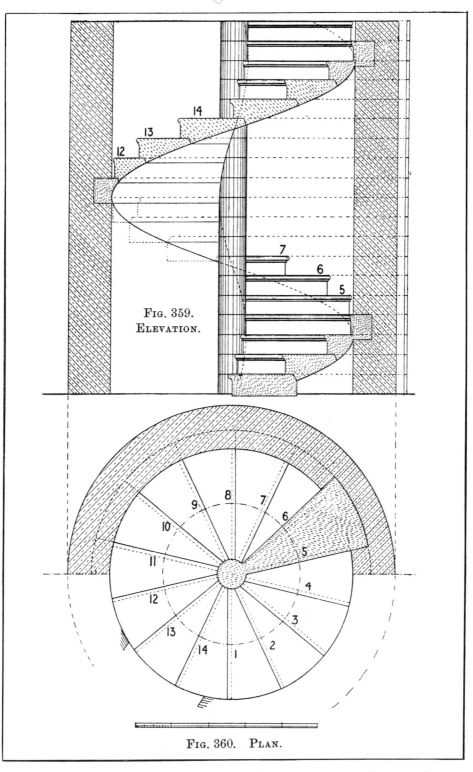

Newel

limited diameter

FIG. 359.
ELEVATION.

FIG. 360. PLAN.

FIGS. 359 AND 360. SPIRAL STAIR WITH NEWEL FORMED ON ENDS OF STEPS.

with steps of rectangular section is to make the back of each step tangential to the newel, with the riser planes placed radially, as in the drawing.

The isometric sketch (Fig. 361) is introduced to show the appearance that the steps present when worked to the required form. The stone-cutting operations, and the manner of obtaining the necessary moulds, will be explained in connection with the steps of the next example (Fig. 362).

II. Spiral stair (Geometrical).—The drawing (Fig. 362) illustrates another spiral stair, but in this instance, in place of the close solid newel, we have an open circular well with a balustrade.

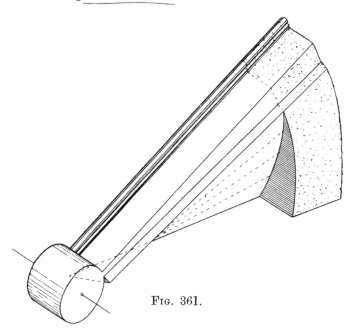

FIG. 361.

The elevation shows that the upper landing is reached by one revolution and a quarter of the spiral. The diameter of the well-hole is 3 feet, a size which allows of the steps at the narrow end under the handrail being $6\frac{1}{2}$ inches wide, which gives ample foothold, and is a suitable dimension for an arrangement of one baluster on each step.

The rise is 6 inches, so that the height reached in one turn with the number of steps (twenty) is 10 feet, which allows liberal head-room.

Practical problems involved in the construction of winding stairs. —Taking the two examples (Figs. 359 and 362) as actual cases to be produced, and supposing the diameter of the stairway, the diameter of the open newel or well, and the height to be reached to be fixed upon, we have to solve the following problems:

3'

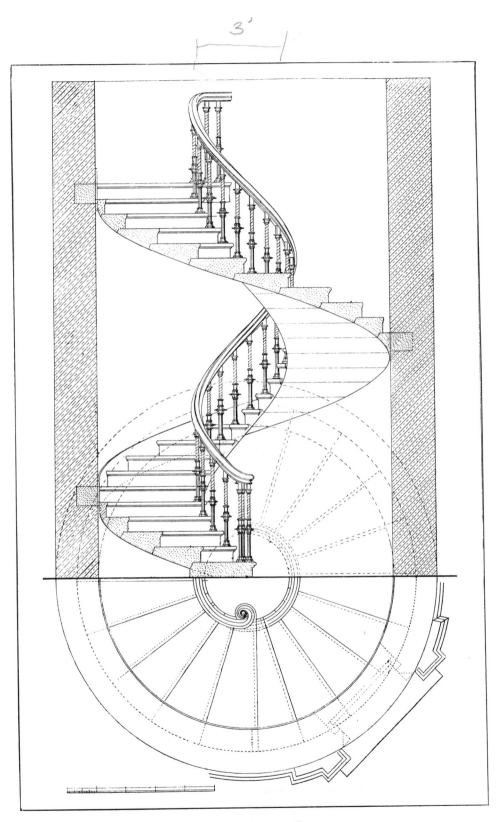

FIG. 362. SPIRAL STAIR—GEOMETRICAL.

Q Q

(1) To arrange the plan with respect to the number of steps, so that the tread and rise will be correctly proportioned to each other along the natural line of ascent.

(2) To make the underside or soffit a helicoidal surface.

(3) To arrange that the lower surface of the joggle joint between the steps be a plane surface, and normal to the soffit at some point along the joint, preferably at the open end of the steps.

Each step, therefore, has to be formed so that, when in its place as a component part of the structure, it will fulfil the above conditions; and we shall see that for this purpose three moulds or their equivalents will be required.

Problem (1) will, in general, be solved by the architect, subject to modifications, if found necessary, by the practical man, who will lay down a full-sized plan of the stair from the small scale drawing furnished to him; and for directions relating to this part of the work the student may again refer to pages 22-25.

The drawings necessary to enable Problems (2) and (3) to be worked out practically are given by Figs. 363-365, which we shall now explain.

Fig. 365 represents to a larger scale the plan of one of the steps of the stair illustrated by Fig. 362, o being the centre of the well, the radial lines $o\,m\,p$ and $o\,n\,q$ being two consecutive riser lines, and $a\,b$ the nosing line. The arc K K represents the plan of the cylindric end of the step at the well, and 1 2 that of the projecting return nosing, while L 4 is the wall line.

Fig. 363 is the development of the section of the step at the wall on the arc L 4, and Fig. 364 is similarly the development of the quoin end on the cylinder, whose plan is the arc $a\,m\,d$.

In order to draw out these developments, commencing with that at the wall line, take a flexible batten and bend it round the arc L 4 in Fig. 365, and copy on to it the points b, p, q, where the arc intersects the nosing and riser lines respectively. Draw any two parallel lines at a distance apart equal to the rise, as P N and R H, Figs. 363 and 364. Spring the batten straight on the upper line, and with it mark the points B, P, Q, corresponding to the points b, p, q at the wall line L 4, Fig. 365. Draw P R at right angles to P Q and join R Q, which latter gives the pitch line at the wall, and the development of the intersection of the soffit surface with the wall is a straight line and parallel to R Q.

Similarly for the narrow or quoin end of the step set off with a batten the points A, M, N, Fig. 364, corresponding to a, m, n in

Fig. 365, and draw the triangle M H N, then the soffit of the step on this development will, of course, be parallel to H N. Having drawn the return nosing and the riser line at N, as shown in Fig. 364, we have

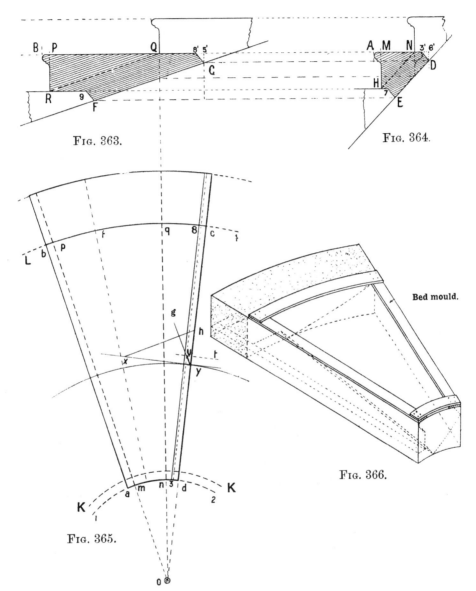

FIG. 363.

FIG. 364.

Bed mould.

FIG. 366.

FIG. 365.

next to determine the distance that the soffit line, D E, should be from H N. We have already laid down a rule, page 284, that the distance from the soffit to the inner angle, as at N in the figure, should not be less than $2\frac{1}{2}$ inches for steps 4 feet long, and this dimension will prove ample in the present case, as the steps are only a little over 3 feet 9 inches, and the soffit line E D in Fig. 364 is therefore drawn $2\frac{1}{2}$ inches from H N agreeably to this rule.

Draw the joint line D 3^1 (Fig. 364) at right angles to the soffit E D and conveniently clear of the return nosing, making the level portion N 3^1 of the joint not less than 1 inch. Set off D E equal to N H, and complete the lower joint E 7 H as shown, then the shaded figure A 3^1 D E H is the mould to apply to the narrow end of the step when formed to the cylindric surface represented in plan by the arc 1 2, Fig. 365.

Since the joint lines, as at E and D, are straight lines, and lie on the helicoidal surface, they are therefore generating lines of that surface, and will consequently appear as radial lines in the plan, Fig. 365. Make, therefore, the distances n 3 and 3 d in Fig. 365 equal to N 3′ and 3′ 6′ respectively in Fig. 364, and draw the radial line o d c, also the line 3 8, parallel to it. Then a b c d is the mould to apply to the top of the step, and is called the *bed mould* (see Fig. 366).

On P Q produced (Fig. 363) set off the distances Q 8′ and 8′ 5′ equal respectively to q 8 and 8 c in the plan, Fig. 365, then a horizontal line through D and a vertical through 5′ discovers by their intersection the point C, through which the soffit line C F is drawn parallel to Q R. Join C 8′, and set off C F equal to Q R, then a parallel line F 9 to C 8′ completes the mould that would apply to the section of the step made by the wall surface. Of course this mould, since the step is tailed 9 inches into the wall, cannot be directly applied like the one at the quoin end of the step given by Fig. 364, but reverse moulds can be made from the shaded section if required.

Although it is sufficiently correct in practice to draw the joint lines C 8′ and D 3′, Figs. 363 and 364 respectively, straight, it will be quite apparent to the geometrical student that they are not really so, these lines being the developments of the intersections of a plane surface with two vertical cylindric surfaces, which are of course ellipses, and do not, when the cylindric surfaces are unfolded, become straight lines.

Remarks.—It will be noticed that the heading joint between the steps as just drawn is only normal to the soffit at the outer end of the step, and that at the wall there is decided obliquity. A perfect heading joint would be one normal to the soffit at every point throughout the entire length of the step, which would require the joint surface to be helicoidal like that of the soffit itself, and which would prove troublesome to make, besides being quite unnecessary for this narrow part of the joint occurring in stair steps. A plane surface normal to the soffit at one point answers the purpose sufficiently well, and is easier made.

In drawing out the moulds, Figs. 363 and 364, we have made the joint normal at the exposed end of the steps (1st) because this simplifies the drawing; (2nd) it is at the end of the steps remote from the wall that there is the greater necessity for the joint being normal to the thrust, as towards the other end which is built into the wall the tendency of the steps to slide over one another grows less; (3rd) since the edge of the joint is only seen at the well it is obvious that it will have a better appearance there when made normal to the line of the soffit.

Sometimes in practice the joint plane is fixed so as to be normal to the soffit at some point about the middle of the length of the step, so as to share the deflection from the normal between the two ends; and when this is aimed at it is an advantage, in cases where the steps are not of the same shape, to take the point at the going line, because the steps being set out along it of uniform width results in a straight line development of the soffit, whatever be the plan form, which makes a normal more easily obtained at this point than at any other. The necessary construction for fixing the plane of the joint in this position is shown in Fig. 365. Let $o\,d\,c$ be the plan of the joint line on the soffit, its position being fixed by the same considerations as before. Through y, the point in which $o\,c$ intersects the going line, draw $x\,y$ perpendicular to $o\,c$. Make $x\,y$ equal to the width of tread as measured on the curve of the going line, and set off from y along $d\,c$ the distance $y\,h$ equal to the rise of the steps. Join $x\,h$ and draw $y\,g$ perpendicular to it: then $y\,g$ is the normal at the point y to the helicoidal surface forming the soffit, and the plane of the joint passes through $c\,d$ and lies on $y\,g$. A line, $u\,t$, parallel to $x\,y$ and at a distance from it equal to that of the joint line $c\,d$ on the soffit from the upper surface of the step, as given by D 6′ in Fig. 364, intersects $g\,y$ at u; then a parallel through the point u to $c\,d$ gives the plan of the intersection of the joint plane with the tread, which corresponds to the line 8 3 obtained by the last method. The intercepts of the arcs 1 2 and L 4 between this line and $c\,d$ give the distances corresponding to 3′ 6′ and 5′ 8′ in Figs. 364 and 363, which enable the joint lines on these moulds to be drawn as before.

Application of the moulds in the preparation of the steps.—Having selected a suitable stone, commence by bringing the intended top of the step to a true plane as a surface of operation. Then apply the bed mould $a\,b\,c\,d$, Fig. 365 (formed by nailing together thin lathes of wood, as shown by Fig. 366), to the dressed surface and scribe all round, leaving 9 inches of the stone beyond the mould for the purpose of building into the wall. Next work the cylindric surface at the narrow or well end of the step square to the tread. Apply the quoin mould (made out of zinc or other suitable material to the outline in Fig. 364) to the curved surface thus formed, keeping its upper edge flush with the tread and bending it close to the concave surface. Scribe in all round the mould.

The whole step may now be worked to these lines scribed on the stone, the lap of the joint and other particulars at the wall being measured from the mould (Fig. 365). To work the soffit or warped surface of the step cut a draft into the end along the line R S, Fig. 367, and sink another draft at the wall line M N. Clear away the bulk of

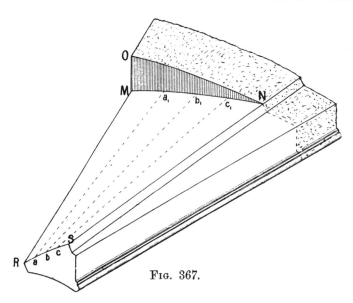

FIG. 367.

the waste material, and cut the draft M N to the accurate depth, using a reverse mould obtained from the line F C, Fig. 363, which in the present case is a straight line, so that any thin, flexible piece of stuff with a straight edge formed on it will answer the purpose, of course bending it against the surface M N O. Divide M N and R S, Fig. 367, into the same number of equal parts, and cut straight drafts between these points, as $a\,a_1$, $b\,b_1$, $c\,c_1$, and work as many intermediate drafts as may be found requisite to finish accurately the entire twisted surface of the step.

A bevel may with advantage be used to form the salient angle on the back edge of the step, applying the stock of the bevel to the tread. The end and front of the step may then be recessed back to form the moulded nosing.

The drawings for obtaining the moulds and the subsequent operations just described will apply equally to the preparation of the steps of newel stairs, such as that in Fig. 361, in which a segment of the newel is formed on each step, only the mould for the end next the newel cannot be directly applied, so that this end has to be dealt with in the same manner as that at the wall, viz., by applying reverse moulds, etc.

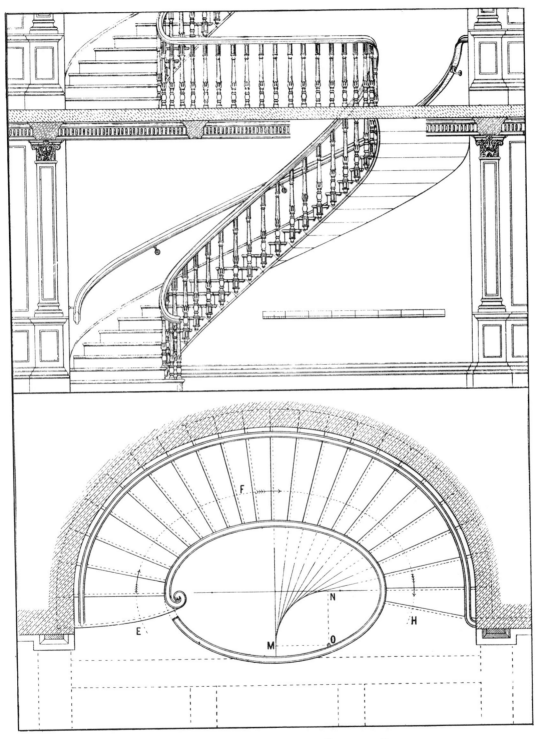

FIG. 368. PLAN AND ELEVATION OF ELLIPTIC STAIRCASE.

III. Elliptic staircases.—In Fig. 368 is illustrated, by plan and elevation, an elliptic staircase with overhanging steps and balustrade. In the plan the ellipse is taken at the centre line of handrail at the well, all the other plan curves being parallel to it.

The treads are set out of equal widths along the curved line of travel E F H, and the riser lines (dotted in the figure) drawn through the points of division and tangent to the circle O M N. This circle is drawn to touch the major and minor axes, the radius being about equal to semi-minor axis. It will be seen that this displaces the riser lines from what may be considered as their natural positions, i.e., normals to the ellipse, as in these latter positions they would be tangents to the evolute of the ellipse, which does not of course coincide with the circle O M N. The method just described of balancing the steps gives a fairly satisfactory graduation of their widths, both at their narrow ends and at the wall, and from the elevation of the stair it will be seen to give also easy falling lines for the soffit.

A similar set of operations to that we have above described in connection with Figs. 363-365 has to be performed with the present example, but since all the steps composing this stair are different, separate moulds are required for each one, which makes the construction of elliptic stone stairs difficult and expensive.

Forming the soffit.—Irregular soffits, i.e., irregular as compared with those of circular stairs, may be generated in two ways, which would entail slight differences in getting out the moulds. (1) The surface may be regarded as generated by a horizontal straight line moving on the line of uniform pitch on the proposed soffit, the plan of which is the line of travel, and in every successive position kept horizontal and tangent to the same cylindrical surface as has been used for determining the directions of the riser lines of the steps. (2) It may be generated by a horizontal straight line moving on two fixed curves, the one curve being a previously arranged falling line at the narrow ends of the steps, the other a similarly arranged falling line at the wall.

It will be found the easier plan to get out the moulds in accordance with the second method here given of generating the soffit surface.

An approximate method of determining the soffit lines, etc., by a modification of the second mode given above for generating the soffit surface, is illustrated by Figs. 369-370, being the enfoldments at the wall and quoin end respectively of the first six steps of the elliptic stair (Fig. 368).

(1.) Draw a complete development of the steps (tread and rise), both at the wall (Fig. 369) and at the quoin end (Fig. 370).

(2.) Draw the soffit line *a e c* at the narrow ends of the steps, and produce the riser lines to intersect this falling line as at *c* and *e*, then level over these points to intersect the corresponding lines on the wall development (Fig. 369) as at *c'* and *e'* at the riser lines 6 and 5 respectively. Similar points being obtained at each riser, draw through them the curve *a' e' c'*, which gives the soffit line at the wall.

(3.) Arrange the joints on the quoin ends (Fig. 370), making them about normal to the soffit line *a e c*, and level over the points where they

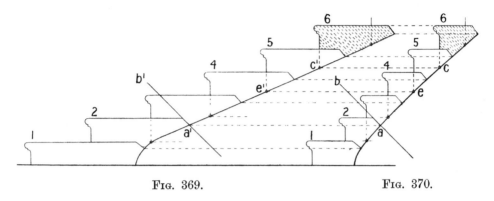

FIG. 369.   FIG. 370.

intersect the soffit surface to the soffit line just found on the wall development; for example, *a* in Fig. 370 is projected over to *a'* in Fig. 369.

(4.) Through the joint points thus obtained draw lines on the wall development parallel to the corresponding joint lines on the development at the other end of the steps (Fig. 370), thus *a' b'* is drawn parallel to *a b*.

This method does not, of course, determine the directions of the joint lines at the wall so as to correspond accurately with the assumed directions at the open end of the steps, but it will be found a sufficiently near approximation for all practical purposes.

CHAPTER XXII

General arrangement.—A quarter-circle stair of this character is shown by Figs. 371, 372, and will serve to illustrate the geometrical methods that should be employed in getting out a *ramp* and *twist* in stone.

The general arrangement and construction of the stair will be sufficiently clear from the elevation and plan furnished by Figs. 371 and 372.

In order to get out the requisite moulds for application to the stones, a full-sized plan of the stair and also a development of each balustrade (say, on its convex side) will have to be made.

Commence, therefore, by laying off the plan, as in Fig. 372, upon a floor or upon boarding specially prepared for setting-out purposes. The plan should show at least the following: (1) the riser lines; (2) thickness of plinth and width of capstone; (3) correct spacings of balusters; (4) horizontal sections of pedestals as they occur at the *start* and *land* of the stair.

Development of long balustrade.—Next proceed to draw the development (full size) of the longer side of the stair. It will be most advantageous to take this development on the convex side, which must be the cylindric surface, coinciding with the outside surfaces of the plinth and capstone, which in this case are arranged so as to have the same width in plan. This development is shown by Fig. 373, and is obtained by first setting out a development of the ends of the steps as they would intersect if produced the outside surface of the plinth, their widths, which are all equal, being got by producing the rise lines in the plan, Fig. 372, to intersect the circle E H F, which is of course the plan of the developed surface. Draw the raking or falling lines representing the edges of the plinth in suitable positions with respect to the development of steps just drawn. Since the ends of the steps are of a uniform width these plinth lines are of course straight lines in the development, being regular helices in the actual stair. The raking lines of the capstone will also be drawn at the desired height above the steps, and parallel to the plinth lines. The springings of the curve should be clearly marked on the development, and in the figure they are shown by the vertical dotted lines at E and F. The outlines of the pedestals may next be drawn agreeably to their positions in plan, and the ramp at the bottom pedestal and the swan neck at the upper one in both the capping and plinth set out. The latter have to be carefully arranged and adjusted, so as to conform to a suitable height of the pedestals on both sides of the stair. The transverse sides of the baluster seatings converge to the common axis of the cylindric surfaces. The baluster seatings are laid off on the developed surface at the widths that they would have if extended to intersect that surface, these widths being obtained by producing the radial lines in plan to cut the circle E F H. These seatings being drawn in the manner described, the heading joints in the plinth and capstone may then be arranged in suitable positions, having, of course, regard to the size of the stones available for the purpose.

A similar development will be required for the other side of the stair. This is shown by Fig. 381, being taken on the convex surface *i.e.*, on the line T M N in the plan, Fig. 372.

At (N), in Fig. 373, is also shown a section of the terrace wall, as well as of the plinth and capstone of the balustrade on the level.

Nature of the heading joints in the plinth and capstone of the balustrade.— One of two forms of heading joints may be adopted, in the plinth as well as in the capstone. (1) These joints may be made plane surfaces, and perpendicular to some one central falling line. (2) They may be made helicoidal or twisted surfaces, *i.e.*, generated by a horizontal line, which moves so that in every successive position it intersects a vertical axis and a directing helical curve.

The latter kind of joint is the most suitable for plinth blocks, and has been adopted in the illustrations.

In the present example, Figs. 371, 372, since the plan is circular and the pitch uniform, these joints will form portions of right helicoidal or screw surfaces, and are therefore of the same character precisely as the twisted surfaces forming the upper sides of the plinths.

To form this kind of joint in wood, for example, in a handrail wreath, would prove quite impracticable, but in stone it does not present much more difficulty in cutting than a joint made to a plane surface. And, moreover, it has this practical advantage that it intersects the cylindrical surfaces or vertical sides, in regular helices, which are of course straight lines on the development of these surfaces, and are therefore easily

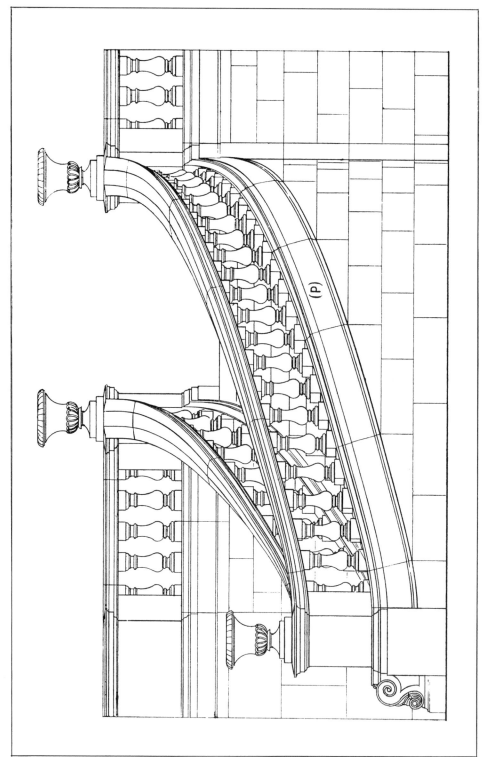

(P)

FIG. 371. ELEVATION OF TERRACE STAIR.

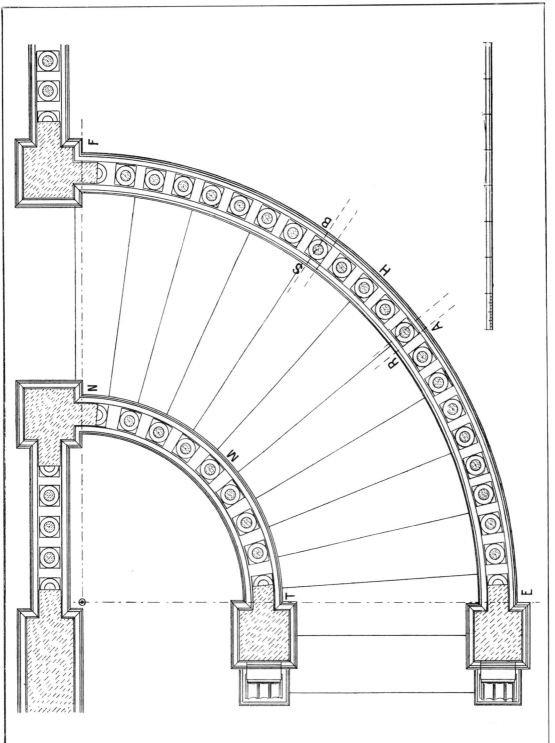

FIG. 372. PLAN OF TERRACE STAIR.

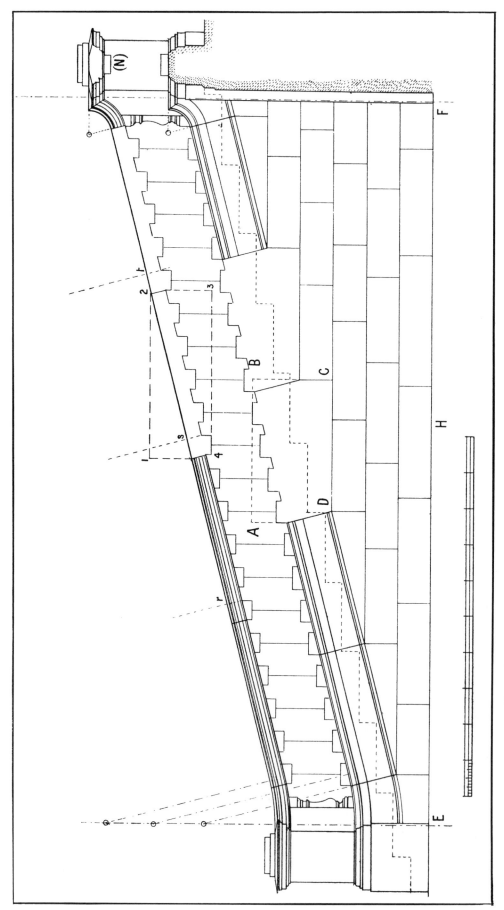

FIG. 373. DEVELOPMENT OF LONGER BALUSTRADE ON THE LINE E H F (FIG. 372).

drawn, whereas plane joints cut the same surfaces in ellipses which do not unfold into straight lines.

When plane joints are adopted they have consequently to be formed antecedently to the cylindrical surfaces, while helicoidal joints are cut after these curved sides have been accurately formed.

Moulds for marking out the plinth blocks.—We shall now describe how to obtain the moulds for the stone plinth when formed with helicoidal heading joints. As an example, take one of the plinth blocks on the long side of the stair, viz., that marked A B C D in Fig. 373. An examination of Fig. 373 will show that the joints are arranged so as to make the several blocks composing the plinth of the same size, and that the length of each block includes four baluster seatings, which are wrought upon it; and, further, that the plinth stones are not cut on their undersides to the rake, but so as to rest on level beds, the stone courses of the supporting wall being continued out at the same level. The horizontal beds are

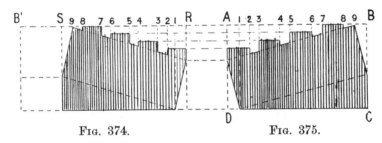

FIG. 374.   FIG. 375.

taken at the levels of the points of intersection of the joint lines with the raking line defining the continuous underside of the plinth.

The heading joint lines in this drawing, Fig. 373, being the developments of regular helices, are, of course, straight lines, and are drawn so as to be perpendicular to the raking helices on that surface, while their positions are chosen preferably, so as to pass through the intersections of the lower faces of the baluster seatings with the upper side of plinth.

A mould is then made of zinc or other flexible material to the extreme outline of the development of the finished stone as given at A B C D, Fig. 373. This mould is shown by the shaded portion of Fig. 375, and is sometimes called a *side mould*.

We have next to make a mould to apply to the horizontal faces of the stone, termed the *bed mould*, which in outline is merely the plan or horizontal projection of the plinth block, and is shown in Fig. 376, being the segment of the plan marked A B S R in Fig. 372.

The lower end of this mould coincides with the radial line A R, at the face of the baluster seating, Fig. 372, while the radial line at its upper end is got by setting off the length A B, Fig. 372, along the plan curve from A to B, Fig. 376. The length of the arc, A B, therefore, of the bed mould, Fig. 376, should be exactly equal to A B, Fig. 372.

Directions for working one of the plinth blocks.—Work the bottom side or intended bed of the stone to a true plane, and the top parallel to

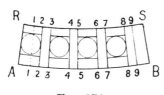

FIG. 376.

it, making the depth equal to B C or A D of the side mould, Fig. 375. Inscribe the form of the bed mould, A B S R, Fig. 376, on each of the prepared surfaces, using means to insure that the position of the mould on the top surface is vertically over that on the under surface. Gradually work off to these lines, the portions of the solid exterior to them, thus bringing the sides to cylindric, and the ends to plane surfaces. This will of course be done in the usual way by cutting straight drafts from points on one side to corresponding points on the other, these being marked on the stone from the bed mould. The solid will then appear as Fig. 377.

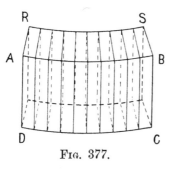

FIG. 377.

Next bend the side mould, Fig. 375, round the convex face of the stone, A B C D, Fig. 377, and scribe in its form, as shown by Fig. 378.

To mark the joint lines, etc., on the concave side; from the point 4, Fig. 378, square a line across the end to intersect the concave face at the point 7, and also draw by means of the bed mould a radial line, 6 5, across the bed of the stone; join 5 7, Fig. 378, by means of a flexible straight-edge, bent close to the surface. This gives the line of the lower joint, and the upper one may be determined in a similar manner.

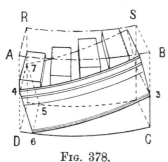

FIG. 378.

The lines of the baluster seatings are marked across the top by means of the bed mould, and squared down the concave side to the raking line of the upper edge of the plinth, the latter being marked on that face with a flexible straight-edge.

The joints are then worked through to the lines, and the baluster seatings formed as shown in Fig. 378. The forms of the mouldings may now be scribed into the joint surfaces and worked to the helical lines on the faces, which can be gauged from the raking line on the top of the plinth, or lined off with flexible straight-edges bent round the surface as may be found most convenient.   The correct contour of the mouldings at intermediate points will be secured by working them to reverse moulds.   The appearance of the finished plinth block is given by Fig. 379.

FIG. 379.

Remarks.—We have shown above how to work the block by using a bed mould and *one* side mould.   Frequently, however, in examples of this kind a *second* side mould is used to mark out the concave side of the stone; but this mould, as we have seen, may be dispensed with when, as in the present case, the falling lines are straight lines in development, since these lines can be scribed in by means of a flexible straight-edge.

For those who prefer to work with two side moulds we have shown in Fig. 374, how the extra mould may be drawn from particulars obtained from the other one, and the bed mould.   To do this make R S, Fig. 374, equal to the stretch out of the concave side, R S, of the bed mould, Fig. 376, copying also the points 1, 2 .... 9 as they occur upon it, and complete the mould by levelling over corresponding points from Fig. 375, as shown in the drawing.

Moulds for marking out the wreathed capstone of balustrade.— The capstone may be prepared in exactly the same way as above described for a plinth block; but that method, though very correct and easy of application is not economical of material, requiring a much greater depth of stone than is absolutely necessary, especially when the capstone is of steep pitch and wrought in long lengths.   The depth of stone required to get out a length of capstone by that method is shown in the development, Fig. 373, of the long wreath by the circumscribing outline 1 2 3 4.

To illustrate a more economical method as regards material we shall take as an example a segment of the capstone of the balustrade on the steep side of the stair, viz., that between the joints *e m* and *f n*, Fig. 381; the rectangle *m n f e* includes the baluster seatings, and is the plain side mould for applying to the convex side of the stone to obtain the circum- scribing wreathed solid.   Here, as in the case of the plinth, the joints are made helicoidal, not plane surfaces.   In the method we are about to describe, the finished stone is regarded as being included between two parallel planes, inclined to the horizontal at an angle to be determined by construction, but which is approximately equal to the pitch angle, and the practical problem to be solved is the determination of a mould (usually termed the face mould), to apply to these inclined surfaces to mark out the stone for cutting its cylindric sides, effecting the same purpose as a bed mould applied to two similarly prepared horizontal surfaces.

Proceed by drawing the plan, *a c m f*, Fig. 380, of the length of cap-

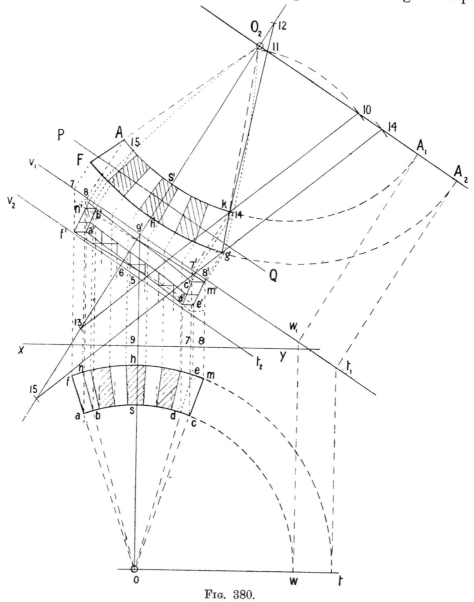

FIG. 380.

stone for which the mould is required, O being the centre of the plan circles. This, in the present example, is just the corresponding portion of the whole plan of the capstone, T M N, Fig. 372, and would be the necessary bed mould for preparing the stone by the method already given for the plinth blocks.

The lines of the joints and those of the baluster seatings are of course radial, converging to the common centre, O, their positions in the plan, Fig. 380, being here determined from the development, Fig. 381. For example, the arc, $f\,m$, in the plan (Fig. 380) is equal to the distance of f from the line $m\,p$ in Fig. 381, and $m\,e$ and $f\,n$ equal to $p3$. The points e and n being joined to the centre O give $a\,b\,n\,f$, the plan of the upper joint surface, and $c\,d\,e\,m$ that of the lower.

Next take a ground line, $x\,y$, at right angles to O h, the bisector of the angle f O m, and set up elevations of the two joint surfaces, namely, $a^1\,b^1\,n^1\,f^1$ and $c^1\,d^1\,e^1\,m^1$. The difference in levels of corresponding horizontal lines of the two joints is the height $p\,m$, Fig. 381; for example, $f^1\,a^1$ of the upper joint is higher than $d^1\,e^1$ by the distance $p\,m$, Fig. 381. It would now prove an easy task, the joints being drawn, to complete the entire elevation of the squared solid as is shown in Fig. 380, but for the purpose of getting out the face mould this is unnecessary, and we have only to inclose the two joint sections by the two parallel lines $v_1\,t_1$ and $v_2\,t_2$, these being the traces of the two inclined parallel planes which give by their distance apart the thickness of stone required for the finished length of capstone. These traces may be drawn as closely as possible to the joints, and even cutting off small corners, but of course taking care to leave sufficient material for the moulded section. It is better, however, to take a stone thick enough to give the complete squared solid.

Produce O h to cut $v_1\,t_1$ and $v_2\,t_2$ at the points 9^1 and 5 respectively, and through 9^1 draw an indefinite line, O$_2$ 15, at right angles to $v_1\,t_1$. Set off on this line the distance 9^1 O$_2$ equal to 9 O in the plan; O$_2$ is then the common centre of the two ellipses forming the edges of the mould. A line, O$_2$ A$_2$, perpendicular to O$_2$ 9^1 is the common line of the major axes of the two curves, and O$_2\,s^1$ and O$_2\,h^1$, set off respectively equal O s and O h in the plan, are the semi-minor axes. To determine the lengths of the semi-major axes we have only to project the points w and t in the plan up to $v_1\,t_1$ at w_1 and t_1, respectively, then $9^1\,w_1$ and $9^1\,t_1$ are the lengths required. These, with the width of the mould $s^1\,h^1$ on the minor axis, furnish sufficient data for striking out with a trammel the two elliptic curves A $s^1\,k$ and F $h^1\,g$, forming the edges of the mould (see Appendix, Problem 18).

The necessary trammels may be found in another way, as follows:

Continue the projectors $c\,c^1$ and $m\,m^1$, Fig. 380, to meet $v_1\,t_1$ in the points 7^1 and 8^1 respectively, and draw the ordinates $7^1\,k$ and $8^1\,g$ perpendicular to $v_1\,t_1$, making $7^1\,k$ equal to $7\,c$ in the plan, and similarly $8^1\,g$

equal to 8 m. The point k just found lies on the inner curve of the mould, and g on the outer. With k as centre and radius equal to the semi-minor axis $O s$, cut the line of the major axis in the points 10 and 11; then k 11 produced to meet the minor axis in the point 12 gives the trammel k 11 12, which will describe the inner curve, k being the tracing point, and 11 and 12 constrained to move along the major and minor axes respectively.

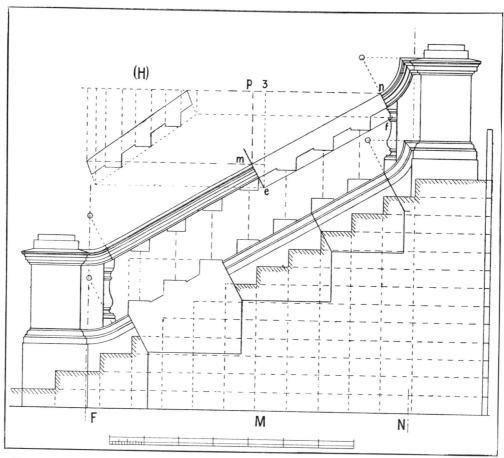

FIG. 381. DEVELOPMENT OF SHORTER BALUSTRADE ON THE LINE T M N (FIG. 372).

Of course the length k 12 of this trammel is that of the semi-major axis, and equal to $O_2 A_1$, found as already described.

By joining 10 k and producing it to cut the line of the minor axis, we may determine another trammel 10 k 13, which would similarly describe the same ellipse. In this case k is the tracing point, the extremities 10 and 13 being guided along the axes. The latter trammel, however, as will be seen in the figure, would prove rather too long for convenient use.

Of course the curves of the face mould may be determined by means of level ordinates, as in Figs. 270-272, to which the reader is referred.

In Fig. 380 we have determined the positions of the baluster seatings on the face mould, the points where they occur on the convex edge being projected from the plan and then joined to the common centre, O_2, of the two ellipses.

Directions for applying the moulds and working a length of the capstone of balustrade.—(1) Form the intended upper side of the stone to a plane surface. Work the under surface parallel to it, making the thickness exactly equal to the distance between the traces $v_1\ t_1$ and $v_2\ t_2$, Fig. 380.

(2) Inscribe the *face mould* on the upper side, and before removing it mark upon the stone the line of the minor axis $s^1\ h^1$, and also any line, such as P Q, drawn at right angles to it, as shown on the mould, Fig. 380. Square these two guide lines, $s^1\ h^1$ and P Q, over the edges of the stone, and draw them on its under side.

(3) Next apply the face mould on the under side, keeping the lines P Q and $s^1\ h^1$ drawn on the mould coincident with the corresponding lines just marked on the stone. Then slide the mould along the line P Q towards the lower end, a distance equal to 6 5, Fig. 380, the distance 6 5 being the intercept on $v_2\ t_2$ between the plumb line $9^1\ 5$, and the square line $9^1\ 6$, both drawn from the common point 9^1 on the upper surface, thus bringing the mould vertically under its position already marked on the upper surface, when the stone is set up to its proper inclination. This being carefully done the form of the mould is scribed in upon this side also.

Note.—The lines F A and $g\ k$, Fig. 380, defining the length of the face mould when drawn on each side of the stone, give the correct lines for forming plumb radial sections, as in Fig. 377, but these provisional sections need not be formed as was done for the plinth block, except with the view of clearing away the bulk of the waste material from the ends of the solid, since the joint proper has to be cut to helical lines given by the side or falling moulds. The actual joint surfaces being helicoidal do not therefore intersect the surfaces of the stone, *i.e.*, the planes of the face mould, in straight lines, but in curves, so that these lines cannot be readily drawn on the mould, nor are they really required in practice. They are, however, shown here by the dotted lines $O_2\ 14$ and $O_2\ 15$ (Fig. 380), drawn on the plane of the mould, and by symmetry the same lines would apply to the under surface, the mould being turned end for end.

(4) Cut the sides of the stone to true cylindrical surfaces, by first pointing off roughly the waste material exterior to them, and then finishing by working straight drafts from points on one side to corresponding points on the other, marked from the face mould, the drafts being of course parallel to the line $9^1\,5$ in Fig. 380.

(5) Bend the side mould $m\,n\,f\,e$, Fig. 381, round the convex side in its correct position, and inscribe its outline, including the baluster seatings on the stone, thus giving the joint lines on the convex side. A mould may be made for the concave side and applied in a similar manner. This latter mould can of course be readily drawn from that of the convex side in the same way as has been shown for the side moulds of the plinth block, Figs. 374, 375. This mould is drawn at (H) in Fig. 381, being projected over from the convex mould $m\,n\,f\,e$.

(6) Work the joints through from side to side to the lines drawn by means of the side moulds, Fig. 381, applying a straight-edge across the surface of the joint in the direction that level lines would take on that surface when the stone is held at its proper inclination. Accuracy in doing this may be secured by dividing the inscribed lines of the joints on each side into the same number of equal parts, and working through to corresponding points.

(7) Next work the top of the stone to the falling lines, bringing it to a right helicoidal surface, by sinking straight drafts from side to side in radial lines marked from the face mould, such, for instance, as the lines of the sides of the baluster seatings. The under side being similarly worked, and the baluster seatings formed thereon, the solid is then ready for being moulded to the required sectional form, which is shown at (N), Fig. 373.

Observations on the above method.—A careful comparison of the two side moulds, Fig. 381, will show that the one at (H) for the concave side is very different in form from that of the convex $m\,n\,f\,e$. For instance, the joint lines on the latter are made perpendicular to the raking lines on that side, while the similar lines on the former show considerable obliquity to each other. This deflection of the joint line from the perpendicular on the concave side becomes more decided as the width of the capstone is increased and the radius of its plan decreased.

At the other side of the stair, where there is a wider sweep, the difference of the two moulds is very small, the joint lines on the concave side being very nearly perpendicular to the falling lines on that side, as will be seen by comparing the two side moulds for the plinth block, Figs. 374 and 375.

The defect to which we are calling attention may be made less noticeable by placing the joint surface so as to be perpendicular to the falling lines occurring on the expansion of the vertical cylindrical surface at the middle of the width, instead of placing it perpendicular to those on the extreme convex side as is done in the diagram. This deflects the joint lines from the perpendicular on both sides of the wreath, but in opposite directions, thus sharing the deviation between them.

This may be effected by a very simple geometrical construction as shown in Fig. 382, and without drawing a complete development of the central surface referred to. Draw A 1 and A 3, Fig. 382, through a

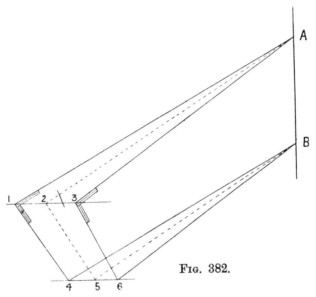

FIG. 382.

common point, A, to represent the development of the falling lines of the convex and concave sides respectively, their inclinations being obtained from Fig. 381. Draw across them any horizontal line such as 1 3. Bisect 1 3 at the point 2 and join A 2. Then the dotted line, A 2, will represent the central falling line.

Through any point B vertically below A draw B 4, B 5, and B 6 respectively parallel to A 1, A 2 and A 3. Also through the point 2 draw the dotted line 2 5 perpendicular to A 2, intersecting B 5 at the point 5, and through 5 draw the horizontal line 4 6. Join 1 4 and 3 6; then A 1 4 is the angle or bevel that the joint line makes with the falling line or edge of side mould on the convex side of wreath, and A 3 6 is similarly the angle of the concave side.

Preparing the capstone when the heading joints are plane surfaces.—In preparing wreathed capstones either for stair balustrades, as in the example illustrated, or to form similar stones for wall copings it will generally be found the easier plan to make the heading joints helicoidal as explained above. They are not unfrequently, however, made plane surfaces, and when this is done the methods that should be adopted for getting out the moulds and bevels and applying them are precisely the same as those applicable to wood handrails.

The sets of lines necessary for this purpose, with full instructions for applying the moulds and bevels, are given in Part II, and more particularly in Chapter XIV, to which the student of the present section is referred.

APPENDIX.

A SHORT COURSE OF PLANE AND DESCRIPTIVE GEOMETRY, ARRANGED TO
BE OF ASSISTANCE AND FOR EASY REFERENCE IN THE STUDY OF THE
SUBJECTS OF "STAIRBUILDING AND HANDRAILING."

GENERAL REMARKS.—The importance of a knowledge of Practical Plane
and Descriptive Geometry to those engaged in the constructive and
mechanical arts can scarcely be over-estimated. This is now very
generally recognized, and in Science and Technical Schools it has of
late years received a large share of attention. It is usually taught in
a general way, without reference to any particular trade or profession,
and its special applications easily follow.

In arranging the following course the principal object has been to
lead the student in the most direct manner to those geometrical principles
and constructions which have immediate application to Stairbuilding
and Handrailing. Although the course as here presented is necessarily
much abridged, it is hoped that the student who has carefully worked
out the problems will have laid a wide enough foundation for a more
extended knowledge of Plane and Descriptive Geometry, as set forth in
advanced text-books dealing with it as a special subject.

In describing the Problems, it is assumed that the student is already
acquainted with the ordinary geometrical terms and the definitions of
plane figures, as well as those of the more common solids.

PLANE GEOMETRY.

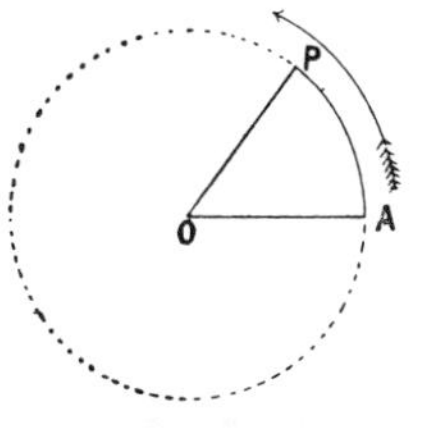

Measurement of angles.—An angle may be regarded
as generated by a straight line revolving, in a given
plane, about one of its extremities. Thus, if the line
O P, Fig. 1, revolve about the point O, and starting
from its initial position O A, stop in the position O P,
it is said to have described an angle A O P. By continuing the motion

FIG. 1.

T T

of O P in the same direction till it again occupies the initial position O A, a complete circle would be generated.

For the purpose of measurement the circle is divided into 360 equal parts, called degrees, and the measure of an angle is the number of degrees it contains.

The protractor is an instrument used for measuring and setting out angles. A common form is that of the semicircular disc delineated in

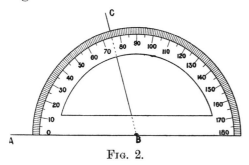

FIG. 2.

Fig. 2. The circumference of the semicircle is divided into 180 equal parts, each of which will thus represent one degree.

To use the protractor to set out any angle, say 75°, with the line A B, Fig. 2. Place the centre of the semicircular disc on the point B, making its diameter coincide with A B, and mark the paper at the division 75. Remove the protractor, and from B draw B C, passing through the mark at 75, then A B C is the angle required.

PROBLEM 1.—*To bisect a given angle.*

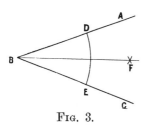

FIG. 3.

Let A B C, Fig. 3, be the given angle. With centre B, and any convenient radius, describe an arc cutting B A and B C in the points D and E. With D and E as centres, and any radius greater than half the distance between them, describe arcs intersecting in F. Then the line B F bisects the angle A B C, *i.e.*, the angle A B F is equal to the angle C B F.

PROBLEM 2.—*To divide a given straight line into any number of equal parts.*

Let A B, Fig. 4, be the given line which is required to be divided

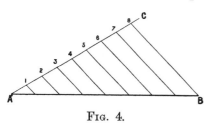

FIG. 4.

into any number of equal parts (say eight). From the point A draw the straight line A C of indefinite length, making any convenient angle with A B. Step off with the dividers any 8 equal parts from A along A C; join B to the point marked 8, and through the other points of division draw lines parallel to B 8, which will divide A B into the number of equal parts required.

PROBLEM 3.—*To divide a straight line, A B, proportionately to a given divided straight line, C D, Fig. 5.*

At A draw a line, A E, of indefinite length, making any convenient angle with A B. Set out along A E the length of C D and its divisions at the points a, b, c. Join E B, and through the points a, b, c draw the lines $a\,a^1$, $b\,b^1$, $c\,c^1$ parallel to E B. Then A B is divided at a^1, b^1, c^1 in the same proportion as C D.

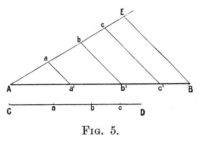
FIG. 5.

PROBLEM 4.—*In a given square to inscribe an octagon.*

Let A B C D, Fig. 6, be the given square. Draw the diagonals A C and B D.

With centres A, B, C, and D, and radius equal to one-half the diagonal, describe arcs cutting the sides of the square in the points a, b, c, d, etc. Join $b\,c$, $d\,e$, $f\,g$, and $h\,a$. Then $a\,b\,c\,d\,e\,f\,g\,h$ is the required octagon.

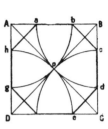
FIG. 6.

PROBLEM 5.—*In a given circle to inscribe a square and an octagon.*

Let A C G, Fig. 7, be the given circle. Draw two diameters, H D and B F, perpendicular to each other, and join H B, B D, D F, F H; then B D F H is the square required.

Bisect the arcs H B and B D in A and C. From A and C draw lines through the centre, O, meeting the circumference in G and E, and join A B, B C, C D, etc.; then A B C D E F G H is the required octagon.

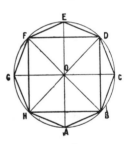
FIG. 7.

PROBLEM 6.—*To describe a circle passing through three given points, A, B and C, which are not in a straight line.*

Join A B and B C, Fig. 8. Bisect these lines by perpendiculars intersecting each other at O. With centre O and radius O A describe a circle which will also pass through the points B and C.

> Note.—To find the centre of a given circle it is only necessary to take any three points on its circumference and proceed as above.

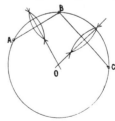
FIG. 8.

PROBLEM 7.—*In a given circle to inscribe any regular polygon.*

Let A C F (Fig. 9) be the given circle, and let the required polygon be a heptagon. Draw any diameter, A 7, and divide it into the same

number of equal parts as the polygon is to have sides (in this case seven).
With the points A and 7 as centres, and the diameter of the circle as radius,

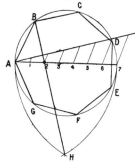

describe arcs intersecting in H. Draw H 2, and
produce it to meet the circle in B. Join A B, then
A B is one side of the heptagon. Take A B therefore in the compasses, and step round the circle,
which will give the angular points of the required
heptagon.

It should be noted that in the above method,
which is an approximate one, the line H B should
be drawn through the *second point* of division on the
diameter, whatever number of divisions there may be.

FIG. 9.

PROBLEM 8.—*To construct a regular polygon of any number of sides,
having a side given.*

Let A B be the given side, and produce it to D, making A D equal
to A B (Fig. 10). With A as centre and A B as radius describe the

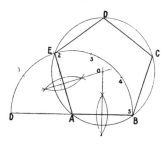

semicircle B E D, and divide it at the points
1, 2, 3, etc., into as many equal arcs as the
polygon is to have sides (in this case five).
Join A E, E being always the *second division*
from the extremity D of the semicircle. Then
A E will be the second side of the polygon.

Bisect A B and A E by perpendiculars meeting in O, which is therefore the centre of the
circumscribing circle of the polygon.

FIG. 10.

With centre O and radius O A describe the circle A B C D E, and
mark off distances B C and C D equal to A B. Join B C, C D, and D E,
then A B C D E is the required polygon.

PROBLEM 9.—*To draw a tangent to a given circle; 1st, at a given point
in the circumference; 2nd, from a given point without the circle.*

Let A C E be the given circle, whose centre is O (Fig. 11).

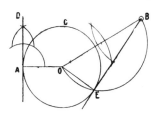

1st. Let A be the given point on its circumference. Draw the radius O A, and through the
point A draw the line A D perpendicular to A O,
and it will be the tangent required; since a
tangent to a circle is always at right angles to
the radius drawn through the point of contact.

2nd. Let B be the given point without the
circle. Join O B, and upon it as diameter
describe a semicircle, B E O, cutting the given circle in E. Join B E.

FIG. 11.

Then B E is the tangent to the circle at E, because the angle B E O, being in a semicircle, is a right angle.

PROBLEM 10.—*To inscribe a circle in a given triangle, A B C, Fig.* 12.

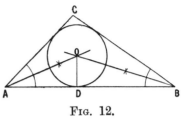

FIG. 12.

Bisect the angles A B C and C A B. The point O, where the bisectors meet, is the centre of the inscribed circle. To find the radius: from O let fall a perpendicular, O D, on any of the sides, as A B. With O as centre and radius O D describe a circle. This circle will be inscribed in the triangle A B C as required.

PROBLEM 11.—*To draw the arc of a circle by means of a template when the centre is inaccessible, the chord and versed sine or rise of the arc being given.*

Let A B be the chord and C D the rise of the arc (Fig. 13). Drive in a nail or pin at A, and also one at B. Take two laths, C e, C f, the

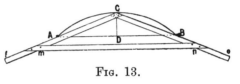

FIG. 13.

length of each not less than the chord A B, and fasten them together at C, so that their outer edges bear against the pins, and intersect at C as shown. For rigidity they may be tied together by a third piece, m n. If the rods are kept steady against the pins at A and B, and at the same time moved to right and left, a pencil held at C will describe the arc of the circle A C B.

The same practical method may be applied to draw an arc of a circle through *any* three given points when the centre is not at a convenient distance.

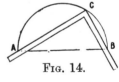

FIG. 14.

Note.—The above method depends upon an important property of the circle, viz., that *the angles in the same segment are equal.* Another application of the same principle is given in Fig. 14, which shows how a semicircle may be described by means of an ordinary square.

PROBLEM 12.—*To find any number of points in the arc of a circle by means of intersecting lines, the chord and versed sine being given.*

Let A B be the chord, and C D the versed sine (Fig. 15). Join A D, and draw A E at right angles to A D, also D E parallel to A B, meeting A E at E. Draw A F at

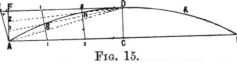

FIG. 15.

right angles to A B, meeting D E at F. Divide A C and E D into the same number of equal parts, numbering the points of division from A and E respectively, and join the corresponding numbers by lines, as 1 1, 2 2.

Divide A F also into the same number of equal parts, as A C or E B, and number from A upwards. Join D 1, intersecting 1 1 at g, and D 2 intersecting 2 2 at h, then g and h are points on the curve which may be traced through the points A, g, h, D. The other half of the curve may then be drawn in a similar manner.

> *Note.*—The method given is mathematically correct, but when the versed sine is very small, as compared with the chord, it is sufficient for practical purposes to draw the ordinates 1 1, 2 2 at right angles to A B. The method thus modified is the one usually practised in laying off the "beam moulds" for the decks of ships.

Another method.—Let A B and C D be the chord and versed sine respectively (Fig. 16). Join A D, and draw D E equal to C D, making

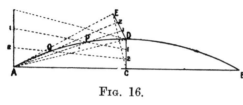

FIG. 16.

the angle A D E equal to the angle A D C. Draw also A F at right angles to A B and equal to twice the versed sine C D. Divide the lines A F, C D, D E, each into the same number of equal parts, and draw the intersecting lines as shown in the figure.

The intersection of the lines 1 1 and 1 A gives a point P on the curve. Similarly, the intersection of the lines 2 2 and 2 A gives another point, Q.

CONSTRUCTION OF THE ELLIPSE, PARABOLA, AND HYPERBOLA.

These curves are produced by plane sections of the cone, but they have certain properties which enable them to be described without reference to their being sections of that solid.

The ellipse is produced by a plane section passing through both sides of the cone.

It is also produced by a plane section of a right cylinder (see Figs. 56 and 59), which makes the geometry of the ellipse of the greatest importance in the practical subject of handrailing.

> *Definitions.*—Lines passing through the centre and terminated by the curve are termed *diameters* or *axes* of the ellipse. When two of these diameters are so related that each is parallel to the tangent at the extremity of the other, they are called *conjugate diameters*. The longest and shortest axes in the ellipse are termed the *major* and *minor* axes respectively, and are mutually at right angles.

PROBLEM 13.—*To draw an ellipse by means of a string when the major and minor axes are given.*

Let A A_1 and B B_1 (Fig. 17) be respectively the major and minor axes, placed so that they bisect each other at right angles. With B as centre and half the major axis, C A, as radius, draw an arc cutting the major axis in S and S_1. Insert a small pin in each of the points S and S_1.

Tie the ends of a piece of string to-gether, so that when laid over the pins and stretched tightly it will lie over the triangle S B S_1. Then by placing a pencil in the doubling of the string, and carry-ing it round in the manner shown, the complete curve of the ellipse may be traced out.

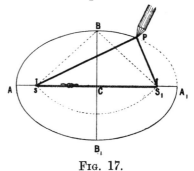

FIG. 17.

The points S and S_1 are called *the foci,* and the above construction is based on the important property of the ellipse, that *the sum of the distances of any point on the curve from the two foci is constant and equal to the major axis;* thus, in the figure, $S P + S_1 P = S B + S_1 B = A A_1$

PROBLEM 14.—*To determine points in the curve of an ellipse by means of the auxiliary circles,*[1] *the axes being given as in the preceding problem.*

Describe a circle on each of the axes (Fig. 18), and on one of these circles (the inner) assume any points, 1, 2, etc. Draw the radii, C 1, C 2, etc., through these points, and produce them to cut the larger circle in corresponding points, 1_1, 2_1, etc. Through the points 1, 2, etc., on the smaller circle draw parallels to the major axis, A A_1, and similarly through the points 1_1, 2_1, etc., on the larger circle draw parallels to the minor axis, B B_1. The intersection

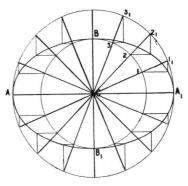

FIG. 18.

of each pair of parallels is a point on the curve of the ellipse, which can therefore be drawn through the points thus determined.

PROBLEM 15.—*To determine points on the curve of an ellipse by means of intersecting lines.*

Let A A_1 and B B_1 be the major and minor axes respectively (Fig. 19).

Construct a rectangle, D E F G, by drawing through the extremities of each diameter lines parallel to the other. Divide A C and A G into the same number of equal parts, and number them 1, 2, etc., from A. Join B with each point of division on A G. Join also B_1 with the

---

[1] The circles described on the two principal axes of an ellipse are called the *auxiliary circles,* that described upon the major axis is termed the *major auxiliary circle,* while that described on the minor axis is termed the *minor auxiliary circle.*

divisions on A C, and produce these lines to meet the corresponding lines drawn from B. The intersections at a, b, c, etc., are the required points on the curve.

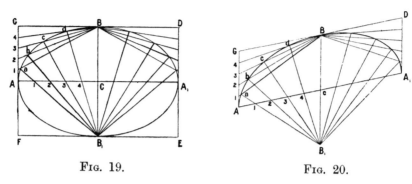

FIG. 19.   FIG. 20.

Precisely the same construction is applied (Fig. 20) to obtain the curve of the ellipse when the conjugate diameters, A A_1 and B B_1, are not at right angles to each other, and, therefore, not the principal axes of the ellipse.

PROBLEM 16.—*To determine points in the curve of an ellipse by means of ordinates, the major and minor axes being given.*

Draw A B (Fig. 21) equal to the minor axis, and at one extremity,

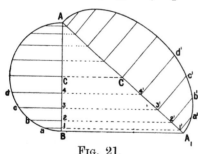

FIG. 21.

B, draw B A_1 at right angles to it. With A as centre and radius equal to the major axis, cut B A_1 at A_1, and join A A_1. On A B as diameter describe the semi-circle, B d A, and divide it into any number of parts at a, b, c, etc. Draw the ordinates $a\,1$, $b\,2$, etc., parallel to A_1 B, and produce them to meet A A_1 in the points 1^1, 2^1, etc. At these points draw the ordinates $1^1\,a^1$, $2^1\,b^1$, etc., at right angles to A A_1, making them equal to the corresponding ordinates in the circle. The curve traced through the extremities, a^1, b^1, etc., of these ordinates is the ellipse required.

PROBLEM 17.—*To draw the tangent and normal to an ellipse at a given point on the curve.*

Let P be the given point on the curve of the ellipse (Fig. 22). Draw the focal distances S P and S_1 P, and produce S P beyond the curve. Bisect the angle S_1 P D by the straight line P T. Then T P is the tangent to the ellipse at the given point P.

The normal at any point is perpendicular to the tangent at the same point. Hence the normal at P can at once be drawn; but it may be found directly, as shown at Q (Fig. 22), by bisecting the interior angle between the focal distances S Q and S₁ Q, the bisector T Q being the required normal.

PROBLEM 18.—*To describe an ellipse by means of a trammel, the major and minor axes being given.*

Take a thin lath, or, if the ellipse is small, a strip of paper, as L (Fig. 22), and from one end, p, measure off the distances pf and pg equal to

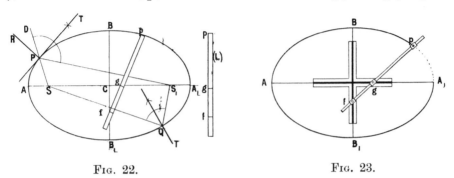

FIG. 22.   FIG. 23.

the semi-major and semi-minor axes respectively.   Place the lath (L), termed a *trammel*, so that f may fall on B B₁ and g on A A₁; the point p will then be in the curve of the ellipse.   By moving it to new positions, and always keeping the point g on the major axis and f on the minor, any number of points on the curve may be obtained.

Fig. 23 shows how the curve of an ellipse may be drawn continuously by the application of the same principle; the points f and g are constrained to move along the two axes by means of two grooves at right angles to each other run on the upper surface of a cross-shaped piece. The cross is temporarily fixed to the material on which the ellipse is to be drawn, with the centre lines of the grooves directly over the axes, as shown in the figure.   In the grooves two studs are fitted to slide freely, and are attached to the trammel at f and g.   As the studs at f and g move along the grooves, the pencil at the free end, p, traces out the curve of the ellipse.

PROBLEM 19.—*To describe an ellipse, having given the minor axis and a point on the curve.*

Let B B₁, Fig. 24, be the minor axis, P the given point on the curve.

Through C draw A A₁ at right angles to B B₁, giving the indefinite line of the major axis.

With P as centre, and radius equal to C B, the semi-minor axis, describe the arc cutting A A₁ in the points h and g.   Join the latter points to P, and produce these lines to meet the minor axis at k and f.

U U

This construction gives two trammels, P gf and h P k, each of which being guided on the axes A A$_1$ and B B$_1$, the point P will describe the ellipse. The former is the ordinary trammel as used in Problem 18 (Fig. 22), where the distance between the two guided points, f and g, is equal to the difference between the semi-major and semi-minor axes; while the guided points h and k in the latter trammel are at a distance apart equal to the sum of these semi-axes.

As the extremities h and k of the trammel h P k are moved along the two axes A A$_1$ and B B$_1$ in tracing out the ellipse, its middle point m obviously describes a circle about C (shown by a dotted line in the figure), while any other point in the length of the trammel will describe an ellipse. We may consequently, in describing the curve, use only one of the axes or guiding lines, and in place of the other use a radial bar, C m, jointed to the middle point, m, of the trammel, and free to rotate about C, the centre of the ellipse.

Similarly, the shorter trammel P gf may be guided by the radial bar C n, and either of the axes. It will be found that the attachment of the radial bar gives greater freedom in describing the ellipse than when the trammel has to be guided on two straight lines.

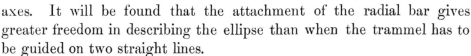

FIG. 24.

In comparing the action of the two trammels here shown, the arrangement of the longer one, h P k, unless the curve is very large, is generally to be preferred, and especially when there is little difference between the lengths of the two axes of the ellipse, as in that case the two guided points, f and g, in the shorter trammel are too near each other to determine its direction with any degree of accuracy.

PROBLEM 20.—*The normal and tangent at any point of an ellipse obtained from the position of the trammel.*

1st method.—Suppose, in Fig. 24, it is required to draw a normal to the ellipse at the point P. Proceed to find the position of the trammel on the axes when it is describing the point P. Thus, from P (Fig. 24), with the semi-minor axis as radius, cut the major axis in h; join h P, and produce it to intersect the minor axis at k; then $h\,\mathrm{P}\,k$ is the longer trammel and is in the position required. Through its extremities, h and k, draw perpendiculars to the axes intersecting at l. Join $l\,\mathrm{P}$ then $l\,\mathrm{P}$ is the normal to the curve at P, and, of course, the line at right angles to it through P is the tangent at that point. The normal may be found by a similar construction with the shorter trammel $\mathrm{P}\,g\,f$; thus, perpendiculars to the axes through f and g intersect at e, which, joined to P, will be in the same straight line as $l\,\mathrm{P}$.

It will be seen that the points l and e are the instantaneous centres about which the trammels $h\,\mathrm{P}\,k$ and $\mathrm{P}\,g\,f$ respectively are momentarily moving, and are the points of contact of the rolling and fixed circles (see Problem 21).

2nd method (*Practical*).—The construction just given leads up to an easy practical method of drawing normals by the application of the radial bar. Thus, referring again to Fig. 24, whatever be the position of P on the curve, the perpendiculars $k\,l$ and $h\,l$ form, with the axes, a rectangle, of which the trammel $h\,k$ is one diagonal, and a line, $l\,c$, the other, both being, of course, of equal length, and bisecting each other at m. Hence, in describing the curve, it is only necessary to attach the radial bar, $c\,m$, to the trammel, as described in the last problem, and have it extended as shown in the figure, so that $m\,l$ may be equal to $c\,m$, when its extremity, l, will always lie on the normal to the ellipse at the point that is being momentarily described.

When tracing out the curve, therefore, the trammel may be arrested in its motion when it has arrived at any specified point (say P), and the normal drawn by laying a straight-edge against l and P.

The same end may be attained by means of the shorter trammel, $\mathrm{P}\,g\,f$ (Fig. 24), by doubling the length of the radial bar, $c\,n$, when its extremity, e, will always lie on the normal to the curve.

Note.—This method may be very usefully applied in masonry for setting out elliptic arches with the trammel, as the joint lines of the *voussoirs* may be obtained simultaneously with the curve itself.

3rd method.—In Fig. 24, if from m, the middle point of the trammel $h\,\mathrm{P}\,k$, the distance $m\,\mathrm{P}$ be set off on the other side of it, as $m\,\mathrm{Q}$, Q is then a fixed point on the trammel, and if joined to C, the centre of the ellipse, gives a line, Q C, which is always parallel to the normal at whatever part of the curve P may be tracing out. Thus, in tracing out the ellipse, the trammel may be stopped at any point, as P, and a line drawn through it parallel to Q C, which is the normal required.

In the shorter trammel, $\mathrm{P}\,g\,f$, the corresponding point Q^1 lies on it produced, $n\,\mathrm{Q}^1$ being of course made equal to $n\,\mathrm{P}$.

It will be observed that C Q¹ is equal to C Q, as well as in the same straight line with it, both being parallel to the normal $l\,e$ at P; and further, that P Q¹ is equal to the longer trammel $h\,k$.

The constructions in the several methods of drawing the ellipse with a trammel that we have already given, and those that we are about to describe, may be all referred to the following principle:

If a circle roll internally, on the circumference of another circle of *twice* its diameter, any point on its circumference describes a diameter of the fixed circle (a particular case of the hypocycloid), and any other point on its plane describes an ellipse (a particular case of the hypotrochoid).

PROBLEM 21.—*Given the major and minor axes of an ellipse, to describe the curve with a trammel moving on any pair of straight lines passing through the centre.*

(1) In Fig. 25 A A¹ and B B¹ are the given axes. Produce C B to Q, making B Q equal to C A, the semi-major axis, and on C Q as diameter

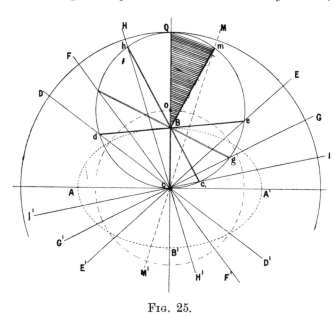

FIG. 25.

describe the circle C f Q. With centre C and radius C Q describe the circle D Q E. If now the smaller circle, C f Q, be rolled internally on the circumference of the larger one, the point B will trace out the ellipse A B A¹ required. Any point on the circumference of the rolling circle will describe a straight line passing through the centre C of the

fixed circle; for example, point d traces out the straight line D d D¹.

Any chord, therefore, of the rolling circle passing through B may be used as a trammel to describe the ellipse, its extremities being guided on the pair of axes appropriate to it. For example, in the figure, d B e is one of those chords taken arbitrarily, and through its extremities d and e and the centre, C, of the ellipse, lines D D¹ and E E¹ are drawn. Now if the ends d and e of this trammel represented by the chord $d\,e$ are moved along these lines into successive positions, the point B will trace out the curve of the ellipse, and the trammel will execute movements precisely the same as if it were clamped to the circular disc in the position shown, and the latter made to roll on the fixed circle, as we have above described.

Similarly other chords, such as $f\,g$ and $h\,c_1$, guided along the lines passing through their extremities and the centre C, the point B will again trace out the same ellipse.

Triangular trammel.—Further, it may be noted that the same ellipse may be described on any pair of lines whatever passing through its centre, C; only the three points of the trammel may not, under these conditions, necessarily lie in one and the same straight line. In Fig. 25 the angular point B of the hatched triangle B Q m will trace out the ellipse, if its other two angular points Q and m are guided on B Q, the minor axis, and the line M M[1] respectively. Or again, one only of these guiding lines may be used, say M M[1], and in place of the other a radial bar joining C, the centre of the ellipse, and the point O on the triangle, which is the centre of the circle C f Q.

Every such triangle formed on the rolling circle with its vertex at B, and having for its base a chord of that circle, will trace out the ellipse. In fact, the straight line trammel is only a particular case of the more general triangular one.

(2) If the point Q, Fig. 25, had been taken on the other side of B on the minor axis and a circle described on C Q[1] (Q[1] not shown, but see Fig. 26) as diameter, another entirely different set of trammels available for striking out the ellipse would be obtained.

Thus, referring to Fig. 26, which shows the same ellipse as Fig. 25. From B set off B Q[1] equal to C A, the semi-major axis, and on C Q[1] as diameter describe the circle C k Q[1], and with centre C and radius C Q[1] draw the larger circle z Q[1] y.

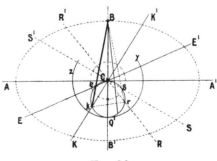
Fig 26.

If now the point B is rigidly attached to the circular disc represented by C k Q[1] it will trace out the ellipse, as the latter is made to roll internally on the circumference of the fixed circle z Q[1] y.

Again, it will follow that any line drawn from B to cut the smaller circle C k Q[1] will form a suitable trammel.

In the figure let B e k be one of these cutting lines, intersecting the circle in k and e, and through these points and the centre, C, of the ellipse draw the lines K K^1 and E E^1.

By now moving the trammel B e k into successive positions, constraining the point e to move on E E^1, and k on the line K K^1, the point B will, as before, trace out the elliptic curve, and the motion of the trammel will in all respects be the same as if it were attached to the rolling circle.

Similarly any other secant of the rolling circle, such as B s r, will trammel out the ellipse on the guiding lines S S^1 and R R^1.

Also any triangle having its vertex at B, and its base a chord of the circle C k Q^1, may be used to describe the curve. Thus the triangle B k r will answer the purpose, k and r being guided on the fixed lines K K^1 and R R^1.

It may be well to observe that the two sets of trammels, as determined in the two preceding figures, are related to each other in the following manner. In Fig. 25 the product of the segments of any chord of the rolling circle, Q f C e, is equal to the product of the semi-major and semi-minor axes, and equal to the product of the whole cutting line and the part without the circle, C k Q^1 r, in Fig. 26. For example: d B $\times$ e B (Fig. 25) = B k $\times$ B e (Fig. 26) = A C $\times$ B C.

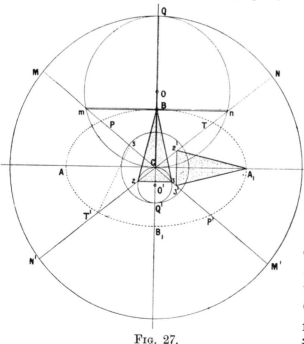

It should be observed also that in Fig. 25 the diameters of the rolling and fixed circles are equal respectively to the sum of the semi-major and semi-minor axes and to the sum of the major and minor axes, while in Fig. 26 they are equal to the difference of the semi axes and that of the whole axes respectively.

Equal-ended trammel and isosceles triangle.—In Fig. 27 the two circles on the diameters C Q and C Q^1 of the two preceding figures are here combined in the same diagram to illustrate a rather useful and interesting case, namely, what may be called an equal-ended trammel. This trammel, m B n, is of course the

FIG. 27.

chord through B at right angles to the diameter, Q C, of the rolling circle, which diameter also passes through B, and which, it will be seen, constitutes the trammel for using on the major and minor axes. It follows, that since the trammel m B n is bisected at B, its half-length is a mean proportional between B Q and C B the semi-major and semi-minor axes. It is guided on the diameters P P¹ and T T¹ symmetrically placed with respect to the principal axes of the ellipse, each of these diameters being equal in length to the trammel itself.

The corresponding trammel in the group belonging to the smaller circle is obviously the two tangents B 2 and B 3, each being equal to B m or B n, the half length of the other trammel. The two tangents B 2 and B 3 form the two sides of an isosceles triangle, B 2 3, shaded in the figure, which will trace out the ellipse on the same axes, M M¹ and N N¹, appropriate to the equal-ended trammel m B n. This triangle is shown in two other positions, namely, A₁ 2¹ 3¹ while tracing the point A₁, and T¹ C 5 tracing the point T¹ on the curve.

PROBLEM 22.—*To draw a parabola by means of intersecting lines, an abscissa of the axis and corresponding double ordinate being given.*

Let A N be the abscissa and P Q the double ordinate (Fig. 28), in their positions as shown. Construct the rectangle P Q R S. Divide P N and P S into the same number of equal parts, numbering them 1, 2, etc., from P. Join A with the points of division

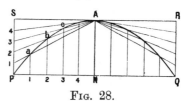

FIG. 28.

in P S, and through the points 1, 2, 3, etc., in P N, draw parallels to A N. The intersections of corresponding pairs of lines give points a, b, etc., on the curve through which the parabola may be traced.

PROBLEM 23.—*To draw a hyperbola by means of intersecting lines when the major axis A A₁, an abscissa of the axis A N, and the corresponding double ordinate P Q, are given* (Fig. 29).

Draw the rectangle P Q R S as in the previous problem. Divide P N and P S into the same number of equal parts, and number them 1, 2, 3, etc., from P. Join A with the points of division on P S, and A₁ with those on P N. Then the intersections a, b, c, d, of corresponding pairs of lines are points on the curve of the hyperbola. The other half of the curve, A Q, may be found in the same manner.

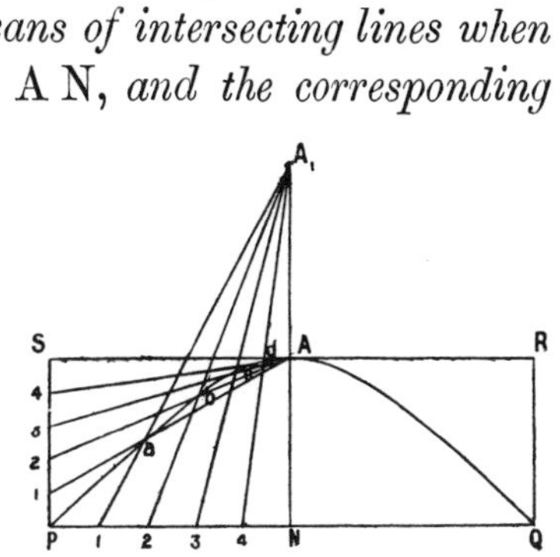

FIG. 29.

Scales

When objects are to be represented by drawings it is seldom convenient, and obviously in many cases impossible, to make them the same size as the objects delineated. In general they are required to be reduced representations of the object; but those parts which include minute and intricate details are often drawn separately full size, and in exceptional cases they may even be enlarged. But whatever size the drawing is to be, a correct representation will be obtained by making every line bear the same ratio to the corresponding line of the object, or, in other words, when every line of the object is proportionately diminished or increased.

Drawings which represent the object diminished or increased in this manner are said to be "drawn to scale," and the ratio referred to represents the "scale" of the drawing. Thus, if a drawing were made in which every 1 foot of the object is represented by 1 inch, it would give the correct relative proportions of the parts drawn to scale. As every linear inch in the drawing represents a true length of 1 foot, it would be said to be drawn to a scale of "1 inch to 1 foot," or to a scale of $\frac{1}{12}$, because it is shown in the drawing $\frac{1}{12}$ of its true length. This fraction is termed the *representative fraction* of the scale, and shows the ratio each line on the drawing bears to the corresponding line on the object delineated.

It should be carefully observed that it is only the *lines* in the drawing and object, or the *linear dimensions*, which bear the relation expressed by the scale. Thus, taking the above example, though 1 inch in the drawing represents a length of 12 inches in the object, 1 square inch of surface on the drawing would represent 144 square inches of area on the object. And further, if a model were made the same size as the drawing, 1 cubic inch of the model would represent 1,728 cubic inches of the actual object.

A scale used in drawing consists of a line accurately divided so as to represent the units of length employed in the measurement of the real object.

A *plain scale* is one which shows equal divisions only. A *diagonal scale* is one which is employed where very minute and accurate division is required.

Problem 24.—*To construct a plain scale of $\frac{1}{2}$ inch to the foot, to measure 7 feet.*

Draw two parallel lines, Fig. 30, a little apart, as shown, and set off with the dividers 7 divisions of ½ inch each, to represent feet. Divide

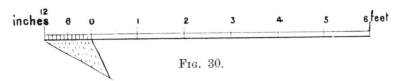

FIG. 30.

the first interval on the left accurately into 12 equal parts, by Problem 2, to represent inches, and figure the scale as shown, placing the zero between the feet and the subdivisions into inches, so that feet are read off to the right of the zero and inches to the left.

PROBLEM 25.—*To construct a diagonal scale showing inches and hundredths of an inch.*

Draw a line, A C, Fig. 30, and set off divisions of 1 inch from A. Divide the first inch, A B, into 10 equal parts, numbering them 1, 2, 3, etc., from B. At A and B erect perpendiculars, and on that, through A, set off any 10 equal divisions, marking them 1, 2, 3, etc., from A, and through these points draw lines parallel to

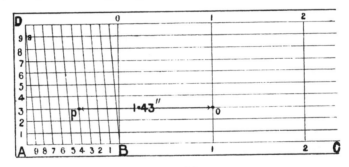

FIG. 31.

A B. Join D 9, and through the other points of division on A B draw parallels to D 9, which completes the scale.

It is clear that 9 a is $\frac{1}{10}$ of A 9, which latter is $\frac{1}{10}$ of an inch, and therefore, 9 a is $\frac{1}{100}$ of an inch. Measurements can therefore be taken from this scale to represent two places of decimals. For example, to find 1·43 inch on the scale, place one point of the dividers on O, that is, on the horizontal line marked 3 and on the vertical division 1. Open the dividers to the point P, where the diagonal line 4 intersects the horizontal line. It is evident that O P is 1·43 inches.

PROBLEM 26.—*To construct a scale of chords.*

A scale of chords is used for setting out and measuring angles. It is an unequally divided scale, which gives the length of the chord of an arc (to a given radius) subtending any angle from 1 to 90 degrees.

On any line, A B (Fig. 32), describe a semicircle, A C B, and divide the quadrant A C into 9 equal parts, each of which will thus represent

X X

10°. Draw the chord A C, which forms one edge of the scale. With centre A describe arcs from each point of division on to the line A C, giving the main divisions 10°, 20°, 30°, etc., on the scale. These primary divisions on the scale are further subdivided to represent 1° by the division into tenths of the corresponding arcs.

The important point to observe is that the common radius of the arcs subtending the angles is given on the scale, being equal to the chord

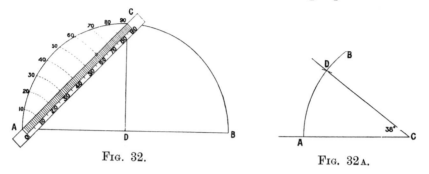

FIG. 32.   FIG. 32A.

of 60°. This enables the circle on which the scale was constructed, and to which the chords correspond, to be reproduced. To use the scale, therefore, in setting out angles, it is only necessary to draw this circle and cut off the chord of the required angle, and join its extremities with the centre. For example, let it be required to draw a line making an angle of 38° with a given line, A C (Fig. 32A): with C as centre and radius equal to the chord of 60° on the scale, describe an arc, A B. Then take the chord of 38° from the scale, and with A as centre cut off its length, A D. Join D C, then A C D is the angle required.

SOLID OR DESCRIPTIVE GEOMETRY.

Solid or Descriptive Geometry has for its object the representation upon a plane surface having two dimensions, viz., length and breadth, the forms of solid bodies which have three dimensions, namely, length, breadth, and thickness, in such a way that, from the representation alone, the true dimensions, form, and relationship of the parts may be accurately inferred.

Since the surfaces of all bodies may be considered as composed of points, the representation of a point is the first step towards the representation of any surface or solid.

Projections of a point.—The orthographic projection of a point on a given plane is the foot of the perpendicular let fall from the point to the plane.   The perpendicular is called the *projector* of the point, and the plane on which the point is projected the *plane of projection* of the point. For example, in Fig. 33 let M N O P represent a plane, B a point, and B *b* a perpendicular let fall from the point to the plane, then the foot *b* of that perpendicular is the *projection* of the point B on the plane M N O P, and B *b* the *projector* of the point.

All that the single projection *b* (Fig. 33) tells us of the actual position of the point B is, that it lies somewhere on the perpendicular to the plane

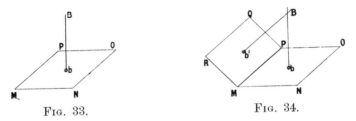

Fig. 33.   Fig. 34.

through the point *b*, but if the projection *b'* of the point B on a second plane, M P Q R (Fig. 34), not parallel to the first, is also given, the position of the point B with respect to both planes can be accurately inferred. For the actual point lies on the perpendicular, through *b*, to the first plane, and also on the perpendicular, through *b'*, to the second plane; the point therefore being at the same time on the two straight lines, will be the single point of their intersection.   A point is thus determined when its projections on two intersecting planes are given, as no other point can have the same pair of projections.

For the purpose of descriptive geometry the two planes are conceived to be at right angles to each other, and named, from their usual positions, the *horizontal* and *vertical planes of projection*, their line of intersection being called the *ground line*.

These two planes of projection, termed also the *co-ordinate planes*, being mutually perpendicular, form by their intersection *four dihedral angles* or *quadrants*, known as the 1st, 2nd, 3rd, and 4th dihedral angles. Limited portions of such a pair of planes are shown in Fig. 35, E F being the horizontal plane, G H the vertical, and X Y their line of intersection. The 1st dihedral angle is the space in front of the vertical and above the horizontal planes of projection; the 2nd, behind the vertical and above the horizontal; the 3rd, behind the vertical and below the horizontal; and the 4th, in front of the vertical and below the horizontal.

One point and its projections are shown in each of the four quadrants, A being situated in the 1st, B in the 2nd, C in the 3rd, and D in the 4th.

Drawings or projections on the horizontal plane (H. P.) are called *plans*, and those on the vertical plane (V.P.) *elevations*. The plan of a point A in space may be marked a, and its elevation a^1.

Though the planes of projection have always to be conceived at right angles to each other, as shown in Fig. 35, it is obvious that drawings can only be made conveniently on one plane, that is, in practice, on one flat sheet of paper, not two at right angles. It is assumed, therefore, that the vertical plane, with the vertical projections upon it, is rotated backwards in the direction of the arrows (Fig. 35) about its intersection, X Y, with the horizontal plane as an axis, through a right angle, till it coincides with the horizontal plane, and forms one plane with it.

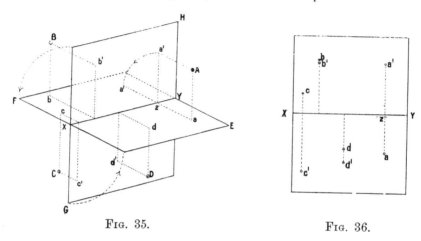

Fig. 35.   Fig. 36.

The two projections (plan and elevation) of any point will, after rotation of the vertical plane, be found to lie on the same straight line perpendicular to the ground line. Fig. 36 shows the planes in the previous figure after rotation, with the projections of the points A, B, C, D on them, as they would be drawn geometrically on a sheet of paper. It has to be constantly kept in view, that the part of the paper below the ground line represents not only the horizontal plane, but also the lower portion of the vertical plane, and that the part above the ground line represents the vertical plane as well as the back portion of the horizontal plane. Consequently a point A, situated in the 1st quadrant, will, after the usual rotation, have its plan below the X Y and its elevation above it, while both plan and elevation of the point B in the 2nd quadrant will appear above the X Y. The positions of the projections of the points C and D in the 3rd and 4th quadrants relatively to the X Y are also shown in Fig. 36.

The plan of a point indicates by its distance from the ground line the distance of the actual point from the vertical plane, and similarly the elevation shows the distance of the point from the horizontal plane. From this fact the plan and elevation of a point can be at once determined, when its distances from the planes of projection are given, by drawing a perpendicular to the ground line X Y, and setting off from the latter along the perpendicular the given distances of the point from the planes of projection. The elevation of the point will be set off above the X Y and the plan below it if the point is situated in the 1st quadrant; if the point is situated in the 2nd quadrant, both plan and elevation above X Y; if in the 3rd, the plan above and the elevation below; and if in the 4th, both below.

It should be observed that in the practical application of descriptive geometry it is generally possible to confine the operations to the 1st quadrant, so that the plan will be below and the elevation above X Y.

Projection of a line.—The projection of a line on a plane is the line which passes through the feet of all the perpendiculars which can be let fall from the line to the plane, and the surface containing the projectors is called the *projecting surface* of the line.

The projection of a straight line on a plane is a straight line, for it is the intersection of the plane in which the projectors of the line lie, with the plane on which the line is projected. In order, therefore, to determine the projection of any straight line it is only necessary to determine the projections of two of its points; the straight line drawn through these two projections will be the projection of the line. For example, in Fig. 37, which is merely a sketch introduced to help the student to better realize a straight line and its projections in their positions with respect to each other and the two co-ordinate planes, the projections of the extremities of the line A B on the horizontal plane are a and b; the line ab joining these points is the projection of the line A B on the horizontal plane. Similarly $a^1 b^1$ is its projection on the vertical plane.

Trace of a line.—The point in which a line or line produced intersects a plane is called the *trace* of the line on that plane. The intersection of a line with the horizontal plane is called the *horizontal trace*, and its intersection with the vertical plane the *vertical trace*.

Inclination of a line to a plane.—By the inclination of a line to a plane is meant the angle which the line makes with its projection on that plane; thus, in Fig. 37, h is the

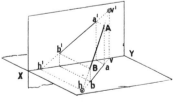

FIG. 37.

horizontal trace and v^1 the vertical trace of the line A B, and the angle A h a, between the line and its horizontal projection, is the inclination of the line A B to the horizontal plane. Similarly the angle B $v^1 b^1$ is the inclination of the same line to the vertical plane of projection.

The projection of a straight line of given length is equal to that line if the latter is parallel to the plane of projection, but less when the line is inclined, the length of the projection diminishing as the angle of inclination increases, becoming a point when the angle reaches 90°, that is, when the line is perpendicular to the plane.

A line may occupy with respect to the two co-ordinate planes any one of the following positions: 1. Parallel to both planes of projection. 2. Perpendicular to either.　3. Parallel to one and inclined to the other.　4. Inclined to both.

In position 1 both projections are parallel to X Y, and equal in length to the line itself; in 2, one projection is perpendicular to X Y and equal in length to the line itself, the other a point; in 3, one projection is inclined to X Y and equal in length to the line itself, the other parallel to X Y and shorter than the line itself ; and in 4, both projections are inclined to X Y, and their lengths less than that of the real line.

PROBLEM 27.—*Given the projections of a straight line, A B, to determine its traces, real length, and angles of inclination to the planes of projection.*

Let $a b$, $a^1 b^1$, Fig. 38, be the plan and elevation of a line, A B. These projections show that the line is inclined to both planes of projection, and therefore will have a trace on each of them if produced far enough.

To find the horizontal trace.—Produce the elevation $a^1 b^1$ to intersect the ground line in the point h^1. This point is the elevation of the horizontal trace, and the point h, where a perpendicular to X Y from h^1 meets the plan $a b$ produced, is the horizontal trace of the line.

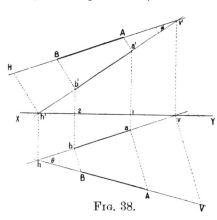

To find the vertical trace. — Produce the plan $a b$ to intersect X Y in v, then v is obviously the plan of the vertical trace, and a projector, $v v^1$, at right angles to X Y from this point meets the elevation $a^1 b^1$ produced in v^1, which is the vertical trace of the line.

To find the true length.—Consider the line A B in its position as represented in the sketch, Fig. 37, resting on its two projectors a A and b B.

FIG. 38.

These lines, together with the plan $a b$, form a four-sided figure standing vertically, two sides of which (the projectors) are parallel to each other, and at right angles to $a b$. Suppose this figure to be rotated about ab into the horizontal plane, its true shape and the real length of A B would then be shown on that plane. Draw therefore the lines a A, b B, Fig. 38, at right angles to ab, and each equal in length to the heights of the points a^1, b^1 respectively above X Y; thus a A and b B will represent the projectors after the rotation referred to. Join A B, then A B is the true length of the line. This process is termed *constructing* the line into the horizontal plane.

To find the inclinations of the line.—If A B (Fig. 38) be produced to meet ab, it will evidently do so in the horizontal trace h already found, and the angle ah A is the inclination of the line A B to the H.P.

In the same figure the line is shown similarly constructed into the vertical plane of projection, giving its real length again, and its angle of inclination H v^1 h^1 to that plane.

PROBLEM 28.—*To determine the plan and elevation of a straight line which shall make given angles, θ and ϕ, with the horizontal and vertical planes of projection respectively.*

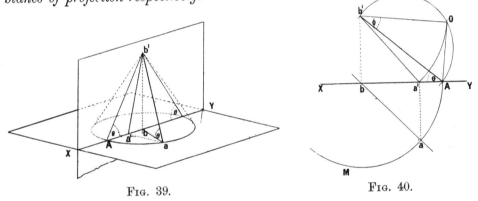

FIG. 39.   FIG. 40.

If we suppose, as shown in the sketch, Fig. 39, a right circular cone standing on its base on the H.P. with its base angle equal to θ; then any generatrix (that is, any line, as b^1 A, drawn from the apex to the base) of this conical surface will make the required angle θ with the H.P., and therefore fulfil one of the conditions of the problem.

We have then only to find out the particular generatrices on this cone which are inclined at an angle ϕ to the V.P. It is convenient to assume the axis b^1 b of this cone in the vertical plane of projection, as shown in the sketch Fig. 39.

At any point A in the ground line X Y (Fig. 40) draw a line A b^1, making an angle θ with it. Take any point b^1 in this line, and let fall the perpendicular b^1 b; then b b^1 is the axis of the cone, b the plan of this axis and centre of the circular base. With centre b and radius b A

describe a circle A M. Then A M is part of the plan of the cone, and
A $b^1 b$ its half elevation. A b is the plan, A b^1 the elevation of a line
inclined θ to the H.P., but *in* the V.P., and therefore making no angle
with the latter. Suppose the extremity A to be moved round the
circle till the line A b makes the required angle ϕ with the V.P. Its
plan will be a radius of the base, but the elevation-length has to be
found by constructing a right-angled triangle, the hypotenuse of which
is the real line, its base the elevation of that line, and the base angle, ϕ,
i.e., the angle of inclination to the V.P. To construct this triangle:
at b^1 (Fig. 40) make the angle A $b^1 o$ equal to ϕ, from A let fall a
perpendicular on $b^1 o$, meeting it in o; then $b^1 o$ is the elevation-length
of the line. With b^1 as centre and $b^1 o$ as radius describe an arc cutting
the ground line in a^1; then $a^1 b^1$ is the required elevation, and a projector
therefore from a^1 at right angles to X Y, meeting the circular base in a,
determines $a b$, the plan of the line.

It will be obvious, in referring again to the sketch, Fig. 39, that on
the surface of the cone there would be four lines which satisfy the conditions of the problem, two in front of the V. P. and two behind it.

A little consideration will make it apparent also that the sum of the
two angles of inclination cannot exceed 90°.

PLANES.—Planes indefinitely extended are generally expressed in
Descriptive Geometry by their lines of intersection with the co-ordinate
planes. These intersections are called the *traces* of the plane, and are
straight lines which meet in one point in the ground line, unless when
the plane is parallel to it.

The intersection of a plane with the H.P. is called its *horizontal trace*
(h.t.), and with the V.P. its *vertical trace* (v.t.)

The position of a plane is determined when its traces are known.

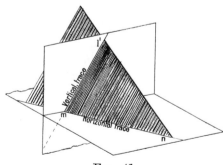

For example, the oblique plane
$l^1 m n$ (Fig. 41) has its position completely determined by its traces $m n$
and $m l^1$.

A plane perpendicular to one of
the planes of projection has its trace
on the other plane perpendicular to
X Y ; a plane perpendicular to both
planes of projection has for its traces
two lines perpendicular to X Y; a

FIG. 41.

plane parallel to one of the planes of projection has a trace on the other
plane of projection only, being a straight line parallel to X Y ; and a

plane inclined to both planes of projection (*i.e.*, making with either an angle less than a right angle) has both its traces inclined to X Y.

In the last case the traces of the plane do not show the angle at which it is inclined to either of the co-ordinate planes, and to determine either of these angles a special construction is required, which is shown in Figs. 42 and 43, and explained in the next problem.

PROBLEM 29.—*To determine the angles which a given plane, $l^1 m n$, makes with the planes of projection, and also the real angle between the traces.*

Definition.—The angle between two planes is the angle contained by two straight lines, one drawn in each plane, from the same point on their intersection, and at right angles to it.

To find the angle of inclination to the H.P.—

From any point a in X Y (Fig. 42) draw $a b$ perpendicular to the horizontal trace $m n$, and $a a^1$ perpendicular to X Y, meeting the vertical trace $m l^1$ in a^1. With a as centre and $a b$ as radius describe the arc b B, and join a^1 B; then the angle a B a^1 is the inclination (θ) of the given plane to the horizontal plane.

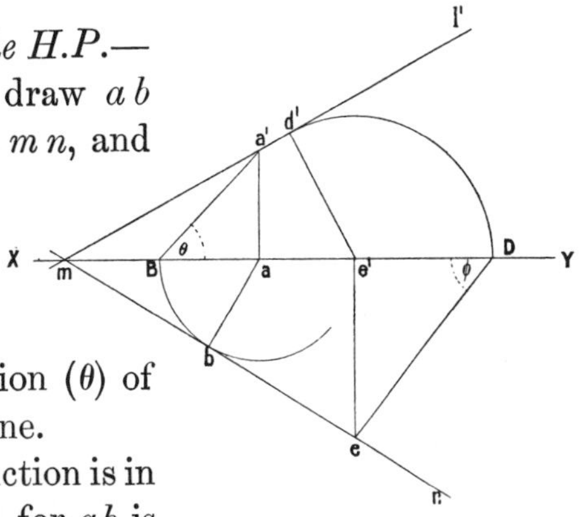

FIG. 42.

It will be obvious that this construction is in accordance with the above definition, for ab is a line on the horizontal plane at right angles to the horizontal trace $m n$, and a line on the oblique plane drawn from the same point, b, also at right angles to the trace mn, would evidently stand over $a b$, forming the hypotenuse of a right-angled triangle, of which $a b$ is the base and $a a^1$ the perpendicular. The angle between the base and hypotenuse of this triangle is clearly the inclination (θ) of the oblique plane to the horizontal plane.

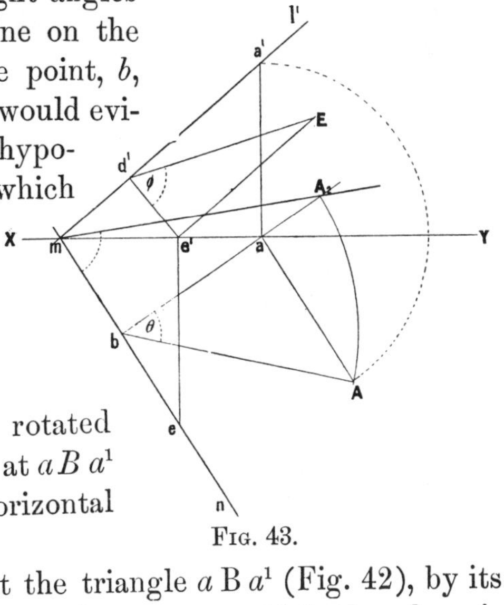

This triangle, $a b a^1$, may be rotated about $a a^1$ into the vertical plane, as at $a B a^1$ in Fig. 42, or about $a b$ into the horizontal plane, as at $a b$ in Fig. 43.

FIG. 43.

It should be observed also that the triangle a B a^1 (Fig. 42), by its rotation about $a a^1$, would generate a right cone to which the plane is tangential, and therefore the base angle, a^1 B a, of this cone is the inclination (θ) of the plane to the horizontal plane.

Y Y

To find the inclination to the vertical plane.—The same principle is applicable to the vertical plane. From any point e^1 in X Y (Fig. 42) draw $e^1 d^1$ at right angles to the vertical trace, and $e^1 e$ perpendicular to X Y, and meeting the horizontal trace in e. With e^1 as centre and $e^1 d^1$ as radius describe the arc d^1 D, cutting X Y in D. Join e D; then e D e^1 is the angle of inclination (ϕ) to the vertical plane.

The triangle e D e^1 might also have been rotated about $e^1 d^1$ into the vertical plane, as shown in Fig. 43.

The real angle between the traces is obtained by conceiving the oblique plane to be rotated about its horizontal trace until it coincides with the horizontal plane, and bringing with it the vertical trace. During rotation all the points situated in the plane evidently move in vertical planes at right angles to the trace (horizontal trace). Hence, in Fig. 43, after the plane $n\,m\,l^1$ has been constructed into the horizontal plane, as described, the point A, which is situated in the vertical trace, will lie on $b\,a$ produced. The real length, b A, marked from b along $b\,a$ produced, will give the point A_2, and the line $A_2\,m$ is the vertical trace constructed into the horizontal plane, and therefore $A_2\,m\,n$ is the real angle between the traces.

> Note.—It will be noticed that $m\,A_2$ (Fig. 43) is equal to $m\,a^1$, and A_2 might have been found by describing an arc with m as centre and $m\,a^1$ as radius, cutting $b\,a$, produced in A_2.

PROBLEM 30.—*To determine the traces of a plane containing three given points (not in the same straight line).*

Let a, b, c, and a^1, b^1, c^1 (Fig. 44), be the plans and elevations respectively of three points, A, B, and C.

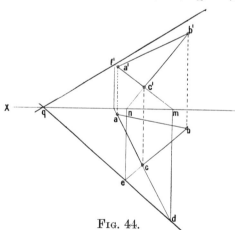

Since the straight lines joining the points lie wholly in the plane, the traces of these lines will be in the traces of the plane.

Join the projections of the points, and we have the triangle $a\,b\,c$ and $a^1\,b^1\,c^1$. The traces of any two sides of the triangle A B C, whose plan and elevation are $a\,b\,c$ and $a^1\,b^1\,c^1$, respectively, will be sufficient to determine the traces of the plane.

FIG. 44.

To work the problem, therefore, produce $a^1\,c^1$ to meet X Y in m, and draw $m\,d$ at right angles to X Y to meet the plan $a\,c$ produced in d. Then d is the horizontal trace of the line A C, and therefore one point on the horizontal trace of the required plane. The trace e of the line B C is similarly found, and the line dq drawn through d and e is the horizontal trace of the plane. Since the vertical trace of the plane passes through q, it is only necessary to find the vertical trace, f^1, of one of the lines C A, then f^1 joined to q is the vertical trace of the plane.

PROBLEM 31.—*To find the projections of the intersection of two oblique planes, mln^1 and mpn^1.*

The point m (Fig. 45), in which the horizontal traces of the given planes intersect, is evidently a point on the plan of the required line; and the point n^1, in which their vertical traces intersect, is a point in the elevation of the required line. Since n^1 is in the vertical plane, its plan is in X Y; and since m is a point in the horizontal plane,

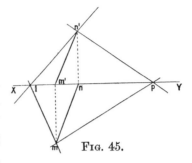

FIG. 45.

its elevation is in the X Y. From the points m and n^1, therefore, draw perpendiculars to X Y, giving points m^1 and n. Then mn and $m^1 n^1$ are the required projections of the intersection of the two planes.

PROBLEM 32.—*To find the point of intersection of a given line and plane.*

Let ab and $a^1 b^1$ (Fig. 46) be the plan and elevation of a line; it is required to find its intersection with the plane mln^1. Assume a vertical plane which shall contain the given line A B. Then, since the line A B is in this vertical plane and intersects the other plane, it must do so in the line which is common to both planes, that is, in their intersection.

Produce ab both ways, meeting the trace lm at c and X Y at d; cd will represent the horizontal trace of the vertical plane containing A B, and dd^1 at right angles to X Y its vertical trace.

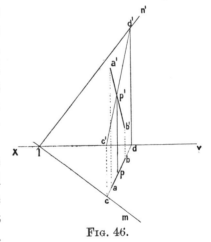

FIG. 46.

From c draw cc^1 at right angles to X Y, and join $c^1 d^1$. Then $c^1 d^1$ is the elevation of the intersection of the two planes. The point p^1, where $c^1 d^1$ crosses $a^1 b^1$, is the elevation of the intersection of the line A B with the plane mln^1, and a projector from p^1 on ab gives the plan p.

PROBLEM 33.—*To determine the traces of a plane perpendicular to a given line, and passing through a given point in that line.*

Let ab and $a^1 b^1$ be the projections of the given line (Fig. 47), p and p^1 those of the given point on it.

Note.—When a line is at right angles to a plane the projections of the line are perpendicular to the traces of the plane, *i.e.*, the plan and elevation of the line are respectively perpendicular to the horizontal and vertical traces of the plane.

The horizontal trace of the required plane will therefore be at right angles to $a\,b$, and its vertical trace at right angles to $a^1\,b^1$. As the plane

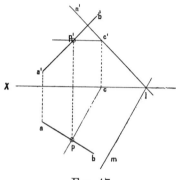

has to contain the point P, it will also contain the horizontal line through p perpendicular to A B. Through p draw $p\,c$ at right angles to $a\,b$ to meet X Y in c. The elevation of this horizontal line is a parallel through p^1 to X Y, and a perpendicular to X Y through c gives the vertical trace c^1 of this level line, and c^1 is therefore a point in the vertical trace of the required plane. A line, $n^1\,l$, drawn at right angles to $a^1\,b^1$ through the point c^1, and $l\,m$ at right angles to $a\,b$, are

FIG. 47.

the traces of the plane, passing through P and at right angles to A B.

PROBLEM 34.—*To determine the angle between any two oblique planes, given by their traces as $m\,l\,n^1$, $m\,p\,n^1$* (Fig. 48).

The angle between two planes is the angle between the intersections formed by a third plane cutting each of the given planes at right angles. The third plane will be perpendicular to the intersection of the two given planes, and will cut them in lines, which are also perpendicular to that intersection. The angle required there-

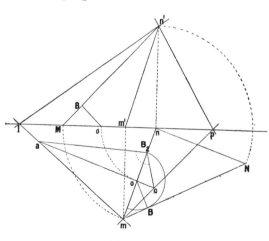

fore will be measured by the plane-angle formed by two straight lines drawn, one in each plane, from a point in their intersection and at right angles to it. If the plane containing these perpendiculars be determined, and constructed about its horizontal trace into the horizontal plane, the required angle will be shown.

To work the Problem.—

Find $m\,n$ and $m^1\,n^1$, the plan

FIG. 48.

and elevation, respectively, of the intersection of the two planes, as in Problem 27. Through any convenient point, o, on $m\,n$, the plan of the intersection of the planes, draw the straight line $a\,o\,c$ at right angles to $m\,n$, meeting the horizontal traces of the planes at a and c. Then construct their intersection $m\,n$, m^1n^1, into either of the planes of projection. In Fig. 48 this is done on the horizontal plane by drawing $n\,\mathrm{N}$ at right angles to $m\,n$, and equal to the projector $n\,n^1$. Then $m\,\mathrm{N}$ is the constructed intersection. From the point o draw $o\,\mathrm{B}$ perpendicular to $m\,\mathrm{N}$ thus found. Set off along $m\,n$, $o\,\mathrm{B}_2$ equal to $o\,\mathrm{B}$, and join $a\,\mathrm{B}_2$, $c\,\mathrm{B}_2$; then $a\,\mathrm{B}_2\,c$ is the angle between the two planes.

Note.—The length $o\,\mathrm{B}$, Fig. 48, is also found by rotating the intersection of the two planes, together with the point o, into the vertical plane, as shown.

PROBLEM 35.—*To determine the distance between two parallel planes given by their traces.*

CONVERSELY.—*To determine by its traces a plane parallel to a given plane and at a given distance from it.*

If two or more parallel planes be cut by another plane, the cutting plane will intersect these planes in lines which will be parallel to one another. It follows, therefore, that parallel planes have parallel traces.

1. Let $v\,t\,h$ and $v^1t^1h^1$ (Fig. 49) be the traces of the given parallel planes.

Draw the traces $a\,\mathrm{B}$ and $a\,a''$ of a vertical plane cutting the other two at right angles, *i.e.*, from any point a on the ground line draw

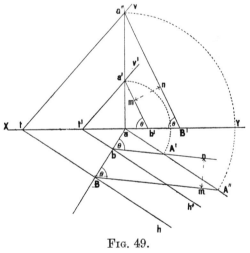

FIG. 49.

$a\,\mathrm{B}$ at right angles to $t\,h$ or $t^1\,h^1$, intersecting them in B and b, respectively, and from a also draw $a\,a''$ at right angles to X Y intersecting the vertical traces in a^1 and a''. Set off from a along the ground line $a\,b^1$ and $a\,\mathrm{B}^1$ equal to $a\,b$ and $a\,\mathrm{B}$ respectively, and join $a^1\,b^1$ and $a''\,\mathrm{B}^1$. The perpendicular distance $m\,n$, between these lines, which are necessarily parallel by the theorem stated above. is that between the two given planes.

In the figure the same result is obtained by constructing the same triangles, $a\,b^1a^1$ and $a\,\mathrm{B}^1a''$, into the horizontal plane.

The construction, it will be seen, is the same as that of finding the inclination θ of the two given parallel planes to the horizontal plane.

Note.—The problem might also have been solved by taking any point in one of the planes and letting fall a perpendicular on to the other. The true length of this line would obviously be the perpendicular distance between the two planes.

2. Referring again to Fig. 49, let $v\,t\,h$ be the traces of the given plane, and $m\,n$ the distance that the required plane has to be from it.

Now since parallel planes have parallel traces, one point determined in either trace will, of course, fix the position of the required plane.

Proceed to find the angle of inclination that the given plane $v\,t\,h$ makes with the horizontal, as $a''\,\mathrm{B^1}\,a$. Then A parallel to $a''\,\mathrm{B^1}$ at a distance $m\,n$ from it cuts the vertical line $a\,a''$ at a^1, and $a^1 t^1$ and $t^1 h^1$ drawn parallel to the vertical and horizontal traces respectively of the given plane are the traces of the plane as required.

SECTIONS AND DEVELOPMENTS.

PROBLEM 36.—*Given a right square prism standing with its base on the horizontal plane, to find the projections and true shape of a section of the solid made by any oblique plane, and also the development of the surface of the prism, showing on it the trace of the cutting plane.*

It was shown in Problem 32 how to find the projections of the point of intersection of a straight line and a plane. The present problem resolves itself into that of finding the intersections of four vertical lines with an oblique plane.

In Fig. 50, let (M) and (N) be the plan and elevation respectively of the vertical square prism placed with one face parallel to the vertical plane, and let $v\,t$ and $h\,t$ be the traces of the cutting plane.

To determine the section, two methods are shown in Fig. 50.

1. Draw a second elevation of the prism on a ground line $\mathrm{X_2\,Y_2}$, at right angles to $h\,t$, as shown at (P).

Through any point (say a) draw a line parallel to $h\,t$, the horizontal trace of the oblique plane, cutting the old and new ground lines in the points 1 and 3 respectively. This will be the plan of a level line lying in the given plane and at a height which is determined by the vertical line 1 2. At the point 3 on the new ground line $\mathrm{X_2\,Y_2}$, erect 3 a'' perpendicular to it, and equal to 1 2, then the line through h and a'' is the vertical trace, and is also an " edge " view of the plane of section.

To obtain the true shape of the section of the prism: suppose the cutting plane folded into the horizontal plane about $h\,t$ as a hinge with the various points upon it. During rotation the points whose plans are a, b, c, and d will move in vertical planes perpendicular to $h\,t$. Through a, b, c, d, therefore, draw perpendiculars to $h\,t$ and set off from it 4 $\mathrm{A^1}$, 5 $\mathrm{B^1}$, 6 $\mathrm{C^1}$, and 7 $\mathrm{D^1}$ equal to $h\,a''$, $h\,b''$, $h\,c''$, and $h\,d''$ respectively, then $\mathrm{A^1\,B^1\,C^1\,D^1}$ is the true shape of the section.

2. By the following method the plane of section is rotated about its vertical trace, $v\,t$, into the vertical plane of projection. To do this, determine the elevation $a^1\,b^1\,c^1\,d^1$ of the section. Draw the plans of level lines lying on the cutting plane through the various plan points a, b, c, d of the section. In this case those through a and b will be sufficient. Their elevations, $2\,a^1$ and $9\,b^1$, intersect the vertical edges of the prism in a^1 and b^1, and—since two faces of the prism are parallel to the vertical plane—parallel lines $a^1\,d^1$ and $b^1\,c^1$ to the vertical trace, $v\,t$, complete the elevation of the section.

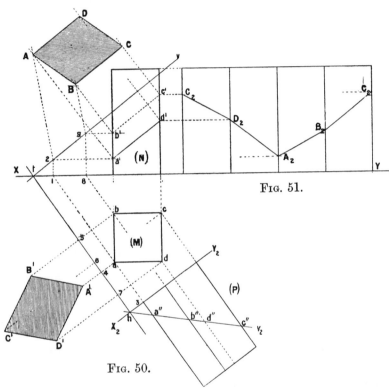

Fig. 51.

Fig. 50.

Through the points a^1, b^1, c^1, and d^1, draw indefinite lines perpendicular to $v\,t$. Then from point 2 in $v\,t$, with $1\,a$ as radius, cut the perpendicular through a^1 at A, and through 9 draw 9 B parallel to 2 A, cutting the perpendicular through b^1 at B. Through A and B draw parallels to $v\,t$, cutting the perpendiculars through c^1 and d^1 in C and D, respectively; then the parallelogram, A B C D, is the true shape of the section of the prism by the plane $v\,t\,h$, and should of course be equal in every respect to $A^1\,B^1\,C^1\,D^1$ as found by the other method.

To determine the development of the cut surfaces of the prism: draw the five vertical lines C_2, D_2, A_2, B_2, C_2 (Fig. 51), at a common distance apart equal to the edge of the square base of prism. The heights of the various points of the section in the elevation are transferred to these lines in the order that they occur, and the lines $C_2 D_2$, $D_2 A_2$, etc., drawn, which gives the trace of the cutting plane on each face of the solid.

PROBLEM 37.—*Given the plan and elevation of a square pyramid situated as in Fig. 52, to determine the true shape of the section made by an inclined plane, and also the development of the cut surfaces of the solid.*

In Fig. 52 the cutting plane is taken at right angles to the vertical plane, so that the vertical trace represents an edge view of the plane,

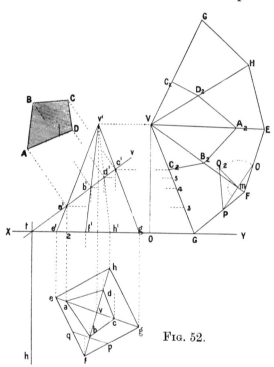

and therefore the elevations a^1, b^1, c^1, d^1 of its points of intersection with the sloping edges of the pyramid lie on vt. Projectors let fall from these points to the corresponding lines in plan determine $abcd$, the plan of the section.

Draw perpendiculars to vt from the points a^1, b^1, c^1, d^1, and make them equal to the distances of the same points in the plan from XY. Thus, for example, $a^1 A$ is made equal to $a\,2$. The figure A B C D is then the *true shape of the section.*

To draw the development. —As shown on the right of the elevation of the pyramid

FIG. 52.

(Fig. 52), construct the right-angled triangle V O G: its base, O G, equal to the plan length vg of a sloping edge of the solid, and the perpendicular O V equal to the axis of the pyramid, the hypotenuse V G is the true length of the slanting edges of the pyramid. On V G construct the isosceles triangle V G F, having G F equal to the edge of the base, and repeat the same construction for the other three equal triangles, making up the figure G H E F G V, which is the required development, and which, if re-folded and placed over the square base, would make up the pyramid.

To determine the section lines on this development, level over the points a^1, b^1, c^1, d^1 in elevation on to V G at 3, 4, 5, and C_2 respectively. Set off from V along V H the distance V D_2 equal to V 5, and join C_2 D_2, and proceed similarly with the lines on the other faces.

Dihedral angle between two adjacent slanting faces of pyramid.—This angle can be very readily determined from the plan and the development just drawn. Thus, at right angles to V F in the development, draw any line, as P m Q, and in the plan set off fp and fq equal to F P or F Q. Then pq is the base of a triangle whose sides, P m and Q m, include the dihedral angle. Hence, with P and m as centres, and radii

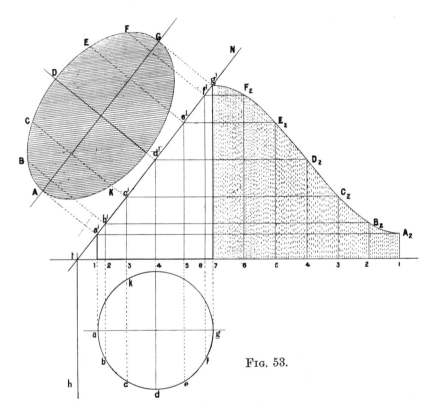

FIG. 53.

equal to pq and m Q respectively, draw the arcs intersecting at Q_2. Then P m Q_2 is the dihedral angle between any two adjacent faces.

PROBLEM 38.—*Given the plan and elevation of a right cylinder, axis vertical, cut by an inclined plane at right angles to the vertical plane of projection, to determine the true shape of the section and the development of the cylindric surface with the line of intersection of the cutting plane upon it.*

To find the section.—Any section of a cylinder made by a plane inclined to the axis is an ellipse. In Fig. 53 the line $a^1 g^1$ is the major axis, and the diameter of the cylinder the minor, from which data the ellipse could be drawn by any of the methods described in Problems 13 *et seq.*

Z Z

Otherwise, in Fig. 53, the plane of section is rotated about the vertical trace t N into the vertical plane. Divide the circumference of the plan circle into any convenient number of equal parts (say twelve). Now, for illustration, take the points c and k, and from their common elevation, c^1, draw a line at right angles to t N. Make c^1 K and c^1 C equal to $3\,k$ and $3\,c$ respectively in the plan ; then C and K are points on the curve of the elliptic section. Other points, D, E, F, etc., are similarly found, and the curve traced through them.

To find the development.—In Fig. 53, $A_2\,g^1\,7\,1$ is the development of the front half of the cylinder below the section ; the other half, which by symmetry is exactly the same, is not drawn.

Set off along the ground line from 7 the distance 7 1, equal to the stretch out of the semicircle (about $3\frac{1}{7}$ times the radius). Divide the line 7 1 into the same number of equal parts (six) as the semi-circumference, and at the several points of division set up vertical lines to intersect the level lines drawn from the corresponding points in the elevation at $A_2\,B_2$, etc. The curve traced through these points A_2, B_2, etc., is the development of the line of intersection of the plane with the cylindric surface, and should be equal in length to the semi-circumference of the ellipse.

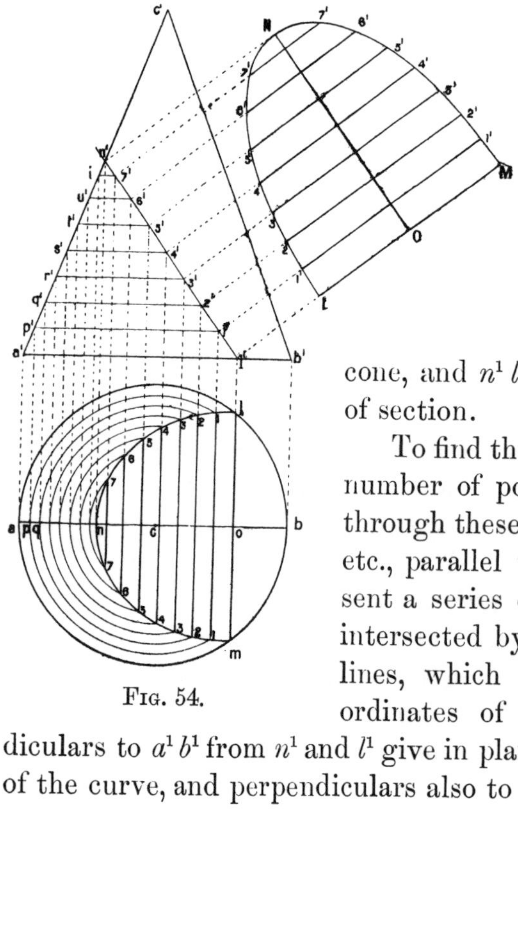

PROBLEM 39.—*To determine the section of a right circular cone by any given plane.*

Let $a\,m\,b$ (Fig. 54) be the plan, $a^1\,b^1\,c^1$ the elevation of a cone, and $n^1\,l^1$ the vertical trace of the plane of section.

To find the plan of the section, assume any number of points, 1^1, 2^1, 3^1, etc., in $n^1\,l^1$, and through these points draw the lines $1^1\,p^1$, $2^1\,q^1$, etc., parallel to the base $a^1\,b^1$. These represent a series of circular sections of the cone intersected by the plane of section in straight lines, which are chords of the circles and ordinates of the curve required. Perpendiculars to $a^1\,b^1$ from n^1 and l^1 give in plan m, l, and n, the extreme points of the curve, and perpendiculars also to $a\,b$ from p^1, q^1, etc., give $c\,p$, $c\,q$,

FIG. 54.

etc., the radii of the plans of the sections. These circles intersect the plans of the ordinates 1 1, 2 2, etc., in the points 1, 2, etc. The curve traced through these points, together with the line $l\,m$, determine the plan of the section.

To find the true form of the section, take any axis, N O, parallel to $l^1\,n^1$, and from the points l^1, 1^1, 2^1, etc., draw the perpendiculars l^1 M, $1^1\,1^1$, $2^1\,2^1$, etc. Make the ordinates L M, $1^1\,1^1$, $2^1\,2^1$, etc., equal to their respective lengths in the plan. The curve drawn through the points 1^1, 2^1, etc., gives the true shape, L M N, of the section.

PROBLEM 40.—*To draw the development of a right circular cone, and to trace upon it the developments of the curves of the ellipse, parabola, and hyperbola.*

A developable surface is one capable of being unfolded or laid out into one plane surface without tearing or buckling. The plane figure produced in this way is termed the development of the surface.

Developable surfaces belong to the class called ruled surfaces, *i.e.*, surfaces which may be generated by the motion of a straight line. If two consecutive positions of the generating line lie in one plane the surface can be developed.

The surface of a right circular cone develops into the sector of a circle, having for its radius the length of the slant side of the cone and its arc equal in length to the circumference of the circular base of the cone.

With v^1 (Fig. 55) as centre and $v^1\,a^1$ as radius draw the arc $a^1\,m$, and cut from it a length, $a^1\,1$, equal to the circumference of the base of the cone (*i.e.*, about $3\frac{1}{7}$ times the diameter); then the $a^1\,v^1\,1$ is the development of the conical surface.

To trace on this development the curves of the ellipse, parabola, and hyperbola produced by the sections d^1 G, $c^1\,5^1$, G 4^1; divide the circumference of the base into any number (say sixteen) equal parts. Join the points of division with centre v, and

FIG. 55.

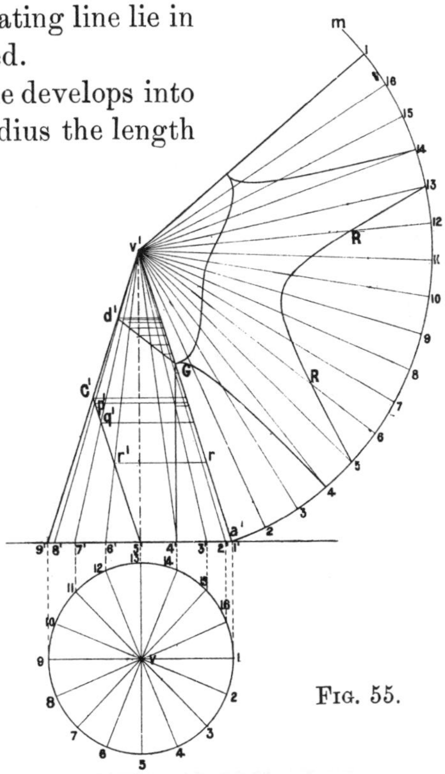

these lines will be plans of generatrices of the cone. Determine their elevations $v^1\,1^1$, $v^1\,2^1$, etc., and the same lines in the development by dividing the arc $a^1\,1$ into the same number of equal parts as the circumference of the base, and joining the points of division with v^1.

It will be seen that the section $C^1\,5^1$ cuts the lines $v^1\,6^1$, $v^1\,7^1$, and $v^1\,8^1$ in the points p^1, q^1, and r^1, respectively. The real distances of these points from v^1, the apex of the cone, set off along the lines $v^1\,6$, $v^1\,7$, and $v^1\,8$ in the development will give points in the curve. For example, to find the points R, R in the development of the curve: draw a parallel to the base through r^1 in the elevation, cutting one of the slant edges of the cone in r. Then $v^1\,r$ set off along $v^1\,6$ and $v^1\,12$ gives the points R R. Points in the other curves may be found in a similar manner.

PROBLEM 41.—*To find the development of the intersection of two right cylindrical surfaces whose axes are in the same plane and at right angles to each other.*

Let $a\,b\,c$ (Fig. 56) be the plan and $a\,e^1 f^1\,b$ the elevation of one-half

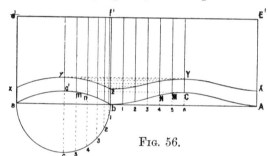

FIG. 56.

of a vertical cylinder, and $a\,c^1\,b$ the elevation of its intersection with a horizontal cylinder of large radius.

The surface of a right cylinder develops into a rectangle, one side of which is equal to the circumference of the circle that serves as the base of the cylinder, and the other equal to its height. Produce $a\,b$ to A, making $b\,$A equal in length to the semicircle $b\,c\,a$ (that is, about $3\frac{1}{7}$ times the radius), and complete the rectangle $b\,$A$\,$E$^1 f^1$. Then $b\,$A$\,$E$^1 f^1$ is the development of the vertical half cylinder.

To obtain the intersection on this development divide the quarter circle $b\,c$ into any number of equal parts, and the half of $b\,$A into the same number, and let vertical lines be drawn as shown through all these points of division. Through the points c^1, m, n, etc., where these lines meet the curve $a\,c^1\,b$, draw parallels to $a\,$A to meet the corresponding vertical lines in the development at C, M, N, etc. The curve drawn through C, M, N, and similarly obtained points, is the development of the intersection of the two cylindric surfaces.

The curve Z Y X is the development of the intersection of another horizontal cylinder having the same axis as the first.

PROBLEM 42.—*To find the development of the intersection of two right cylindrical surfaces, the axes of which are in the same plane, but not at right angles to each other.*

Let T R g and a K L^1g (Fig. 57) be an elevation of the two cylindric surfaces (one of which is horizontal) on a plane parallel to that containing the two axes, and R S O^1 an end elevation. Only a part, R g_1 S, of the horizontal cylinder is drawn, and the curve $d_1 g_1 x_1$ is the end elevation also of the curve of intersection of the two cylinders. To obtain the intersection $a d g$ on the side elevation: with centre, o, and radius, o K, equal to that of the base of the inclined cylinder, draw a semicircle, K 3 L^1, and divide it into an even number of equal parts (say six). Through these points draw lines 1 b, 2 c, etc., on the surface of the cylinder and parallel to the axis $o d$. Draw also these lines on the end elevation, and let them meet the curve R g_1 S in the points e_1, f_1, g_1. Through the points d_1, e_1, f_1, g_1, draw horizontal lines meeting the corresponding generatrices of the side elevation in the points a, b, c, d, e, f, g. The curve drawn through these points is the elevation of the intersection of the two cylinders.

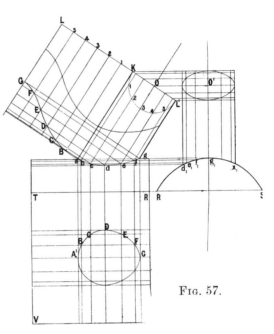

Fig. 57.

To obtain the development of the intersection, unfold the surface of the inclined cylinder about a K, as in the previous problem, and from the points a, b, c, etc., draw lines at right angles to the axis O d, cutting the corresponding generatrices on the development in the points B, C, D, E, etc. The curve drawn through A, B, C, D, etc., is the development of half of the intersection; the other half is not drawn, being the same as that just found.

The surface, T V S R, of the horizontal cylinder is unfolded about T R, and the full development of the intersection is shown upon it.

It need hardly be pointed out that R S in this development is the stretch out of the arc R g_1 S.

PROBLEM 43. *On a given right cylinder, to determine by its projections a helix of given pitch.*

The curve traced on the surface of a right cylinder and intersecting successive generatrices at a constant angle (that is, when the tangent at any point of the curve makes a constant angle with the generator of the cylinder through the point of contact) is called a helix.

The pitch of a helix is the distance between two consecutive intersections of the curve on the same generatrix.

From the definition of the curve it follows that when the surface of the cylinder and the helix are developed into one plane the latter becomes

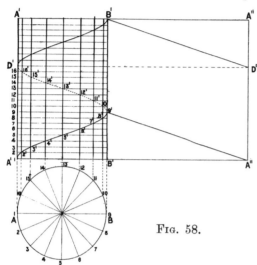

FIG. 58.

a straight line; and the development of a complete revolution forms the hypotenuse of a right-angled triangle, of which the perpendicular is the pitch, and the base equal to the circumference of the circle representing the cylinder upon which the helix is traced.

Let A B be the plan, and $A^1 B^1$, $B^1 A^1$, the elevation of the cylinder (Fig. 58). Divide the circle into any convenient number (sixteen) of equal parts. The points of division will represent the plans of generatrices of the cylinder at equal angular distances round the axis. Draw the elevations of these generatrices. From A^1 in the elevation mark $A^1 D^1$ equal to the pitch, and divide it into the same number (sixteen) of equal parts, marking them as shown. Then parallels to the ground line through these points will intersect the elevations of the generatrices through 1, 2, 3, etc., in points 1^1, 2^1, 3^1, 4^1, etc., on the elevation of the required helix.

The figure shows one revolution and a half of the helix, together with a development of the front half of the cylinder with that of the helix drawn upon it.

INDEX

INDEX

CHECK LIST OF ENGLISH LANGUAGE
BOOKS DEALING IN PART OR WHOLE
WITH STAIRBUILDING OR HANDRAILING

_____. A NEW SYSTEM OF HAND RAILING, CUT SQUARE TO THE PLANK, WITHOUT THE AID OF FALLING MOULDS. A New and Easy Method of Forming Hand Rails. Containing a Large Number of Illustrations of Hand Rails, with Full Instructions for Working Them. By an Old Stair Builder. New York: 1885. Revised and corrected edition. Industrial Publishing Society. 65pp. 26 wood engravings. Also, Philadelphia: David McKay 1906. Probably originally edited by Paul Hasluck.

Ashpitel, Arthur. HANDRAILS AND STAIRCASES. A New and Improved Method of Finding the Lines for Handrails . . . . . London: John Weale 1851. 52pp and 44 plates.

Austin, Ken. CONTRACT JOINERY. London: Northwood Books. 1981. 168pp.

Badzinski, Stanley Jr. STAIR LAYOUT. New York: Sterling Publishing Co. 72pp.

Banks, Joseph. AN ORIGINAL, INDEPENDENT AND LIBERAL TREATISE OF STAIRCASING. London: 1823

Banks, Joseph. A NEW AND IMPROVED TREATISE ON HANDRAILING. Manchester: 1836

Banks, Langley. THE JOINERS COMPANION TO A NEW SYSTEM OF HANDRAILING, NAMELY THE SQUARE CUT. Manchester: The Author. 1853. iv & 48 plates.

Collings, George. A PRACTICAL TREATISE IN HANDRAILING, SHOWING NEW AND SIMPLE METHODS FOR FINDING THE PITCH OF THE PLANK, DRAWING THE MOULDS, BEVELLING JOINTING UP AND SQUARING THE WREATH. London: 1882

Cresswell, Frank O. HANDRAILING AND STAIRCASING. 1886

Cupper, R.A. THE UNIVERSAL STAIR BUILDER. New York: 1851 29 plates.

Davidson, Ellis. DRAWING FOR CARPENTERS AND JOINERS. London and New York: Cassell & Co. 1870 and numerous reprints.

De Graff, Simon. THE MODERN GEOMETRICAL STAIR-BUILDERS GUIDE. Philadelphia: F. Bell. 1845. 73pp. 23 plates (4 folding). Also 1854 and 1856.

Dowsett, John F. STAIRBUILDING AND HANDRAILING. "The Analysis, Setting Out and Making of Wreathed Handrails by the Square Cut, Normal Sections and Easing in the Wreath Methods. London: The Library Press 1929. 239pp. 40 plates and 208 figures in the text. A good though scarce title.

Easterbrook and Monckton. AMERICAN STAIRBUILDER. 1859.

Ellis, George. MODERN PRACTICAL STAIRBUILDING AND HANDRAILING. 2 vols. London: B.T. Batsford. 1932. A well known but scarce title.

Ellis, George. MODERN PRACTICAL JOINERY. London: B.T. Batsford. 1902 379pp. Numerous editions. One of the finest English joinery books.

Foad, E.V. PURPOSE MADE JOINERY. London: Van Nostrand Reinhold. 1982. 204pp.

Forbes, William. THE SECTORIAN SYSTEM OF HAND RAILING. 1873.

Godfrey, W.H. THE ENGLISH STAIRCASE: An Historical Account of the Characteristic Types to the End of the 18th Century. London: 1911. 38 plates and brief text.

Gould, Lucius D. HANDRAILING. 1875

Gould, Lucius D. THE ART AND SCIENCE OF STAIR BUILDING. New York: William Comstock. 1885. 77pp. 36 engraved plates.

Halfpenny, William. ART OF SOUND BUILDING. London: 1725.

Hasluck, Paul. ed. PRACTICAL STAIRCASE JOINERY. Philadelphia: David McKay. 1903 & 1907. 160pp.

Hasluck, Paul. ed. PRACTICAL HANDRAILING. Cassell & Co. 1905. 160pp.

Hatfield, R.G. THE AMERICAN HOUSE CARPENTER. New York: John Wiley. 1844. 254pp. 32pp of illustrations. This title went into a number of editions.

Hodgson, Fred. STAIR BUILDING MADE EASY. New York. 1884. Numerous editions.

Hodgson, Fred. COMMON SENSE STAIR BUILDING AND HANDRAILING. New York: Frederick J. Drake. 1903. 195pp. Numerous editions.

Jeays, Joshua. ORTHOGONAL SYSTEM OF HANDRAILING. 1864.

Lafever, Minard. THE MODERN PRACTICE OF STAIRCASE AND HAN-
DRAIL CONSTRUCTION. New York: D. Appleton. 1838. 47pp. 15 plates.

Langley, Batty. BUILDERS COMPLETE ASSISTANT. 1738.

Loth, C. Edward. THE PRACTICAL STAIRBUILDERS COMPLETE TREA-
TISE ON THE ART OF BUILDING STAIRS AND HANDRAILS. Troy New
York. 1868.

Mannes, Willibald. DESIGNING STAIRCASES. New York: Van Nostrand Reinhold. 1982. 144pp.

Marwick, Thomas Purvis. THE HISTORY AND CONSTRUCTION OF STAIR-
CASES. Edinburgh: J&J Gray. 1888 138pp.

Monckton, James H. NATIONAL STAIR-BUILDER. 1872

Monckton, James H. STAIRBUILDING IN ITS VARIOUS FORMS AND THE
NEW ONE PLANE METHOD OF DRAWING FACE MOULDS AND UN-
FOLDING THE CENTRE LINE OF WREATH. New York: John Wiley &
Sons. 1888

Mowat, W. & A. A TREATISE ON STAIRBUILDING AND HANDRAILING.
London: 1900.

Moxon. MECHANICAL EXERCISES. 1693.

Newlands, James. THE CARPENTERS AND JOINERS ASSISTANT. Edinburgh
and London: Blackie and Sons. 1860. 291pp. 115 plates.

Nicholson, Peter. CARPENTERS ASSISTANT. 1792. Numerous editions through
the 19th century.

Nicholson, P. A TREATISE ON THE CONSTRUCTION OF STAIRCASES AND
HANDRAILS. 39 plans. London: 1820. 2nd ed. 1847.

Nicholson, M.A. CARPENTER, JOINER, AND BUILDERS COMPANION.
1826.

Perry. HANDRAILING. 1858.

Pocock, William. MODERN FINISHINGS FOR ROOMS: A SERIES OF DE-
SIGNS FOR VESTIBULES, HALLS, STAIRCASES, ETC. London: 1881

Price, Frances. BRITISH CARPENTER. London: 1733. Numerous editions and
highly regarded.

Reynolds, Louis Ethan. A TREATISE ON HANDRAILING. New Orleans: Hinton & Co. 1849. 95pp. 20 plates. One of the very few joinery books published in the South.

Riddell, Robert. HANDRAILING SIMPLIFIED. Philadelphia: 1850. 12 plates, 10 pp.

Riddell, Robert. THE ELEMENTS OF HAND-RAILING. C. 1855. This title went through a number of editions by various publishers. The 3rd edition was published in 1860 and contained 26pp and 22 plates.

Riddell, Robert. THE CARPENTER AND JOINER, STAIR BUILDER AND HAND-RAILER. Edinburgh: Thomas C. Jack. ND. c. 1860-1870. Apparently the 2nd edition. 125pp. 57 plates of which the last four are cardboard models.

Riddell, Robert. THE MODERN CARPENTER AND BUILDER. NEW AND ORIGINAL METHODS FOR EVERY CUT IN CARPENTRY, JOINERY, AND HAND RAILING. Philadelphia: Howard Challen. 1867 for the 4th edition. 40pp. 14 plates.

Riddell, Robert. THE CARPENTER AND JOINER AND ELEMENTS OF HANDRAILING. c. 1860. Numerous editions. By 1869 the ELEMENTS OF HANDRAILING was in its 11th edition.

Riddell, Robert. THE NEW ELEMENTS OF HAND-RAILING. Rev. ed. Philadelphia: Claxton, Remsen and Haffelfinger. 1871. 126pp. 41 plates, 13 of which appear for the first time.

Riddell, Robert. MECHANICS' GEOMETRY, PLAINLY TEACHING THE CARPENTER, JOINER, METAL PLATE WORKER, IN FACT THE ARTISAN . . . . Philadelphia: Claxton, Remsen and Haffelfinger. 1874. Apparently identical to the edition published in the same year by A.J. Bicknell in New York. 156pp. 52 plates, 4 cardboard models.

Riddell, Robert. LESSONS ON HAND RAILING FOR LEARNERS. Philadelphia: Claxton, Remsen and Haffelfinger. 1876. 32 plates with text for each. Riddell states that this book does not replace his previous books but is rather a completely new system of lines.

Rothery, Guy. STAIRCASES AND GARDEN STEPS. London: T. Werner Laurie. ND. c. 1910, xii & 250pp. Frontis and 38 plates.

Sherratt, P.J. THE ELEMENTS OF HAND RAILING. 38 plates. 1900.

Sherratt, P.J. STAIRBUILDING AND HANDRAILING. ND. c. 1860.

Swan, Abraham. THE BRITISH ARCHITECT: OR THE BUILDERS TREASURY OF STAIRCASES. London: 1745.

Swan, Abraham. BUILDERS COMPLETE ASSISTANT. London. 1750.

Talbot, Anthony. ed. HANDBOOK OF DOORMAKING, WINDOW MAKING, AND STAIRCASING. New York: Sterling Publishing Co. 1980. 256pp. This is a combined edition of DOORMAKING FOR CARPENTERS AND JOINERS; WINDOW MAKING FOR CARPENTERS AND JOINERS; and ELEMENTARY STAIRCASING.

Twiss, William. HANDRAILING ON THE BLOCK SYSTEM . . . . Manchester: Abel Heywood and Son. 1878. 30 + 1 pp. 4 folding plates. A scarce book on the subject.

Williams, Morris. STAIR BUILDERS GUIDE. New York: David William Co. 1914. 256pp. This title was reprinted twice in the 1920's.